Mass Communication in the Modern Arab World

Mass Communication in the Modern Arab World

Ongoing Agents of Change Following the Arab Spring

Edited by Naila Nabil Hamdy and Philip Auter

ROWMAN & LITTLEFIELD
Lanham • Boulder • New York • London

Published by Rowman & Littlefield
An imprint of The Rowman & Littlefield Publishing Group, Inc.
4501 Forbes Boulevard, Suite 200, Lanham, Maryland 20706
www.rowman.com

86-90 Paul Street, London EC2A 4NE, United Kingdom

British Library Cataloguing in Publication Information Available

Library of Congress Cataloging-in-Publication Data
Names: Hamdy, Naila Nabil, 1958- editor. | Auter, Philip, 1963- editor.
Title: Mass communication in the modern Arab world : ongoing agents of change following the Arab spring / edited by Naila Nabil Hamdy and Philip Auter.
Description: Lanham, Maryland : Rowman & Littlefield, 2022. | Includes bibliographical references and index. | Summary: "This book introduces, explains, and explores communication in the modern Arab world. Focusing on contemporary times and the lasting effects of the Arab Spring, the book reveals how the unceasing growth of media and communication technologies have acted as agents of change and provides evidence of mass communication's potential to transform societies and cultures"— Provided by publisher.
Identifiers: LCCN 2021040404 (print) | LCCN 2021040405 (ebook) | ISBN 9781538140031 (cloth) | ISBN 9781538199183 (paper) | ISBN 9781538140048 (epub)
Subjects: LCSH: Mass media—Arab countries. | Mass media—Arab countries—Influence.
Classification: LCC P92.A65 M375 2022 (print) | LCC P92.A65 (ebook) | DDC 302.230917/4927—dc23
LC record available at https://lccn.loc.gov/2021040404
LC ebook record available at https://lccn.loc.gov/2021040405

Contents

Introduction

The Arab Region's History and Current State

Naila Nabil Hamdy and Philip Auter

As this book went to press the situation with the ongoing spread of the coronavirus (COVID-19) that started in Wuhan, China, at the end of 2019 had been in full swing for over a year. By March 11, 2020, the World Health Organization (WHO) declared the outbreak a pandemic as the new disease spread quickly around the world. A few days later the Arab world had reported its first 3,449 cases and 75 deaths as a direct result of the infection (Arab Center 2020).

International government reactions varied widely. In the Arab world, responses ranged from severe restrictions on people's movements to closure of airports. The numbers of new infections are reported daily in most countries, although for different reasons—ranging from downplaying the potential impact of the virus to lack of testing abilities—several countries have underreported their cases. Against the chronology of the coronavirus outbreak and its dizzying spread, as the data surrounding increases rolled in, the public in the region panicked and the demand for information skyrocketed. At the same time, governments needed to disseminate essential information to the public as they recognized the importance of reaching their citizens and dispelling dangerous misinformation and rumors.

Communication and media rose to the forefront, becoming actors in the public health crisis, relaying information and health awareness campaigns and generally mobilizing societal action to fight the pandemic. The news media in particular have placed this "war" on the virus on the top of national agendas in each of the countries where the pandemic has been taken seriously. Because of the heavy coverage of the disease and its consequences for individuals and society, the pandemic has become of great concern to the public. As McCombs and Shaw (1972) assert, the media tell us what to think about by highlighting certain issues. In much of the Arab region, broadcast news was dominated by the topic, and the popularly viewed evening talk shows were exclusively dedicated to minute-by-minute updates on related health issues, economic consequences, and potential methods for avoiding the virus and fighting back. And this remained the case for the initial first few months.

In most countries that function under authoritarian media systems, the information is mostly provided by, or at least guided by, the government. In the case of transnational news media, much of the information on individual countries has been influenced by the agenda of the dominant nations who control media discourses. Social media played a similar role. Unlike the days of previous epidemics such as H1N1 and MERS, or the political upheavals such as those witnessed during the Arab uprisings, social media are no longer the space for loud voices or alternate information. This time, ministries of health and other governmental associations are better equipped to communicate information online. Yes, you could still view dissenting opinions and criticism, but social media conversations are no longer dominated by the opposition.

Misinformation and disinformation have been circulated, and complex conspiracy theories have exhibited a cancerous growth among social media users; but on the other hand, governments have also used this medium to inform the public, control the panic, and dismiss harmful rumors. That is not to say that the virus has not been used as a weapon of division in the battle for influence in the region. Governments have used deliberate misinformation campaigns to gain dominance over their rivals. The health crisis was used to fuel Sunni–Shiite hostility and discredit the Turkey–Qatar axis (Bulus 2020). As social media have matured, many of the same communication tools that had been used predominantly for entertainment, engagement, and socializing were being used by employees and students who were teleworking and learning during their home confinement time. Individuals also read, forwarded (reposted), and created humorous memes about the COVID-19 pandemic, which may have helped them to process the major events occurring in their lives.

Meanwhile, in the midst of the pandemic, the United States was struggling with protests resulting from the killing of African Americans by the police, and also a highly controversial election. All sides of these issues and events were using the traditional media—and especially social media—to present arguments, ambiguous information, and in some cases outright falsehoods. Many in the United States resisted believing in the pandemic, and this also became a point of contention. Although the election was called by most media outlets in November 2020, Joseph R. Biden was not declared the winner of this closely contested election until mid-December, when the Electoral College finally voted. And even then, the false rhetoric persisted, and tensions continued to build. On January 6, the U.S. Capitol was stormed by protestors who had just left a Trump rally and it was breached for the first time since the U.S. Civil War.

Communication technologies and access to media are not uniform across the Arab region. Nor are the political environments that shape and often govern media systems identical. In fact, it is often at times of crisis that similarities and differences are highlighted. It is conceptually challenging to use the term "Arab communication" without implying that we are looking at a unified whole. Most Arab media have a history of being rooted in the concept of the nation-state, even though the common language, and the largely common religion and culture of Islam, have given the landscape a sense of Arab integration. As noted by longtime observers, Arab media systems are molded by the national political cultures in which they function (Rugh 2007). One view is that changes in media are often a reflection of changes in the domestic political contexts rather than the result of new technologies or other variables—such as political and social change. But other observers, for instance Hafez (2014), have also noted that Arab media have developed at a much faster pace than the Arab political systems. This resulted in triggering democratization, despite periodic political setbacks, putting the media together with civil society at the forefront of political and societal changes.

Traditionally, most Arab media have been known to be dominated by the state or state-sponsored power elites and characterized by insulation from the outside world. A significant change occurred in the 1990s with the introduction of satellite television and the development of the Internet. These technological revolutions brought new content to the Arab world, but also a wave of liberalization and privatization. Arab governments consciously allowed, and even promoted, these changes in order to counter global and transnational competition.

After 1996, Al Jazeera's chilling effect with their open discussions, taboo breaking, and empowerment of marginalized voices pushed governments toward further opening channels of communication. For the first time a small Gulf state was using a television station as a political tool to position itself as a major player in the region through its broadcasts. Funded by their government, this station could disseminate ideas and coverage of topics previously not discussed as long as it was not inside Qatar. The popularity of this content and open discussion led Al Jazeera to become a prominent media outlet in the region. After the September 11, 2001, attack on the United States, Al Jazeera became a major global news leader.

At this point, the other major players in the region decided to follow Al Jazeera's example. The growth of television channels and the increase in talk show programming occurred at an unprecedented rate. Arab audiences were glued to their TV sets watching, hearing, participating, and interacting with ideas hitherto unknown to this region.

It is not that party press, strong journalism, or diverse opinions had been absent before. They did exist, but not in audio-visual outlets, which—except in Lebanon—were owned by governments and tightly controlled. As government regulations loosened, a dynamic public sphere emerged almost unintentionally across the Arab region, expressed in radio and television and aided by the introduction of the Internet (Hafez 2014). Governments were focused on using the Internet to capitalize on the perceived economic benefits of the new technology. They were therefore not monitoring it in the same ways they typically monitored the traditional media. It may not have occurred to them that this new communication channel could be used to present unrepresented voices, diverse views, and even public dissent.

As has been the case in the past, developing media ultimately affect traditional media agendas. For several years ahead of the Arab Spring the media systems were liberalizing, and a new dynamic between Internet activists and mainstream media journalists and professionals was already apparent. Unheard voices and sidelined issues raised on blogs and other social media spilled onto traditional media content, creating an unusual marriage of new and old ideas in popular new private stations that were viewed nationally and regionally (Hamdy 2009). The media may have indeed moved ahead of political change by the Arab Spring breaking point.

Scholars have proposed typologies and classifications to analyze the media in the region. In his book *The Arab Press*, first published in 1979, William Rugh primarily divided the region into three categories: the "mobilization press," which included Algeria, Egypt, Libya, Sudan, Iraq, and Yemen; the "loyalist press," which included Jordan, Saudi Arabia, Bahrain, Qatar, Oman, Tunisia, the United Arab Emirates, and Palestine; and the "diverse press" existing in Lebanon, Kuwait, and Morocco (Rugh 1979). In the influential update to his work, *Arab Mass Media: Newspapers, Radio, and Television in Arab Politics* (2004), Rugh updated his typology to include the addition of a transitional category that encompassed the changing media systems of Egypt, Jordan, Tunisia, and Algeria. He also moved Yemen to the diverse press category (Rugh 2004).

Similarly, Douglas Boyd's 1999 analysis of the Arab region's broadcast organizations takes a close look at national systems with special emphasis on Egypt and Saudi Arabia. Egypt was important because of its early position as an influential media developer and informational leader in the region, Saudi Arabia because of its wealth and political power. The two countries recognized their weight in the pan-Arab media discourses and the Arab media scene early on. Other scholars, such as Mohammad Ayish (2003), put forth what he referred to as a normative Arab–Islamic perspective identifying constructs that assume the nature of communication in the region, finding patterns that are formalistic, indirect, hyperbolic, asymmetrical, metaphysical, and orally biased. This perspective emphasizes the relationship between communication and culture.

Noha Mellor (2014) finds that the Arab region has a unique media system that is marked by commercialism and business interests that encourage profits but do not allow for much free speech. Adopting liberal economic values while controlling social and political ones, Arab states accordingly continue to promote media production as long as it does not support political activism. Thus, Mellor examines the media through a political economy perspective.

Scholars have also been inspired by the success of Hallin and Mancini's work in *Comparing Media Systems* (2004), using the comparative analysis approach to analyze Arab media (Hafez 2014, Richter et al. 2020) and guide their research. The three models that they propose—the Mediterranean or Polarized Pluralist Model, the North/Central European or Democratic Corporatist Model, and the North Atlantic or Liberal Model—were designed to assess more democratic Western countries. Nonetheless, several Arab media scholars have found these analytical frameworks useful in studying some aspects of the Arab region. For instance, Hafez (2014) finds that countries like Lebanon, Tunisia, and Egypt (at the time of this writing) align with the Mediterranean Model, while countries like Jordan, Algeria, Yemen, and Morocco—despite state control of media and lack of political pluralism—follow the model of Southern Europe.

Hafez (2014) also notes that industry professionalism may not have been comparable to Europe, but was evolving and had developed in the Arab region, with evidence that democratic journalistic values were present prior to the 2011 uprising (Ramaprasad and Hamdy 2006). The various typologies have often been critiqued for being too Western for application to the Arab region, or rejected for lack of evidence that there is such a thing as a distinct Arab/Muslim media classification.

Arab media studies changed significantly after the 2011 upheavals. In Tunisia, Egypt, Libya, Yemen, and other neighboring countries, media studies began to focus more on how traditional and social media lead political transformations. The interest was not localized to the region, though. Western scholarly journals suddenly became extremely interested in research on "change in the Arab world."

By 2019 there was a second wave of protests—in Sudan, Algeria, Lebanon, and Iraq—and interest in the role of media appeared to wane. It may be too early to tell whether these new events have gained the same interest from scholars. This may be because of the failure of most of the 2011 revolutions, but it could also be that the second wave, although extensively covered by Arab media, failed to capture the imagination of as many people around the region and internationally as did its predecessor.

It is not that the media are less critical to the region, but that there has been an important change since the 2011 uprisings. These protests had directly affected the media landscape in several key countries—even as the media had helped to shape the protests. Both traditional and digital media mushroomed in quantity, but just as many of the democratic transitions failed, the media mostly lost their focus and their credibility with the public.

CURRENT TRENDS

Several emerging trends characterize Arab media these days. While the political context across the region has always varied, in the post-2011 era differences have been complex and, in some cases, exacerbated by wars and internal strife. Yet there are several noteworthy trends: (1) the decline in popularity of transnational or pan-Arab media coupled with the rise of private ownership and viewership in national contexts, (2) increase in digital media and connectivity options, and (3) a shift in media consumption among youth.

Firstly, pan-Arab satellite television stations such as Al Jazeera and Al Arabiya and later the digital media domain (blogs, social media networks, etc.) had contributed to a rise or even a resurgence of long-forgotten transnational Arab and Muslim identity. This movement has been heralded as the new Arab public space—decreasing the importance of the national identity (Nisbet and Myers 2010). But this powerful link between Arab transnational media and Arab identity has been disrupted as new and old national media became immensely more popular. Transnational media lost their force when they got involved with regional power struggles and presenting very one-sided coverage. Prominent instances of this include the dispute between Saudi Arabia and Qatar, where the media advocated self-serving ideologies. Similarly, during the Syrian and Libyan civil wars they went as far as campaigning for favored rebel groups (Lynch 2015). In fact, there has been a resurgence of nationalism in several Arab countries, resulting in a greater focus on nationalism and unity to the exclusion of other countries, and therefore a rise in national media.

Although the transnational media and the pivotal actors in the Arab media landscape, such as Saudi Arabia, UAE, Egypt, and Qatar, remain important, there has been an evolution of local media spurred by leaders who wanted to fast-track the media liberalization moment that began many years ago (Guaaybess 2013). As these identity conflicts unfold, the political nature of Arab media becomes more and more evident. The surge of private ownership, and in particular satellite television, has ended state monopoly but has not ended the politics. The majority, if not all, of these outlets have specific agendas that either reflect the owner's stance or are heavily influenced by government policies.

In Egypt, during the period between 2011 and 2013, media wars on TV reflected the divisive political struggles in the country, causing TV broadcasting to become a polarizing factor between Islamists, liberals, and others, with content going as far as blatant hate speech and encouraging incitement to violence. After the change of regime, when General Abdel Fattah al-Sisi became the president of Egypt, government restrictions on the media increased. Despite this, audiences have continued to prefer national stations, particularly after the once popular Al Jazeera took a one-sided position in support of the Muslim Brotherhood and lost much of its credibility. The popularity of private television is significant given that 98% of Egyptians have access to television. Pre-2011 stations such as Dream TV, El Mehwar, Al Hayat, and Sada Elbalad, as well as post-2011 additions such as CBC and On E, have large audiences and have survived despite the unstable advertising revenues and small-scale competition from a revamped state television network. Audiences will switch to Sada Elbalad or CBC Extra for live coverage of local news and commentary on popular talk shows. The fact that the private stations are not completely free from government influence has not driven their audiences away. In the meantime, the national identity is being reinforced by the media.

In Algeria, several private channels were launched after the introduction of the 2012 media law which allowed for a more diverse, albeit controlled, media environment. Owned by both preexisting media groups and prominent businessmen, the new channels have proved to be successful in creating a new national public—particularly by providing a new choice of national and regional news. These new news channels, like Echorouk, Ennahar, and Dzair News, gained quick credibility among an audience that previously had no trust in national media (Sarnelli and Kobibi 2017).

Tunisia—which has emerged from the 2011 uprisings as a democratizing nation—has also had reforms in its media regulations, resulting in an increase in media and press freedoms. But the transition has been fragile, and despite legislation protecting media independence and the emergence of self-regulatory bodies in the early days, the new rules have not been fully implemented. Powerful figures associated with the former Ben Ali regime and others associated with the current government have hindered much of the progress despite the 2014 establishment of the Independent Broadcasting Authority. Nonetheless, Tunisia is currently home to two public television channels and twelve private channels, some of which are broadcasting without a license in response to political and economic constraints. Similar to Egypt between 2011 and 2013, Tunisian television channels also became polarized, aligning themselves with their chosen ideologies. Additionally, major political groups such as Ennahda and Nidaa Tounes own their own stations to promote their own agendas (Lynch 2015). Several private stations are widely viewed, including Elhiwar Ettounsi, Nessma TV, and Hannibal, alongside the reformed state stations of Wataniya, despite reports of polarization, political affiliation, and bias caused by economic interests.

In countries that managed to escape the domino effect of the initial 2011 uprisings, such as Jordan and Morocco, the royal rulers avoided the massive protests seen elsewhere by proposing moderate reforms and using media controls to serve their self-interests. Limited media liberalizations allowed for privatization of broadcast, mainly radio for Morocco and TV for Jordan, and has allowed citizens more local choice. In the meantime, the failed states of Libya and Yemen also saw an explosion of private stations aligned with various political factions (Lynch 2015). As destructive as they are, these stations have been influential in fostering a discordant public opinion.

The current landscape is dominated by local channels, but transnational media still maintain a presence. Although many of these giants have launched new localized channels, like MBC Masr or the more recently launched Al Hadith news station, they no longer command the hearts and minds of the Arab street as they did in the past.

Arab viewers also have the choice of watching international broadcasters such as Al Hurrah, Radio Sawa, BBC, CNN, Deutsche Welle, France 24, Russia Today, and CCTV. While these outlets do have a moderate viewership, it tends to be composed primarily of the cultural elite and may not be widespread enough to negatively impact viewership of local media.

Another clear trend in the Arab media landscape is the marked increase in digital media and their accessibility. Internet penetration and adoption in the Arab region was slow in comparison to more developed countries, but that has quickly changed. According to recent figures, the number of Internet users in the region is now more than 125 million, or 48% of the population, with an annual growth rate of 30%, and more than 53 million using social media actively (Internet World Stats 2017). Improved infrastructure, rapid expansion of Internet connectivity, and affordable devices have spurred this growth, and not just in the more affluent economies of the Gulf states. In fact, countries like Morocco and Sudan have seen some of the highest growth rates.

According to Northwestern University in Qatar's 2017 media usage survey, the Arab world has seen dramatic changes in Internet penetration, media use, and attitudes toward issues such as online privacy and free speech. This groundbreaking study found that Internet penetration had grown dramatically in Jordan, Lebanon, and Tunisia. It also found that smartphone ownership growth paralleled increased Internet use and that 83% of Lebanese, Qatari, Saudi, and Emirati nationals own a smartphone. At the same time the number of Arabs who watch TV has declined modestly, but newspaper and magazine readership and radio listening have decreased dramatically. Furthermore, Arabic is more frequently used than previously, indicating an increase in Arabic-language Internet users and possibly Arabic-language digital media content (Northwestern University in Qatar 2017).

Arab citizens have become more and more dependent on social media platforms not just for societal communication, but also for education, business, entertainment, news, advertising, public relations, and marketing. The gaming industry is growing and several countries—specifically Palestine and Egypt—have a vibrant startup culture. Such technological changes have also meant that Arabs now have a choice of video content through platforms such as YouTube, Netflix Arabia, Saudi-owned Shahid.net, and the more recent Egyptian WatchIT, increasing their access to visual content beyond traditional TV.

Given the preference for visual media, what implications will this have on the cultural, social, and political environments of the region? With so many choices, individuals may become unplugged from a mediated national consciousness. Further, such a large amount of media content can offer individuals the opportunity to immerse themselves in only one type of programming—which can reinforce a more singular and less open-minded perspective.

As stated earlier, most Arab communication research has studied the digital media through the prism of the 2011 uprisings. Focus has been on the new media technologies and their facilitation of new forms of journalism, alternate opinions, dissident political activism, the circumvention of state control of information, the mobilization of protests, and the shaping of opinion. Other aspects of digital media effects have been mostly ignored. The time has come when media scholars should take a step back and look at the wider picture. Digital media are increasing not only in quantity, but also in the ways they are being used. The Arab region's population is about 400 million, with more than half of the population under 30 years old. This unprecedented "youth bulge"—the term used to describe how the proportion of Arab youth compares to older groups—is increasingly engaged with digital media. Because of this youth trend, and the fact that young people tend to be early adopters of new technologies and intensive users of digital media, we should be keeping an eye on how the younger generations consume, interact with, and create media. The rapid expansion of user-generated content in the Arab region in the past decade, mostly disseminated via social media, has significantly altered the cultural and political landscape.

Consumption is changing among young people. For example, according to the 2017 survey by Northwestern University in Qatar, more and more youth are consuming news digitally and moving away from the print press. While television is still the most popular news platform, at least a third of the youth responding to the survey said they access news content via social media, often from non-news organizations. Importantly, youth also share news extensively via digital channels. As governments have increased the surveillance of Facebook and the blocking of websites (OpenNet Initiative), and become more knowledgeable about using social media networks for their own benefit and to influence public opinion, the younger generation has been moving to encrypted sites such as WhatsApp because they are concerned about the authorities monitoring their online activity.

THE STRUCTURE OF THIS BOOK

The following chapters represent a snapshot of the rapidly evolving communication landscape in the twenty-first-century Arab world. They represent current trends and will document these events for history. We are presenting a selection of nineteen chapters in a volume focusing on key issues in the current media landscape of the Arab world. The contributions represent twenty-first-century media communication trends in a number of individual countries as well as the region as a whole.

Part I: In the Beginning: Historical, Political, and Societal Issues Leading Up to the Arab Uprisings

Part I focuses on some of the historical, political, and societal events that have occurred since the Arab Spring uprisings by looking at the enabling circumstances that may have caused changes in the region. So many accounts of the Arab Spring begin with the young street vendor Bouazizi's act of protest igniting uprisings, or the Facebook invitation to a rally that was answered by hundreds of Egyptians. These responses were mobilized by social media that spread waves of demonstrations across the Arab world. Yet the authors of the first part of the volume prefer to put the story of the storm in a deeper historical context.

Leonard Ray Teel analyzes journalism documentation of nongovernmental organizations' (NGOs) activities in the region in the period between the United Nations Global Conference held in Cairo in 1994 and the Arab Spring. One of the reasons Egypt had been chosen to host the conference was that the country had seen a growth of NGOs and grassroots movements that were concerned with problems important to society and unaddressed by the government. The Cairo meeting marked the beginning of six workshops involving the media and NGOs conducted from 1999 to 2004, moving from Cairo to Casablanca, Ramallah, Amman, Dubai, and back to Cairo. NGOs became news shapers when stories of their wide-ranging societal interests and goals were told by journalists to the public, helping develop awareness of the role of civil society in assisting people with unmet needs and paving the way for larger democratic aspirations on the part of the public.

Tayeb Boutbouqalt's chapter uses a wide range of multidimensional and transdisciplinary approaches to evaluate the emergence of new media in the Moroccan media landscape. He attempts to explain how this emergence may have been triggered by the 2011 protests that swept through the Middle East and North Africa, as well as how that impacted Moroccan society. His work traces historical developments, taking the reader through a remarkable account of the relationship between the country's society at times of intense exchange of information through both peace and unrest—from precolonial times all the way to the start of the third millennium and the rapid evolution of the media with the onset of the digital revolution. Boutbouqalt finds similarities in the ways that the colonial occupation of the twentieth century and the digital revolution in the twenty-first impacted Moroccan society.

Kamal Hamidou's work on the establishment of the radio and television broadcasting networks in Algeria and their ensuing expansion also addresses the historic context of the growth of broadcast media throughout the French colonial occupation, up to what he describes as their partial emancipation in 2012. In his insightful analysis we are offered a glimpse into how broadcast media development has been intertwined with the political and military agenda that facilitated the use of broadcast messages for political purposes throughout the history of Algeria. He highlights a continuous authoritarian effort to indoctrinate and mobilize citizens even to this day.

Part II: Governing Bodies: Media Influence, Power, Ownership, and Control

In Part II the authors address the complex systems of media power, ownership, and control, and how they are coupled with legal rules and regulations. Both formal and informal methods of media control are explored, in addition to the ways in which governments utilize media to advance their own image and promote nation building.

Noha Mellor reviews two analytical approaches—critical political economy and cultural studies—and delves into a dissection of the media–capital nexus that underlies most media in the Arab world. The complex media scene connects the local, regional, and global media, capital, and national security interests, making it difficult to analyze the Arab media as an independent field. The author finds that ownership patterns cannot be viewed as privately owned versus state-owned, not just because of these connections but because they cannot be seen as separate from the political and security fields and thus cannot be compared to similar models in the Western world. Nonetheless, Mellor examines media ownership in Egypt, Saudi Arabia, and Syria, illustrating the unusual interchangeability of this connection and offering the reader enough historical background to understand what led to the current circumstances. She uses examples of ownership patterns illustrating the close association between media, capital, and security to underscore her point.

In discussing Egypt's 2014 Constitution, Inas Abou Youssef highlights the twelve articles granting freedom of expression; access to information; freedom of thought, opinion, and the expression thereof; and freedom of the press. The constitution established three bodies to handle media in the country, develop a new media policy, and reform the media, with an emphasis on state media. The three bodies were formed by 2016: the Supreme Council for Media Regulation (SCMR), the National Press Authority (NPA), and the National Media Authority (NMA). Scrutinizing their roles, Abou Youssef is able to explain the not-so-positive impact that the three organizations had had on Egypt's press and media system in general by 2018.

Part III: The Politics of Influence: Making Policy and Swaying Public Opinion

Part III addresses two sides of the same coin—influencing public opinion. The chapter authors look at how policy makers in the Arab region and also the United States attempt to sway public opinion to suit government agendas.

Hesham Mesbah and Deanna Loew study the U.S.-based public relations activities of key Middle Eastern countries and their communication strategies as they attempt to sway U.S. public opinion, policies, and laws. They use FARA (Foreign Agent Registration Act) reports to identify the relationship between the levels of democracy and transparency in the countries under study and their PR tactics. Their chapter analyzes the activities of Egypt, Israel, Saudi Arabia, and Turkey to see if the level of democracy found in each of these countries impacts their PR plans.

Fran Hassencahl assesses the credibility and effectiveness of the Radio Sawa station, which was launched by the U.S. government as part of an overall strategy to influence public opinion in the Arab world. She questions the wisdom of choosing a U.S. model of radio broadcast and addresses the challenges faced by the station since its 2002 launch. She writes about how the U.S. model of popular music with news breaks on the half hour was accepted by young audiences and how regional stations later adopted the format—but without news from the U.S. perspective. Hassencahl also questions the reliability of audience data and whether there is enough solid evidence to make proper informed decisions about radio programming.

Part IV: The Pendulum of Progress: Top-Down and Participatory Media's Role in Development Communication

Part IV is dedicated to the role of media in development communication. The term "development" has evolved over time to include various growth areas, ranging from human development to economic and technological development. After decades of propositions and theories of varying success, scholars in the twenty-first century shifted to communication strategies that promote sustainable development.

Abeer Salem analyzes the shift in development communication, comparing the traditional development paradigm to the sustainability communication approach, tracing the evolution globally and comparing the two approaches within an Arab regional context. The author explains how the focus shifted from a deterministic to a sustainable perspective by becoming a recognized participatory process that targets the improvement of the quality of human life in an environmentally accountable way. By reviewing the United Nations Millennium Development Goals (MDGs) and moving to the United Nations Sustainable Development Goals (SDGs), she presents an assessment of the changes that took place in the Arab region. Salem draws attention in her chapter to the great importance of information and communication technology (digitization) for realizing the ambition of the 2030 SDG agenda to be inclusive and not leave anyone behind.

Information and communication technology (ICT) has been identified as a catalyst to achieve the United Nations SDGs. The UAE (an emerging economy) not only leads the GCC and the Arab region but is on the same global level as advanced regional economies such as Southeast Asia, Europe, and North America. Oshane Thorpe highlights the efforts of the UAE government in adopting ICT for e-governance and the promotion of public participation in the government's determination to promote inclusiveness and transparency and step toward achieving happiness and well-being, which is at the top of the government policy agenda. However, he does question the validity of assessing the readiness of the UAE to measure happiness effectively, and makes recommendations for citizen-centric approaches to e-governance.

Because community media represent a fundamental role in the development process, in the next chapter Hend El-Taher's work shows the link between community media and human development, focusing on the important role played by the media in democratization, social struggles, and awareness raising. The author writes about the experience of a local newspaper in the rural area of Upper Egypt. Despite the success of the experiment, the project faced many challenges, such as financial sustainability and the lack of skilled journalists willing to join a local enterprise.

Saddek Rabah's chapter presents a rare analytical framework based on the evolution of social media in Algeria in the authoritarian environment that characterized the Algerian regime until recently, while explaining how the country resisted the wind of revolt that had blown over from its neighbors in 2011. Rabah surveys the related laws, regulations, and debates, as well as the potential of both the Internet and social media, not only in aiding development but in democratizing the public space and the Internet. He also discusses social media's ability to erode the authority of the government. Just after Rabah submitted his chapter for publication in this volume, the delayed revolt happened. In 2019 Algeria was brought back into the spotlight after decades of international and regional media isolation with protests that have been live-tweeted, live-streamed on Facebook, and spread on YouTube.

Part V: Major Moves: Convergence, Globalization, and Technological Change

Convergence, globalization, extraordinary technological change, and the cultural, social, economic, and political effects of technological advancement have transformed the media industries in the Arab world. The confluence of these factors calls for a revisit of the media industries in the region. Part V of this collection helps readers understand today's media environment in an ever-evolving Arab world despite the existing challenges. These contributions offer us a preview of the future of professional media.

Mohammad Ayish provides the reader an overall picture of the Arab world that viewed the media industry in the three postcolonial decades as a key driver and accelerator of socioeconomic and cultural development. That idea directly caused governments to launch state broadcasting systems and expand press institutions of all ownership types, with the mission of informing their public of government development goals while promoting and engaging citizens with state ideologies. With the emergence of satellite television and the Internet in the 1990s, the governing regimes lost their grip as the digital environment drove a shift away from a monolithic media landscape toward a more pluralistic one. Ayish's chapter discusses the impact of disruptive digital innovations on the region's traditional media systems and considers the effect on interconnected areas and spaces such as organizational structures, performance, media education, and relations with society.

In recent years, videogaming has become the world's largest entertainment industry. Its revenue exceeds that of global film production. Karin Wilkins and Kyung Sun Lee discuss the explosive growth of interactive digital gaming and e-sports within the MENA region. They explore new trends in production and distribution within the global industry, including localization strategies of global game development, co-production, and creation of alternate narratives that are embedded within an individual region's cultural and geographic context. The authors show that the emergent gaming ecosystems consist of cultural texts that should be studied within the context of their production and consumption.

Television remains a primary entertainment and information medium in the Arab region despite the availability of new online sources. Tara Al-Kadi focuses her work on the Egyptian broadcast industry in the post-2011 era because of its importance as part of the mediated Egyptian culture. Al-Kadi's chapter explores the perceptions, attitudes, and experiences of audiences toward television as it remains an agent of socialization, reflecting and preserving cultural values and beliefs. Drawing on critical and theoretical perspectives concerned with realism and critiques of materialism and commercialization, Al-Kadi provides insightful information on audience experiences in Egypt.

Ahmed El Gody's chapter on modern journalism describes the changing nature of news production in Egypt because of the integration of social media, user-generated media, and other facets of networked journalism—a term that describes new forms of technologically driven practices that have come into existence since the 2011 uprisings. He explores the ways in which Egyptian media outlets have expanded their presence on social media and have used social media as a tool to engage with their audience. El Gody considers the changes in newsmaking and distribution, and the possibilities that may arise from participatory journalism. He also sheds light, in broad terms, on how the shift to the new environment can allow news organizations to perform the critical function of mediating information transactions within society.

Part VI: Cultural Evolution: Media's Effects on Societal Norms and Expectations

Part VI of this volume emphasizes the effect of communication on culture—both intracultural and transcultural—in the Arab world through a broad understanding of media effects, including media selection, media reception, meaning construction, and effects on the individual and societal levels. These effects can be reinforced by both traditional media and digital media, as posited by the chapters in this section.

By exploring the image of the United Arab Emirates among the non-Arab expatriates residing in the country, Khaled Gaweesh has updated and expanded Hofstede's cultural dimension theory, bringing significant insights to the field of cross-cultural communication. The UAE has a special character, since its population includes a huge number of expatriates from many nations faced with a spectrum of new circumstances to which they must adapt. They must live in a multicultural, multireligious environment that is somewhat open but is still governed by a very traditional Muslim citizenry. This makes it the ideal situation to study the image of the UAE in the eyes of its non-Arab residents and to explore the variables that influence the image built by these expatriates. Such information has become increasingly important for a government that seeks to make the UAE an appealing destination.

The emergence of social media and online environments has brought changes in the way people construct and reconstruct their identities and build an online self. In her chapter on women's self-representation, Meriem Narimane Noumeur applies Goffman's dramaturgical theory of self-representation and social interaction to reveal how Algerian women present themselves through social media sites. Attempting to understand the degree of gendering effect on women in using and sharing on social media, Noumeur uncovers how the women are depicting and managing their virtual identities through Facebook. She also looks at the ways in which the women construct identities and how they establish their online presence.

Aliaa Dawoud provides a particularly interesting case study of media representation of public opinion through an examination of user comments posted on the YouTube version of an Egyptian talk show. The subject of this particular show was Tunisian president Beji Caid Essebsi's proposal to establish equal inheritance between men and women under Tunisian law. This suggestion, highly controversial in the Islamic world, is seen as a challenge to the Sharia law on inheritance. Featuring an Islamic scholar and a secular journalist, the episode examined the proposed (and later enacted) law. The comments space in YouTube functioned as an intellectual forum for intense discussion of various viewpoints. Dawoud's analysis of the comments examines public sentiment on the legislation and the wider, dominant Islamic ideology behind it.

The concept of watching television has undergone a major transition as audiences in the Arab world have flocked to nontraditional viewing platforms for content. Azza Ahmed's work focuses on the phenomenon of binge-watching, which has been on the increase with "anytime/ anywhere" access to media. The content of streaming services is mostly Western, making the issue of cultural erosion more salient than ever. Following a review of the literature, Ahmed sheds light on three recent studies conducted in the UAE investigating this behavioral phenomenon, and considers the implications of binge-watching of global media for cultural identity.

ACKNOWLEDGMENTS

A book such as this one is designed to be used both as a way to delve into Arab media in the twenty-first century and as a supplement in international and global communication courses. It is intended for communication scholars and graduate students, although some advanced undergraduate students may find it useful, as may scholars in related disciplines. University libraries may wish to add this volume to their reference collections as a comprehensive resource on communication in the Arab world. It can serve as a starting point for discussions about recent Arab media issues. It represents only one moment in time, however, and we encourage the reader to continue looking at the latest scholarly work on the subject.

We are grateful for all the contributions from so many colleagues who produced the excellent work that makes up this book. We would especially like to express our gratitude to Leonard Ray Teel, emeritus professor at Georgia State University, founding member and first president of the Arab-U.S. Association for Communication Educators (AUSACE), and the founding editor of the *Journal of Middle East Media*. We would like to acknowledge AUSACE for bringing many media scholars together—including the two editors of this book. We would also like to thank our predecessors in this history of covering communication in this important region of the world, many of whom we first connected with at an AUSACE conference.

Finally, we hope that you find this book useful and enjoyable. Perhaps you will be one of the future contributors to research on media use in the Arab region.

REFERENCES

Arab Center, Washington, DC. 2020. "The coronavirus pandemic and the Arab world: Impact, politics, and mitigation." March 24, 2020. http://arabcenterdc.org/policy_analyses/the-coronavirus-pandemic-and-the-arab-world-impact-politics-and-mitigation.

Ayish, M. I. 2003. "Beyond western-oriented communication theories: A normative Arab-Islamic perspective." *Javnost—The Public* 10 (2): 79–92. https://doi.org/10.1080/13183222.2003.11008829.

Boyd, D. A. 1999. *Broadcasting in the Arab World: A Survey of the Electronic Media in the Middle East.* 3rd ed. Ames: Iowa State University Press.

Bulus, N. 2020. "Coronavirus becomes a weapon of disinformation in Middle East battle for influence." *Los Angeles Times*, April 8, 2020. https://www.latimes.com/world-nation/story/2020-04-08/coronavirus-becomes-new-front-in-middle-east-battle-for-influence.

Guaaybess, T. 2013. "Introduction: A Return to the National Perspective." In *National Broadcasting and State Policy in Arab Countries*, edited by T. Guaaybess, 1–12. New York: Palgrave Macmillan.

Hafez, K. 2014. "Arab and Western Media Systems Typologies." In *Media Evolution on the Eve of the Arab Spring*, edited by L. Hudson, A. Iskandar, and M. Kirk, 235–50. Palgrave Macmillan Series in International Political Communication. New York: Palgrave Macmillan. https://doi.org/10.1057/9781137403155_15.

Hallin, D. C., and P. Mancini. 2004. *Comparing Media Systems: Three Models of Media and Politics.* Cambridge: Cambridge University Press.

Hamdy, N. 2009. "Arab citizen journalism in action: Challenging mainstream media, authorities and media laws." *Westminster Papers in Communication and Culture* 6 (1): 92–112.

Internet World Stats. 2017. https://www.internetworldstats.com.

Lynch, M. 2015. "After the Arab Spring: How the media trashed the transitions." *Journal of Democracy* 26 (4): 90–99. https://doi.org/10.1353/jod.2015.0070.

McCombs, M., and D. Shaw. 1972. "The agenda-setting function of mass media." *Public Opinion Quarterly* 36 (2): 176–87.

Mellor, N. 2014. "The two faces of media liberalization." *Mediterranean Politics* 19 (2): 265–71. https://doi.org/10.1080/13629395.2014.915914.

Nisbet, E. C., and T. A. Myers. 2010. "Challenging the state: Transnational TV and political identity in the Middle East." *Political Communication* 27 (4): 347–66. https://doi.org/10.1080/10584609.2010.516801.

Northwestern University in Qatar. 2017. "Media use in the Middle East." Accessed April 27, 2020. http://www.mideastmedia.org/survey/2017.

Ramaprasad, J., and N. N. Hamdy. 2006. "Functions of Egyptian journalists." *International Communication Gazette* 68 (2): 167–85. https://doi.org/10.1177/1748048506062233.

Richter, C., I. Dupuis, and H. Badr. 2020. "Media pushing for political transformation: A comparative analysis of issue contestation in Poland before 1989 and Egypt before 2011." *International Communication Gazette* 83 (4): 326–46. https://doi.org/10.1177/1748048520915833.

Rugh, W. A. 1979. *The Arab Press.* Syracuse, NY: Syracuse University Press.

———. 2004. *Arab Mass Media: Newspapers, Radio, and Television in Arab Politics*. Westport, CT: Praeger.

———. 2007. "Do national political systems still influence Arab media?" *Arab Media & Society*, May 2007. https://www.arabmediasociety.com/wp-content/uploads/2017/12/20070523081944_AMS2_William_A_Rugh.pdf.

Sarnelli, V., and H. Kobibi. 2017. "National, regional, global TV in Algeria: University students and television audience after the 2012 Algerian media law." *Global Media and Communication* 13 (1): 57–83. https://doi.org/10.1177/1742766517694473.

I

IN THE BEGINNING

Historical, Political, and Societal Issues
Leading Up to the Arab Uprisings

Arab Regional Civic Action before the Arab Spring

A Media–NGO Study from Casablanca to Dubai

Leonard Ray Teel

Tucked inside Egypt's seaport of Alexandria is the city's cherished oasis from noise and fumes—its historic Rose Garden. Created from a nineteenth-century French architect's design, the Rose Garden has enchanted generations with its beauty and incense. The garden's royal pedigree dates back to the plan by Jean-Pierre Barillet-Deschamps, architect and chief gardener of Paris during the reign of Emperor Napoleon III.

Given such a history, the Rose Garden's devotees were astonished to learn that Alexandria's city government approved condemning part of the garden for a parking lot for a new intercity bus depot. The decision was already approved at the top by Alexandria's governor Ismail El-Gawsaqi.

Citizens soon organized in opposition. In early 1994 the Rose Garden's Friends of the Environment Association, a nongovernmental organization (NGO), went to court and sued the governor. The Friends' NGO, founded in 1990 to provide the garden with constant care, was one of hundreds of NGOs established in the 1990s across Egypt and the Middle East to organize citizen action on problems ranging from education to poverty and the environment.

For the court fight, the Garden's NGO hired a prominent lawyer, Egypt's former attorney general Mohamed Abdelaziz Elgendi. Their lawsuit temporarily stalled the governor's plan, but the Friends worried they would lose because the governor contended the bus station was a public necessity. Even Elgendi worried: "I wouldn't expect success will be on our side" (el-Essawy 1999).

But the NGO found legal support from a new Egyptian environmental law, Law 4, that favored green spaces. Law 4 was approved by the national government to reduce Egypt's serious air pollution by (1) promoting development of new green spaces and (2) prohibiting destruction of existing green spaces.

In court, Elgendi argued that Law 4 now protected the existing *green space* of the Rose Garden and that paving the garden for a parking lot would be *illegal*. "What will be the feelings of all these people if they don't have this garden to breathe?" Elgendi asked. "Several thousands visit the Garden daily. . . . Today, I want to ask Governor El-Gawsaqi: What would be the condition of those residents if they did not have the Garden to spend time and vent their life pressure in?" (el-Essawy 1999).

Despite the court battle, the case drew little public attention until an enterprising Cairo journalist, Mahmoud el-Essawy, wrote in *Al-Ahrar* in 1997 that Alexandria's Rose Garden lawsuit was "the first test case of the new Law 4" (el-Essawy 1997).

In 1999 the court rejected the Alexandria governor's plan, thus preserving all five hectares (12.35 acres) of the Rose Garden. By then, Alexandria had a new governor who changed the plan, locating the intercity bus station nearer to the road to Cairo. "The joint campaign," el-Essawy emphasized to the workshop attendees, "succeeded in saving the garden."

The court's landmark ruling had two other significant effects for citizens and NGOs. First, the court justified the authority of the national government to administer the new environmental protection Law 4 against city governments. Second, the court recognized the *legal status* of an NGO to represent citizen groups.

That legal victory in 1999 surprised the Friends of the Garden NGO as well as Alexandria's governor. The case evidenced that *private citizens*—relatively powerless against governments—gained legal influence when they joined as a *community of interest* in an NGO. The Garden NGO, representing a *community*, had used a *democratic* method to successfully challenge an *authoritarian* decision.

MEDIA–NGO WORKSHOP IN CAIRO, SEPTEMBER 1999

The *Al-Ahrar* journalist, Mahmoud el-Essawy, retold the story of the Rose Garden's NGO at the first of six pan-Arab media–NGO workshops, this one hosted in the renowned Al Ahram Regional Press Institute in Cairo. His audience included twelve Egyptian NGO representatives and twelve Egyptian journalists assembled to document increasing NGO activities across Egypt.

The inclusion of journalists was a key aspect of the workshop because reporting on *non-governmental* organizations was not a standard journalistic practice, as was reporting on the *government* agencies. NGOs generally expressed concern about the lack of press coverage. "Nobody knows us," complained one NGO representative. "Even if we give them something, they don't publish it. We need to let them know the kind of work we do and give us a chance to ask for help. Without the press we are not known to the public. There wasn't even one single story, wasn't even one newspaper speaking about NGOs." In fact, the NGOs received little or no publicity largely because they were generally unskilled in the public relations practice of attracting media attention. Journalists could argue that the NGOs' stories were not *news* and that the NGOs thought of journalists as public relations outlets (NGO–Media Workshop, 1999).

The workshop's keynote speaker was Dr. Amani Kandil, the prominent director of the Arab Regional NGO in Cairo. She noted that Egypt's increased NGO activity was a key reason why the United Nations had chosen Cairo for its Global Conference in 1994 that attracted 20,000 delegates to advance the worldwide NGO movement. By 1999, Kandil said, NGOs in Egypt had surpassed the "tipping point" of development and were a mainstay—with about 14,000 registered NGOs and foundations rooted "in generosity, voluntary initiatives, philanthropy and community service." NGOs had become a significant asset of the nation, she said, because they provided pathways for citizens to deal with societal problems not adequately addressed by government (Kandil 1995, 9–10).

Numerous NGOs now addressed women's issues—marital abuse, underage marriages, and the right to divorce, among others. Some advocated girls' education and discouraged child labor. Some assisted with micro-loans to start small businesses or provide clean water. Others helped the homeless or addressed physical handicaps or aided victims of war and drug abuse.

On the workshop's first day the twelve journalists paired with twelve NGO representatives and then worked together for three days, researching and writing about the organizations' work and interviewing people being helped. The journalist Moushira Moussa and photographer Mohamed Wassim portrayed the work of the Hope Village that rescued Cairo street children by providing housing and education. A notable success was a street boy named Ahmed who had now graduated from college and had become a role model (Moussa 1999, 6–7). Other journalists documented the work of an NGO that aided victims of the infectious Nile River blindness, and another NGO that helped five blind girls learn to play the violin and perform as a quintet.

In less populous Upper Egypt, where medical care was often unavailable, the Association of Egypt's Medical Development had secured private and government funding for technology and training. Another NGO, the Childhood and Development Association, dealt with "entrenched gender norms" that devalued girls' education (Wendoh 2013, 156).[1] Promoting literacy for girls, the association established a community school in 1995 and had notable success in persuading parents to let girls continue into upper grades and learn about occupations other than agriculture. One farmer's daughter, 10-year-old Laila Soliman, told the Egyptian journalist Amany Bassyouny, "I would like to become an engineer when I grow up" (Bassyouny 1999, 1).

The Cairo workshop model was subsequently replicated in Casablanca, Ramallah, Amman, Dubai, and a second time in Cairo. Overall, journalists working with NGOs published more than eighty stories, creating a regional picture of the Arab NGO grassroots movement. Those stories were published after workshops in cooperating newspapers in Cairo and Casablanca in 1999, in the Palestinian Territory in 2000, in Jordan in 2001, in the United Arab Emirate of Dubai in 2003, and in 2004 again at the Al Ahram Regional Press Institute in Cairo.

CASABLANCA: OCTOBER 1999 AT *AL-ITTIHAD AL-ICHTIRAKI*

The Moroccan journalist Abdel Khalek Shabou wrote about the impact of increased migration to Europe upon families left behind. His story focused on a Bedouin woman named Fatima, whose husband deserted her and their three small boys, selling the family cow for travel money and joining his friends emigrating to Europe.

Fatima worked jobs common for women with only three years of schooling. Herding sheep and working in fields, she strapped the baby to her back and dragged another boy by his hand while the oldest boy stayed home to tend their house and chickens. Fatima's outlook improved after a friend told her of a scheduled visit to her town by an NGO, the Local Partnership and Development Foundation. Fatima explained her idea for starting a business raising sheep and the foundation granted her a micro-loan to buy two sheep (Shabou 1999, 1).

"Fatima's sheep increased in numbers and she started turning a profit," said the Development Foundation's president, Lillian Guillan. Fatima repaid the loan, and the foundation granted a larger loan to expand her business. Fatima gained further support to start a community cooperative for raising sheep and making wool products—a business employing orphaned girls and school dropouts who learned wool yarning and small-carpet weaving. Looking forward, Fatima planned to train more of the town's girls—a "school for all."

At the NGO, Ms. Guillan said, "It's time to admit the importance of micro-credits as an effective tool in combating poverty and reducing the severity of unemployment" (Shabou 1999, 1).

Other Moroccan journalists wrote about NGOs assisting with the lack of clean water in rural areas, physical disabilities, and violence against women. Muhammad Ridwan focused on Raqiyya, who with her five children rejoiced because the family "finally has clean water." The NGO Teeska had arranged to install a water pump powered by solar energy.

Muhammad Hird and Khalid Tawrel wrote about young men and women being helped by the Moroccan Organization for Physically Handicapped (al-Widadiya al-Magrabiya li-l-Mua'qin).

Abdelrahim al-Hariti focused his story on a project for young girls in rural Chefchaouen by the Democratic Society for Moroccan Women. As in Egypt and elsewhere, the NGO worked to persuade mothers who refused to send their daughters to school on a bus with boys. The NGO's women emphasized that keeping girls home from educational opportunities was "not beneficial to them or the girls."

Muhammed Mafouz wrote about wives who found refuge at the Center for Listening and Legal and Psychological Guidance for Women Victims of Violence. According to the NGO, the women fled husbands who beat, scalded, and threatened them with knives ("Closeness" 1999, 2, 7).

RAMALLAH: JUNE 2000 AT *AL-AYYAM*

In the Palestinian National Authority, numerous NGOs established programs supporting community education, counseling, mental health, job training, agriculture, and legal aid for the rights of landowners. At the Palestinian Center for Counseling in Beit Hanina, near Jerusalem, staff helped find jobs for young unemployed or underemployed men and women. Palestinian journalists Nizar al-Ghoul and Haitham Muhammad noted that the many youths aided by the center seemed unable to cope in society. The center's program official, Rima Salah, said the young people they saw suffered from an inability to deal with society, leading them to drop out of school. Salah said the dropout rate in Arab Jerusalem was as high as 52%.

One young man who came to the center when he was 17, Ali al-Sheikh, recalled that he "did not know how to talk with others and I was isolated." But in leading a center campaign against drug abuse, he demonstrated organizational abilities. Ali said that when he stood at the podium as a public speaker, he surprised those who knew him as a loner: "Now I feel the importance of my existence. I feel that I am important in society" (al-Ghoul and Muhammed 2000, 6 [Arabic], 10 [English]).

In a rural Palestinian area southeast of Nablus, a Palestinian farmer was helped to realize his dream of growing apples as his father had done. The veteran journalist Mohammed Daraghmeh wrote that Ibrahim Abu Sbaih gained support from the Palestinian Relief Committee (PARC) after "the clear success" of three sample apple trees. "The lack of fruit production encouraged the relief committee to adopt this project to spread the cultivation of apples in areas such as Qublan," Daraghmeh wrote. The village was suitable because the land is among the highest above sea level in Palestine. Abu Sbaih's success encouraged PARC to support other villagers. In all, thirty-five families planted 15,000 apple trees. According to PARC, its "sustainable development program improves access to food through multiple initiatives like urban home gardens . . . and projects such as a farm-to-table program" linking farmers with consumers in Gaza (Daraghmeh 2000, 7).

Preventing demolition of Palestinian homes has been the goal of the Palestinian Society for the Protection of Human Rights and Environment (LAW), an NGO that provides legal aid eligible to argue in Israeli courts. The journalist Kawthar Salam wrote how LAW interceded in court when the home of the Palestinian family of Samih Jaber in agricultural al-Baqa'a was targeted for demolition by the Israeli government. "I was haunted by nightmares," Jaber's wife, Fathiyah, told Salam. Fathiyah said she imagined the sound of Israeli bulldozers demolishing the house over the heads of her five children. "I would get really scared and come closer to my little child and hug him to my chest as if someone was kidnapping him from me. How many times did I stand witness to the demolition of the neighboring houses of my relatives." Salam noted that Jaber's family claimed inheritance of that land dating back to the Ottoman Empire, but the LAW society had lost its case in a lower court. On appeal, four years later, the NGO won a ruling from an Israeli higher court to prevent the demolition.

The field investigator for LAW, Fahmi Shahin, said the NGO would continue to defend families. But he noted a continuing demolition trend affecting hundreds of Palestinians. He said that in the first four months of 2000, Israeli authorities issued 189 demolition orders to families in the Hebron area, where ten houses were demolished in 1999. In that year, LAW succeeded in stopping thirteen demolitions (Salam 2000, 1 [Arabic], 12 [English]).

AMMAN: MAY 2001 AT *AL-RA'I*

The Jordanian journalist Aman al-Sayeh focused on the story of Hania, a 14-year-old Palestinian girl who had been transferred from Gaza by way of Egypt to a hospital in Amman. Hania was a victim of a remnant of war in Palestinian Gaza—an unexploded landmine.[2] Hania had been living with her mother and sister in Gaza's Nuseirat Refugee Camp. After school, she was taking the family's four sheep to graze when she stepped on the landmine, triggering an explosion. "I was sitting at home," Hania's mother told al-Sayeh, "and I heard a loud noise and the walls and the earth were shaking. I didn't know that the victim of this was my daughter."

After first aid, Hania was transported for treatment in Jordan, traveling the roundabout route through Gaza's southern Rafah border crossing into Egypt and then by air to Amman. There she was treated in the Islamic Hospital and attended by members of an NGO, the Women's Division of the Islamic Action Front. The head of the Women's Division, Arwa Kilani, told al-Sayeh that the division "covers the costs of the wounded who cannot be treated in Palestinian hospitals." Ms. Kilani said their mission was to serve the Palestinian cause and bring the stories of these wounded to the world. In her hospital bed, Hania told al-Sayeh, "I would have felt more pain and hurt if I lost one of my sheep." At the hospital Hania learned that the NGO had arranged to take her to Iraq to be fitted with prosthetic feet (al-Sayeh 2001, 1 [Arabic], 12 [English]).

Across Jordan, the problem of child labor is an official national concern. A study by the National Task Force for Children, titled "Child Labor in Jordan," documented hazards children face, notably as victims of accidents and physical and sexual abuse. On Amman's main streets, children spend days and nights in unsafe conditions, usually to help their families.

Interviews with working children revealed unstable home situations. The Amman journalist Fatima Smadi focused on 12-year-old Fahd, who daily walked between cars at traffic lights, competing with other boys as he peddled pastries and chewing gum by the stick (two pieces for five piasters). "My dad used to be a merchant," Fahd told Smadi, "but he went to jail more than once for forging checks." Fahd said his income helped his family while his older brother had a regular job to pay the rent. "This work is not a shame or forbidden," Fahd said, "but it's work with no future. And I am sick, and at night I have fever because of tonsillitis." Quitting is not a solution: "How can I feed my family?" (Smadi 2001, 1, 12). Nine-year-old Mosa told Smadi, "My dad is married to three women and he divorced my mother. He gives us 40 JDs [Jordanian dinars] at the end of the month. Although my mom works, this isn't enough." Abed, 13, said his father was sick, his mother had no work, and he had a handicapped brother and two other brothers who went to jail because of a fight. Abed shivered as he spoke: "I always sell chewing gum and corn in front of schools, and I live with my family in one room" (Smadi 2001, 1, 12).

A Jordanian government task force concluded that Jordan needed a long-term plan and amendment of laws that would allow children to work under certain conditions to help support their families. One task force project, "From One to Another," engaged working children to meet and talk among themselves about their problems, leading them to make decisions that can prevent abuse. In another "Generations" project, the task force organized mixed teams of street children and non-working children to discuss their situations with each other. "This way," said Sadiq Khawaja, with the task force's documentation department, "it makes the children able to be partners in spreading knowledge of the risks of child labor and making programs to reduce this problem" (Smadi 2001, 1, 12).

DUBAI: DECEMBER 2002 AT MEDIA CITY

As Dubai's leaders developed the Arab world's richest seascape with a man-made island and skyscrapers, some environmentalists were troubled by an underside to rapid development. By 2002, the impact of Dubai's accelerated growth on the ecology of both the Arabian Gulf and the desert had become a focus for environmental protection undertaken in part by NGOs.

In this context, the workshop hosted by Zayed University in Dubai's Media City focused on a mix of NGOs and Dubai government agencies (Rodrigues 2002, 4). Stories written during the workshop in December 2002 were featured in a special bilingual publication, *Earth Scream*, on February 4, 2003, on the UAE's fifth annual National Environment Day ("Workshop" 2003, 8).

The workshop's stories about environmental impact on the Gulf focused on five issues: overfishing of baby sharks, destruction of coral reefs by an alien sea creature, pollution in the nearby desert, protection of native birds, and the impact on sea turtles' nesting areas from the Palm Jumeirah island megastructure jutting into the Gulf.

The alien sea creature in the Gulf—the crown-of-thorns starfish—was a recognized menace, attacking one of Dubai's treasured coral reefs. One private NGO, the Emirates Diving Association, headed by Ibrahim Al Zu'bi, sponsored a Coral Monitoring Project to deal with the starfish. He said the starfish suck the life fluid from living coral, leaving sections of the reef as a skeleton so brittle that, when struck, the reef breaks like glass. Zu'bi said his association planned to expand the monitoring project, which has sponsored dives to catch starfish in five treasured locations: Snoopy Island, Coral Gardens, Martini Rock, Sharm Rocks, and Hole in the Wall (Al Zu'bi 2003, 7).

Another NGO campaign against overfishing of sharks contends against local and international appetites for shark cuisine, as journalist Dominic Rodrigues of the daily *Gulf Today* reported. Baby sharks are an established delicacy when boiled and sautéed in herbs and spices in a dish called *geshid*. Shark fins also are cooked in soups and sold for as much as $100 a bowl; shark fins are also exported, notably to Southeast Asia. Sharks' livers also are coveted for waterproofing boats, noted Dr. Saif al-Ghais, with another NGO, the International Union for the Conservation of Nature. "Little do these consumers know," he said, "that they are contributing to the decline—and possible extinction—of the shark species" (Rodrigues 2003, 7).

Without sharks, the balance of nature in the Gulf could change unfavorably, Dr. al-Ghais said.

> The shark is considered the dominant predator in the marine ecosystem and removing them will cause an environmental vacuum. Sharks are likely to be replaced by another predator like the barracuda, whose presence may lead to decline or adversely affect other species of marine creatures. Sharks as a species ... play a very important role in keeping the marine environment clean by eating sick and weak sea creatures, and thus maintaining a healthy balance of the fish species in the sea. (Rodrigues 2003, 7)

Laila Yousef al-Hassan, with the government Environmental Research and Wildlife Agency, focused on protected birds and a failed attempt to smuggle several into Dubai as bait for falconry. That was, she said, "one environmental crime that has a happy ending." She also reported the smuggling of seventeen severely dehydrated houbara bustards, an endangered species now seldom found in Dubai. The bustards, discovered in sacks stuffed under seats of a vehicle, were treated and scheduled to be transferred to the rehabilitation center at the Al Ain Zoo, to be released before the start of their migration season (al-Hassan 2003, 7). In winter, when the birds migrated from north Asia to Pakistan, they were met by Arabs on shooting vacations, providing Pakistanis with a source of income.[3]

The environmental problem posed by discarded plastic bags was personified in Dubai by the death of a beloved cow. As reported in Dubai's *Earth Scream*, a 75-year-old deaf and mute widow named Mahra depended on her cow for subsistence. While grazing at the edge of the desert, her cow ate a plastic bag and died choking. "The cow was very dear and close to my aunt," said Mahra's niece, Selma al-Koutbi. "It used to give my aunt company in her loneliness. It drew smiles on her face and gave her a lot of love and hope." When the story was broadcast on radio, Ms. Koutbi said, "Many people proposed to replace the lost cow ... but my aunt never forgot her loss caused by plastic, which to her constitutes an enemy to humans, animals and plants" ("Plastic bags" 2003, 1 [Arabic], 8 [English]).

A decade later, a campaign to ban the bags got more support. The Ministry of Environment and Water reported that plastic bags caused half of camel deaths each year. From 2013 onward, the UAE ruled that plastic bags "must be biodegradable" as directed by the Emirates Authority for Standardization and Metrology, which also deals with date palm fruit and grocery labeling. And in 2020, the Dubai International Airport (DXB) and Al Maktoum International Airport (DWC) banned all single-use plastics (including knives, forks, and spoons) throughout their terminals.

CAIRO: JUNE 2004 AT AL AHRAM REGIONAL PRESS INSTITUTE

During this second Cairo media–NGO workshop at the Al Ahram Regional Press Institute, all Egyptian NGOs were operating under increased surveillance from the national government. In 2002, the government passed Law 84 regulating all such organizations. The law specified new restrictions on NGOs, provided for dissolving them, and threatened up to a year's imprisonment for those committing a gross violation of law or the public order or morality (Herrold 2016).

That 2004 media–NGO workshop revealed significant new NGO activities assisting citizens. One story focused on the Egyptian Development and Environment Youth Association campaign to protect children from life-threatening danger from contaminated medical waste carelessly discarded. The journalist Hisham Younis interviewed 9-year-old Ayman in his hospital room. The boy told how he found discarded medical gloves in a government hospital's garbage dump near his soccer field and wore those gloves as he played goalkeeper. Now in the hospital, he was being treated for a deadly hepatitis-B infection that attacked his liver, causing severe pain, fatigue, and lack of concentration. Ayman said his playmates also retrieved discarded syringes from the dump and used them as toy weapons. When his schoolmate Walid visited, Ayman told him, "I am so sad because I couldn't attend the [final] exam."

The Youth Association's president, Dr. Magdi Alam, said their study determined that 16% of hospital wastes are hazardous. The garbage dump, he said, "becomes a hub for diseases." His NGO offers technical training and supervision. Classes at al-Mansoura Hospital had seventy staffers being taught how to deal with medical wastes "either by burning them in a special crematory or by grinding them" (Younis 2004, 1 [Arabic], 8 [English]).

Another issue raised at the workshop was a woman's right to divorce. While Egyptian women have the legal right to divorce (*haq al-esma*), it can be shameful for the bride's family if she insists on that right as part of the marriage ceremony. As the Egyptian journalist Ossama Khaled reported, one NGO—the New Women's Study Center's Youth Forum—helped women with this dilemma. Dr. Rimi Hosni, chairperson of the forum, said the group includes about twenty-five women and aims to give women awareness of basic rights and ways of obtaining them.

Two of the Youth Forum's women, Yaffa and Ahlam, said they had rebelled against tradition by insisting on divorce rights before their weddings. Another bride, Lamia Lotfy, recalled the "very strange" situation during her wedding to her fiancé, Salah, in a Cairo mosque. Before the wedding, Lamia had set several conditions, including the right to work, to travel, and to divorce. Her husband acquiesced to all her conditions, but her family members considered the right to divorce as shameful, Lotfy said. "We were all going to have the marriage procedures completed. Suddenly, my father and my uncle screamed at me, and the minister and the invited people were all rejecting the mere idea of my having divorce rights in my own grip" (Khaled 2004, 8 [Arabic], 10 [English]).

Dr. Hosni said it is "almost impossible for one to speak about the rights of women in a society where the main actors are men. It is equally impossible to speak about a woman's right to divorce. In spite of the fact that the right is legal from the religious point of view, women are denied it." No official statistics exist about the number of women who have insisted on *haq al-esma*, but Dr. Hosni said two unofficial studies report that in 1995 the number reached 3,000 (Khaled 2004).

"The problem," said Yaffa, "has mainly been how to face a reserved society that rejects these strange ideas like a woman getting the right to divorce. I think I'm completely different from the other girls in my own generation. The way I was brought up was totally open. This open upbringing gave me the chance to know what my rights are and what my duties are." When she met her husband, Mohammed, she agreed with him on all the conditions for the marriage. "When we came to marry, we had already reached a common ground to the point that Mohammed did not object to my having the right to divorce." Still, she said, the minister and all the attendants from her own family and Mohammed's family were shocked at the demand. In marriage, Lamia, Yaffa, and Ahlam said they are happy and plan to stay married—that the right to divorce is just that, a right (Khaled 2004).

In Asyut in rural Upper Egypt, staff at the Center for Hearing Female Victims have dealt with violence involved with broken marriages. Its director, Azza Kamel, said the center's mission is to "help women who have been victims of violence." She told journalist Walaa Sharawy the story of one desperate mother named Fekreya, who, abandoned by her husband, showed up at the center with little more than her infant daughter after months of fighting off cold and hunger.

Fekreya said she was 25 years old and had been abused since she was 14—beaten and locked up, sexually assaulted, mistreated in marriage, then left with a crying baby and no money for shelter or food. When the center stepped in, Ms. Kamel said, it told Fekreya about her legal rights, filed a lawsuit to get financial support from her husband, found her a place to live with her daughter, and through its educational workshop trained her as a kindergarten teacher. Fekreya recalled: "I was about to throw my daughter anywhere to protect her from her mother's torment. I sold everything I owned, even blankets protecting me from the cold of winter. I am now able to work, raise my child and support her. She is now in a better condition" (Sharawy 2004, 8 [Arabic], 11 [English]).

POSTSCRIPT: IN MEMORY OF THE CONTRIBUTIONS OF GEBRAN TUENI AND DR. MONA KHALAF

In 1999, one of Lebanon's preeminent news executives, the late Gebran Ghassan Tueni, publisher of one of the nation's most widely read daily newspapers, *Al-Nahar*, asserted proudly that Lebanon had the Arab world's "freest press"—able to speak truth to power.[4]

At the same time, one of Lebanon's leading advocates for women's rights, the late Dr. Mona Khalaf of Lebanese American University (LAU), carried that free-press idea forward in her work. She encouraged and developed bonds between journalists and NGOs that were assisting with Lebanon's recovery from more than fifteen years of civil war. In September 1999 at LAU in Beirut, Dr. Khalaf conducted an inspirational media–NGO workshop that became a model adopted for the AUSACE media–NGO workshops I directed from 1999 to 2004 that are the focus of this chapter.[5]

During Dr. Khalaf's workshop, I witnessed the potential for outstanding cooperation between journalists and NGOs. One of Lebanon's veteran journalists, Najia al-Houssari, a Middle East correspondent for the London-based Arab daily *al-Hayat*, initiated a media–NGO collaboration that, four years later, freed a young girl from the women's prison. During the workshop, two women representing an NGO, House of Hope (Dar al-Amal), told al-Houssari that a teenaged girl named Hanan whom they met in Lebanon's women's prison at Baabda had been sentenced for the murder of her newborn baby. Hanan told them she was innocent.

Al-Houssari followed up with stories about Hanan's case. After four years, she reported that an attorney's investigation uncovered the truth. The girl's parents in south Lebanon had altered her birth certificate to show that she was of age to be married, then arranged to marry her into another family. The investigation indicated that a member of that family raped her and, when her child was born, it was killed, but not by her, though she was charged with murder. In Hanan's defense, Dar al-Amal's legal counsel argued that the criminal justice system had overlooked her actual age and mental condition. In 2003, Ms. Al-Houssari reported: "The girl was released a couple of days ago, after she was declared innocent and had spent four years in prison." In 2004 in Cairo, Najia Al-Houssari was honored by AUSACE as the "Arab Journalist of the Year."[6]

Hanan's story is a textbook case of "girls at risk"—girls aged 15–19 who live in rural areas or in countries in conflicts and who are beyond the scope of projects that normally help young girls. In "Too Young to Be Women, Too Old to Be Girls," Seri Wendoh focused on the rising trend of violence against girls in poverty: "Gender inequality, undervaluing of girls, gender-based violence, sexual exploitation, and deepening poverty are key drivers" (Wendoh 2013, 155).

AUTHOR'S NOTE AND ACKNOWLEDGMENTS

As evidenced by the six pan-Arab media–NGO workshops, NGOs across the Arab world were addressing a widening range of basic societal needs. Where possible, NGOs intervened to help alleviate poverty, hunger, and unemployment. Across the region, NGOs assisted with microfinance, economic development, water purification, health care, women's rights, education for girls, and children's healthcare.

This demonstrative media–NGO project could not have succeeded without the assistance of more than a hundred journalists and NGO representatives and sponsors—notably the cooperative Arab news organizations which hosted the workshops: the Al Ahram Regional Press Institute in Cairo, *al-Ittihad al-Ichtiraki* in Casablanca, *al-Ayyam* in Ramallah, *al-Dustur* and *al-Ra'i* in Amman, and Media City in Dubai. Other institutional support was provided by university faculty with the Arab–U.S. Association for Communication Educators (AUSACE. org) in the participating countries, and by the Georgia State University College of Arts and Sciences and its Department of Communication, the GSU Center for International Media Education (CIME), and the U.S. Bureau of Educational and Cultural Affairs, specifically Thomas Johnston.

Arabic–English translations were kindly provided by Henrietta Aswad, Dr. Wael Kamal, Dr. Hesham Mesbah, Mohammed Daraghmeh, Dr. Issam Mousa, and (no relation) Laila Mousa. Thanks to my wife Katherine Winfield Teel, MFA, who kept me on track with intellectual support and encouragement.

Early drafts were critiqued by faculty referees with the Association for Education in Journalism and Mass Communication (AEJMC) and the American Journalism Historians Association, and a previous version was presented at the 23rd annual AUSACE conference at the University of Louisiana at Lafayette.

NOTES

1. Wendoh served as senior technical officer at the International Planned Parenthood Foundation.

2. Handicap International (HI), an NGO, published a report in 2015 citing a lack of awareness of landmines among young boys and girls (Boedicker 2015). The HI report listed the various ways adults and children are warned about explosive remnants of war (ERWs) but added that "only 29% of those that had seen ERW had actually reported it."

3. One of the attractions of the houbara is the alleged aphrodisiac quality of its flesh that "ranks somewhere between Spanish fly and Viagra" (Conniff 2014).

4. Gibran Ghassan Tueni, interview with Leonard Ray Teel in the *Al-Nahar* newspaper office in Beirut, October 21, 1999. Tueni, the managing director and leading columnist for *Al-Nahar*, was murdered on December 12, 2005, when a bomb targeted his armored car.

5. Media–NGO one-day workshop and discussions were held at LAU on October 21, 1999.

6. Najia al-Houssari, telephone interview with Leonard Ray Teel, April 2003.

REFERENCES

Bassyouny, A. 1999. "Laila challenges illiteracy." *Al Halina*, Al Ahram Regional Press Institute, Cairo, September 1999.

Boedicker, N. 2015. *Bombs Under the Rubble: Study of Awareness of Explosive Remnants of War [ERWs] among the Population of Gaza.* Lyon, France: Handicap International. https://www.handi cap-international.org.uk/sites/uk/files/documents/files/2015-01-report-gaza-bombs-under-the-rubble -handicap-international.pdf.

"Closeness." 1999. *Al-Ittihad al-Ichtiraki*, October 28, 1999.

Conniff, R. 2014. "These birds are dying so that rich, powerful men can improve their sex lives." TakePart, February 7, 2014. http://www.takepart.com/article/2014/02/07/sex-drive-rich-men-killing -bird.

Daraghmeh, M. 2000. "Three trees turned into groves that cover the mountains of Qublan: Abu Sbaih dreamed of growing apples." *Assiraj*, June 2000, Arabic edition.

el-Essawy, M. 1997. "Alexandria governor violates the environmental law." *Al-Ahrar* (Cairo), April 27, 1997.

———. 1999. "'Success Park' in Alexandria: Symbol of resistance; Friends of Environment's 5 years of victory." *Al Halina*, Al Ahram Regional Press Institute, Cairo, September 1999.

al-Ghoul, N., and H. Muhammed. 2000. "Ala' is reborn." *Assiraj*, June 2000, Arabic and English editions.

al-Hassan, L. 2003. "Endangered birds are recovering well." *Earth Scream*, February 4, 2003, English edition.

Herrold, C. 2016. "NGO policy in pre- and post-Mubarak Egypt: Effects on NGOs' roles in democracy promotion." *Nonprofit Policy Forum* 7 (2): 189–212.

Kandil, A. 1995. *Civil Society in the Arab World.* Johannesburg: CIVICUS.

Khaled, O. 2004. "Women's divorce rights." *Egyptian Tale [Hadutu Masria]*, Al Ahram Regional Press Institute, Cairo, May 2004, Arabic and English editions.

Moussa, M. 1999. "The hope road: Two million kids fight for survival in Egypt's streets." *Al Halina*, Al Ahram Regional Press Institute, Cairo, September 1999.

NGO–Media Workshop. 1999. Opening discussion of NGO–media relations. Casablanca, October 5, 1999.

"Plastic bags pose an environmental threat: The story of Mahra's cow and a lonely widow." 2003. *Earth Scream*, February 4, 2003, Arabic and English editions.

Rodrigues, D. 2002. "Eco-workshop calls for people-centered media." *The Gulf Today*, December 16, 2002.

———. 2003. "Hunting baby sharks to extinction." *Earth Scream*, February 4, 2003, English edition.

Salam, K. 2000. "Sameeh Jaber's family stays under his roof: Al Baqa'a between the threat of demolition and the cancerous settlements." *Assiraj*, June 2000, Arabic and English editions.

al-Sayeh, A. 2001. "Explosion stole Hania's feet." *Al-Azem*, May 2001, Arabic and English editions.

Shabou, A. K. 1999. "Fatima defies! Fighting poverty with microcredit loans." In "Closeness," *al-Ittihad al-Ichtiraki*, October 28, 1999.

Sharawy, W. 2004. "Escaping from a life of violence." *Egyptian Tale [Hadutu Masria]*, Al Ahram Regional Press Institute, Cairo, May 2004, Arabic and English editions.

Smadi, F. 2001. "Child labor in Jordan." *Al-Azem*, May 2001, Arabic and English editions.

Wendoh, S. 2013. "Too Young to Be Women, Too Old to Be Girls: The (Un)changing Aid Landscape and the Reality of Girls at Risk." In *Aid, NGOs and the Realities of Women's Lives*, edited by T. Wallace, 155–56. Rugby, UK: Practical Action Publishing.

"Workshop brings together the world of storytellers." 2003. *Earth Scream: A Special Supplement*, Emirates Media and Zayed University, February 4, 2003.

Younis, H. 2004. "Infectious game . . . the medical waste shoots at children." *Egyptian Tale* [*Hadutu Masria*], Al Ahram Regional Press Institute, Cairo, May 1, 2004, Arabic and English editions.

Al Zu'bi, I. 2003. "EDA programme keeps an eye on the crown of thorns starfish." *Earth Scream*, February 7, 2003, English edition.

2

Moroccan Communication Systems from the Era of Public Screamers to the Era of Facebook

Tayeb Boutbouqalt

At the outset, it is worth raising the question, "Can we talk about a Moroccan communication system?" Truth be told, the question is quite burning and controversial. Its treatment presupposes not only an adequate application of systemic analysis to a vast field of multiform communication, but also the existence of a certain number of distinctive features. This makes the Moroccan communication system a structured whole with multiple properties and various elements, which interact and intersect according to some given principles. It is a complex and very broad subject which deserves in-depth research based on a broader theoretical framework, calling upon a multidisciplinary team to work in networks. It is sufficient to say that the following points of investigation are therefore only a rough outline with the aim of highlighting the specifics of this system.

SYSTEMS THEORY

We cannot pretend to provide a thorough analysis of the Moroccan communication system if we content ourselves with an isolated case or superficial reading about the sociocultural specificities of Moroccan society. It is therefore imperative to widen the horizon of the investigations by taking Morocco in whole or in part as an object of research. The labyrinthine field of communication requires a methodology based on multidimensional and transdisciplinary approaches, backed up by the general systems theory (von Bertalanffy 1968). This non-exhaustive theoretical framework deserves to be clarified methodologically: it is necessary to insist on the existence of two diametrically opposed approaches featuring different origins and conflicting underlying theoretical assumptions.

The first approach is Khaldounian. It is based on the concept of *al-assabiyya* (clan spirit/solidarity of the tribal group) as it was developed by the famous historian and sociologist Abd al-Rahman ibn Muhammed ibn Khaldoun (1332–1406) in his classic work, *al-Muqaddima* (Ibn Khaldoun 1967–1968).

To this authority, it is necessary to add the considerable works of three great contemporary Moroccan intellectuals, who have provided complementary and very enlightening scientific contributions: the insightful and forward-thinking contributions of the late Mohammed Abed al-Jabri (1935–2010); the remarkable production in the humanities and social sciences of the late Mahdi Elmandjra (1933–2014); and the vast historical-political and sociocultural synthesis of the historian Abdalla Laroui (b. 1933).

The second approach is a Western-centric approach represented by fairly rich and diversified intellectual productions. Their common denominator consists of a more or less condescending and dominating look. Several examples can be cited as investigations that purport to be innovative and generally respectful of modern scientific methodology. The goal here is not to make their critical analysis, though in all cases critical thinking must be the basis of any objectified interpretation. These sources cover practically the whole of the twentieth century and their pertinence and relevance cannot be called into question. Although different, their observation methods are broadly complementary and very useful for understanding the Moroccan communication system as a whole.

A brief chronological presentation of the aforementioned sources is as follows: 1908—the ethnographic reflections of Edmond Doutté (1867–1926); 1923—the comparative psychosociological considerations of Louis Brunot (1882–1965); 1926—Edvard Alexander Westermarck's (1862–1939) field surveys focused on the cultural analysis of the Moroccan tribal fabric; 1955/1978—the thesis of Jacques Berque (1910–1995); 1958—the vast and very instructive fieldwork by Daniel Lerner (1917–1980); 1968—the comparative case study of Clifford Geertz (1926–2006); 1969—the anthropological investigation of Ernest Gellner (1925–2015) devoted to the Moroccan Amazigh of the Atlas; 1975—the analysis of the Moroccan political regime by John Waterbury (b. 1939); 1979—an enlightening segmentary research by Paul Pascon (1923–1985) on the socioeconomic, political, and cultural instances of social formation in Morocco; 1982—Mark Tessler, "Morocco: Institutional Pluralism and Monarchical Dominance," in *Political Elites in Arab North Africa: Morocco, Algeria, Tunisia, Libya, and Egypt*, edited by I. William Zartman, et al.; 1993—Henry Munson Jr., *Religion and Power in Morocco*; 1994—John Waterbury, "Democracy without Democrats? The Potential for Political Liberalization in the Middle East," in *Democracy without Democrats? The Renewal of Politics in the Muslim World*, edited by Ghassan Salamé; 1997—Mark Tessler, "Kingdom of Morocco," in *The Government and Politics of the Middle East and North Africa*, edited by David E. Long and Bernard Reich; 2000—Guilain Denoeux, "The Politics of Morocco's Fight against Corruption," *Middle East Policy* 6 (2); 2002—Dale F. Eickelman and Armando Salvatore, "The Public Sphere and Muslim Identities," *Archives Européennes de Sociologie / European Journal of Sociology / Europäisches Archiv für Soziologie* 43 (1); 2004—William A. Rugh, *Arab Mass Media: Newspapers, Radio, and Television in Arab Politics*; 2012—Taylor Dewey, Juliane Kaden, Miriam Marks, Shun Matsushima, and Beijing Zhu, *The Impact of Social Media on Social Unrest in the Arab Spring: Final Report*.

Far from being exhaustive, the above sources nevertheless represent a sample of scientific studies depicting their object, Morocco, as a multifaceted human sociohistorical entity. Their contribution to the understanding of the Moroccan communication system cannot be underestimated.

THE MOROCCAN COMMUNICATION SYSTEM IN ACTION

The aim of the present overview is to lay the background foundation for a better understanding of the specifics of this system. Starting from a general observation, we note that relations between members of Moroccan society have historically been characterized by direct contacts, during which there is an intense exchange of information of all kinds. In peacetime as well as in times of unrest, Moroccan information circuits generally work very well. It is clear that the affective factors have always been decisive in the perceptual management of space/time. This means that for Moroccans, proximity information has been for centuries anchored in the neighborhood, from a spatial point of view. At the same time, ties of kinship, tribal affiliation, and religious convictions have had their role to play from an emotional point of view. News from distant lands was peddled by caravan traders, pilgrims returning from the Holy Places, travelers across the country for various reasons, and nomads, mostly transhumant pastoralists who moved in search of water sources and good pastures for their herds.

The amalgamation of news from distant regions with local news was done in privileged places through interactive exchanges: the *suq*s (generally weekly markets bearing the name of the day and the locality where they take place); the *mussem*s (annual customary socioeconomic and cultural festivals); mosques (meeting places for daily prayers, religious festivals, and any event requiring the mobilization of the community); *zawiya*s (Muslim brotherhoods with multiple socioeconomic, political, and religious functions); water sources (any water point where Moroccans, especially women, used to go to fetch water); and the *hammam* (also called "Turkish bath" or "Moorish bath"), whose function is eminently sociocultural as it is not limited to bodily cleansing.

These were the most important traditional centers of education and dissemination of information for Moroccan public opinion. People visited these places regularly, which enabled a continuous exchange of information from various but generally reliable sources. With the diversity of these meeting points, the cross-checking and verification of information was done fairly consistently and within relatively short periods. The rapid circulation of this information, without written support, intrigued the European colonizers, who, with considerable irony, named this system "Arab telephone."

Functioning via direct human contact, these main centers of information and education of Moroccan public opinion operated freely until the beginning of the twentieth century. It is worth noting that in such centers, information was free and thus acquired by any Moroccan out of simple natural human curiosity under the pressure of the needs and traditions in vogue in society at that time.

Religious and popular festivals and other public or private ceremonies offered Moroccans multiple opportunities to meet, and to express their feelings and exchange opinions on all matters of concern. This in turn helped to maintain the flow of this uninterrupted exchange of information. The whole formed a dynamic communication system where the written medium stood at a respectful distance behind all that was verbal. The Moroccan communication system was fundamentally characterized by the oral tradition, which has remained for a very long time the privileged channel of transmission of all Moroccans from generation to generation, exactly like in other African cultural spheres (Vansina 1985).

Undoubtedly, illiteracy and the near-absence of an adequate technical infrastructure explain this duration: the printing press was introduced in Morocco only in the second half of the nineteenth century and its impact was very weak. In fact, until the beginning of the twentieth century, Morocco had neither a railway nor a modern road network. Writing remained the prerogative of a handful of Moroccan scholars: *ulema*, *fuqaha* (Muslim scholars and experts in Islamic jurisprudence), and senior officials of the Makhzen (Moroccan administration). Although confined to a limited sphere, letters were exchanged and most often accompanied by comments and information communicated orally by a *raqqas* (messenger/postman). The urgent press releases from public authorities were most often brought to the attention of the populations by human voice, in the form of brief statements read by *al-barrah* ("public screamer"). The screamer usually had to repeat the message several times in front of a target group of inhabitants in a given space.

As for the credibility of such information sources, note that rumors have always occupied, even today, a preponderant place in the Moroccan communication system. A "fact" amounted to a rumor that could actually be proved.

THE MOROCCAN COMMUNICATION SYSTEM AT THE TIME OF THE *RAQQAS*

Before the twentieth century, Morocco had both a public and a private organized mail management service. It was provided by private agents called *raqqassa*. These private agents were pedestrians who were responsible for delivering the mail entrusted to them to the places of its destination within a given area. A *raqqas* could cover an average distance ranging from forty to fifty kilometers per day. For every one hundred kilometers on foot, they received an average salary corresponding to forty French francs (1867 value).

In each city, the *raqqassa* had their *amin* (chief), a former *raqqas* himself, to whom they had to pay 2.5% of their salary. It was the *amins* who organized and managed the entire service; for example, they always had a sufficient number of *raqqassa* ready to leave for any given destination if the needs of the service required it. The chiefs were personally responsible for the letters and the deposits that were given to them. They strictly entrusted these items to men physically and morally able to accomplish such missions. This activity, therefore, appeared to be a "liberal profession" subject to customary practices and rules in force. However, its legal status remained uncertain: the administrative authorities (Makhzen) constantly called upon these agents, who perfectly fulfilled the task of a public service which was not officially recognized. Many of them were purely and simply agents exercising their function on a permanent and exclusive basis for the benefit of administrative services, in their capacity as "civil servants" (Boutbouqalt 1996, 116).

During a certain historical period, the *raqqassa* provided the entire postal service of the Moroccan government, as well as that of the foreign consulates established in Morocco. The ever-increasing need for communication, accentuated by the development of economic and administrative activities of the kingdom, and the insufficient means employed to satisfy this need pushed Sultan Moulay Hassan (1873–1894) to consider the creation of a central postal service. The organization and coordination of the activities of this service were the object of the royal decree of November 22, 1892 (Champredone 1984, 39). It was on this date that *raqqas* was recognized as a profession and integrated into the "public service sector."

This new system took over the structures of the previous one, giving them a more official character to make them more effective; for example, messages were delivered under the authority of the post office *umana* (*raqqassa* chiefs) in the main cities of Morocco. The wages of these agents were paid, in part, from a 5% fee levied on customs taxes. Inside the country, their wages were deducted from the *mustafadat* (income from taxes on state property).

The assets and conditions required to exercise this appreciated and coveted profession were a good physical constitution, an experiential knowledge of the geography of Morocco, good moral qualities, and a good reputation based on seriousness and confidence. Sultan Moulay Hassan's postal initiative heralded the introduction of a vast modern communication system in Morocco, which was, however, aborted by the actions of an invading colonial movement (Boutbouqalt 1996, 115–16).

THE FLOW OF INFORMATION BETWEEN ORAL TRADITION
AND THE SACREDNESS OF THE WRITTEN WORD

Although oral tradition largely dominated the circulation of information, the written word had always enjoyed a "sacred" status for different reasons. First, since the conversion to Islam of almost the entire Moroccan population, the most widespread manuscript in all of Morocco has been the Quran. Second, official legal documents, such as real estate titles, were usually drawn up; therefore, their diction exhibited their sanctity. Expressions like "May Allah venerate/bless your parents" were and still are very common. Nowadays, they are generally pronounced during courteous exchanges between Moroccans. Moreover, before the advent of digital communication all public or private letters usually began with the expression "Praise be to God, In the name of God, the Compassionate, the Merciful." Therefore, the written word has remained the symbol of the sacred and holds authority that is both legitimate and binding.

Certain Sufis, including Ibn Arabi (1165–1240), Jabir Ibn Hayyan (721–815), and especially the Shiite Muslims, invented a "mystical science of letters" (*jafriyya*) where eschatology and clairvoyance arise. This mysterious force of writing has even been exploited maliciously by sorcerers of all kinds. This is why, even today, there are still charlatan "healers" who transcribe formulas, enigmatic in nature, at the bottom of a bowl and then mix them with springwater before administering them to their patients. The mixture is believed to have an effective therapeutic power against their suffering. In terms of superstition, it is not uncommon to find, in certain regions of Morocco, people who believe in wearing a talisman to drive out "evil spirits" and to symbolically protect against the "evil eye."

In short, the value of writing in Moroccan society in past centuries can only be explained in a very small part by the scarcity of paper. The introduction of the European colonial press in Morocco shook up this communication system, without, however, being able to undermine its basic foundations.

GENERAL STRATEGY OF FRENCH COLONIAL PROPAGANDA IN MOROCCO

From 1912 to 1956, Morocco was under European colonial occupation, predominantly French. The official establishment of the Protectorate of the French Republic in Morocco in 1912 was the never-denied foundation for the entire propaganda policy of the colonial system. Official statements by political and military authorities, taken up and amplified by the media at the time, continuously exploited this general pattern of propagandist information that prevailed from the start of the occupation until the independence of the country.

This is why 1912 is historically regarded as the reference year for this general strategy of French colonial propaganda in Morocco. It was the year in which the treaty of Morocco was signed by the Protectorate of the French Republic. The main strategic outlines of this colonial propaganda were twofold. The first depicts an independent Morocco pre-1912 as having an obscure past and emphasizes traits like barbarity, anarchy, backwardness, underdevelopment, and misery. The other depicts post-1912 Morocco under French domination as having a bright future while highlighting ideas like civilization, order, progress, guaranteed development, and wellbeing (Boutbouqalt 1996, 178).

THE ARCHETYPES OF COLONIAL DISCOURSE

Situated, as it was, at the gates of Europe, could Morocco escape from its colonial hold? Colonial propaganda campaigns used to present this country as resistant to "civilization," a country inhabited by a "fanatic" and "xenophobic" population. A terrified European public ended up believing it. All the possible attributes to denigrate the cultural identity of the Moroccan people were abundantly repeated, thus offering to European public opinion many "justifications" to colonize or "civilize" the country from things such as barbarism, anarchy, fanaticism, and xenophobia. Moroccan society, culture, and political power were treated by the European media of the time as an anachronism.

> Moroccan society is little more than a bad meeting of tribes. These tribes live side by side without merging, without penetrating each other, exchanging more gunshots than good methods, and with them the idea of nationality is as absent as that of obedience to a common chief. This chief exists, however, but one would seek in vain to find points of analogy to him with any representative of a European state. (Leblanc 1906, 9; author's translation)

After a few trips to Morocco at the beginning of the twentieth century, Eugène Aubin published the results of his investigation in several newspapers: *La Renaissance Latine*, *La Revue de Paris*, *Le Journal des Débats*, and *La Revue des Deux Mondes*. He brought together all of his propagandist thinking in a book in which he described Morocco as follows:

> I was allowed to observe Moroccan feudalism, that is to say a kind of Holy Empire, frozen in Islamism, with its incoherent federation of tribes, its customs from another age and its complicated play of religious influences; all things that make Morocco the most extraordinary of Muslim states and give it a disconcerting character for the newcomer. (Aubin 1904, iv)

According to this propaganda, Morocco, like other countries of North Africa, had suffered a civilizational delay because of Islam. The Islamization of the Maghreb was interpreted as the source of all the misfortunes of North Africa. Colonial propaganda considered this historic event as the origin of handicaps, preventing the realization of any project aimed at the economic and social development of the Maghreb. "The doctrines of Islam are, moreover, opposed to any progress; Muslims declare that they have nothing better to do than to keep the traditions of their ancestors" (Leblanc 1906, 13).

What characterized Morocco, according to this propaganda, was its secular anarchy. The newspaper *Le Radical*, dated January 15, 1908, did not hesitate to give this definition of Morocco: "Morocco is not a nation: it alone is ten, twenty countries ready to turn against each other and thus create the most inextricable of anarchies."

THE INTRODUCTION OF THE EUROPEAN COLONIAL PRESS IN MOROCCO

Since the expedition of Napoleon Bonaparte (1769–1821) to Egypt in 1798, the press has always been considered a valuable accessory to the execution of all French colonial policy. The occupation of Algeria in 1830 and Tunisia in 1881 demonstrated this fact (Boutbouqalt 1996, 53–63).

Long before the country's official colonization, Morocco was the scene of a hostile and aggressive European press, over which the Moroccan political power had no means of control, either legal or political. In this regard, the complaints repeatedly made by the Moroccan administration at the end of the nineteenth century had been futile and even ridiculous (Boutbouqalt 1996, 40–52).

Two fundamental observations characterized this European press that was launched in Morocco at this time. First, a concentration in time and space. Between 1883 and 1900, more than 80% of European newspapers in Morocco appeared in Tangier. As for the few Spanish newspapers published in Ceuta, Melilla, and Tétouan, they had irregular and brief appearances, and a very small audience.

Second, almost all of these newspapers were written by Moroccan Jewish journalists who were "protected" by one European power or another. While defending their own interests, such journalists were not independent as they put themselves at the service of colonial powers and therefore may have felt obligated to government interests. This was particularly true because of their closeness to those in the position of economic powerbrokers. This helped to directly facilitate the ideal European transmission of ideas.

In the name of protecting Morocco against the barbarism of the government and people, this press was able to actively engage in Morocco's path of reforms and progress in the name of civilization. This was particularly effective because there were no regulations governing the activities of the press at the time.

The languages in which these periodicals were written were Spanish, French, and English. The geographical proximity of Spain—reinforced by its occupation of the Moroccan cities of Ceuta and Melilla in 1415 and 1497 respectively—the British occupation of Gibraltar since 1704, and the French occupation of Algeria since 1830 were propitious for the involvement of these countries in a contest of influence. Morocco was no longer able to defend itself effectively and preserve its sovereignty.

After Tangier, this press would move to Casablanca and Rabat. Its development was closely linked to the colonizers whom it praised, and thus contributed to acceleration of its extension. Mainly because of the First World War, this press had to slow down its activities considerably. After the Armistice of 1918, it witnessed a real progression, which was to culminate at the end of 1929, the start of the great world economic crisis.

In a study devoted to "the French-language periodical press in Morocco from its origins to 1929," Roger Falcou looked at the classical archetypes of colonial discourse irreparably glued to the image of Morocco. For him, the introduction of the French press was a "benefit" by which Morocco could be torn from its "medieval anarchy." He said:

> Imagine, Roger Falcou invites us, on the brink of the twentieth century, five million inhabitants, cut off from the world, separated by their division into tribes, by the persistence of dissent and the periodic revolts of "rouguis." Material life was most rudimentary. No source of information, no means of dissemination, runners traveling on foot, the "Rekkas" carried the correspondence. As for the rumors circulating by word of mouth via the "Arab telephone," they provoked violent reactions and explosions of anarchy. One event may have shaken Morocco from its torpor: the appearance of the press. It seems to have set the stage for the prestigious development which, under the aegis of France, was to transform this medieval land, traditionally closed to external influences, into a modern nation. (Falcou 1956, 7)

In relation to the general content of the French colonial press in Morocco, the main Protectorate newspapers stood out above all in matters of local controversy and in all matters relating to the defense of colonial private interests. Overall, the French colonial press in Morocco was a business press: publicity had come in overwhelmingly, like the revival of the colonial economy in the aftermath of the First World War (Boutbouqalt 1996, 304).

The colonial press strategy was to maintain a gap between private colonial interests and the general French propaganda policy necessary for the advancement of the colonial enterprise. This problem was easily resolved when the Maroc Soir (Mas) press group got hold of the press sector with the firm support of the first Resident General of the French Protectorate in Morocco, General Lyautey. The few newspapers demonstrating a certain critical spirit or pushing the art of controversy very far were subjected to a repressive legal regime, which governed the press in a selective manner. The Protectorate press as a whole was a propaganda press, not a news press in the literal sense. One could only speak of "information" accidentally through the shocks of local controversies, or following a general counter-propaganda action dictated by the colonial power.

The Havas agency, of which the current Agence France Presse is the heir, had opened its first office in Tangier in 1889. With the establishment of the Protectorate regime in 1912, and as the colonial troops gained ground, the activities of the Havas agency followed the same pattern. The action of Havas was most often confused with that of the French colonial authorities in Morocco (Boutbouqalt 1994).

CINEMA AND RADIO PROPAGANDA

The primary objective of the introduction of cinema and broadcasting in Morocco was to strengthen the impact of colonial propaganda targeting the indigenous populations. The forerunner of film propaganda in Morocco was none other than General Lyautey. His successor, Théodore Steeg, organized radio propaganda by inaugurating the Radio Station Maroc in February 1928 (Boutbouqalt 1994, 448). The colonial authorities presented these new media as "achievements" made for the benefit of Moroccans. The possibility that these two media could work for the intensification of propagandist activities was perceived very early by the General Residence in Rabat, which gave them first-rank importance.

On December 13, 1916, General Lyautey was appointed Minister of War; he left Morocco for his new ministerial functions in Paris. He did not resume his powers as Resident General in Rabat until March 1917. On February 22, 1917, during his time in France at the head of the Ministry of War, the Cinematographic of Morocco was created in accordance with his directive and thus attached to the occupation troops of Morocco. Its mission was not only to intensify propaganda in indigenous circles, but also to maintain the morale of colonial troops.

On May 17, 1919, Lyautey proposed the creation of a new service called Groupe Cinématographique du Maroc. He was very happy with the results obtained from this new colonial propaganda tool. Furthermore, he wrote to the Minister of War in Paris: "The results of these various tests have been very satisfactory. It was recognized that the cinematographic sessions could be given in good conditions to the front occupation troops, despite the communication difficulties. In addition, the cinematograph is more successful with the indigenous populations and constitutes an excellent means of propaganda" (Lyautey 1919).

General Lyautey considered cinema "an educational tool for our protégés" (*Bulletin d'information* 1945). This "education through cinema" was a pure propaganda operation consisting of defending the image of France as a "protective power" for Moroccans, which is why Lyautey relied heavily on this new means of propaganda: "Appropriate views and films will certainly leave in the new minds of the Moroccan natives deep traces as to the vitality, the strength, the wealth of France. We can hope that this campaign is likely to give birth in

Moroccans to a feeling of admiration for France, which will certainly increase their confidence in us" (Boutbouqalt 1996, 461–62).

At first very uninformed, then skeptical and somewhat hesitant, the Moroccans ended up accessing a new medium in a relatively short time: broadcasting. The adoption of this innovation went through the five classic stages: knowledge, persuasion, decision, implementation, and confirmation. This intercultural contact of the diffusionist type (Rogers 1983) would very quickly prove to be a double-edged sword, in the sense that it would strengthen the arsenal of colonial propaganda while indirectly enlightening the Moroccans on the situation they were in.

In 1930, Europeans living in Morocco had 2,630 radio receivers while Moroccans had only 19. However, the Moroccan public quickly became interested in this new medium: the number of radio receivers owned by Moroccans increased to 7,000 in 1939 and to 16,968 in 1945. Radio Maroc was a new means of colonial political action. It was judged by the political and military leaders of the Protectorate to be of invaluable use both internally, by making life easier for the colonists while fooling the colonized, and externally, by counterattacking all radio propaganda from foreign sources hostile to France (Boutbouqalt 1996, 448–59, 510).

Colonial propaganda by means of television was very short-lived. On May 29, 1951, the General Residence granted a concession to a French private company to introduce television in Morocco. The latter, officially incorporated on June 24, 1952, took the name of Telma. This company was authorized to transmit and relay images and/or video signals, as well as sound signals which could accompany them. It was subject to double financial and technical control. For example, the hours of its broadcasts had to be approved by the colonial authorities in charge of propaganda services. The duration of the broadcasts had to be at least twenty hours. Television commercials were authorized but should not exceed 10% of the transmission time. The financial resources consisted of income from advertisements and the proceeds of various special taxes or annual fees.

The project was begun in September 1952. Telma broadcast its first programs on February 23, 1954, from Casablanca. At that time, this city had more than 700 television receivers. To begin with, Telma planned to prepare three hours of broadcast each day: one hour in French, one hour in Arabic, and one hour in English for an American audience in Morocco. It is important to note that at that time the American presence in Morocco had just been reinforced following the concession of five military bases, which the Protectorate had granted to the government of the United States. By the beginning of October of that same year, in 1954, the number of declared receiving stations had reached about 4,000. The unexpected political evolution of Morocco toward its independence put an end to the activities of this new additional means of colonial propaganda (Boutbouqalt 1996, 531).

The Havas agency, the Mas press group, the Cinematographic Section of Morocco, and Radio Maroc were the main pillars of the propagandist activities of French colonization in Morocco. The main goals of the French Protectorate's information policy in Morocco were to boost the morale of the colonial troops, encourage the establishment of new settlers, stifle the voices of Moroccans, and combat all anti-French propaganda (German, Bolshevik/Communist, Islamic/Nationalist). It was not until after the First World War, thanks in particular to the Rif War, that international public opinion began to be informed about the concrete reality of the devastating activities of European colonization in Morocco (Boutbouqalt 1992).

FREEDOM OF EXPRESSION, THE NERVE CENTER OF THE NATIONALIST REACTION

The introduction of the colonial press in Morocco provoked the reaction of Moroccan public opinion, which manifested itself through a nationalist press and associative, political, and union organizations, all united for the same objective: independence. The main obstacle encountered by young Moroccan nationalists in their political struggle was the almost total absence of freedom of expression and especially the freedom of the press. No Arabic-language newspaper could appear without prior authorization, which was always revocable. In addition, for any "Moroccan" periodical written in French, the manager had to be of French nationality (Boutbouqalt 1996, 420–30). One might wonder why the French were relatively "forgiving" toward Moroccan nationalists desiring to express their ideas in the language of the colonizer.

Three factors were advantageously exploited by the French colonizers. First, Arabic was officially considered by colonial France as a foreign language in Morocco. Then, the French allowed the colonial power to "demonstrate" to international public opinion that France remained faithful to the spirit of the Protectorate treaty signed in Fez on March 30, 1912, with a view to legitimizing its occupation of Morocco under international colonial law. By giving the floor to Moroccan nationalists, even if not in their mother tongue, France was signaling its intention to remain the "guarantor" of the political rights of Moroccans and of the evolution and advancement of the country under French supervision within the framework of international colonial agreements. Finally, any nationalist publication in French should not only strengthen the prestige of the "protector" state, but above all allow the colonial authorities to better control the reactions of a Moroccan public who had no free and independent forum where opinions could be expressed.

It was not until August 4, 1933, that the first nationalist newspaper appeared in Fez, under the title *People's Action*, with the nationalist Mohamed ben Hassan El Ouezzani (1910–1978) at its head. In its edition of October 20, 1933, this newspaper proposed the date of November 18 of each year for the celebration of the feast of the throne, in an attempt to commemorate the sovereignty of Morocco under the reign of Sultan Mohammed V. A few weeks later, the colonial power banned this first Moroccan nationalist newspaper. Thanks in particular to this nationalist media action, in 1934 Sultan Mohammed V appeared officially as the indisputable leader of the nationalist movement in Morocco under French–English–Spanish occupation.

Relatively better treated than those in the French zone, the Moroccan nationalists who established themselves in the northern zone occupied by Spain benefited from a certain leeway in their journalistic initiatives. This situation was mainly due to a certain hidden competition between the two colonial powers. In fact, in both areas, nationalist newspapers were constantly censored, suspended, or banned. This is why the leaflet appeared to the Moroccan nationalists as a reliable medium to circulate their ideas and thus display their independence beliefs. In this regard, the mosque remained more than ever the privileged place for fostering awareness and circulating information to the Muslim audience in Morocco.

The mobilization of public opinion was a major event in the history of the Moroccan nationalist movement as a result of the deportation of Sultan Mohammed V on August 20, 1953. In this regard, two French authors, contemporaries of the last events of the French occupation of Morocco, give this testimony:

> The Moroccan crowds are mobilizable, capable of an impressive discipline: few peoples have given such striking proofs of collective will and union in the face of an objective such as the boycott of French tobacco in 1954–55. To deprive oneself of smoking to express a collective refusal while

inflicting a blow on the opponent's trade seems to us a demonstration of maturity and energy much more significant than this or that act of terrorism committed by a small group with a questionable cause. (Lacouture and Lacouture 1958, 293)

It was this peaceful process of nationalist engagement—the revolution of the king and the people—against colonial propaganda that contributed significantly to the liberation of the country in 1956.

ASSESSMENT OF COLONIZATION

In its September 1953 issue, the American magazine *Look* published an article by William O. Douglas, a justice of the U.S. Supreme Court. The article details Douglas's trip in the French-occupied zone of Morocco and describes the situation in which the Moroccan people found themselves under French colonization: "Morocco is only a country where 9,000,000 inhabitants are enslaved by 350,000 Frenchmen who have no other concern than 'milking the Moroccan cow' for their strict profit. To this end, they monopolized agriculture and industry while trying to keep the natives in misery and ignorance" (Boutbouqalt 1996, 544).

With regard to the assessment of the results of French colonization in all North African countries that were under the French Protectorate, Lucien Sève underlined how much colonial propaganda tried to distort the results of this largely negative work on all levels.

Certainly, there are appearances tirelessly mocked up by colonial propaganda which could make one believe the opposite: industrial and agricultural achievements, development of urban life and means of communication, sanitary or educational measures, etc. It is therefore easy to show photos of beautiful new schools, or roads, or active ports. But first of all, this propaganda is very discreet on the overall balance sheet. It would rather show a photo of such a school, for example, than say what is true: there is no school for almost nine-tenths of the school-age Muslim population. It shows such a hospital, but it does not say that this hospital has a hundred beds for a Muslim population of 200,000 inhabitants, etc. But above all, these achievements are not a function of the colonized people, but a function of the need for colonial exploitation. (Boutbouqalt 1996, 545)

In quantitative terms, it is very difficult to assess the exact impact of the media propaganda of the French Protectorate in Morocco between 1912 and 1956. We can roughly establish statistics on the readers of the newspapers of that time. We also know the overall number of listeners of the Radio Maroc station and the number of spectators of films screened during the same period, but we cannot know exactly what the Moroccan public thought of these propagandist campaigns, apart from their negative impact on the Moroccan resistance movement. What is certain is that these same campaigns did, by a reactive mechanism, provoke an awareness of Moroccan public opinion by mobilizing it to achieve one single objective: the independence of the country.

THE MOROCCAN MEDIA LANDSCAPE IN THE AFTERMATH OF THE COUNTRY'S INDEPENDENCE

A careful and thorough reading of Morocco's evolution in the postcolonial phase up to the current day allows us to draw a conclusion that specialists have great difficulty refuting: the independence of Morocco in 1956 oscillated bitterly between half-failure and half-success. The problem of the Moroccan Sahara and the enclaves that remained in the hands of the Spanish are today the salient points of a half-aborted Moroccan independence.

In any case, Morocco, a young, independent state, has managed to organize itself as a modern state with all the necessary markers of its sovereignty. The hope of building a free, modern, and independent Morocco was the hallmark of a feverish atmosphere for an entire population. However, the new Moroccan political leaders who acceded to power after the partial liberation of their country had no experience in the management of the affairs of a modern state to which they so strongly aspired. At most, they expressed enthusiasm overflowing with the bitter taste of ill-gotten independence.

The old Makhzen organization was no longer viable, and the young Moroccans who came to power further solidified this fact. They had only a heavy legacy from the colonial administration with its legal arsenal, economic apparatus, press, and organizational and bureaucratic structures. They loosely adopted the Protectorate organizational model. It seems that it was in the context of negotiations aimed at otherwise perpetuating colonial power, in the form of a Néoprotectorat, that this decision was made. This can be traced in the fallacious slogan forged by the French government under the famous name of "independence in interdependence." This was how the neocolonial Moroccan state was born—into a subdued dependence that still felt the effects of the actions of the French Republic. This Republic, more than ever, was faithfully committed to the constantly readjusted redeployment of its classical colonial strategy: *la pénétration pacifique*—the hidden invasion.

THE YEARS OF FALSE LEADS AND DASHED HOPES

Like the French colonial power, the new Moroccan authorities paid particular attention to the media. Like the Protectorate, the new government exercised a strict and severe monopoly over the information sector. The nationalist movement, on the other hand, split into several factions which established themselves as political organizations opposed to power, and more particularly, to the institution that embodies it: the monarchy.

For these vital forces in the country, the fight for independence against the colonizer became a fight against the regime for democracy. Everything was played out for almost half a century in the field of human rights and public liberties in an atmosphere of merciless tension and struggle. The opposition partisan press practiced radical journalism in the face of a political power that did not intend to yield anything in the field of freedom of expression. Several newspapers were censored or outright banned. A good number of journalists were brought to justice or even tortured for two major reasons. On the one hand, they did not play the game and sang the praises of a power falsely displaying pluralist liberalism. On the other hand, they bet too much on a democratic ideal whose objective conditions for achievement were not met.

Morocco's mass media in the aftermath of the country's independence, mainly the audiovisual system and the Maghreb Arab Press Agency, were under the direct and highly centralized control of a resolutely autocratic power. In November of 1956, Radio Maroc was attached to a ministerial department responsible for information and tourism. The national information agency, MAP, was inaugurated in 1959 as a symbol of Moroccan media sovereignty in the political realm. With the arrival of television in 1962, the public audiovisual system was reinforced for the almost exclusive benefit of official state policy. It is thus sufficient to say that the overflowing enthusiasm displayed by Moroccan public opinion after the "departure" of the French had quickly fallen into oblivion under the weight of so many dashed hopes.

In the recent history of Morocco, this period from the 1960s to the 1990s is rightly described as the "Years of Lead": blind police repressions, abductions and tortures, unfair trials, frequent strikes by students and workers, mass riots, states of emergency, military attempts to overthrow the monarchical regime, muzzled opposition press, political detainees by the hundreds, state apparatus plagued by corruption, and the like.

The Equity and Reconciliation Commission (IER) was responsible for shedding light on this troubled period in the history of contemporary Morocco. The IER confirms that it has received 16,861 files to study, including 9,779 cases of serious human rights abuses. One hundred seventy-four people died during arbitrary detention or disappearance between 1956 and 1999 (IER, online reports). For civil society actors, including the Moroccan Association for Human Rights, these figures are far from reflecting reality. The figure of around 3,000 killed during this period, also known as the "Years of Embers," is frequently put forward.

DEMOCRATIC PROCESS AND TRANSFORMATION OF THE MOROCCAN COMMUNICATION SYSTEM

The 1990s were marked by an in-depth reform of the Moroccan political system. A long democratic process began to take place. This process was closed and required considerable time and effort for those involved. A grave concern for the respect of human rights and fundamental freedoms occupied a huge place both in political discourse and in the decisions of the powers aimed at reforming the institutions. At the same time, a wind of freedom began to blow on the media field through a series of events.

The proclamation of the National Charter of Human Rights in Rabat and the creation of a Human Rights Advisory Council in 1990, followed by the release of political prisoners and their return from exile in 1991 and 1994, was the catalyst. This was enhanced by the opening of the audiovisual means to electoral campaigns related to legislative and municipal elections in 1992; the organization of the first national symposium on information and communication with a view to introduce structural reforms in the Moroccan media field in 1993; and the introduction of two constitutional revisions as preludes to a democratization of the system in 1992 and 1996. Additionally, the establishment of a Minister of Communication and a government spokesperson in 1994, plus the so-called independent press appearing in the form of *Maroc hebdo* in 1991, *Assahifa* in 1997, and *al-Ahdath al-Maghribia* in 1998, supported the process. And finally, access to power of the first opposition government under the name of "alternation government" in 1998 added fuel to this media reform movement.

After the death of King Hassan II (1961–1999) on July 23, 1999, King Mohammed VI succeeded him with the firm will to consolidate the foundations of the building of the rule of law. On October 12, 1999, in Casablanca, in a speech delivered to the heads of the regions, the *wilaya*s, the prefectures and the provinces of the kingdom, the executives of the administration, and the representatives of the citizens, King Mohammed VI defined the "new concept of authority." It was, in fact, the start of a vast program of progressive and peaceful institutional reform in Morocco at the dawn of the twenty-first century.

RESTRUCTURING OF THE MEDIA FIELD

At the start of this third millennium, two significant facts characterized the evolution of the Moroccan media field: the liberalization of the airwaves, thanks to new audiovisual laws, and the liberation of speech for Moroccan citizens, thanks to the digital revolution, which thus allowed them to have direct access to information via social networks (Ministry of Culture and Communication, legal texts, etc.).

A new era of consolidation of the state of rights in the contemporary sense of the term began with the constitution of 2011. The clauses and provisions of this new constitutional charter provided for human rights in their universal sense and stated that freedom of expression and freedom of the press are substantial. The country seems certain to make a historic break with its recent past, where the most basic rights and freedoms of the citizens were flouted. The reforms of the system are under way and everything seems to indicate their irreversibility, despite some rigidities linked mainly to bureaucratic apparatuses and the slow change of mentalities at the systemic level.

Today, Morocco has nine domestic television channels, including one private channel (Medi1TV) and eight public channels: TVM, TVM Satellitaire, Arriyadiya, Arrabiâ, Al Maghribiya, Assadissa, Tamazight TV, and the regional channel Laâyoun TV. Compared to television, the radio landscape has changed significantly, in terms of both form and content. It is made up of more than thirty radio stations, including fifteen in the public or semi-public sector: Radio 2M, Radio Nationale, Radio Amazigh, Rabat Chaine Inter, Radio Mohammed VI of the Holy Quran, and ten regional radios. There are nearly twenty private radio channels: Medi1 Radio, Atlantic Radio, Radio Sawa, Hit Radio, Radio Aswat, Casa FM, Cap Radio, Chada FM, Radio Plus Marrakech and Agadir, five MFM radios (Atlas, Saïss, Souss, Oriental, and Moroccan Sahara), Luxe Radio, Radio Mars, Medradio, and Medina FM. On the other hand, the web radios that make a timid appearance from time to time are likely to seriously upset the current radio landscape.

With regard to audiovisual audiences, statistics for the past three years (2017, 2018, 2019) indicate that Moroccans spend an average of just three hours watching television daily. For radio, the daily listening time is just below three hours.

Meanwhile, the paper press is sinking irreparably into a crisis brought about by the digital revolution. Faced with a vertiginous decrease in circulation and sales and a sharp drop in advertising revenues, almost all Moroccan newspapers have been forced to turn to digital formats, with far from satisfactory results.

In recent years, there has been a constant but anarchic proliferation of news websites. In accordance with the provisions of Chapter 3 of the Press and Publishing Code, any electronic newspaper is obliged to submit a prior declaration of publication within legally established deadlines. As of May 9, 2019, according to the Ministry of Culture and Communication, the total number of newspapers that had carried out this procedure had reached 892, of which less than 50% were deemed to be in conformity with the legal provisions in force. Having counted on online advertising revenue, these newspapers are facing competition from social networks, which monopolize a large part of the online advertising market (Ministry of Culture and Communication, legal texts online).

In short, a new configuration of the Moroccan communication system is shaping up with glaring problems and uncertainties. Under the pressure of the digital revolution, combined with the effects of globalization, the classic rules of the linearity of the modes of production, distribution, and consumption of information are no longer valid.

PUBLIC OPINION, THE MAIN LEVER FOR DEMOCRACY IN MOROCCO

Moroccan public opinion has never felt as strongly supported or as highly valued as it is today in social networks. Moroccans are showing extraordinary enthusiasm for these new media, as if to take revenge on decades of domination by traditional media that were seen as globally corrupt and fundamentally not very credible. This new information and communication technology, against the backdrop of rampant globalization, added to the wind of the "Arab Spring" that blew on Morocco by generating a movement of vast and deep waves of protests against the endemic dysfunctions of the established powers (Movement February 20). These were the exogenous factors that had such a definitive effect on the active awareness of the Moroccan masses in the digital era (Dewey et al. 2012, 24–25).

According to the National Telecommunications Regulatory Agency (ANRT), 60% of the Moroccan population is connected to the Internet, one of the highest rates in Africa. According to several sources, Morocco is among the top ten countries in the world in terms of annual growth in traffic on social networks like Facebook, LinkedIn, and YouTube (Iraqi 2018). These data are confirmed by the 2019 edition of the annual digital report published by Hootsuite, with a definite upward trend in terms of Internet and social media users (Kemp 2019).

Accordingly, the penetration rate of Internet access in Morocco is above the world average, at 57%. At the African level, Morocco is ahead of South Africa (54%), Nigeria (50%), and Egypt (49%). Morocco has 22.57 million Internet users, representing a penetration rate of 62%. There are 17 million Moroccan users of social networks, representing a penetration rate of 47%. The 18–24 and 25–34 age groups make up the majority of Moroccan Internet users.

This same source indicates that the most active users of social media platforms and messaging applications in Morocco are WhatsApp (81%), Facebook (76%), YouTube (60%), Instagram (45%), FB Messenger (43%), Snapchat (25%), Twitter (17%), Skype (15%), LinkedIn (5%), and Pinterest (4%).

Google remains the most used browser in Morocco, with more than 71 million visits per month, according to the ranking established by this report.

It is perfectly normal for such upheavals to generate new perceptions and new behaviors vis-à-vis media flows and established powers. Moroccan public opinion is no longer what it used to be. Its quantitative and qualitative transformation is due, in part, to the immediate impacts of the digital revolution. A boycott movement demonstrated in a singular way the omnipotence of social networks in mobilizing the masses. On April 20, 2018, a surprising boycott campaign, via Facebook, targeted three consumer brands: Oulmès Mineral Waters, Afriquia petrol stations, and dairy products from Centrale Danone. The effort was an immediate success: 70% to 80% of the Moroccan population responded favorably by refraining from purchasing the targeted brands.

Governments have taken a long time to respond, and when they do, they have indirectly shown that they are unable to effectively manage communication crises in the digital age. If from a technological point of view control of the media sphere by the state is no longer possible, it should also be stressed that, from a legal and ethical point of view, this control is unacceptable for any political regime seeking to respect human rights in their universal sense.

MEDIA EDUCATION AS AN ANTIDOTE TO HARMFUL
SOCIAL MEDIA PRACTICES IN MOROCCO

Since 2015, cases linked to the activities of terrorist groups, mafiosi, racketeering, pedophilia, and prostitution have been flooding Moroccan social networks, carrying more and more sensational data and facts on a daily basis. Of course, the irresponsible and malicious use of social media can be highly destructive to a whole value system of a deeply conservative society, which is the case for Moroccan society. And it is not because of the absence of a legal framework or of ethical charters of journalistic activities that such a phenomenon invades social networks in Morocco. The law relating to the protection of individuals with regard to the processing of personal data, for example, has existed since 2009, but everything suggests that Moroccan Internet users are not informed of the provisions of this law. Its article 57 stipulates:

> Anyone who proceeds, without the express consent of the persons concerned, to processing of personal data which, directly or indirectly, reveals racial or ethnic origins, political, philosophical, or religious opinions, trade union membership of persons, or health-related information, is liable to imprisonment from three months to one year and/or a fine of 50,000 to 300,000 DH. The same penalties apply to anyone who processes personal data relating to offenses, convictions, or security measures. (Loi 09-08 2009)

It seems increasingly clear that only a long-term strategy, based on media education, could effectively contribute to gradually lowering this production of harmful content from Moroccan social networks. This could be achieved by massively engaging them in the path of modern state democratic reforms.

In any case, the beginnings are already promising: as a space for debate and free speech, conducive to the development of a true participatory democracy, social networks have enabled the Moroccan public to discover themselves, promote themselves, and act outside of the relative field of free expression. A sense of effective national solidarity has manifested itself through social media in a fairly dynamic way, and on multiple occasions. This is how we witnessed the emergence of electronic platforms (crowdfunding) to rescue the victims of the deadly floods of Guelmim in 2014. In January 2018, Moroccan Internet users utilized different social networks to offer help to the poor residents of a landlocked village in the southern part of the country, Ksar Ait Ben Haddou. This outreach ultimately collected food, clothing, and blankets for the residents. They also offered various means to help residents cope with a severe winter marked by heavy rainfall and snowfall. This mobilization was reported, hour by hour, through Facebook pages and hashtags on Twitter specially created to carry out this humanitarian action.

In September 2019, Hajar Raissouni, a journalist, was sentenced to one year in prison for "illegal abortion." The reaction of Moroccan Internet users was quick: many messages of support circulated on social networks, with the hashtags #freehajar, #LiberezHajarRaissouni, and #SoutienHajarRaissouni. Representatives of Moroccan civil society disseminated petitions under the title of "Kharija Ala L'Qanun," "Hors la loi," or "Outlaws" to denounce the "liberticide" laws of the Moroccan Penal Code while calling for openness of a "national debate on individual freedoms." This e-mobilization was not limited to Morocco; support for Hajar Raissouni also came from abroad. Ultimately, the result of this campaign was a royal pardon, which ended the journalist's imprisonment.

CONCLUSION

It is obvious that any communication system is intimately linked to the socioeconomic, political, and cultural specificities of the society or the country to which it is attached. Consequently, any communication system is a fairly faithful mirror of the historical evolution of the entity of which it is an integral part. Morocco is no exception to this rule; its communication system bears the indelible traces that have marked its evolution from its most distant past to the most recent changes of the present time. If the substratum of Moroccan cultural identity has remained relatively intact over the centuries, it is clear that successive revolutions of the information and communication systems have influenced it more or less deeply.

Two strong tremors significantly shook the Moroccan communication system: the colonial occupation in the twentieth century and the digital revolution in the twenty-first century. In both cases, the Moroccans first tried to understand the functionalities of the new technologies that had been imposed on them, before adapting them to their own needs while remaining attached to the secular achievements of their sociocultural identity. Generally speaking, it can be emphasized that social networks have completely de-structured the classic pattern of sending and receiving information: linearity seems to have given way definitively to interactivity. But every coin has two sides: the almost unlimited freedom of expression on social networks has been accompanied by a very strong tendency to manipulate and therefore to discredit the message.

The notion of "sharing" is often hammered by the users of these networks and thus has something of a connotation of "fake news." Given this paradigmatic change in the globalized media field, a crucial question arises for Morocco: Are social networks strengthening or disintegrating Moroccan sociocultural and political identity? In the current state of available data, the answer to this question does not seem so simple. In the absence of sufficient data, we are not likely to draw a definitive conclusion, although it can certainly be affirmed that nothing will be similar to before. The whole problem seems to reside a priori in the capacity to adapt in order to meet these challenges.

REFERENCES

Aubin, E. 1904. *Le Maroc aujourd'hui*. Paris: A. Colin.

Berque, J. 1978. *Structures sociales du Haut-Atlas*. Paris: Presses universitaires de France.

Boutbouqalt, T. 1992. *La guerre du Rif et la réaction de l'opinion publique internationale, 1921–1926*. Casablanca: Imprimerie Najah El Jadida.

———. 1994. *Les agences mondiales d'information, Havas Maroc, 1889–1940*. Rabat: Imprimerie El Maârif Al Jadida.

———. 1996. *La politique d'information du Protectorat français au Maroc, 1912–1956*. Casablanca: Les Editions Maghrébines.

Brunot, L. 1923. "L'esprit marocain: Les caractères essentiels de la mentalité marocaine." *Bulletin de l'enseignement public du Maroc*, no. 45: 35–59.

Bulletin d'information et de documentation, no. 9. 1945 (November). Le cinéma au Maroc.

Champredone, R. 1984. *Histoire des grands services publics au Maroc*. Toulouse: Presses de l'Institut d'Etudes politiques de Toulouse.

Denoeux, G. 2000. "The politics of Morocco's fight against corruption." *Middle East Policy* 6 (2). http://www.mepc.org/journal/0002_denoeux.htm.

Dewey, T., J. Kaden, M. Marks, S. Matsushima, and B. Zhu. 2012. *The Impact of Social Media on Social Unrest in the Arab Spring: Final Report*. Stanford, CA: Stanford University.

Doutté, E. 1908. *La société musulmane du Maghrib: Magie et religion dans l'Afrique du Nord*. Maisonneuve J. et Geuthner.

Eickelman, D. F., and A. Salvatore. 2002. "The public sphere and Muslim identities." *Archives Européennes de Sociologie / European Journal of Sociology / Europäisches Archiv für Soziologie* 43 (1): 92–115.

Elmandjra, M. 1988. *Maghreb et francophonie*. Paris: Economica.

———. 1996. "La décolonisation culturelle, défi majeur du XXIe siècle." *Futuribles*, no. 213 (October 1, 1996).

Falcou, R. 1956. *La presse périodique de langue française au Maroc des origines à 1929*. Paris: Bibliothèque de la Fondation Nationale des Sciences Politiques.

Geertz, C. 1968. *Islam Observed: Religious Development in Morocco and Indonesia*. Chicago: University of Chicago Press.

Gellner, E. 1969. *Saints of the Atlas*. Chicago: University of Chicago Press.

Ibn Khaldoun, A. 1967–1968. *Discours sur l'histoire universelle*. Translated by V. Monteil. Beirut: Commission internationale pour la traduction des chefs-d'œuvre.

Instance Equité et Réconciliation. "Synthèse du rapport final." Accessed June 23, 2019. http://www.ier.ma/article.php3?id_article=1496.

Iraqi, Fahr. 2018. "Maroc: le débat public à l'heure des réseaux sociaux." *Jeune Afrique*, July 2, 2018. https://www.jeuneafrique.com/mag/586195/culture/maroc-le-debat-public-a-lheure-des-reseaux-sociaux.

Al Jabri, M. A. 2011. *The Formation of Arab Reason: Text, Tradition and the Construction of Modernity in the Arab World*. London: I. B. Tauris, in association with the Centre for Arab Unity Studies.

Kemp, S. 2019. "Digital 2019." We Are Social, January 30, 2019. https://wearesocial.com/global-digital-report-2019.

Lacouture, J., and S. Lacouture. 1958. *Le Maroc à l'épreuve*. Paris: Seuil.

Laroui, A. 1970. *L'histoire du Maghreb: un essai de synthèse*. Paris: Librairie François Maspero.

———. 1977. *Les Origines sociales et culturelles du nationalisme marocain, 1830–1912*. Paris: Maspero.

Leblanc, A. 1906. *La politique européenne au Maroc à l'époque contemporaine*. Paris: A. Pedone.

Lerner, D. 1958. *The Passing of Traditional Society: Modernizing the Middle East*. New York: Free Press.

Loi 09-08. 2009. "Dahir no. 1-09-15 du 22 safar 1430 (18 février 2009) portant promulgation de la loi no. 09-08 relative à la protection des personnes physiques à l'égard du traitement des données à caractère personnel." Bulletin Officiel no. 5714 du 7 rabii I 1430 (March 5, 2009), 345.

Lyautey, H. 1919. Lettre au ministre de la Guerre, du 17.05.1919. Archives du Service Historique de l'Armée de Terre, Château de Vincennes.

Munson, H. 1993. *Religion and Power in Morocco*. New Haven and London: Yale University Press.

Pascon, P. 1979. "Segmentation and stratification in Moroccan rural society." *Economic and Social Bulletin of Morocco* 138–39: 105–19.

Rogers, E. M. 1983. *Diffusion of Innovations*. New York: Free Press.

Rugh, W. A. 2004. *Arab Mass Media: Newspapers, Radio, and Television in Arab Politics*. Westport, CT: Praeger.

Tessler, M. 1982. "Morocco: Institutional Pluralism and Monarchical Dominance." In *Political Elites in Arab North Africa: Morocco, Algeria, Tunisia, Libya, and Egypt*, edited by I. W. Zartman, et al., 72–91. New York: Longman.

———. 1997. "Kingdom of Morocco." In *The Government and Politics of the Middle East and North Africa*, edited by D. E. Long and B. Reich, 91–108. San Francisco: Westview Press.

Vansina, J. 1985. *Oral Tradition as History*. Madison: University of Wisconsin Press.

von Bertalanffy, L. 1968. *General System Theory: Foundations, Development, Applications*. New York: George Braziller.

Waterbury, J. 1975. *Le Commandeur des croyants*. Paris: Presses universitaires de France.

———. 1994. "Democracy without Democrats? The Potential for Political Liberalization in the Middle East." In *Democracy without Democrats? The Renewal of Politics in the Muslim World*, edited by G. Salamé, 23–47. London and New York: I. B. Tauris.

Westermarck, E. A. 1926. *Ritual and Belief in Morocco*. New Hyde Park, NY: University Books.

3

Radio and TV Broadcasting in Algeria from Origins to the Present Day

Birth, Development, and Obstacles

Kamal Hamidou

The advent and development of radio and TV broadcasting in Algeria is spread over two distinct historical periods: the first occurring under the French colonization from 1923 to 1962, and the second occurring after Algeria's independence in 1962 (Cheriet 1969). During both periods, Algeria's political history deeply affected the evolution of these two media-heavy geographical and technical developments, the orientation of their programs and contents, and the societal role they have been assigned (Hamidou 2003). To further understand the extent of this impact, we will adopt both historical and analytical approaches. First, we will trace the birth of radio and television in Algeria during the French colonization period. Once this has been established, we will track its development from the country's independence to the present day. Our end objective is to highlight the most important historical stages in order to understand their evolution until now. We will also take a look at the political factors that influenced their development.

1923–1945: BIRTH OF A PIONEER COLONIAL RADIO IN AFRICA

Algeria was among the first few countries in the world to experience broadcasting at the beginning of the twentieth century. The first steps toward the advent of Algerian radio were taken under the French colonization in the beginning of 1923. It began with the initiative of a few radio amateur members of the Algiers Radio Club (*Echo d'Alger*, June 1, 1923), led by Georges Jougla and M. Martin. Jougla and Martin launched a TSF (cordless phone station) aimed at relaying music concerts transmitted from the Eiffel Tower transmitter in Paris to some initiated receivers (*Echo d'Alger*, January 20, 1923). The two technicians benefited from technical equipment offered by Maison Colin, a major musical instrument store founded in Algiers by Paul Colin.

In July 1923, Maison Colin took responsibility for the technical installation and development of TSF transmission in Algiers. Algiers's TFS network was then annexed to Maison Colin's services (*Echo d'Alger*, July 3, 1923) under the technical management of Mr. Martin and Mr. Morali. The new TSF network used an 8 dB signal-to-diffuse ratio twice a week on a

410-meter wavelength, with a 50-watt transmitter and a 35-meter antenna, covering an area of about 50 kilometers in Algiers and its surroundings.

At the end of 1924, the radio station used a 190-meter wavelength transmitter to begin broadcasting twice a week in the evening. In 1925, the station broadcast a major boxing tournament and displayed live rounds results, thus becoming the first sports broadcast in Algeria. The following December, Maison Colin launched the Radio Alger station. The station began a regular broadcast on Thursdays and Mondays from 8:45 p.m. to 10:00 p.m. This station operated under Algiers's Post, Telegraph, and Telephone (PTT) administration. These groups also brought another official station, also called Radio Alger, into service. In January 1926, the General Government decided to take over this station and rename it Radio Algérie, relegating its management to the PTT. A few months later, this station was again renamed Radio Alger and placed under the responsibility of the French General Government in Algeria.

In July 1939, when an official decree turned the official metropolitan French Radio Diffusion into an autonomous administration, Radio Alger was released from the PTT's supervision and merged with the French national radio through an official order published on November 2, 1945 (Documents Algériens 1954). In 1953, Radio Alger broadcast its programs in three languages—French, Arabic, and Kabyle—and addressed an audience of nearly 255,000 people. Of these, 184,000 (72%) were French colonists and 71,000 (27.8%) were Algerian natives. At the time, Radio Alger broadcast from both the medium-wave transmitters installed in Algiers, Oran, and Constantine, designed to cover the northern part of the Algerian territory, and two short-wave transmitters designed to cover the south of the country. Nonetheless, numerous regions were not covered—due either to the lack of sufficiently powerful transmitters or to natural barriers such as mountains.

1956–2019: FROM UNDERGROUND STATIONS TO THE FULLY INDEPENDENT ALGERIAN RADIO

Algerian Radio was born around the year 1956, during the launch of the Voice of Fighting Algeria and amid the national liberation struggle. This radio broadcast its programs through a medium-wave transmitter purchased from an American officer working for the U.S. Army on the U.S. naval base at Quneitra in Morocco (Chellouch 2012). This transmitter was installed on a truck that moved along the border strip between Morocco and Algeria during broadcasts to avoid being localized and destroyed by the French army. The Voice of Fighting Algeria was essentially launched to thwart the propaganda diffused by the colonial force's media. Its broadcast stopped in 1957, resuming in 1959. This radio operated using short wavelengths of 25, 35, and 49 meters, and broadcast its programs every day from 8:00 p.m. to 10:00 p.m. in three different languages: Arabic, French, and Kabyle.

In tandem with the Voice of Fighting Algeria, Algerian natives were used for Voice of Algeria programs presented by Algerian journalists working in Morocco, Tunisia, Cairo, Libya, Damascus, Baghdad, and Kuwait. All these sources broadcast programs in three languages (Arabic, French, and Kabyle), targeting not only the Algerian people but also French citizens and international public opinion.

After Algeria's independence in 1962, Algerian Radio faced a big challenge owing to the collective departure of the French employees, who suddenly left their positions at the colonial radio, mainly for security reasons. The journalistic team and technicians in charge of the Voice of Fighting Algeria had to handle the transition and ensure the continuity of the post-independence Algerian radio programs, which they successfully did, but not without difficulty. On August 1, 1963, a formal decree published by the Algerian government placed the post-independence Algerian radio under the authority of the Ministry of Information. Furthermore, it assigned a public service mission to the post-independence Algerian radio and television and merged them into a new structure called the Algerian Radio-Diffusion and Television (RTA) Company.

Between 1962 and 1986, Algerian radio presented its programs in the country's two national languages, Arabic and Kabyle, as well as in three foreign languages: French, English, and Spanish. After its independence, the Algerian government invested in new broadcast methods aimed at expanding the coverage to the entire Algerian territory. This was achieved using short waves, medium waves, long waves, and, later, frequency modulation and satellite diffusion. Starting in 1965, more-powerful radio transmitters were installed to ensure better coverage of the national territory and to broadcast international programs abroad. The south of the country was then equipped with a network of radio transmitters receiving Algiers programs via Intelsat satellite.

In 1986, the RTA underwent a restructuring process that led to the creation of four independent companies: the National Sound Broadcasting Company (ENRS), the National Television Company (ENTV), the National Audiovisual Production Company (ENPA), and the National Broadcasting Company (ENTD). This restructuring gave the National Sound Broadcasting Company a relative organizational and financial independence, which allowed it to develop its own means of production. Through the political openness and liberalization process initiated in 1989 by the Algerian government, Algerian public radio took up a public, industrial, and commercial status, following Executive Decree No. 91-102 issued on April 20, 1991, which led to its development on a remarkable scale.

In terms of technical development, the government executed a major operation of renewing and modernizing equipment and tools for the purpose of bringing Algerian radio in tune with the standards, techniques, and tools used by the major radio services internationally. In 2010, a studio digitalization program and a means of production were also initiated. The technical modernization effort was a continuation of the diversification and geographical relocation plan launched in 1991. The professional development component was not neglected either: in 2012, Algerian radio inaugurated a training center in Tipaza to provide professional enhancement and development for both journalists and technicians in radio broadcasting.

Today, the Algerian radio landscape is composed of fifty-five public radio channels, forty-eight of which are local radio stations, and three national channels that broadcast their programs in different languages. The main channel, Channel 1, was nationalized in 1962 and broadcasts programs in Arabic not only to the whole Algerian territory, but also to the Mediterranean area and the MENA region. Channel 2 is another general channel, launched in 1948 under the French colonization and nationalized in 1962. It broadcasts in Berber languages with five dialect variants: Kabyle, Shenoui, Shaoui, Mozabi, and Targui. Channel 3, a general channel launched in 1926 during the French colonization and nationalized in 1962, presents its programs exclusively in French. In addition to the national channels, twenty-one other local radios present their programs in Arabic, and twenty-seven broadcast in regional Berber languages, namely Kabyle, Shaoui, Chelhi, Mozabi, Zennati, Hessani, Ouargli, Targui, and Shenoui.

In addition to the previously mentioned channels, four other thematic channels have been launched (Chellouch 2012) since the liberalization that was initiated in Algeria with the constitution of 1989. The first is Radio Quran, specializing in the broadcast of religious programs. Launched in 1991, this channel features its programs on medium waves as well as on frequency modulation waves. The second, launched in 1995, is Radio Culture. This channel specializes in artistic, historical, and cultural programs. It broadcasts on medium waves as well as on frequency modulation waves. The third channel is Jil FM, specializing in programs based on songs and light debates targeting young audiences. Launched in 2012, Jil FM has become the most popular Internet radio channel in Algeria. In addition to the Internet, the station broadcasts its programs on frequency modulation in the center of Algeria and on medium waves to the rest of the country. The last thematic station is Radio Algérie Internationale. Launched in 2007, the station is dedicated to news and political programs, as either analyses or debates. Its programs are presented in four languages: Arabic, French, English, and Spanish. The station is broadcast through the Internet, frequency modulation waves, medium waves, and satellites.

1956–1962: EARLY ADVENT OF TELEVISION AT THE HEIGHT OF THE NATIONAL LIBERATION WAR

The formal advent of Algerian TV occurred in 1956, during the French colonization in the Algiers region and its surroundings. This was two years after the National Liberation War in 1954. In fact, the first steps were taken in December 1954 (Bab El Oued Story, n.d.), barely a month after the war's onset. Aware of the role that television could play in the propaganda efforts that targeted the minds of both the indigenous and European populations, the French colonists installed a 50-watt transmitter in Cap Matifou (currently Bordj Al Bahri) in the Algiers suburbs, using the standard VHF 819 lines. In 1957, this transmitter's signal strength was raised to 500 watts, with a diameter of 100 kilometers to the east, west, and south, to cover Algiers's outlying areas. Two years later, another transmitter was installed in the Sidi Ali Bounab Mountains between Bordj Menaiel and Tizi Ouzou to cover the center regions located in Great Kabylia. In 1961, the broadcast area was extended to the interior zones after the installation of a 500-watt transmitter at the top of the Shreya Mountains overlooking Blida City to cover the Metidja region and beyond.

In western Algeria, the first transmitter, with a 50-watt antenna, was installed in 1958 in the town center of Oran. It was reinforced in 1961 by another transmitter installed in Tessala, which had a 500-watt antenna intended to cover the region beyond Sidi Bel Abbes City. The Algerian eastern zone had to wait until 1960 to witness the installation of its first transmitter with a power of 50 watts. However, no effort was made in the direction of the huge Sahara zone in the south of Algeria during the first years of Algerian TV broadcasting.

These programs, mainly sports magazines, reports, and films as well as theater, music, opera, information, variety, and children's programs, were presented mostly in French and Arabic. Because no transmission relay was possible with the French national channel RTF, the programs were entirely made in Algiers. According to a report by Rogers Vaurs, the Advisor of the Foreign Affairs Ministry at the French Embassy in the United States, in terms of audience, only 50,000 households in the region of Algiers and Oran were equipped to receive TV programs in 1960 (Correspondance de la presse 1960). Most were European, given that no more than 6,000 Algerian natives owned a TV receiver (Hamidou 2003). On June 30, 1962, the French RTF presented its last live edition of the evening newscast a day before the self-determination referendum. On October 28, 1962, three months after the declaration of independence on July 5, 1962, Algerian Broadcasting became independent from the French authority. The Algerian administration then took over all the RTF infrastructure and buildings by force.

1962–1963: FROM THE NATIONALIZATION OF THE RTF TO THE ADVENT OF THE INDEPENDENT ALGERIAN TV: RTA

The year 1962 is considered the second birth of radio and TV broadcasting in Algeria. The Algerian government's radio and television takeover caused political clashes between the new national authority and the previous colonial authorities. In fact, the French government tried to make the Algerian government pay for their takeover of the RTF facilities, buildings, and equipment.

The French government's strategy was to convince the Algerian authorities that the RTF was an independent corporation in France without any control from the French state. Therefore, the French authorities' first intention was to put the RTF buildings and facilities at the Algerian government's disposal in the framework of a one-year renewable leasing period instead of giving a free permanent retrocession. Furthermore, the French government tried to get the Algerian authorities to pay the debts contracted by the RTF in Algeria. It also tried to impose on the Algerian authorities the obligation to broadcast programs in French at least half of the on-air time. Finally, the French negotiators also required that France remain the sole master of radio broadcasting in Algeria, since no memorandum of understanding on the RTF's transfer to Algerian sovereignty had been signed.

The Algerian government refused to meet the conditions laid down by the French authorities, arguing that radio and TV broadcasting in independent Algeria were a matter of national sovereignty. When the Algerian authorities decided to forcibly seize the RTF buildings and to nominate Mohamed Safer as the director of the new Radio-Télévision Algérienne and Khaled Safer as the new editor in chief, the RTF decided to repatriate all its employees to France, creating a sizable diplomatic crisis between the two nations. Finally, on January 22, 1963, the two corporations agreed to sign a technical cooperation agreement to ensure a smooth transition between the two institutions (Accords bilatéraux franco-arabes, 1963).

The official birth of the independent Algerian television RTA occurred on October 28, 1962, as the Algerian army took control of TV buildings in Algiers. The new Algerian authorities' first act of sovereignty was to turn the "Here Algiers" signal (used by the RTF) into "Here the Algerian Radio and Television" after interrupting the transmission from France (Belkhiri 2014). The second act was the decision to place Algerian television under the administrative supervision of the Algerian Ministry of Information through a decree issued on June 22, 1963. In August 1963, the "RTA" logo was officially created by Decree No. 63-684. The same decree established the RTA's new administrative hierarchy, its nature, and its prerogatives in terms of budget and mission character.

1967–1988: THE ERA OF NETWORK EXTENSION AND ADMINISTRATIVE RESTRUCTURING

After Algeria's independence, rapidly expanding the Algerian radio and TV networks became a national priority. At that time, mass media were widely considered a key factor for social change and for industrial and agricultural development by the developing countries, encouraged by some international organizations. Therefore, the Algerian government signed various technical cooperation agreements with Egypt, the USSR, Czechoslovakia, and Yugoslavia. Their purpose was to train the RTA employees and to help Algerian technicians extend the Algerian TV network's diffusion capacities.

The triennial and quadrennial development plans drawn up between 1967 and 1977 granted the RTA an ample budget to extend its TV coverage to the east, the west, and the Great Algerian South. Several new transmitters and wireless backhaul relays were installed in Annaba, Constantine, Sétif, and Béjaïa in the east; in Chlef, Boumerdès, and Tizi Ouzou in the center; and in Metlili, Mechria, and Nador in the west. Because of the vastness of the Great Algerian South, the Algerian government opted for satellite broadcast. In 1970, an agreement was signed by the RTA with the Intelsat Corporation to launch the DOMSAT program, aimed at covering the whole south of Algeria with TV satellite broadcast. Fourteen wireless backhaul relays were installed in cooperation with the American International System Corporation and the Japanese Mitsubishi Electric Corporation. These relays were installed in Béchar, Beni-Abbas, Adrar, Ouargla, Ghardaïa, El-Oued, Tamanrasset, Timimoun, Ain Salah, El Golea, Djanet, Reggane, and Hassi Messaoud. They were all connected to the main satellite reception station in Lakhdaria. Today, the TV broadcast coverage in the Algerian territory is estimated at around 97%, with the exception of specific zones where wireless backhaul relays cannot work properly because of natural barriers (Grine 2017).

In 1986, following Decree No. 86-147 issued on July 1, 1986, the RTA underwent its first restructuring. The *RTA* logo was replaced by the *ENTV* logo. ENTV remained the only Algerian national television channel until 1994. Later, with Law No. 91-100 issued on April 24, 1991, ENTV was set up as a public establishment of an industrial and commercial nature called the EPTV Group. Since that time, it has been administered by a directory board and entrusted with a clearly defined public service mission. *EPTV* became the new logo for the Public Establishment of Algerian Radio and Television. This major restructuring led to the creation of four autonomous entities. The first one is the ENRS, in charge of radio broadcasting. The second one is the ENPA, in charge of producing programs for the different public channels. The third is the ENTD, in charge of broadcasting. Last is the ENTV, now in charge of the use, maintenance, and development of the technical means of production, staff training, and conservation and management of audiovisual archives.

Today, the EPTV network is composed of five channels: one terrestrial channel called "Télévision Algérienne," which broadcasts over-the-air and digital terrestrial television (DTT), and four other channels that use satellite broadcasting. Three of them are generalist channels: the major one is Canal Algérie, a channel that broadcasts in French to the Algerian community in the Western countries. The second is Algérie 3, a channel that targets the Algerian community in the Arab world, and the third is Algérie 4, which targets the Berber audience in Algeria and abroad. Only one channel is thematic, 5, which is dedicated to the Quran and religious programs.

2010–2019: A HESITANT CONVERSION FROM HERTZIAN BROADCASTING TO DIGITAL BROADCASTING

In 2010, the Algerian government launched a program to introduce digital terrestrial television to enhance the diffusion quality. According to the Algerian Minister of Communication, Hamid Grine, 85% of the Algerian territory was covered by DTT in 2017, after the installation of seventy DTT broadcasting stations.

It is important to mention that digitalization was not a choice for the Algerian state; it was an obligation imposed on all countries by the International Telecommunication Union (ITU) (Télédiffusion d'Algérie, n.d.). Indeed, the ITU had set the deadline of June 17, 2015, for the

African and Middle Eastern countries to completely stop the use of analog broadcasting on the VHF band (174–230 MHz). In addition, the ITU set the deadline of June 17, 2020, to halt the use of digital broadcasting on the UHF band (470–862 MHz). The Public Broadcasting Company of Algeria (TDA) broadcasts five TV programs in SD format, as well as five national radio channels on the UHF band. The DTT deployment on the UHF band in Algeria will make it possible to stop the analog broadcasting on the VHF band and, therefore, to abide by the 2020 deadline set by the ITU.

Digitalization started in Algeria in 2010 with the installation of seven DTT broadcasting stations, covering around 25% of the territory. In 2013, this rate rose to 55% of the national territory, thanks to the installation of fifty new DTT stations. In October 2015, EPTV launched its first channel in high definition, by simulcasting the A3 channel via Nilesat. To make the Algerian DTT project possible, the Algerian government planned to install 34 broadcasting stations throughout the national territory, in addition to 450 rebroadcasting stations in the south. The TDA laid out a three-step plan to install 107 transmitters and 100 repeaters. The first step consisted of establishing one DTT station in each major region in the center, the east, and the west. The second step consisted of launching five new terrestrial television stations in the south. The last step was dedicated to the generalization of DTT by acquiring the rest of the equipment and linking the different networks, which required the installation of new intermediary sites to connect the High Plateau (*Liberté*, 2009). Unfortunately, the generalization of DTT in Algeria slowed down in 2018 due to technical issues caused by the lack of digital receivers. Indeed, most Algerian citizens cannot afford new digital receivers or new television sets.

A SPECIFIC BIRTH CONTEXT THAT FAVORED THE POLITICAL "INSTRUMENTALIZATION" OF RADIO AND TV

In Algeria, the development of radio and TV broadcasting was based on the potential of these major media as societal and political control tools. Therefore, radio and television rapidly came under different types of political pressure. Their political programs were subjected to significant political control and censorship, either under the French colonial administration or under the Algerian independent government. In the beginning of 1948, the Algerian colonizing assembly attempted to create monitoring committees inside the Algerian Radio station to control the contents of radio broadcasts. Even though this control was later refused by the French Parliament, it is known that the General Governor of Algeria maintained total control of the political programs broadcast by Radio Alger.

After the outbreak of the independence war in 1954, censorship began to grow. Alain Resnais was among the few French journalists who dared denounce the practice of censoring at that time. In an interview published in 1958, he stated: "We are free to say and to write whatever we want, given that we do not speak about gendarmes, police and military, magistrates and ministers, and given that we do not raise issues related to the current political situation" (Resnais 1958, 13). Through this political censorship of radio and TV broadcasts, the French government wanted to maintain a standardized perception of colonization within a society characterized by an incoherent social fabric and led by dominator/dominated relationships. Broadcast-heavy media, therefore, had a prominent role in the French colonizing efforts to alienate the native population as well as to justify colonization for the European population (Chevaldonné 1978, 15).

The situation did not change after Algeria's independence. Five days after independence, the Algerian state decided to ban the publication, sale, and distribution of many French or Algerian newspapers that were viewed as contributors to the French interests in the country. In addition to this ban, the Algerian government provided clues about its willingness to institute a certain uniformity in the media discourse. The decision to nationalize three major newspapers, *La Dépêche d'Algérie*, *Oran Républicain*, and *L'Écho d'Oran*, was released in November 1962 and was quickly followed by the launch of two new publications, *Révolution Africaine* and *Révolution et Travail*.

At that time, the Algerian government's priority was to unify the vision, beliefs, and actions of the Algerian citizens for the purpose of derailing any counterrevolutionary attempt and involving the Algerian people in achieving future revolutionary goals. Therefore, the presidency, the National Liberation Army (ALN), and the National Liberation Front (FLN) took complete control of the Algerian media. In the aftermath of the coup d'état of June 19, 1965, the Ministry of Information was created to oversee all publications and broadcasting programs.

In the formal texts and in the official statements made by the political leaders, journalists were considered mere officials serving the Algerian state and revolution. In an interview published in 1968, President Houari Boumédiene declared, "The role of [the] national press raises the problem of the function of the journalist and his role. To fulfill his mission, the journalist must defend an idea. The journalist must define for himself whether he is for or against the revolution. In revolutionary Algeria, he can only be revolutionary and committed, because he is the spokesperson, the defender, and the voice of the Revolution" (Scagnetti 2012, 62). Therefore, in the terms used by Noha Mellor (2008), the journalist's role was perceived as that of a mediator between the single political party and the Algerian citizens, with a final goal of "fostering the ideals of the socialist revolution and the objectives of national development and social change" (Kirat 1987, 74).

Decision No. 528-68, released in September 1968, reinforced the definition of journalists as "loyal servants" to the state and the revolution by establishing that journalists "should exercise their functions in a militant option." Furthermore, the press code promulgated on February 6, 1982, reflected on the media's gradual tutelage as well as on journalists' enslavement in socialist Algeria. Its first article stated that "the information sector is one of the national sovereignty sectors. Under the leadership of the National Liberation Front Party and within the framework of the socialist options defined by the National Charter, information is the expression of the will of the revolution." The second article also specified the totalitarian understanding of the right to information by stating that "the right to information is exercised freely within the framework of the country's ideological options, the moral values of the Nation and the orientations of the Political Direction."

In fact, such a conception of cultural and ideological uniformity was not unique to Algeria at that time. Until the 1800s, it was prevalent in the Arab world as a whole, while decision-makers prioritized the reinforcement of the national identity and collective belonging after the Arab countries' independence (Mellor 2014). The problem with this conception came from the fact that the Algerian national identity is considered as a fixed entity that could only suffer from any mingling of its national identity with foreign cultures, specifically in terms of the deterioration of the citizens' sense of belonging. It is important to mention here that, at that time, many Arab and African countries implemented developmental plans and awareness-building programs for their population. As a result, there was no space for criticism or free speech. Information was considered a tool for collective promotion and mobilization. Thus, in the minds of the political decision-makers, it was natural that information should be controlled and monitored. Journalists had to serve the dominant political parties and the state (Perret 2005).

After the revolt of October 5, 1988, and the political reforms that followed in 1989, Algeria experienced a brief democratic period and political pluralism in the field of media work. Unfortunately, radio and television did not experience the same broad openness that occurred in print media. Indeed, between 1989 and 1991 under the reformist Mouloud Hamrouche's government, Algeria experienced an extraordinary media openness. Amid the rise of the Islamic Front of Salvation (FIS), the new director of Algerian television, Abdou Bouziane, authorized the introduction of political broadcasts, including the famous political program *Face à la Presse*. With debate programs of this kind, the RTA became the first television company to present contradictory broadcast debates between Islamists and democrats in the Arab world.

Notwithstanding, the general strike launched by the FIS in 1991 and the numerous sit-ins held in Algiers created serious security problems, causing the deaths of more than eighty FIS activists and an unspecified number of military forces. These tragic events led the government to definitively lock the audiovisual sector, wrongly accused of being the initiators of political troubles. Therefore, EPTV became the "only child" or the "orphan," as it is popularly called in Algeria—His Master's Voice, as it were—speaking the standardized propaganda language from 1991 to the present day.

THE AUDIOVISUAL LANDSCAPE'S SLIGHT AND UNASSUMED OPENNESS TO PRIVATE CHANNELS

Algeria is the last Maghreb country that needs to liberalize its broadcasting sector, even though openness has been promised several times since the 1990s (Sarnelli and Kobibi 2017). Algerian citizens had to wait almost twenty years after the liberalization of political life in 1989 for a timid legislative text that ambiguously announced the broadcasting sector's openness to private investors. Although in the press Algerian decision-makers had expressed their willingness to open the audiovisual sector since 1991, the Algerian people had to wait until 2011 to see the first regular broadcast of a private TV channel, Echorouk TV. The second private TV channel was Ennahar TV and was launched in 2012.

In fact, these private channels were not the first. The very first attempts to launch private channels occurred long before the promulgation of the Organic Law of 2012, which provided a timid opening-up of the Algerian broadcast landscape. In 1996, the Mehri Group, one of the biggest fortunes in the country, tried to create a TV channel targeting an Algerian audience but, in the end, it was the new Algerian "golden boy" Abdelmoumen Khalifa who effectively launched the first private Algerian TV channel, Khalifa TV, from Paris in 2002.

This channel met a tragic end after Khalifa's setbacks with the Algerian justice system in 2003. In the meantime, Nacer Kettane, encouraged by the audience of his radio channel Beur FM in France, launched a TV subsidiary channel targeting the Algerian audience in Algeria and abroad, with the support of many Algerian and foreign economic groups. This channel's broadcasting was stopped in 2004 after the presidential elections. It shared the same fate as the second version of Khalifa TV, which attempted an unsuccessful rebroadcast from London under the name KTV.

Under the Arab Spring's pressure on the Algerian political system, Algerian decision-makers decided, with a certain reluctance, to allow the creation of private channels. The Organic Law of 2012 (JORA 2012) stipulated in article no. 61 that "[a]udiovisual activity is carried out by public institutions, public sector companies, and organizations and companies under Algerian law." Article no. 4 stated that "information activities are carried out in particular by the public-sector media, the media created by public institutions, the media owned or created by political parties or approved associations, and the media owned or created by Algerian legal entities whose capital is held by natural or legal persons of Algerian nationality." In fact, the 2012 Organic Law did not clearly specify that audiovisual broadcasting was open to private investors. Furthermore, the decision to open the door to private investors, published in October 2017, was immediately frozen in November 2017 under the fallacious pretext of avoiding media interference in the 2019 presidential elections (which had in fact occurred during the 2004 and 2014 electoral campaigns).

The Algerian oligarchy, which took complete control of the Algerian political system after independence, has not yet conceived a democratic vision of Algerian society that would allow adversarial debates and a real multiparty system. Sixty-seven years after independence, decision-makers still consider that the major media should be kept under control. They still think that media contents should remain uniform to disseminate a discourse that promotes one-track thinking through a permanent effort of indoctrinating and mobilizing Algerian citizens.

This orientation was reflected by the public media that covered the October 1988 protests. These protests caused hundreds of deaths and injuries among Algerian citizens, but the sole public channel was not allowed to report this event; instead, the ENTV's editorial board chose to speak about the dramatic developments in Algiers's streets only during the main newscasts. In the journalists' comments, protesters were criticized and stigmatized. The real reasons for the anger and revolt were neither reported nor analyzed. In contrast, international news channels placed major emphasis on this event by mobilizing all their material and human resources to report the revolt live. The public channel only mobilized its archive teams to release old scientific or animal documentaries. The sole public channel always tends to deny reality. This trend is also visible in the coverage of the recent national protests against President Bouteflika's fifth mandate, which started in February 2019.

The public TV channels have deliberately failed to report the protests, considering them non-events or negatively commenting on them. This lack of public-service reporting led reporters from public TV and radio to stage a sit-in protest inside the TV assembly point on February 27, 2019. Their purpose was to denounce censorship and appeal for respect for the public mission allocated to the public major media. Since Algerian decision-makers take a totalitarian approach to the role of state-controlled media, this led them to close two private channels. The first was Atlas TV on March 12, 2014, which was officially accused of broadcasting without any formal approval. The second was El Watan TV on October 12, 2015, which was charged with broadcasting an interview with the former FIS president, Madani Mezrag. In this interview, Mezrag threatened President Bouteflika with a severe reaction if his government refused to accredit his political party.

More than fifty private Algerian TV channels are currently broadcasting in Algeria. Most belong to newspaper groups created after the removal of the print sector's monopoly in 1989. These TV channels can be classified into three groups. The first includes the general TV channels such as Echorouk TV, KBC TV, Al Jazairia TV, Al Bilad TV, Beur TV, Al Hoggar TV, and Port TV. The second includes thematic channels such as Echorouk News, Dzair News, El Watan TV, and El Hoggar News TV (news channels); Al-Haddaf TV (specializing in sports programs); Samira TV (specializing in cooking); and Djurdjura TV (specializing in children's programs). The third includes advertising channels such as Algeria 24 and Algeria Shop.

However, the nascent Algerian private broadcasting landscape still suffers from two main problems. The first issue is the absence of a legal framework for private TV channels, which would have protected them from arbitrary actions. Because of this lack, all Algerian private TV channels must broadcast into Algeria from abroad and under foreign law, namely, from Jordan, Bahrain, Tunisia, the United Kingdom, or France. Only five TV channels have received a partial accreditation from the Ministry of Communication, allowing them to work as foreign channels in Algeria: Echorouk TV, Ennahar TV, Dzair TV, Al-Jazairia TV, and Al Hoggar TV. The other channels broadcast without any accreditation from the Ministry of Communication, which weakens their position and results in violating the legislation.

The second issue is the collusion between private TV-channel owners and politicians or businessmen. Since decision-makers fear media freedom and want to keep the major media under control, they have permitted only a few people to launch TV channels. Influential businessmen such as Ali Haddad, Mahieddine Tahkout, Isaad Rebrab, Reda Mehegueni, Ayoub Ould Zmirli, and a few others control most Algerian TV channels. They finance them with billions of dinars to serve their own interests and to win the favor of current high political leaders. Algerian citizens call this group "the band." In 2016, Reporters Without Borders denounced this collusion by pointing out "the birth of a media oligarchy serving occult economic and political interests."

The recent increasing conflict of interest between the political elite and some "golden boys" at the head of the major media in Algeria fostered corruption and reinforced the lack of separation of powers within the state. This dangerous collusion is one of the reasons why Algerian citizens are currently protesting and requesting changes in Algeria's entire governmental system. They demand a new political system as well as a media system with more integrity, more democracy, and an effective separation of powers.

CONCLUSION

Since the beginning, radio and television have been at the core of all the strategic interests in Algeria, both under the French occupation and under the Algerian government administration after the country's independence. Media were limited to a few urban geographical areas and were mainly intended for the European population. However, the French administration quickly became aware of the interest in generalizing the media to include native Algerians. The media were therefore used to justify the colonization, which was based on a dominator/dominated relationship. After the 1962 independence, the new Algerian authorities seemed to place the development of the national radio and television broadcasting networks at the very heart of the country's development plans. The objective was to use these two major media to strengthen national ties and promote the political and ideological commitment of all Algerian citizens to the achievement of the Algerian revolution's objectives.

In both periods, the "instrumentalization" of radio and television affected their development in Algeria both positively and negatively. The need to generalize their use has positively influenced their birth and development, since Algeria was one of the first countries to establish radio and television networks. In fact, the country benefited from the fastest development and the most extended networks in the history of television in the region. However, the hegemonic vision of both the French and the Algerian authorities crushed the networks' evolution by turning them into tutelary control bodies.

The functions and missions assigned to these two media are part of the authorities' logic, which promotes one-track thinking through a permanent effort to indoctrinate and mobilize

Algerian citizens. This conception of the role of the major media deeply affects the functioning of radio and television in Algeria. Current decision-makers continue to defend a totalitarian approach to the media's role; thus, they aspire to maintain Algerian society in a state of complete political isolation that will allow them to maintain their total control of the country for a long time to come.

REFERENCES

Accords bilatéraux franco-arabes. 1963. "Protocole concernant la coopération technique dans le domaine de la radiodiffusion et de la télévision." January 23, 1963. http://fothman.free.fr/Accbitxt/Cult/dz_cult/dzcult230163/dzcult230163.html.

Bab El Oued Story. n.d. "La Télévision d'Algérie a un an d'existence." Accessed January 24, 2019. http://babelouedstory.com/voix_du_bled/television_musulmane/television_musulmane.html.

Belkhiri, R. 2014. *Introduction to the New Media: Concepts, Methods and Applications.* Algiers: Jossour.

Chellouch, M. 2012. "Algerian radio, birth and course." Radio Algérienne. Accessed January 25, 2019. https://www.radioalgerie.dz/culture/sites/default/files/pdf/Koteyb%20Radio%2016%20dec%202014.pdf.

Cheriet, L. 1969. "La radiodiffusion et la télévision en Algérie." Bachelor's thesis, IFP, Paris II University.

Chevaldonné, F. 1978. "Le cinéma français en Afrique du Nord, naissance et fonctionnement d'un code." *Revue des deux écrans* 8 (12): 15–29.

Correspondance de la presse. 1960. *Bulletin quotidien d'information et de documentation professionnelle*, no. 2478 (July 1960).

Documents Algériens. 1954. "La radiodiffusion en Algérie 1946–1953." Service d'information du Gouverneur Général de l'Algérie, Série politique numéro 28, February 15, 1954.

Echo d'Alger. January 20, 1923. "A l'aide d'un simple récepteur à cristaux, les radio-concerts de la Tour Eiffel sont entendus à Alger."

Echo d'Alger. June 1, 1923. La TSF et les amateurs.

Echo d'Alger. July 3, 1923.

Grine, H. 2017. "L'année 2017 sera celle du développement de la TNT en Algérie." Radio Algérienne, January 16, 2017. http://www.radioalgerie.dz/news/fr/article/20170116/100339.html.

Hamidou, K. 2003. *Télévision, intégration et changement socioculturel en Algérie: Problème des implications socioculturelles et idéologiques de la télévision à l'aune de son instrumentalisation par le politique* [Television, integration and sociocultural change in Algeria: The issue of the socio-cultural and ideological implications of television measured in terms of its instrumentation by politics]. Lille: Presse Universitaire du Septentrion.

JORA (Journal Officiel de la République Algérienne). 2012. "Loi organique no. 1205 du 18 Safar 1433 correspondant au 12 janvier 2012 relative à l'information." Accessed February 27, 2019. https://amb-algerie.fr/wp-content/uploads/2014/04/LOI-ORGANIQUE-N%C2%B0-12-05-DU-12-JANVIER-2012-CORRESPONDANT-A-L%E2%80%99INFORMATION.pdf.

Kirat, M. 1987. "The Algerian News People: A Study of Their Backgrounds, Professional Orientations and Working Conditions." Doctoral dissertation, Indiana University.

Liberté. 2009. "La TNT en Algérie à partir de 2010." November 11, 2009. https://www.liberte-algerie.com/actualite/la-tnt-en-algerie-a-partir-de-2010-71453.

Mellor, N. 2008. "Arab journalists as cultural intermediaries." *Press/Politics* 13 (4): 465–83.

———. 2014. "The two faces of media liberalization." *Mediterranean Politics* 19 (2): 265–71.

Perret, T. 2005. *Le temps des journalistes: L'invention de la presse en Afrique francophone.* Paris: Karthala Editions.

Resnais, A. 1958. "Refuser de se taire." *Témoignage Chrétien*, no. 716 (March 1958): 13.

Sarnelli, V., and H. Kobibi. 2017. "National, regional, global TV in Algeria: University students and television audience after the 2012 Algerian media law." *Global Media and Communication* 13 (1): 57–83.

Scagnetti, J. C. 2012. "Etat média et émigration en Algérie sous l'ère Boumédiene 1965–1978." *Cahiers de la Méditerranée* 85-2012: 59–70.

Télédiffusion d'Algérie. n.d. "Passage à la TNT." Accessed January 15, 2019. http://tnt.tda.dz/fr/node/3085.

II

GOVERNING BODIES

Media Influence, Power, Ownership, and Control

4

Analyzing Media Power in the Arab World

Noha Mellor

Traditional liberal theory portrays the role of media as a watchdog that holds the state accountable. This model, however, does not take into account the other shareholders. Therefore, it does not guarantee "a check on the abuse of all sources of power in both the public and private realms" (Curran 2005, 124). While state media can be accused of aligning with official policies, private media can be argued to compromise institutional independence or downgrade investigative journalism in favor of lighter and more popular genres (Curran 2005, 129). In the case of Arab media, private media ventures have contributed to increasing competitiveness among local and regional media outlets, although it can be argued that these media are fettered by the state.

Looking at Arab media power through this narrow lens of private versus public is too simplistic. The argument here is that the Arab media scene is far more complex, given the intertwining of local, regional, and global media and capital, in addition to the fact that national security interests play a pivotal role in shaping the media power. This interconnectedness of the regional economy and its integration into the global economy, coupled with national security interests, makes it rather difficult to analyze the Arab media as an independent or autonomous field.

There are two main approaches that dominate the analysis of media power, namely, the political economy and cultural studies. To better understand these approaches, this chapter will also lay out the specificities of the Arab media scene, highlighting the media–capital nexus that underpins most media rules in the region. The subsequent sections will examine media ownership in Egypt, Saudi Arabia, and Syria, aiming to demonstrate the interchangeability of this nexus.

MEDIA POWER

Two approaches have roughly dominated the analysis of the role of media power: critical political economy and cultural studies. Indeed, the analysis of media power cannot be confined to the external power of wealth; it also includes the power of the media to generate meaning from within its practices. Media power must, therefore, be analyzed as power over the media (who funds them and who is heard) as well as the power of the media to shape meanings (Hardy 2014, 197). For example, it was feared that media moguls such as Rupert Murdoch, whose media empire exists in both the United Kingdom and the United States, would hamper diversity of views, which triggered inquiries on media ownership and its relationship to pluralism (Valcke et al. 2015, 3). The concentration of media ownership in the United States in a few hands was regarded as an anti-democratic force that curtailed pluralist views and debates (McChesney 2000).

The power of the media is thus not merely symbolic, since "coercive and symbolic power are frequently combined" (Hardy 2014, 196), such as in war reporting. For example, in the Arab world, during the 1930s and 1940s, German, Italian, and British broadcasting stations targeted Arab audiences to influence their perception before and during World War II (Valcke et al. 2015, 3). Herman and Chomsky (1988) sum up the main pressure factors on media output in their well-known model, based on selected filters: business interests of media corporations; advertising and commercialization; professional practices such as reliance on political sources; and the consensus among sources, news institutions, and journalists.

The economic component refers to concentrated media ownership, which leads to (1) common interests between media firms and the political and business elites, and (2) uncritical media coverage of certain cases. The economic factor also refers to advertising as the main source of income for many outlets; consequently, media firms are not permitted to produce content that antagonizes their main advertisers. The media, moreover, often rely on experts and official sources for commentaries. This could mean that such voices, including those of officials, would be viewed as unbiased specialists, which is not always the case. The model generally suggests that media outlets manufacture consent that serves the interests of the political and business elites as a result of the economic and institutional pressures on media institutions.

Arguably, the dichotomy between privately owned and state-owned media in the Arab region cannot be compared to similar models in the United States or Europe. This is because capitalist classes in the MENA do not have the same powers as those of their Western counterparts. Moreover, the region provides a vivid example of yet another filter, namely "national security." The main argument in this chapter is that Arab media, whether pan-Arab or local, should be analyzed through the prism of security in addition to economic interests, otherwise known as the "media–capital–security nexus."

The media–capital–security nexus is defined as the intertwined neoliberal and national security interests manifested in the Arab media industries, and illustrated in both ownership patterns and media output. The chapter will focus on this dynamism through examples of ownership patterns, beginning with a discussion of this intertwining of media, capital, and security.

THE MEDIA–CAPITAL–SECURITY NEXUS

The thriving Arab media scene is often claimed to be the result of a combination of the Gulf's wealth, particularly from Saudi Arabia, and the unifying written language. During the colonial era, "Britain encouraged the concentration of power within the hands of individual rulers who were connected to a wider ruling family and could trace their origins back to one of the Arabian Peninsula tribes" (Hanieh 2011, 5). The GCC states currently host a new capitalist class that has evolved from small, family-based trading activities to conglomerates whose activities span the whole region (not just the GCC market) and extend internationally (Hanieh 2011, 2). Saudi Arabia is the largest and wealthiest GCC state, contributing half of the region's GDP, although smaller states such as Qatar and the UAE have higher GDP per capita (Hanieh 2011, 3). The concentration of media owners in the GCC states means the dominance of Gulf capital, not only in the structural media development in the region but also in articulating mass media messages.

The Gulf region, including Saudi Arabia with its massive oil wealth, has been tightly integrated into the world economy since the entry of the U.S. oil companies into Saudi Arabia in the 1930s. The United States maintained control over the oil by linking oil with its currency (Hanieh 2011, 54). GCC-based businesses managed to expand regionally and transnationally, owing to historical and strong tribal connections, with each large family forming "a transnational network for economic collaboration" (Weiner 2016, 5). Ministers were drawn from prominent families, in return for their families' support (Weiner 2016, 7). In Saudi Arabia, all members of the royal family carry the title "prince," which bestows huge benefits on its members and, as a result, ensures the concentration of power held by the most influential family members (Weiner 2016, 7). There are some Saudi princes who have even established their own media outlets to reflect a certain image, such as liberal or moderate (Al-Rasheed 2005, 44).

The Arab region represents a unique case of a media system where media businesses seem to thrive on increasing advertising revenues, despite the limits on free speech. Thus, while Arab investments, particularly by the Gulf states, have increased and several states have launched media cities as free zones to encourage more investments, rigid media laws and self-censorship are still the norm across the region (Mellor 2014).

National security is another important factor in analyzing Arab media. National security interests can refer to state interests; societal interests, such as the survival of a population and protection of values; and regime interests, such as the protection of tenure of existing rulers, who possibly see themselves as a symbol of the state as a whole (Korany et al. 1993, 26). These interests both overlap and are merged together in the Arab world. The security interests of individual states can be mixed up with those of other states in the region, or the Arab community as a whole (Korany et al. 1993, 27). The colonial legacy, for instance, has been held responsible for the arbitrary borders between now-sovereign states such as Kuwait and Iraq, or Qatar and Bahrain.

Arab regimes have been accustomed to citing national security as the reason behind reducing individual and political freedom, in order to protect not only the state but also the whole region from external pressures that aim to undermine the sovereignty of Arab states (Korany et al. 1993, 27). What exacerbates the arguments for protecting national security is the fact that many states in the region have been involved in war at some point in their modern history, such as the wars against Israel (1948, 1967, 1973) and against neighboring countries such as the Gulf War of 1991, as well as the 2003 war and the post-2011 civil wars in Syria, Libya, and Yemen. Security discourse, in fact, enables authorities to justify exceptional measures to counteract certain threats in order to protect the values, citizens, or state's sovereignty (Buzan and Wæver 2003). Following the 9/11 attacks in 2001, for example, Arab states found new reasons to impose more control over media industries in the name of protecting their nations from terrorism.

National security discourse is often linked to the so-called conspiracy theories that claim that the state's sovereignty is being threatened by external actors. Conspiracy theories in the Arab world are often linked to the region's colonial history, and to the European economic, political, and military interventions. This history also influences recent arguments that depict the United States as continuing the same colonial motivations (Gray 2010, 79). Conspiracy theories are also prevalent in media discourse, whether local or pan-Arab outlets. Such theories are prevalent in other parts of the world too, such as fears of Russian or Chinese threats in the United States (Gray 2010, 165–66).

The military plays a pivotal role in sustaining security discourse, especially in developing countries. The military has been seen as the catalyst for modernization and progress, owing to its organizational capacity and patriotic mission. Within the Arab context, the army officers in Egypt, for example, were seen as great modernists (Cook 2007, 14–15). Egyptians see their army as the vanguard of the nation, and their leaders, from Nasser to al-Sisi, as the saviors defending the nation, not only from potential external threats but also from internal groups such as the Muslim Brotherhood (MB), who appeared to prefer power over the national interest (Mostafa 2017, 12).

Nasser used to embellish his speeches with references to grand concepts, such as liberation and unity. This made him the savior not only of Egypt but also of the post-independence Arab world (Mostafa 2017, 24). During Nasser's rule, Egyptian popular culture, including film, songs, and drama, depicted the military favorably, thus enforcing its high status (Mostafa 2017, 50). The 1973 war added to the national euphoria and pride in the Egyptian army, with numerous films and dramas depicting its heroism (Mostafa 2017, 126). These heroic depictions have made it difficult for critics to voice their opinions against military interventions without being accused of betraying their nation. Since Nasser's rule, the Egyptian army has consequently enjoyed a special status as the vanguard of the nation. The army served as a vehicle of progress in the postcolonial era. This is why al-Sisi capitalized on those former depictions, increasing his public support with photographs of Nasser next to al-Sisi's in Tahrir Square after 2013.

This support for the military was displayed by journalists, who declared their unequivocal support for the national army. One example of this support was documented during the "Sisi leaks," or the leaked conversations that took place in the office of al-Sisi's chief of staff in 2015. These were broadcast by the Muslim Brotherhood's channel in Turkey, Mekameleen, as well as Al Jazeera Arabic (Kingsley 2015). These leaked conversations revealed the power of the military over the media. The Egyptian media followed the official military line, although many journalists claim that they did not need to be forced or persuaded to defend al-Sisi and the army's policies. One famous broadcaster said, "Defending al-Sisi during that phase is not an accusation but an honor and a national duty" (cited in Kingsley 2015).

The Egyptian army is also known for its deep ties to the United States. It has depended on U.S. military and economic aid since 1988. The army acknowledged that help, arguing that it was essential to develop Egypt's defense capacity (Cook 2007, 81). The army, therefore, brought in new lucrative deals, not only with the usual partners in the GCC states but also with China and Russia (Mostafa 2017, 126). The GCC states generally play a pivotal role in their investments in Egypt and its neoliberal development. These may be direct investments or indirect transfers in the form of migrant workers' remittances to Egypt (Hanieh 2013). Military entrepreneurs controlled lucrative deals with their ties to GCC partners, such as the Kuwaiti group Kharafi and Sons (Abul-Magd 2016, 29–30). The army has sought to take advantage of the neoliberal economic measures to expand their business empire since Mubarak's era (Abul-Magd 2016, 24). The al-Sisi leaks of 2015 revealed a request to Saudi Arabia to deposit the sum of $10 billion in U.S. dollars directly into the military's coffers, rather than via the Central Bank of Egypt, and an equal amount from the UAE and Kuwait.

During Hosni Mubarak's rule (1981–2011), Gulf capital was injected into numerous real estate projects and land purchases. Following the 2011 uprising, Qatar played a role in sustaining the Egyptian economy under the short rule of the MB. On the other hand, Saudi Arabia and the Emirates played a more pivotal role in stabilizing the economy following the toppling of Morsi in July 2013 (Hanieh 2013). Egypt held an investors and donors conference in 2015, hoping to raise 100 billion in U.S. dollars in line with Egypt's Vision 2030. However, the death of the former Saudi king Abdullah, and the succession of King Salman, was marked by less enthusiasm for injecting money into the Egyptian economy, save for a modest U.S. $4 billion (El-Gamal 2016, 4). Indeed, financial support from the GCC states has slowed down in the last few years and, since 2016, has been linked to an IMF loan subject to the Egyptian economic reform program. The decision of the Egyptian military to limit its assistance to the Saudi-led war in Yemen also contributed to dampening Saudi Arabia's willingness to invest in Egypt (El-Gamal 2016, 7).

This intertwining of capital and security interests is evident in the analysis of Egyptian media in terms of media capture, or the state/army's control of the media landscape, as will be discussed in the following section.

EGYPT: INTERVENTION IN THE NAME OF SOVEREIGNTY

The Egyptian press was mostly privately owned prior to the 1952 revolution. However, after 1952, Nasser's regime aimed to nationalize the media to align with its policies. The first television broadcast in Egypt was launched in 1960 with two main channels. Consequently, with its already thriving cinema industry, Egypt later also became well known for its television dramas.

The first satellite channel, the Egyptian Satellite Channel (ESC), was launched in December 1990 in the wake of the 1990–1991 Gulf War that followed Iraq's invasion of Kuwait in August 1990. CNN ratings rose among Arab audiences who followed the American channel, looking for updates about the course of the war when Arab channels refrained from providing any. The popularity of CNN was arguably the catalyst needed to shake up the Arab media scene. Since then, it has witnessed an explosion in the number of satellite channels competing among themselves in offering new genres, such as debates and live news reports, similar to those offered by CNN (Mellor 2007, 50–51).

Mubarak worked on liberalizing the media sector in the 2000s as part of the liberal economic policies he embarked on beginning in the 1990s. His goal was to further integrate Egypt into the global economy (Rizk 2016, 884). The liberalization and privatization processes began with the telecommunication sectors as far back as 1998, while private broadcasters were allowed to establish their own channels in 2001, with Dream TV the first private satellite channel (Rizk 2016, 884). Satellite television channels, including Dream TV and al-Mehwar (set up in 2002), could deliver cultural programs but were not permitted to provide their own news services (Rizk 2016, 898). Other channels followed, including al-Hayat TV, ONTV, and CBC, owned by Mohamed al-Amin, who also owns shares in al-Nahar TV (Rizk 2016, 905). The state-owned Egyptian Radio and Television Union (ERTU) partially owns shares in the various private outlets based in the Media Production City in Greater Cairo.

In 2004, the private newspaper *al-Masry al-Youm* was launched in an attempt to revive privately owned press, which was nationalized under Nasser's rule. *Al-Masry al-Youm* was founded by a member of al-Wafd Party, Salah Diab, along with a group of businessmen such as Ahmed Bahgat, the owner of Dream TV, and Naguib Sawiris, the previous owner of ONTV. The newspaper is claimed to have the highest circulation figures of any newspaper in Egypt, arguably peaking in 2011 (Rizk 2016, 890). Given the high operational costs, media ownership has usually been in the hands of a few wealthy businessmen as the main "anchor investors" (Rizk 2016, 884). The 2014 constitution generally allows the creation of newspapers by notification to the Shura Council (upper house of parliament), and not by authorization. How this process would help liberalize the press market is still unknown.

The Egyptian military tightened its grip on the Egyptian media after 2013. This form of media capture is defined as the government's intervention to "influence the gathering, dissemination, and reporting of news content" and can be viewed as either coercive or non-coercive (Cárdenas et al. 2017, 4). The coercive form happens when there is direct state intervention in news production via the use of violence to close an outlet. Non-coercive media capture refers to media institutions themselves refraining from reporting certain information. The latter form can also include controlling the media by distributing state advertising funds (Cárdenas et al. 2017, 4).

Private advertisers could also weigh in media institutions' decisions to publish certain information that may be against the interests of those advertisers. Different media have different markets; for instance, television may have a larger share of the market compared to the press or radio. It is debatable, therefore, whether the Egyptian state has actively sought to control the television sector rather than the shrinking press market, especially since several newspaper editors claim that some papers distribute only 7,000 copies, and the total circulated copies of all newspapers is around 300,000 daily (Meghawer 2018).

Portions of the media audiences apparently approve state censorship according to their ideological stances (Cárdenas et al. 2017, 12). Tavana (2017), for instance, found that a slight majority of Egyptians (56%) believed that freedom of expression was guaranteed to a medium or greater extent, despite the low ranking of Egypt on Western media indices. A more recent survey conducted in Morocco, Tunisia, Egypt, and Jordan (Teti et al. 2019) shows that respondents had a holistic understanding of democracy, reflecting the dichotomy between verbal support and practical action. Respondents supported democratic means such as free elections, yet there was a gap between those who supported democracy as the best political system and those who believed their country was ready for it. Drawing on Egyptian patriotism, President al-Sisi urged citizens to donate to a state fund that he had created called "Long Live Egypt" (Abul-Magd 2016, 23).

The recent economic enterprises by the Egyptian military generally enjoyed massive media coverage, which supported the new projects as further steps for military self-sufficiency in order to ease the state budget (Abul-Magd 2016, 30). The expansion of military enterprise has intensified following al-Sisi's ascension to power and the launching of the "Made in Egypt" campaign. This campaign promotes local products manufactured by military enterprises, thereby foregrounding the role of the military in national development (Noll 2017). Since the 1990s, the Egyptian military enterprises have been in competition with civilian ones, with the military businesses managing to expand their economic and international cooperation, such as with the GCC states. They justify this expansion by pointing to the role of the military in controlling prices and products to protect customers (Noll 2017).

SAUDI MEDIA: REGIONAL MEDIA HEGEMONY

During Nasser's rule in the 1950s and 1960s, the Saudi rulers saw a powerful means of propagating Islamic preaching and counterbalancing the Nasserist socialist attack on the Arab monarchies in mass communications. This prompted the Saudi state to launch its Voice of Islam radio broadcast as a counterbalance to the Egyptian Voice of Arabs broadcast. The Saudi government launched two TV stations from Jeddah and Riyadh in 1965. The second channel was intended to target educated Saudi elites fluent in English and French as well as expatriates working inside the kingdom. It thus functioned as a bridge connecting the expatriate community to Islamic preaching (Mellor 2009).

The current media policy, originally decreed in 1963, revised in 1981, and revisited in 2013, declared its main aim to be guarding Islam in the hearts of people, encouraging obedience to the rulers, and serving the public interest. This implies refraining from anything deemed "sinful" (Saudi Ministry of Media, n.d.).

Following the restructuring of the Saudi media market in 1963, several Saudi businessmen launched media ventures abroad. London proved a favorable headquarters for many such ventures, including the newspaper *al-Sharq al-Awsat*, launched by two Saudi brothers, Hesham and Mohamed Hafez, in 1978. The two brothers bought the British Central Press Photo building in central London to serve as the headquarters for *al-Sharq al-Awsat*, thus mirroring the success of the *International Herald Tribune*. The newspaper claims the largest circulation among pan-Arab dailies and includes a large number of advertisements (Mellor 2007, 94). It is said to adopt the official Saudi views, although the owners have argued that their publications are based in London in order to ensure a neutral view on Arab issues (Mellor 2007, 134–35). The newspaper is part of a large portfolio of publications owned by the Saudi Research and Marketing Group (SRG).

Other Saudi conglomerates set up outlets abroad, beginning with the ARA Group, which launched MBC channels in London in 1991. Two years later, Dallah al-Baraka launched ART channels, and al-Mawared Company launched Orbit in 1994. Prince Al-Waleed bin Talal has become known in world media through his business ventures, particularly his buyout of shares in several media corporations, including News Corporation, Time Warner, LBC, and various Arabic newspapers. He launched his Rotana channels in 2003, beginning with Rotana Music, followed by Rotana Clip with an SMS service for young viewers, and Rotana Classic and Rotana Gulf for Gulf music (Mellor 2009). Saudi-funded media have generally expanded well beyond the kingdom in the name of serving the country's interests, as well as the business and ruling elites whose interests are intertwined with global enterprises.

Several pan-Arab satellite channels, whether based in Cairo, Dubai, or Doha, each claimed during 2013 to have the largest audience share, aiming to attract a larger share of the pan-Arab advertising market. This led to a public spat among those channels about the credibility of audience ratings. Al Jazeera claimed to be the most watched news channel, based on a survey conducted by IPSOS. On the other hand, the Saudi-funded al-Arabiya raised doubts about the validity of that survey, especially with the absence of reliable real-time audience data; it claimed that its own commissioned research showed that al-Arabiya is the most watched among Arab expatriates in the UAE (Jones 2013).

IPSOS, unsurprisingly, faced a backlash in Egypt; its office in Cairo was closed down in 2017 on the grounds that the company did not follow health and safety rules or conduct adequate risk assessments. It was rumored that the real reason was to conceal IPSOS's use of media data in the Middle East after it consistently showed Saudi-funded TV channels to be the most watched among Egyptian audiences, in preference to the Egyptian channels (Abul Eineen 2017). The company resumed operating in Egypt in 2019.

According to WikiLeaks' Saudi Cables (2015), Saudi Arabia controls its image by buying loyalty from leading media outlets across the world, including North America, Australia, and Europe. Those outlets comprise local Arab and regional pan-Arab outlets, and the Saudi control usually takes the reward and punishment approach, or what the documents call "neutralization and containment." The former strategy refers to buying the loyalty of international outlets to "neutralize" them—in other words, to make them refrain from publishing negative news or criticism about the Arabian kingdom (WikiLeaks 2015). The containment approach refers to buying the loyalty of the journalists themselves, so that they praise the kingdom and are ready to attack critics of Saudi Arabia.

To facilitate this strategy, the kingdom purchases hundreds or even thousands of subscriptions in selected publications, in return for praise or restraint from attacking Saudi Arabia. An example cited in the Saudi Cables took place in November 2011 when the Egyptian ONTV station, owned by the Egyptian magnate Sawiris, hosted the Saudi opposition figure Saad al-Faqih. That episode prompted the Saudi embassy in Egypt to intervene and investigate the case with Sawiris. Buying loyalty can cost any amount, ranging from a few thousand U.S. dollars for a small outlet in a developing country, for instance, to millions of dollars, depending on the outlet and its influence and status (Eid 2017).

In 2018, numerous Saudi media tycoons, including Prince Al-Waleed bin Talal, owner of the Rotana Group, and Waleed al-Ibrahim, owner of the MBC, together with hundreds of other royals and businessmen, were held against their will in the Ritz hotel in Riyadh and accused of corruption. Their release was allegedly subject to undisclosed deals with the crown prince, paying for their freedom with their wealth and media holdings. As a result, the crown prince, whose family already owns and controls the SRM group, tightened his control over the broadcasting media as well as the digital content produced in the Arabian kingdom (Khashoggi 2018).

The Egyptian and Saudi cases have illustrated this intertwining of capital, security, and media. The following section looks at a different example of Arab media, namely Syrian media, which have witnessed much upheaval since the outbreak of the Syrian civil war in 2011.

SYRIAN MEDIA: THE GLOBAL–LOCAL INTERCONNECTEDNESS

Syrian national television was first launched as a joint venture between the Syrian and Egyptian revolutionary unitary governments in 1960, during the short-lived union between the two countries (1958–1961). The broadcasting sector was regulated in 1951 through Decree No. 68. It has been amended several times; for example, it was amended in 2001 (Decree No. 50) to allow commercial and private ownership of radio and television stations, though this was limited to entertainment shows.

After Hafez al-Assad died in 2000, he was succeeded by his son Bashar al-Assad, who began his rule by promising more media freedom. This allowed the establishment of private media outlets and the release of hundreds of political prisoners (Panos Institute 2010). The prime minister and the minister of information still held the right to issue or revoke licenses for reasons relating to public-security interests. Several FM radio stations have obtained licenses since that amendment (Panos Institute 2010, 49), including Arabesque, Sham FM, and al-Madina FM. They were generally prohibited from broadcasting news and political debates, but Sham FM used to broadcast radio shows based on interviews with local officials (Marrouch 2014, 16).

The Syrian media landscape has been rather chaotic since 2011, with tens, and later hundreds, of groups reporting on the ground, and developed with external funding into more organized media outlets (Issa 2016, 5). Newspapers and radio services flourished in rebel-held areas due to the lack of electricity and access to web-based media services. It is estimated that the majority of independent media (72% out of 39 outlets, including press and broadcasting) are classified as traditional media, whereas the majority of pro-opposition media outlets are based online (63%) outside Syria, targeting the Syrian diaspora and Syrian refugees abroad (Issa 2016, 14).

According to a survey of the active media in Syria since 2011, there were 343 active media organizations by 2015, but many of them faced closure due to the withdrawal of donor funding (Free Press Unlimited 2016, 4). The two main donors were the Association for the Support of Free Media (ASML) and the Syrian NGO Basma, which provided training courses for journalists. Basma was created in 2012 by the Qatari-British company Access Research Knowledge (ARK) and was active until late 2013 (Dollet 2015, 6). The European Union has also backed several media projects through the European Instrument for Democracy and Human Rights. The E.U. states have provided support through a number of international organizations such as CFI, Internews, Free Press Unlimited, Reporters Without Borders, IREX, Institute for War and Peace Reporting, and International Media Support (Dollet 2015, 6). It is argued that the lack of transparency in donors' funding strategies resulted in "unhelpful competition between the different newspapers" and it was, therefore, difficult "to foster cohesion and a spirit of solidarity under these conditions" (Dollet 2015, 13).

It is not only the opposition media in Syria that depend on global links with Western donors for their survival. The Syrian state itself also depended on favorable regional and global coverage in both the Russian and Iranian media in order to support its influence (Zuhur 2016, 209). Gulf money was also said to play a key role in the Syrian civil war. This included Kuwaiti individuals campaigning to raise millions of U.S. dollars to pay for wages and arms for the jihadi fighters, who ran their own media activities. Saudi Arabian nationals were also reported to allow donations to be collected for the same purpose (Zuhur 2016, 208).

The Syrian government claimed that its new constitution granted freedom of expression and prevented the monopoly of the media inside Syria, but it still gives the state the right to ban content that is deemed to be harmful to national unity. The government still has the sole right to grant media licenses to organizations operating within the government-controlled areas. The Emergency Law was repealed and was replaced by the Counter-Terrorism Law. This virtually reinstated the state's emergency powers to arrest civilians accused of promoting terrorist activities.

CONCLUSION

We have argued that Arab media power, in terms of ownership patterns, for example, does not fall neatly within the dichotomy of privately owned versus state-owned media. We can thus see two important trends in the MENA region: (1) local and global interconnectedness and interdependence, and (2) the media–capital–security nexus embraced by public and private media professionals and promoted by the Arab governments. It is difficult in this case to analyze the Arab media market as an independent field, separate from the political and security fields.

In Saudi Arabia, private media ownership has been tolerated, but the royal family, and currently the crown prince, has always held a strong grip on the Saudi-funded media, both inside and outside the kingdom. In Egypt, the government has historically worked with the business elites as well as state bureaucrats. The cooperation of this Egyptian elite class was not due to threats or the use of coercive power; instead, the state has had to bargain with businessmen using various forms of clientelistic relationships with private enterprises (El Tarouty 2015). The division between private and public media was rather superficial in Syria. However, since the 2011 uprisings, the Syrian media scene has witnessed a great upheaval caused by the competing interests of Western media donors. All of these economies, but particularly the Egyptian and Saudi ones, are deeply integrated into the global economy, which adds to the lack of autonomy of the market field.

Therefore, the fact remains that, despite cultural and geographical proximity, MENA is far from being an economically integrated region (El-Gamal 2016, 6). Although the region shares a written language, converging cultural norms, and historical trajectories, unlike other entities such as the European Union, the rivalry and competition for national security interests among the Arab states makes full regional economic integration difficult. This includes the media field, although an intra-regional collaboration could yield tangible benefits in meeting national and regional security concerns.

In an unregulated mediascape, jam-packed with factional and partisan media, it is a challenge for any outlet to provide a forum for a free exchange of ideas and criticism. The way forward could be through collaboration rather than rivalries, such as potential cooperation between pan-Arab media outlets and local media. The use of local expertise and resources when covering local events, producing joint documentaries, creating joint pools of training resources, and agreeing on a set of joint professional standards would go a long way toward meeting regional collaboration and security concerns. The irony is that the Arab States Broadcasting Union (ASBU) actually has a committee whose function is to manage collaboration among Arab television channels in order to coordinate output and provide new visions for intercultural communication—a degree of collaboration that has never really materialized. The result is that local and regional media are likely to remain unstable ventures that depend on political backing for their survival in the name of national security. However, once the backing is gone, so is the news.

REFERENCES

Abul Eineen, A. 2017. "Egypt orders to close down the IPSOS office in Cairo" (in Arabic). Reuters Arabic, July 16, 2017. https://ara.reuters.com/article/topNews/idARAKBN1A10J8.

Abul-Magd, Z. 2016. "Egypt's Adaptable Officers: Business, Nationalism, and Discontent." In *Businessmen in Arms: How the Military and Other Armed Groups Profit in the MENA Region*, edited by E. Grawert and Z. Abul-Magd, 23–42. Lanham, MD: Rowman & Littlefield.

Buzan, B., and O. Wæver. 2003. *Regions and Powers: The Structure of International Security*. Cambridge: Cambridge University Press.

Cárdenas, P. J., A. Declercq, M. S. Lai, and N. Rasquinet. 2017. *The Political Economy of Media Capture*. Master of Public Administration (MPA) Capstone Report, London School of Economics.

Cook, S. A. 2007. *Ruling but Not Governing: The Military and Political Development in Egypt, Algeria, and Turkey*. Baltimore, MD: Johns Hopkins University Press.

Curran, J. 2005. "Mediations of Democracy." In *Mass Media and Society*, 4th ed., edited by J. Curran and M. Gurevitch, 122–49. London: Hodder Arnold.

Dollet, S. 2015. *The New Syrian Press: Appraisal, Challenges, and Outlook*. CFI Media Development. https://www.cfi.fr/sites/default/files/etude_presse_syrienne_EN.pdf.

Eid, G. 2017. *The Princes' Media (I'lam al-umraa)*. Arabic Network for Human Rights Information (ANHRI).

Free Press Unlimited. 2016. *Syria Audience Research 2016*. https://www.freepressunlimited.org/en/news/syria-audience-research-2016.

El-Gamal, M. A. 2016. *Discordant Egyptian and Saudi Visions 2030 and the Forgotten Quest for MENA Economic Integration*. Houston, TX: James A. Baker III Institute for Public Policy of Rice University.

Gray, M. 2010. *Conspiracy Theories in the Arab World: Sources and Politics*. London: Routledge.

Hanieh, A. 2011. *Capitalism and Class in the Gulf Arab States*. New York: Palgrave Macmillan.

———. 2013. *Lineages of Revolt: Issues of Contemporary Capitalism in the Middle East*. Chicago: Haymarket Books.

Hardy, J. 2014. *Critical Political Economy of the Media: An Introduction*. London: Routledge.

Herman, E., and N. Chomsky. 1988. *Manufacturing Consent*. New York: Pantheon Books.

Issa, A. 2016. *Syria's New Media Landscape: Independent Media Born Out of War*. MEI Policy Paper 2016-9, December 2016. Middle East Institute, Washington, DC.

Jones, R. 2013. "Arabic news channels in spat over audience share." *Wall Street Journal* (blog), June 18, 2013. https://blogs.wsj.com/middleeast/2013/06/18/arabic-news-channels-in-spat-over-audience -share.

Khashoggi, J. 2018. "Saudi Arabia's crown prince already controlled the nation's media. Now he's squeezing it even further." *Washington Post*, February 7, 2018. https://www.washingtonpost.com/ news/global-opinions/wp/2018/02/07/saudi-arabias-crown-prince-already-controlled-the-nations -media-now-hes-squeezing-it-even-further.

Kingsley, P. 2015. "Will #SisiLeaks be Egypt's Watergate for Abdel Fatah al-Sisi?" *The Guardian*, March 5, 2015. https://www.theguardian.com/world/2015/mar/05/sisileaks-egypt-watergate-abdel -fatah-al-sisi.

Korany, B., P. Noble, and R. Brynen, eds. 1993. *The Many Faces of National Security in the Arab World*. New York: Palgrave Macmillan.

Marrouch, R. 2014. *Syria's Post-Uprising Media Outlets: Challenges and Opportunities in Syrian Radio Start-Ups*. Reuters Institute for the Study of Journalism, University of Oxford.

McChesney, R. W. 2000. *Rich Media, Poor Democracy: Communication Politics in Dubious Times*. New York: New Press.

Meghawer, M. 2018. "Raising the price of newspapers in Egypt" (in Arabic). *Arabi21*, August 9, 2018. https://bit.ly/2rKfxvG.

Mellor, N. 2007. *Modern Arab Journalism: Problems and Prospects*. Edinburgh: Edinburgh University Press.

———. 2009. "The Rise of a Media Kingdom." In *The Kingdom of Saudi Arabia, 1979–2009: Evolution of a Pivotal State*, 10–12. *Viewpoints* Special Edition. Middle East Institute, Washington, DC.

———. 2014. "The two faces of media liberalization." *Mediterranean Politics* 19 (2): 265–71.

Mostafa, D. S. 2017. *The Egyptian Military in Popular Culture: Context and Critique*. London: Springer Nature, an imprint of Palgrave Macmillan.

Noll, J. 2017. "Egypt's armed forces cement economic power: Military business expansion impedes structural reforms." *SWP Comments* 5 (February 2017), German Institute for International and Security Affairs. https://www.swp-berlin.org/en/publication/egypts-armed-forces-cement-economic-power.

Panos Institute. 2010. *The Syrian Media Environment: A Stability*. Collection Media pour le pluralisme en Méditerranée. Paris: Panos Institute.

Al-Rasheed, M. 2005. *The Reform Dilemma in Saudi Arabia in the 21st Century* (in Arabic). London: Saqi.

Rizk, N. 2016. "Egypt." In *Who Owns the World's Media? Media Concentration and Ownership around the World*, edited by E. M. Noam, 883–941. Oxford: Oxford University Press.

Saudi Ministry of Media. n.d. Regulations. Accessed September 19, 2021. https://www.media.gov.sa/ en/document-library.

El Tarouty, S. 2015. *Businessmen, Clientelism, and Authoritarianism in Egypt*. New York: Palgrave Macmillan.

Tavana, D. 2017. "Egypt five years after the uprisings." *Arab Barometer*, July 20, 2017. https://www .arabbarometer.org/wp-content/uploads/Egypt_Public_Opinion_Survey_2016.pdf.

Teti, A., P. Abbott, and F. Cavatorta. 2019. "Beyond elections: Perceptions of democracy in four Arab countries." *Democratization* 26 (4): 645–65.

Valcke, P., R. G. Picard, and M. Sükösd. 2015. "A Global Perspective on Media Pluralism and Diversity: Introduction." In *Media Pluralism and Diversity: Concepts, Risks and Global Trends*, edited by P. Valcke, M. Sükösd, and R. G. Picard, 1–19. New York: Palgrave Macmillan.

Weiner, S. J. 2016. *Kinship Politics in the Gulf Arab States*. Issue paper no. 7, July 22, 2016. Arab Gulf States Institute, Washington, DC.

WikiLeaks. 2015. "Buying silence: How the Saudi foreign ministry controls Arab media." Accessed September 19, 2021. https://wikileaks.org/saudi-cables/buying-silence.

Zuhur, S. 2016. "Syria's Army, Militias, and Nonstate Armed Groups: Ideology, Funding, and Shifting Landscape." In *Businessmen in Arms: How the Military and Other Armed Groups Profit in the MENA Region*, edited by E. Grawert and Z. Abul-Magd, 197–216. Lanham, MD: Rowman & Littlefield.

5

The Egyptian Media System in the Post-Transitional Period

Challenges Facing Media Reconstruction

Inas Abou Youssef

The 2014 Egyptian Constitution included twelve articles granting freedom of opinion, expression, and the press, and mandated three bodies to be in charge of media. These bodies would enact new media policies and oversee reconstruction of different media bodies, especially state- and government-owned outlets.

Two years later, the three bodies were formed. The Supreme Council for Media Regulation (SCMR) had the responsibility of setting a new media policy and strategy regulating media in Egypt; the National Press Authority (NPA) was responsible for reconstruction of state-owned newspapers; and the National Media Authority (NMA) was responsible for reconstruction of the Radio and TV Union.

The escalating crisis of the Egyptian media became abundantly evident in 2017 and 2018, with public and private media outlets facing financial, administrative, and professional crises. One event among these crises was the expulsion of more than 700 journalists from various private newspapers, 350 of them from one single newspaper (Farag 2017). Journalists also faced obstacles in practicing their profession. Difficulty obtaining information from official sources prevented coverage on certain issues, to the extent that a large number of journalists left the profession rather than risk being in trouble with the law.

Approximately fourteen unlicensed satellite channels ceased operation (Salim 2018) and others were threatened with closure. Many television programs were canceled, and the ownership of networks has shifted from businessmen to companies, usually with governmental links. The Freedom House report on Egypt in 2018, discussing digital rights during the second quarter of 2018, stated that the total number of blocked websites in Egypt had risen to at least 503. Egyptian authorities began extensive blocking of sites in May 2017, and no specific governmental body was identified as responsible. The charges included dissemination of false news, the use of social networks to disseminate ideas of a terrorist group, and threat to national security (Freedom House 2018).

This chapter will describe and analyze the Egyptian media landscape during the formation of the new media bodies, including new legislation, new bodies regulating the media in Egypt, problems facing professional practices, changes in ownership profile, and challenges facing the reconstruction of state-owned media.

LEGAL FRAMEWORK: NEW LEGISLATIONS REGULATING MEDIA AND WEBSITES

Although the transitional articles in the Constitution provided that the issuing of media laws was to be considered a priority, this legislation was postponed for a long time.

The first law concerning the press and media-regulating bodies was enacted on December 24, 2016—two years after the Constitution was enacted. Egyptian president Abdel Fattah al-Sisi issued Law No. 92/2016, declaring the formation of three bodies responsible for the functioning of media in Egyptian society. Two days later, he issued Law No. 93/2016, concerning the establishment of the Media Syndicate, a demand from professional journalists that had been denied by the Mubarak regime for decades. The Egyptian media witnessed a state of instability for six months until the president announced the names of the members of the Supreme Council for Media Regulation, the National Press Authority, and the National Media Authority. However, it did not issue any regulations that would enable these bodies to function (RSF 2019).

The state of confusion continued because the newly formed bodies had no new regulations to follow. They were obliged to apply laws that had been enacted before the ratification of the Constitution. In August 2018, the president ratified Law No. 180/2018, which included the regulations needed for the three bodies to function, and the earlier legislation was abolished.

As published in the Official Gazette, Article 1 of Law 180/2018 states that the provisions of the law shall apply to all printed media, electronic media, and websites, except personal accounts. Article 2 stipulates that all media outlets and existing websites were to bring themselves into conformance with the provisions and regulations of the law within six months from the date of the ratification. These provisions included placing sizable amounts of money on deposit in one of Egypt's licensed banks.

Media owners objected strongly to the new conditions. The deposit amounts were enormous, the bank procedures were lengthy and complicated, and the deadline was far too short. According to Article 35 of Law No. 180/2018, private daily newspapers were required to deposit 6 million pounds; weekly newspapers, 2 million pounds; monthly newspapers and daily regional newspapers, 1 million pounds; weekly regional newspapers, 400,000 pounds; and monthly regional newspapers, 200,000 pounds (SCMR 2018). Electronic newspapers were required to have a capital of 100,000 pounds, half of which had to be deposited in a licensed bank in Egypt before they could begin business.

The purpose of the deposit was to guarantee the coverage of major expenditures, especially its employees' wages and salaries, in case of any threat to the company's finances. However, its potential effect was to restrict journalistic activity to wealthy businesspersons and the upper class, contradicting the freedom of expression guaranteed in the Constitution.

NEW BODIES REGULATING THE MEDIA

Supreme Council for Media Regulations (SCMR)

According to the SCMR website, the council's responsibility is to protect diversity of opinion by preserving freedom of expression, and to ensure the independence of the media in accordance with the provisions of the Constitution and the law. The council grants licenses for media outlets, sets professional standards, and evaluates media performance. According to the law, the council is considered an independent entity (SCMR 2018).

The SCMR consists of a president and twelve members holding the positions of vice-president of the State Council Court, the head of the Protection of Competition and Prevention of Monopolistic Practices, a representative of the National Telecommunication Regulatory Authority, four media practitioners, four public figures (two with media backgrounds), and one professor of media. Although membership in the SCMR is based upon nominations of the State Council Court, Parliament, the Press Syndicate, the Electronic Media Syndicate, and the Supreme Council of Universities, the main challenge is that the president has the final decision in selecting among the nominated members.

The SCMR is assigned fourteen tasks, including the expression of opinions on (but not drafting or voting on) drafted laws and regulations related to media in Egypt. The council also receives notifications of the establishment of newspapers; grants the necessary licenses for the establishment of audio, visual, and digital media; sets professional standards; and ensures that media institutions and journalists comply with these standards and professional ethics. Among other tasks, they establish and implement the auditing system for sources of funding for the media and press institutions, to ensure the transparency and integrity of this funding and to monitor its implementation jointly with the concerned bodies and agencies.

The SCMR is also responsible for imposing sanctions on any media entity that violates the obligations stipulated in its license or permit, in accordance with the procedures specified in the sanctions regulations established by the Supreme Council (*Masrawy* 2020). Unfortunately, to this point in time the council has been mainly concerned with imposing punishments and closing media outlets, while nothing is happening in terms of protecting press freedoms or maintaining a mechanism to audit funding and achieve transparency for institutions that are supposed to monitor transparency in other bodies in society.

The National Press Authority (NPA)

President Sisi ratified the Law of the National Press Authority No. 179/2018 on August 31, 2018. The law includes definitions for press organizations, including newspapers and websites. It explicitly states that every news organization should declare its editorial policy mission, vision, and goals and its political, social, and cultural affiliations, as well as the professional criteria adopted and implemented in their organization. The law includes a definition of an electronic site as a page, link, or electronic application licensed and owned by a national press organization, through which the content is provided, whether textual, audio, visual, fixed, mobile, or multimedia (Essam El Dean 2018).

The NPA is composed of nine members: a president, chosen by the president of Egypt; a vice-president, chosen by the Council of Administrative Affairs of the State Council; a representative of the Ministry of Finance, selected by the Minister of Finance; two experienced members and public figures, also selected by the president of Egypt; two members representing the state-owned press organizations, nominated by the Journalists Syndicate board from outside its membership; and a representative of workers in press organizations and media institutions, nominated by the General Bar of Press Printers Syndicate from outside its membership. Finally, an experienced public figure is nominated by Parliament from outside its members (State Information Services 2018).

The end result, however, is that the president of Egypt is effectively appointing all of the members, either directly or from among candidates nominated by bodies whom he himself has appointed.

The National Press Authority is specifically assigned twenty-one tasks. They include:

- Expressing opinions on draft laws and regulations related to the field
- Monitoring the economic and administrative performance of the state press institutions
- Appointing the heads of the boards and the editors in the state-owned publications and appointing members of the boards of trustees and seven members of the general assembly of these news organizations
- Setting rules, regulations, and standards for evaluating performance, as well as internal, financial, and administrative regulations
- Conducting a comprehensive periodic evaluation of all the departments and publications of the press organizations and making any necessary corrections (*Egypt Today* 2018)

The question of loyalty and favoritism arises when the NPA has the upper hand in closing or combining publications and appointing editors. Exacerbating this problem is the fact that the law does not specify the term of service for the editors in chief at national newspapers. The NPA has the right to evaluate these editors' performance and terminate them at will.

The second major challenge facing the NPA is how to reconstruct newspaper organizations in a professional culture that refuses to combine or close any of these publications. Despite the huge losses and deficits that they are now facing, each individual publication insists on keeping the same status it had before the 2011 revolution.

The National Media Authority (NMA)

The National Media Authority was established by Law No. 178/2018 (State Information Services 2018). It is an independent body authorized to make all necessary modifications in the management of previously government-owned radio and TV. It consists of eight members, similar to the structure of the NPA.

The law assigns twenty-two tasks to the NMA, many of them resembling those of the NPA. The tasks for which it is solely responsible relate to the nature of electronic media, such as monitoring audio and video international broadcasting, confirming the status of stations and transmissions, avoiding any failures of transmission and seeing that they are corrected immediately, and meeting the technical transmission needs of both radio and TV stations to ensure a high standard of operation. It also monitors the management of companies owned by the NMA and audits their operations, evaluating their performance and ensuring that they achieve the target investment revenues. The NMA also develops and implements plans and programs related to the audio and video transmission projects and the maintenance of audio, video, and news studios (RSF 2018).

One of the controversial issues concerning the structure of both the NPA and the NMA is that their functions do not differ much from what they were under the now-canceled Law No. 92/2016. Some of the complaints about the old law made by journalists and other media professionals were not dealt with by the new legislation, the most important of these being the dominance of government appointees in all three of the new bodies. This runs counter to the notion of the independence of press and media promised by the Constitution.

THE CRISIS IN MEDIA PROFESSIONALISM

In terms of recent professional media practices in Egypt, eight main controversial issues or challenges appear to have led to the crisis in media professionalism. These issues are the lack of transparent editorial policies, deterioration of professionalism, increasing politicization in news coverage, sensationalist programming, the overlap between advertising and media content, lack of diversity and experience, a decrease in press freedom, and changes in media ownership.

Lack of Transparent Editorial Policies

Despite the fact that Law 179/2018 regulating newspapers and Law 178/2018 regulating electronic media clearly state that mass media should make their editorial policies public, this requirement is not generally followed. More than 90% of media outlets have no published professional code. (The exceptions are the private newspapers *al-Masry al-Youm*, *al-Watan*, and *al-Shorouk*.) Even those that do have code books do not seem to enforce adherence to their standards.

Media organizations are supposed to serve as the watchdogs of society, and therefore should be demanding transparency from state organizations. However, they themselves fail to declare their sources of funding, blinding the public to the media's real loyalties. This lack of transparency has prompted many other bodies in the country to intervene in evaluating the media, calling for suspending programs, shutting down channels, and firing anchors, without reference to any professional standards because, in effect, there are none.

Deterioration of Professionalism

Complaints about the lack of professional standards in Egyptian media have come from diverse and sometimes opposing bodies in society, including the president of Egypt, government officials, NGOs, academic institutions, and opposition bodies as well, though they differ in the reasons for their complaints. One striking feature of this phenomenon is the lack of news verification. Lamentably, many journalists and reporters—particularly those who appear on talk shows—rely more on social media as sources of their news. News sites recycle Facebook and Twitter content without any verification. For example, the SCMR fined seven news sites 250,000 pounds in December 2018 for publishing lies and fake news without any verification (SCMR 2018).

News Coverage from Polarization to Politicization

Since January 25, 2011, the media have played an essential role in the polarization of the public. Today we are witnessing such a degree of politicization of news coverage that it extends even into sports. The main problem with this kind of coverage is that it turns the media into a propaganda tool for the personal interests of the owners or anchors. One dangerous consequence of this type of coverage is the increased use of hate messages against people, countries, or other specific groups.

Producing Sensational Programs versus Quality Programs

Many complaints have been filed with the Supreme Council of Media Regulation against talk shows focusing on sensational, sexual content, as well as drama productions that do not abide by the media code of ethics for the holy month of Ramadan. For instance, the SCMR issued Resolution No. 34/2019 to suspend the controversial *Sheikh al-Harah* show from broadcasting on any media outlet, whether electronic or digital. The SCMR also threatened to close or withdraw licensure from the channel broadcasting Sheikh al-Harah's show (SCMR 2019). The monitoring committee of the SCMR sent warnings to twelve satellite channels, declaring that the council would impose sanctions because of the sexually suggestive content in four of the dramas broadcast on these channels (Mostafa 2019).

Some might object to these strict resolutions, especially since the council, until now, had not issued any resolution defending freedom of the press, diversity in media content, or the integration of citizens' opinions into media coverage.

Advertising That Overlaps with Media Content

Advertising has been integrated with media content for more than three decades, compromising the credibility of media platforms. Specialized informative advertising pages in newspapers and television programs—in particular, medical programs—are in fact embedded with advertisements from governmental bodies or medical clinics without disclosing that fact to readers or audiences.

One of the reasons the national media were accused of corruption before the revolution is because they ignored their main jobs as watchdogs of society and instead became a tool in manipulating the public in order to please their advertisers. Although this behavior had only been apparent in state-owned media, it spread to private media after the revolution, as a consequence of the lack of funding that followed the political upheaval.

Lack of Diversity and the Firing of Experienced Media Professionals

The Egyptian media are heading rapidly toward concentrated ownership. As a result of this concentration, media content has become mostly homogenous. The diversity of media that the country witnessed immediately following the 2011 revolution, which did not favor the ruling authorities or the owners whose interests were aligned with those authorities, did not last. The obvious result of this large-scale change in ownership has been the decline in political content and the absence of dissenting opinions in favor of expansion in cooking, entertainment, sports, and talk-show programs.

Another important reason for the decline in professionalism is the exclusion of longtime, experienced, professional press and media practitioners in favor of people lacking professional skills, and imposing the interests and instructions of media owners in providing coverage that they themselves know is lacking professionalism. In 2017, more than 590 journalists were fired from private and partisan newspapers, television channels, and radio stations (Farag 2017).

As for electronic media, there are no definite statistics concerning the number of media practitioners who lost their jobs. Observers can see for themselves the rotation of media icons who were transferred from one channel to other, others who were given a mandatory break, and some who were dismissed after the end of their contracts. Examples of these cases are many: Lamis Hadidi left her show with CBC, and Mona Shazly and Mahmoud Saad replaced their political talk shows with socially oriented human-interest shows. On the other hand, after his suspension, the shutting down of his channel, and his dismissal from Parliament, Tawfik Okasha returned to present a talk show.

Decrease in Press Freedom

Reporters without Borders (RWB), also known under its original name, Reporters sans Frontières (RSF), is an international, nonprofit, nongovernmental organization based in Paris that conducts political advocacy on issues relating to freedom of information and freedom of the press. Established in 1985, RSF issues an annual Press Freedom index evaluating press freedom in 180 countries around the world.

Along with the index, RSF calculates a global indicator and regional indicators that evaluate the overall performance of media in countries and regions (in the world and in each region) as regards media freedom (RSF 2018). The index utilizes mainly the following categories to measure press freedom in a country:

- The diversity of the media and the extent to which they represent society
- The independence of the media and the extent to which they are free from questionable funding or governmental influence
- Work environment and self-censorship
- The legal framework for media and informational activities
- The degree of transparency in institutions that produce news
- The quality of the infrastructure that supports the production of news and information
- Violations and violence against journalists

The 2019 index indicated that Arab countries and the Middle East in general were very serious black zones, lacking press freedom and endangering journalists. Egypt was ranked no. 163, losing two positions from 2018 (RSF 2019).

Changes in Media Ownership

Since 2016, the Egyptian media have witnessed a change in ownership from individuals to a type of company that shares ownership with governmental bodies. The sale of private newspapers and private satellite channels has thus grown remarkably.

Alam al-Masrin (Egyptian Media Group), a corporation with very strong relations with the state, has taken over many media outlets in Egypt. Until 2018, this corporation owned the following TV satellite networks: DMC, CBC, al-Hayat, ONTV, 90/90 radio, and the Mobtaba news website. Many of the shares of Egyptian Media Group are owned by Eagle Capital for Financial Investments.

Many of the traditional owners of private media networks in Egypt have left the business. The prominent multimillionaire Naguib Sawiris, who owned shares in nearly 60% of newspapers and private satellite channels before the January 2011 revolution, no longer has any assets in the market. Sawiris sold the ONTV channels to millionaire Ahmed Abu Hashima, who sold them in turn to the Egyptian Media Group after a few months. Businessman Mohamed al-Amin also sold the CBC network to the Egyptian Media Group.

In 2017, Eagle Capital bought Ahmed Abu Hashima's shares. Osama al-Sheikh replaced Abu Hashima as chairman of the board but was then himself replaced by Tamer Morsi, who is still chairman today. Eagle Capital for Financial Investments is headed by Dalia Khurshid, former minister of investment and wife of Central Bank governor Tariq Amer (AFTE 2018).

The recent changes have enabled the Egyptian Media Group to acquire financial and administrative control of nearly 85% of the private media influencing public opinion in Egypt. While certain Egyptian officials claim that the Egyptian Media Group intends only to organize media outlets, it is clear that the true aim of the recent mergers and acquisitions of various satellite channels for new owners is to control the media. The purchases of newspapers and private channels by Eagle is estimated to be 60% of the company's total worth, at a cost of 600 million pounds to be paid over two years (AFTE 2018).

Certainly, this new style of ownership and the new owners will control the identity and form of the private media in Egypt. The new owners also control the future of the profession, which suffers from clandestine changes of ownership, the failure to disclose the policies of the new owners, and the absence of a media system that regulates both the public and private media.

CHALLENGES FACING THE RECONSTRUCTION OF STATE-OWNED MEDIA

The Egyptian state owns fifty-two newspapers, twenty-two television channels, and thirty-two radio stations. Since 2011, the reconstruction of the national media has accrued debts of more than 40 billion pounds and caused the layoff of about 50,000 workers.

The RTV networks are 28 billion pounds in debt, with a total of 37,000 employees whose salaries exceed 220 million pounds every month (Zain 2017). The debts of the national newspapers continue to increase, as the government's direct debt is 12 billion pounds and the debts for the Social Security program represent 2 billion pounds. Their monthly deficit is between 10 million and 65 million pounds, according to the size of the organization (Essam El Dean 2018).

The core problem lies in the confrontations between the government and media organizations. The government agencies refuse to reduce or reschedule any of the debt, while the media organizations that consider themselves part of the government think they should be tax-exempt. This claim is based upon a 1962 resolution by the late president Gamal Abdel Nasser, who considered the media as a part of the government and exempted them from taxes. The debt of the press institutions and commercial banks exceeds 3 billion pounds. Only three news organizations—al-Gomhoriya, Dar al-Hilal, and Dar al-Ma'arif—succeeded in rescheduling and renegotiating their debts with the commercial banks, reducing billions of pounds of debt to tens of millions of pounds (Essam El Dean 2018).

Another challenge is linked to the administration and management problems within these organizations. For more than four decades, these organizations relied on the state to solve their financial problems. Now they are facing complex managerial situations for which they are unprepared. These organizations lack many essentials: specialists in press administration; clear editorial policy; clear job descriptions; a culture of competition and marketing; continuous training of editors, journalists, administrators, technicians, and other employees; adherence to professional standards; achieving job satisfaction; and setting standards for promotion (Abou Youssef 2012). National media organizations also suffer from nepotism in the recruitment of editors and reporters, which results in less-qualified reporters who cannot compete with those who are working in private channels. Editorial policy and decision-making should be the job of editors and senior editors and no one else.

Media organizations simply lack the strategy, vision, mission, standards of performance, and measures for their performance. This situation of administrative failure led the NPA to consider merging some publications and selling some of the companies owned by these news organizations to reduce the debts. News organizations opposed the idea of mergers, insisting they should continue as they are (Farag 2017). In order to support their position, many news organizations are trying to establish commercial projects as new sources of finance. This is an attempt to maintain the status quo without bothering to set new editorial policies, appoint qualified reporters, or set adequate administration policies in order to help them compete in the media market.

The last challenge facing state-owned media is that despite the large number of state-owned newspapers and national channels, the media outlets have been suffering from a decline in numbers of readers, viewers, and listeners. This has been reflected in the disappearance of some publications, especially periodicals and specialized books published by press organizations. Daily and weekly newspapers were forced to reduce the number of pages in all their papers by about 25% in order to reduce expenditures for paper, ink, and other supplies. Circulation rates have dropped dramatically: one of the main national (governmental) dailies has dropped to 5,000 copies a day, and another national weekly sells fewer than 300 copies (Zalaky 2018). Advertisers are also shying away from all governmental media.

All of these factors have caused the public to lose trust in the media and further tarnished their credibility with the spread of rumors and fake news on social media. This has come at a time when social media are gaining access and credibility among the public.

Most of the press and media editors attribute their weakening public influence to the lack of financial resources allocated by the state to the national news organizations. Furthermore, they are under great pressure from the government to reconstruct their organizations within only three years. On the other hand, experts from the NPA are convinced that the real problem is not financial resources, but the inability to develop attractive content that gratifies the needs of the public and to recognize reasons for their own decline other than the supposed reluctance of younger people to read (Farag 2017). The loss of influence on the Egyptian public remains a real crisis, threatening the survival of many national newspapers and media channels, regardless of whether the reason is government intervention, poor funding, mismanagement, or inability to develop content.

CONCLUSION

The 2014 Egyptian Constitution granted the right to freedom of press and expression, devoting twelve articles to the media. One of these articles created new bodies to replace state- and government-owned media. The articles also seem to support a certain theory of social responsibility. According to this theory, the media function as watchdogs of the society, regulating themselves in such a way as to guarantee freedom to the press and social responsibility toward society.

To the contrary, however, the media system in Egypt has functioned as a neo-authoritarian system, with a very high concentration of ownership shared between businessmen and governmental bodies. This type of ownership results in a sense of self-censorship among both owners and the journalists themselves. Despite attempts to reset the media system in Egypt, it still does not have a strategy or an integrated vision of its role in society and its responsibilities and loyalties to the public rather than to the state or other entities.

For thirty years, from 1964 to 1996, the press and media were state-owned and private enterprises were banned from entering the media market. This resulted in the dominance of the authoritarian view of the role of the media in society. Even after private ownership was permitted, businessmen and other corporations who owned the media acted as if they were simply taking the place of state ownership. The new owners perceived the media as vehicles to advance their own interests, not as entities with a responsibility to society as a whole.

Media audiences and the public have continued to be the weakest parties in this relationship. Both are incapable of preserving their right to communicate and are prohibited from having access to mainstream media. The audience is either ignored or underestimated by the owners and anchors, although they are ultimately the real funders of the private media. On the other hand, syndicates are very ineffective. The Journalists Syndicate is still functioning according to a nearly fifty-year-old law that is incompatible with recent developments in the print-media field and with developments in society.

The electronic media syndicate law, which was issued in 2018, is still a work in progress. The syndicate itself is not functioning and has no real effect on the ground. This complex situation has resulted in all parties to the communication process—journalists, readers, and audiences—becoming passive participants, entirely at the mercy of the media owners. It explains why the only priority, in any discussion of the media system in Egypt, is how to deal with financial deficits and find new sources of funding. No one is concerned about presenting a vision for reform and reconstruction that will make the Egyptian media more attractive to both Egyptian and regional audiences.

Until now, all of the active actors in the media—owners, new media organizations, and editors in media organizations—have been trying to find financial solutions to maintain the status quo. What is needed instead is a radical solution that enables the media to truly function as watchdogs of the society and to support its claim for freedom. Unfortunately, the journalists themselves are completely ignored by all parties in charge of the media in Egypt.

REFERENCES

Abou Youssef, I. 2012. "Trends of Egyptian reporters towards the reconstruction of governmental media in Egypt after the 25th of January revolution." *Egyptian Public Opinion Research Journal* 1 (11): 125–83.

AFTE. 2018. Accessed January 15, 2018. http://www.afteegypt.org.

Egypt Today. 2018. "Sisi ratifies National Press Authority law." August 31, 2018. https://www.egypt today.com/Article/1/56924/Sisi-ratifies-National-Press-Authority-law.

Essam El Dean, G. 2018. "Press and media law on track: A long-awaited law on the press and media is now in parliament's hands." Accessed May 22, 2019. https://www.elwatannews.com/news.

Farag, E. 2017. "Contemporary Issues in Interdisciplinary Studies in Media." Roundtable discussion, 6th conference, Mass Communication Faculty, Ahram Canadian University, Cairo.

Freedom House. 2018. "Freedom on the Net: June 1, 2017–May 31, 2018." Accessed May 22, 2019. https://freedomhouse.org/country/Egypt/freedom-net/2018.

Masrawy. 2020. "Know it: 24 duties to Supreme Council of the Press." July 30, 2020. https://www.mas rawy.com/news/news_egypt/details/2020/7/30/1843147.

Masrawy. 2021. "A communique from the National Authority of Media in response to the Osama Hekal minister of information declaration about accumulative debts." Accessed April 2021. https://www .masrawy.com/news/news_egypt/details/2021.

al-Masry al-Youm. 2017. "The *Official Gazette* publishes Media Syndicate Law." January 3, 2017. https://www.almasryalyoum.com/news/details/1066931.

Mostafa, A. 2019. "The Supreme Council of Media decides to suspend Sheik el-Harah's program for a year." *Masrawy,* May 26, 2019. https://www.masrawy.com/arts/tv-theater/details/2019/5/26/1574671.

Presidential Decree No. 158/2016. 2016. Accessed May 20, 2019. http://scm.gov.eg/17937-2.

Press and Media Law. 2018. Law No. 180/2018. Accessed May 22, 2019. http://scm.gov.eg/17937-2.

RSF (Reporters sans Frontières). 2018. "World Press Freedom Index." Accessed May 28, 2019. https://rsf.org/en/world-press-freedom-index.

———. 2019. "Regulators without Regulation." Accessed May 30, 2019. https://egypt.mom-rsf.org/en/context/law/regulatory-authorities.

Salim, A. 2018. "Interview with the Secretary General of the Supreme Council of Media Regulation." Accessed May 22, 2019. https://www.e3lam.com.

SCMR (Supreme Council of Media Regulation). 2018. Accessed May 20, 2019. https://wipolex.wipo.int/zh/text/578755.

———. 2019. Accessed May 28, 2019. http://scm.gov.eg.

State Information Services. 2018. Accessed May 22, 2019. https://hrightsstudies.sis.gov.eg.

al-Waqa'i' al-Misriyya. 2016. Law No. 93/2016. Retrieved May 22, 2019. https://www.almasryalyoum.com/news/details/106693.

Zain, H. 2017. Interview in *Al-Masry Al-Youm*, "Governmental media is sick, audience don't trust it." August 21, 2017. https://www.almasryalyoum.com/news/details/1180649.

Zalaky, E. 2018. "Role of media manager in digital age." Lecture presented at training session organized by Women in News, WAN-IFRA, American University in Cairo, June 2018.

III

THE POLITICS OF INFLUENCE
Making Policy and Swaying Public Opinion

6

Public Relations of Key Middle Eastern Countries in the United States

Does Democracy Make a Difference?

Hesham Mesbah and Deanna Loew

The presence and influence of the United States in the Middle East increased significantly after World War II in general, and, specifically, with the end of the Cold War era. In return, the strategic importance of the United States for key Middle Eastern countries was heightened with the collapse of the Soviet Union and the emergence of the United States as the sole international superpower. The governments of such countries have sought to lobby American law- and decision-makers to polish their public images and enhance their economic interests by engaging several U.S.-based public relations (PR) firms and employing their well-tested PR tactics in the United States. Although most of the Middle Eastern countries are ruled by centralized, authoritarian regimes, they are able to take advantage of the decentralized American political system to target U.S. public opinion and interact with the process of political decision-making.

The present study explores how specific key Middle Eastern allies differ in their use of international public relations in the United States according to their own ranking as functioning democracies. Israel, Egypt, Turkey, and Saudi Arabia can be classified among the key allies of the United States in this part of the world. Israel and Egypt stand out as the biggest recipients of U.S. aid in the region. The United States brokered a historic peace agreement between these countries in 1979, which ended more than thirty years of wars and enmity. Turkey is the only Middle Eastern NATO member and, in 2015, became the first Middle Eastern country to host a G20 summit meeting. Saudi Arabia is the "largest U.S. Foreign Military Sales (FMS) customer, with over $129 billion in active cases" (U.S. Department of State 2020).

Israel, Egypt, Turkey, and Saudi Arabia spend millions of dollars each year on public relations, legal/economic counseling, and media watch contracts in the United States. In 2013, the Saudi Arabian government was the fourth-biggest-spending influencer of U.S. politics (Itkowitz 2014). From 2017 through 2019, Saudi Arabia was ranked fifth on a list of governments spending large amounts of money to influence U.S. politics and foreign policy, with a total spending of almost $52 million (Center of Responsive Politics 2020). The present study examines whether the political structure of each of these four countries has a bearing on its differing international public relations strategies in the United States.

THEORY AND LITERATURE

In 1938, the U.S. Congress passed the Foreign Agents Registration Act (FARA), which required agents representing foreign clients or governments to disclose all their activities and the financial details of these actions on behalf of those clients. The U.S. lawmakers were particularly concerned about the large number of U.S.–based PR and propaganda activities that aided the interest of the authoritarian Nazi Germany before World War II (U.S. Department of Justice 2016). This sheds light on the fact that the political structure of governments determines their international communication strategies.

Contacting, engaging, and influencing the makers of policies and laws has always been a primary and persistent international PR tactic for both wholly democratic and less democratic nations. Lee has reported that contacting U.S. legislators was the most common PR activity between 1997 and 2003 (Lee 2006). For less democratic countries, the emphasis is expected to be higher on image creation, polishing, and/or restoration. Zaharna (2000) suggested that authoritarian political regimes have a greater tendency to use image restoration strategies and assert their political unity, while a democratic, non-authoritarian political structure is more susceptible to strategies of lobbying and public advocacy.

Several former leaders of dictatorships, such as General Machado of Cuba, Ferdinand Marcos of the Philippines, "Papa Doc" Duvalier of Haiti, and King Hassan of Morocco, employed PR firms for the purpose of improving their image in the United States. Teodoro Obiang, the brutal dictator of Equatorial Guinea who acquired his power through a bloody military coup in 1979, spent millions of dollars to transform his image in the U.S. media from a "venal autocrat into a solid American ally" (Kurlantzick 2010).

In 1987, the government of Brunei conducted an international PR campaign aimed at improving the image of the sultan (the head of state) personally, rather than the image of the sultanate (Grunig 1993). Another earlier example of the use of international PR by an emerging nation can be seen in India's campaign in 1951, just four years after its independence. The Indian government hired Edward Bernays to change the country's image from one of man-eating tigers, sacred cows, untouchables, and exotic religious sects to that of a young, emerging democratic state (Grunig 1993).

While developed nations are more focused on human rights and democratic ideals in their public diplomacy, less democratic countries use advocacy as one of their major message strategies in their endeavor to establish favorable reputations and attract foreign investments (White and Radic 2014). White and Radic analyzed the websites of the foreign ministries of eight European nations that were candidates to join the European Union (E.U.), including that of Turkey. They found that the most common message strategy was an informational attempt to show political and economic stability. The authors posed a question about the relationship between the level of democracy and types of public diplomacy messages. Another study analyzed the tweets of top Turkish officials in 2012. The results showed that the tweets used an advocacy approach, which aimed at portraying Turkey as a European, democratic, progressive, secular, and Muslim nation. The authors suggested that these Turkish leaders sought to highlight the Western orientation of Turkey in order to enhance its chances to win membership in the E.U. (Uysal et al. 2012).

The literature also shows that some African and Arab nations have employed U.S. PR firms to seek counseling on economic agreements, lobby members of Congress, and cultivate business partnerships with American companies (Davis 1977; Duncan 2005). However, some Arab countries, most notably Kuwait and Saudi Arabia, have felt the need to expand their international PR activities since 9/11 in order to distance themselves from any connection with terrorism groups. In 2002, Saudi Arabia spent more than $15 million to promote its supposed commitment to the "war against terrorism" (Duncan 2005).

Other developing countries shifted their emphasis from politics-focused international PR into business-oriented PR. Such a shift is not a new phenomenon, as evidenced by Johnson (2005), who analyzed five decades of Mexico's PR activities in the United States (1902–1951) and concluded that Mexico has moved from using publicity into employing strategic planning and lobbying. Throughout this period, however, the focus was primarily on coaxing tourists, businesspeople, and influential Washington politicians to put their faith in Mexico.

Less democratic nations tend to use international PR to support their positions in their internal political conflicts. Grunig (1993) noted that British, Swiss, and U.S. firms represented both the Nigerian government and the secessionist province Biafra during the civil war in 1967. Both warring factions tried to either influence media coverage or reach out to political leaders in other countries.

Over the decades, several countries have sought to promote unethical causes or used unethical, and sometimes illegal, tactics in their international PR campaigns. During its fight to maintain control of Angola in the 1960s, Portugal used an international PR campaign to attempt to divert American opinion away from supporting Angolans desiring to liberate their nation from a colonial power (Marcum 1969).

The apartheid government of South Africa expended millions of dollars in 1973 to undertake media relations activities in the United States. This was done in an attempt to convince U.S. policy makers and voters that economic sanctions on South Africa would hurt its black population most. The campaign ended in what is termed the "Muldergate scandal," named for the South African Minister of Information Connie Mulder. It consisted of bribing international news agencies and, specifically, giving John McGoff, an American newspaper publisher, $11.5 million in order to purchase the *Washington Star* newspaper, which he ultimately failed to do. This was for the sake of counteracting the impact of the *Washington Post*, which espoused an anti-apartheid position (Windrich 1989). In 1983, the apartheid government of South Africa had also invited senators and American journalists on all-expenses-paid trips to South Africa, as part of its "See for Yourself" PR program (Windrich 1989).

A more recent international PR scandal in 1990 occurred when the royal family of Kuwait hired the D.C. firm of Hill and Knowlton to mastermind a campaign aimed at persuading Americans to send troops to liberate Kuwait from the Iraqi invasion. The firm arranged for a Kuwaiti girl (whose last name was not released out of security concerns) to give a sworn testimony before a congressional committee about the supposed atrocities committed by Iraqi soldiers against babies in a neonatal unit of a Kuwait hospital. She testified that the Iraqis committed atrocities such as taking premature babies out of their incubators and throwing them on the floor. This lurid story captured the attention of the American media for months. It was later discovered, in January of 1992, that the girl was the daughter of the Kuwaiti ambassador to the United States, and that she might not have even been in Kuwait at the time the atrocities supposedly occurred (Mickey 1997).

Such practices show that the political and economic structure of foreign governments leaves its mark on the way they craft their message strategies and prioritize their international PR activities. The "Circuit of Culture" model identifies five factors that shape the construction of meaning in international PR (Curtin and Gaither 2007). The first and the last factors in this model pertain to both the organizational and cultural functions of international PR, which is notable here. The first factor is identity, which pertains to the creation of an organizational or national image. The last factor consists of the "cultural values that underlie how public relations campaigns are produced, packaged, and consumed" (Curtin and Gaither 2007, 288).

As suggested in the model, countries use public relations not only to achieve strategic goals, but also to create a cultural discourse (Curtin and Gaither 2005, 107). This cultural discourse bears the imprint of the country's cultural and political economy. Verčič et al. (1996) have also identified five environmental variables that determine the public relations strategies in any given country. These variables are: political ideology, economic system (including the level of development of the country's economy), degree of activism (the level of pressure organizations face from internal political activists), culture and the media system, and nature of the media environment in the country. In a country where the government owns and controls the mass media, "the government becomes the target of most PR efforts" (Taylor and Kent 1999, 137).

Taylor and Kent (1999) suggest that while American PR theories are rooted in democracy and capitalism, PR activities practiced in other nations are rooted in a different set of values, and those values are translated into a different style of conducting PR. In the cases where a political system does not value public opinion and is not influenced significantly by it, one might expect a one-way, propagandist style of public relations. Accordingly, the political and economic resemblance between the foreign principal (foreign country) and the host country is suggested to secure success for the international PR activities. Hence, it is argued that "the greater the cultural resonance between two countries, the more a government will successfully push its frames into the second country's media" (Sheafer and Gabay 2009, 451). Accordingly, Israel's PR activities in the United States are said to have a more powerful impact than those of its Middle Eastern counterparts, since Israel is viewed by many Americans as being more closely associated with the Western ideals of free enterprise and democracy (Page and Bouton 2006).

The impact of international PR is measured in terms of the amount and tone of media coverage and the economic outcome. Manheim and Albritton reported that "after Argentina, Indonesia, South Korea, the Philippines, and Turkey had hired PR firms, positive coverage of each country in the *New York Times* increased" (1984, 655). Lee also studied the PR activities of ninety-seven countries listed in the FARA report in 2002. He found that the dollar amount of PR contracts signed by those countries was significantly related to the prominence of their coverage in the media (Lee 2006). Positive media coverage was shown to be related to the feelings the U.S. public held toward a country (Lee and Hong 2012). Zhang and Cameron (2003) did not report an improvement of the image of China in U.S. media after its PR campaign in 2000 but did detect a limited decrease in the amount of unfavorable news coverage about China in mainstream U.S. newspapers.

The economic outcome of international PR is measured according to its success with enhancing business relations and investments. Lee and Kim (2010) detected a positive relationship between the number of PR contracts in the United States and the number of inbound U.S. tourists and direct investments by U.S. businesses in the client's host country. In a subsequent study (2018), the same authors reported that international PR expenditure had a significant effect on favorable economic outcomes. They measured these outcomes in terms of U.S. imports from a client country and the level of direct foreign investment by U.S. firms in three countries: Japan, the Philippines, and Belgium.

This body of research shows that the political/economic structure of a client country may be expected to determine its international public relations activities. Countries that rank lower on the World Democracy assessment might be more concerned about improving their image and polishing the image of their political leaders. They might also apply the propagandist, one-way communication style which is used domestically to their international PR strategies. Accordingly, less democratic countries could put more emphasis on appealing to policy and lawmakers, rather than appealing to the general public opinion, in order to achieve their specific economic and political objectives. In this context, the present study seeks to answer the following questions:

RQ1: What is the agenda of U.S.-based public relations activities of key Middle Eastern countries in the twenty-first century?

RQ2: Do less democratic/transparent Middle Eastern countries tend to use international PR to target law/decision makers more than they target the general audience?

RQ3: Do less democratic/transparent key Middle Eastern countries have a more politically laden agenda of international public relations activities compared to their more democratic counterparts?

METHOD

To answer these questions, the researchers analyzed the U.S.-based PR activities documented by the Department of Justice under FARA for four key Middle Eastern players, in the period 2001 through 2017 (the FARA data for 2018 have not been completed as of this writing). Some Middle Eastern countries, especially Saudi Arabia, have felt the need to conduct image-restoring PR activities in the United States after 9/11. The four countries under analysis—Egypt, Israel, Saudi Arabia, and Turkey—became major partners with the United States in the war on terror after the 9/11 attacks. According to the U.S. Census, U.S. foreign trade with these countries has more than doubled in the twenty-first century. In October 2015, Egypt and Israel were among the most significant trading partners with the United States (U.S. Census 2015).

The FARA documents contained a total of 1,147 entries for these four countries over the seventeen years monitored for the present study. Content analysis was used to categorize and identify the international public relations activities of the four countries. Each entry represented the unit of analysis, and each unit was analyzed according to several categories, such as the year of a country's PR activities, the nature and target of the activities, and the expense of the activity. The foreign agent who is represented by these activities was coded based on how it was identified on FARA entries and the registration forms. Those agents were mainly governments, state-owned companies, corporations, political parties, educational/research institutions, and nonprofit organizations. For the sake of our analysis, those agents were later coded dichotomously as either government (GOV) or nongovernment (NGOV) agents. For example, political parties and nonprofit organizations from any of the four countries were coded as NGOV, while state departments and ministries of trade or tourism from those countries were coded as GOV. Both researchers coded those categories separately, and the alpha reliability of their coded entries was .81, showing a substantial level of inter-coder reliability.

The registration form adopted by the U.S. Justice Department asks registrants (PR agencies) to identify whether they will engage in political activities on behalf of their foreign clients. The data collected from this item were used to dichotomize the activities of those registrants into political (POL) and nonpolitical (NPOL). All PR activities that sought to target U.S. officials for political and military objectives were coded as POL. Such political activities included

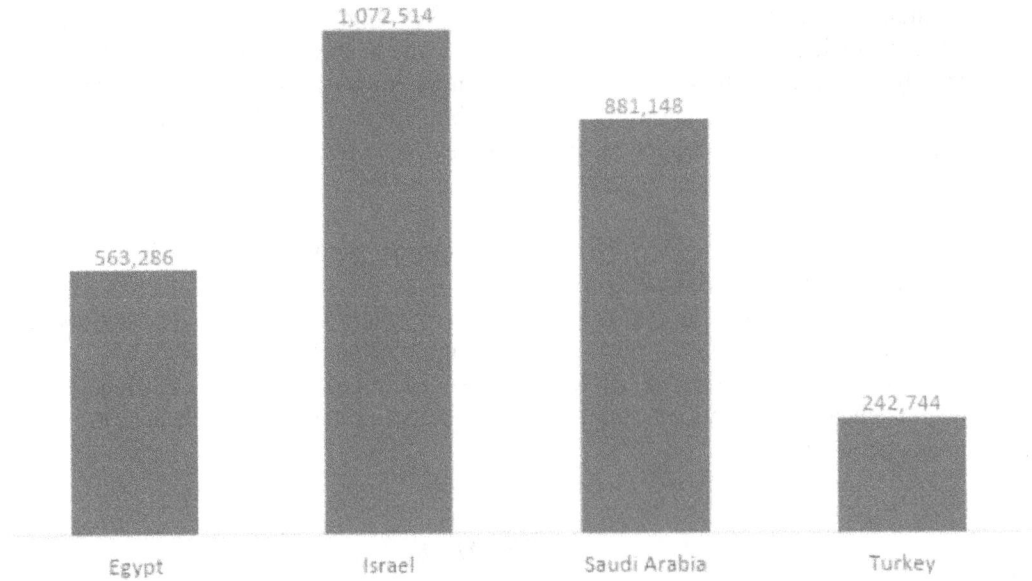

Figure 6.1. Average annual spending on U.S.-based PR activities by key Middle Eastern countries from 2001 to 2017.

seeking consultation on U.S. policies, strengthening/discussing bilateral relations with the United States, seeking advice on military procurement, lobbying decision-makers and lawmakers, monitoring U.S. government activities, discussing arms sales requests, discussing visits of government officials, promoting commitment toward fighting terrorism, promoting efforts to establish democracy and human rights, and arranging meetings between the officials of a foreign client and members of Congress and congressional staffers.

Information about the public relations programs/campaigns of those foreign agents are registered with the Justice Department biannually. Registrants (PR corporations/agencies) must fill out a registration form for each campaign/program separately. However, some registrants fail to provide all requested information. For instance, about 31% of the entries analyzed in the present study did not include information about the total expense of the PR programs/campaigns they reported. Almost 47% of the Saudi entries did not include such data, whereas around 20% of the entries about the PR activities of Egypt, Israel, and Turkey were lacking in the same data. To compensate for these missing expense data, we have estimated the average annual spending on public relations activities in the United States by each country. Figure 6.1 shows that Israel had the highest average of spending on public relations in the United States from 2001 to 2017 (M = $1,072,514), followed by Saudi Arabia (M = $881,148), while Egypt (M = $563,286) and Turkey (M = $242,744) came third and fourth, respectively.

The level of democracy (the independent variable) was measured by aggregating the scores that each of the four countries received in each year of the study, as assessed by the level of its freedom of the press, general freedom, civil liberties, and political rights in the country. The assessment was part of an annual survey conducted by Freedom House, an independent organization dedicated to monitoring freedom and democracy around the world. Freedom House assesses the level of democracy in each country by allocating two numerical ratings on a scale from 1 (most free) to 7 (least free) for political rights and civil liberties. The two ratings are based on scores assigned to twenty-five indicators, as the surveyed politicians and journalists from each country answered questions about the transparency and accuracy of voter registration, the confidentiality of voting, allegations of vote rigging, the freedom of candidates to contact their target audiences, the independence of the election commissions, the level of harassment and intimidation of opposition leaders, and other related indicators (Freedom House 2016).

We have also added the scores that each country received each year on the Corruption Perceptions Index (CPI), which measures the perceived levels of public-sector corruption worldwide on a scale from 0 to 10 (Transparency International 2015). The higher the score, the higher the level of transparency. According to the scale adopted by Freedom House, the higher the score, the lower the level of freedom. In order to fit the scores of this index into our composite measure of democracy, we have subtracted the score of each country from 10, yielding a measure of its level of corruption. For instance, if a country has originally received a score of 9 for its transparency, then its level of corruption would be 1. The higher the score, the higher the level of corruption. Accordingly, the main independent variable of the present study (the level of democracy) was measured based on the aggregate scores of press freedom, general freedom, civil liberties, political rights, and transparency. The higher the score, the higher the level of dictatorship and the lower the level of democracy. Cronbach's Alpha was calculated to be .94, showing a significantly high level of reliability of this composite measurement.

RESULTS

Figure 6.2 shows that Saudi Arabia was the most active foreign agent (in terms of number of registered FARA entries) during the period of analysis (2001–2017), followed by Turkey. However, Israel had the highest average of spending on U.S.-based public relations activities, followed by Saudi Arabia. There was a surge in the Saudi spending right after the 9/11 attacks, as Saudi Arabia sponsored several government and media relations campaigns in the United States to polish its image, which had been tarnished because most of the suspects in the 9/11 attacks were Saudi nationals. For Egypt, there were two periods of peak spending over its PR activities in the United States: during the presidential elections in 2005 and 2014.

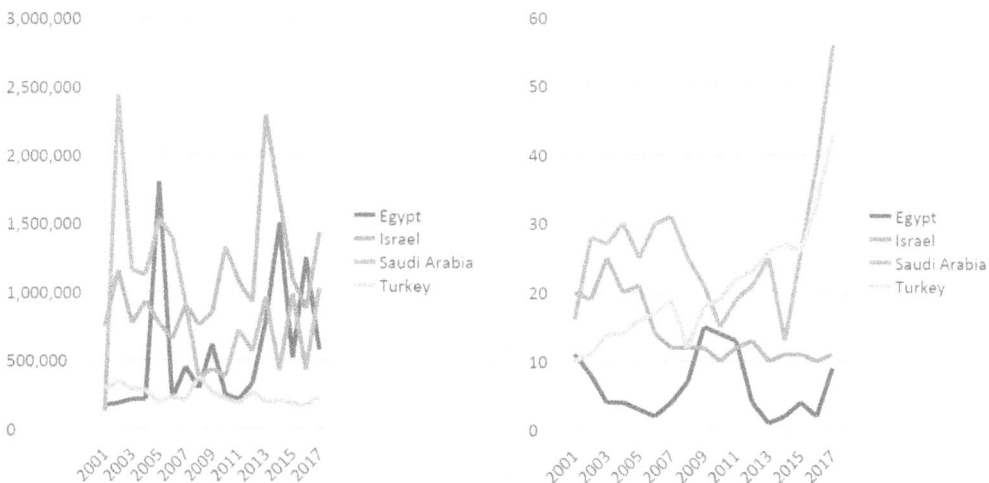

Figure 6.2.   Middle East countries from 2001 through 2017 according to average expense (left) and number of campaigns/PR programs (right) per year.

Figure 6.2 also shows that Turkey kept a stable level of spending on the same activities throughout the period of analysis and increased its programs and activities, and consequently spending, steadily from 2009 to the end of the analysis period.

To identify the agenda of PR activities of those four countries in the United States from 2001 through 2017 (RQ1), the authors content-analyzed the type of activities conducted by those countries according to the registration forms used by the Department of Justice. After identifying a total of sixteen categories of activities, we merged several similar categories, such as merging marketing with advertising and promotion of investment with the promotion of services and trade.

The main categories referred to several activities, as follows:

- Lobbying and legal services. Meetings with members of Congress and congressional staffers to discuss policies and regulations related to bilateral relations, pending foreign aid, U.S. political activities in concern of the foreign client, taxation, counterterrorism policies, and trade legislations affecting trade agreements between the foreign client and the United States.
- Public relations. Strategic plans to communicate messages with key media outlets and the general public, event planning, participation in events, speeches, meetings with diaspora communities, creation of educational and cultural activities, regular monitoring of media outlets or news about the foreign client, and compilation and distribution of information materials.
- U.S. policy consultant. Political consulting, advice on bilateral relations, advice on lobbying and anti-lobbying for the foreign client, and consultations on the World Treaty Organization (WTO).
- Media relations. Arranging conference calls and luncheon meetings between officials from the foreign client and either social media partners or editorial boards of specific U.S. media outlets, drafting op-ed pieces in response to negative media reports about the foreign client, arranging press conferences, and inviting U.S. journalists to visit the country of the foreign client.
- Promotion. Meetings with federal agencies and business leaders; seminars and media placements to promote trade, tourism, and investments in the country of the foreign client.
- Government relations. Contacts with government officials for nonpolitical purposes, such as obtaining contracts, subcontracts, research programs, and grants.

RESEARCH: INFORMATION GATHERING FOR THE FOREIGN CLIENT

Table 6.1 shows that lobbying and seeking legal services and consultations represented the main activity on the agenda of global public relations of those four Middle Eastern nations, especially Saudi Arabia. Israel was more interested in using both mass media and social media in disseminating news and promotional materials to encourage Israeli trade and tourism, organizing events, establishing relations with the U.S. government to seek funds and grants, and reaching out to the Jewish community in the United States. Israel was also the least interested in directing its public relations programs toward seeking consultations about U.S. policy, compared to the other three nations, who showed a substantial interest in that type of activity. The Republic of Egypt sought to obtain more consultations about U.S. policy and establish more

Table 6.1. Types of U.S.-based public relations activities performed by specific Middle Eastern countries, 2001–2017

	Egypt		Israel		Saudi Arabia		Turkey		Total	
	N	%	N	%	N	%	N	%	N	%
Lobbying/legal services	35	30%	127	42%	332	58%	193	45%	687	48%
Public relations	28	24%	105	35%	118	20%	112	26%	363	26%
U.S. policy consultant	27	23%	1	0%	84	15%	70	16%	182	13%
Media relations	18	16%	28	9%	32	6%	42	10%	120	8%
Promotion	8	7%	28	9%	9	2%	10	2%	55	4%
Gov. relations	0	0%	10	3%	0	0%	0	0%	10	1%
Research	0	0%	0	0%	0	0%	3	1%	3	0%
Total	116	100%	299	100%	575	100%	430	100%	1420	100%

media relations. Turkey showed a significant interest in both lobbying and conducting public relations and media-related activities.

A closer examination of the public relations activities over the analysis period (2001–2017) of those four countries reveals the following distinctive aspects.

Diverse Players

The data show that not only does international public relations offer opportunities for governments and diplomatic missions to reach foreign publics and decision makers, but it also extends similar opportunities to other beneficiaries, such as corporations, nonprofit organizations, and political activists. According to the FARA records during the analysis period, 112 different foreign clients from Egypt, Israel, Saudi Arabia, and Turkey initiated and sponsored public relations programs in the United States. Those clients were coded into six categories as shown in table 6.2.

Governmental sources in Egypt, such as the state department, ministries of both tourism and trade, and consulates, are the principal sponsors of lobbying activities and public relations programs in the United States. Most such programs and activities focused on establishing and maintaining relations with the legislative and executive branches of the U.S. government, seeking consultations on U.S. policies, and conducting media relations and public relations

Table 6.2. Type of sponsors of U.S.-based PR programs from Egypt, Israel, Saudi Arabia, and Turkey during the analysis period (2001–2017)

	Egypt		Israel		Saudi Arabia		Turkey		Total	
	N	%	N	%	N	%	N	%	N	%
Government	92	86%	137	57%	306	68%	286	82%	819	72%
State-owned company	8	7%	16	7%	91	20%	6	2%	116	10%
Nonprofit organization	0	0%	43	18%	13	3%	6	2%	60	5%
Corporation	5	5%	27	11%	14	4%	7	2%	58	5%
Political party	2	2%	3	1%	0	0%	44	12%	51	4%
Research center	0	0%	16	7%	23	5%	0	0%	39	3%
Total	107	100%	242	100%	447	100%	349	100%	1143	100%

campaigns. Starting in 2012, all Egyptian lobbying and PR activities in the United States were performed solely by the Egyptian government and its embassy in Washington, D.C.

The lobbying strategies of the Egyptian government in the first decade of the twenty-first century are characterized by an economic turn. From 2003 to 2009, the Alexandria Cotton Exporters in association with the Ministry of Trade and Industry authorized BSMG Worldwide to coordinate a campaign for advertising the quality of Egyptian cotton and communicating with opinion leaders, federal agencies, and Congress members. According to Kostyaev (2013), these lobbying efforts "succeeded in the cancellation of American and European quotas on [the importation] of Egyptian cotton."

In addition to governmental sources, three other types of sources had FARA entries during the period of analysis. EgyptAir, a state-owned company, authorized Hill and Knowlton in 2001 and 2002 to commemorate and monitor the media coverage of the anniversary of the crash of EgyptAir 990 that took off from John F. Kennedy Airport on October 31, 1999, and plummeted into the Atlantic Ocean sixty miles south of Nantucket. In 2003, another agent (Vemer, Lipfert, Bernhard, McPherson & Hand, Chartered) was hired to consult with federal agencies and the legislative branch about the legal issues that had arisen from the crash of EgyptAir 990. Hill and Knowlton conducted five programs for the Information Technology Industry Development Agency (ITIDA), another Egyptian state-owned company, from 2007 to 2012 to promote the industry of information technology in Egypt.

No other corporations from either the public or private sectors in Egypt engaged in U.S.-based public relations programs, although FARA records display several entries from one oil corporation from Egypt. This particular client is the Cairo-based office of Challenger Limited, a Libyan oil company that sponsored several public relations programs in order to help the Libyan government strengthen relations with the United States and assist the former Libyan leader Gadhafi with public events and his speech at the United Nations in 2009.

FARA records also show two entries by the National Democratic Party (NDP), which was led by the former president of Egypt Hosni Mubarak until he was ousted in 2011. Ahmed Ezz, an industry tycoon and a leading figure at the NDP, signed a contract in 2007 with Qorvis Communications in order to highlight the economic and political reforms in Egypt and secure coverage in U.S. media of the annual conventions of the NDP. In its registration form, Qorvis Communication did not link Ezz to either the Egyptian government or the NDP. Ezz was registered as a private businessman and "the majority whip of the National Democratic Party" (U.S. Department of Justice 2007).

Compared to the governments in Egypt, Saudi Arabia, and Turkey, the Israeli government accounts for the least amount of U.S.-based lobbying and PR activities. Most of those activities were sponsored by the Israeli Ministry of Tourism. Two nonprofit Israeli organizations, the Executive of the World Zionist Organization in Jerusalem and the Jewish Agency of Israel, spent more than $175 million on coordinating public relations programs directed toward the Jewish community in the United States. The Executive of the World Zionist Organization hired the World Zionist Organization–American Section, Inc., to coordinate PR programs annually for the entire period of analysis. By the same token, the Jewish Agency–American Section, Inc., was the sole PR agent coordinating the PR programs of the Jewish Agency of Israel in the United States.

Israeli military, communications, and informatics companies were the third-most-active Israeli clients in the U.S.-based media outreach and branding campaigns. For instance, Enavis Networks launched PR programs in the United States in 2001, one year after its establishment. This Israeli telecommunications company sought to position itself in the U.S. market as a leader in its field. The Israeli corporations were less focused on lobbying strategies and more focused on establishing relations with U.S. media, drafting press releases, and monitoring media coverage. The same is true for state-owned Israeli companies, such as El Al Airlines, which coordinated programs to either promote travel to Israel or manage its own crisis when some of its pilots went on a semi-strike in 2016.

Israeli universities and research centers, such as the Hebrew University of Jerusalem and Yitzhak Rabin Center for Israeli Studies, were also active in organizing PR programs in the United States from 2001 through 2007 with the objective of obtaining contracts and research grants/programs for Israeli scientists and seeking funding for the construction and operation of these institutes. To the contrary, Saudi universities and research centers started to sponsor PR programs in the United States in 2007 in order to advertise their publications, recruit faculty, develop and maintain websites, monitor social media, expand outreach to U.S. media, and attract students worldwide.

In 2007, the Saudi Aramco oil company signed a contract with Fleishman-Hillard, Inc., for around $6.4 million in order to launch a PR campaign for the opening of King Abdullah University of Science and Technology (KAUST) in 2009, which was financed by Aramco. KAUST was branded as the first mixed-gender university in Saudi Arabia. Two years prior to its launch, KAUST hired Pillsbury Winthrop Shaw Pittman, LLP, in order to receive legal advice and assistance for the development of a peaceful, commercial atomic energy program and to coordinate negotiations with vendors.

Other Saudi FARA entries pertained to the Organization of Islamic Cooperation (OIC), a nonprofit organization whose headquarters are in Saudi Arabia. The OIC sponsored several lobbying and public relations programs starting in 2012. In addition, the giant Saudi oil and petrochemical companies, such as Aramco and SABIC, have been significantly active in sponsoring lobbying and public relations programs in the United States during the analysis period. Aramco used its in-house public relations agency, Saudi Petroleum International, Inc., in conducting the majority of its lobbying and PR programs in the United States. The registration forms of this in-house agency did not provide much information about the activities it performed and the expenses of such activities. However, SABIC authorized Hill and Knowlton to coordinate all its registered lobbying, media outreach, and public relations activities in the United States during the analysis period.

In 2010, the Saudi private sector debuted its lobbying and PR programs in the United States. The Saudi holding company Kingdom 5-KR-215, which is totally owned by the Saudi billionaire Prince Al-Waleed bin Talal, signed a contract with International Merchandising Corporation (an affiliate with WME/IMG agency) to organize a PR and branding campaign in the United States. This Saudi holding company sponsored annual contracts with the same registrant throughout the analysis period for a total of $8.5 million. Part of the campaign was to establish an Al-Waleed Program that offered research grants for early-career faculty to conduct research in Islamic studies.

Unlike Saudi Arabia and Israel, Turkey did not have any FARA records during the analysis period registered for Turkish universities or research centers. The Turkish government and its embassy and consulates in the United States sponsored most of the lobbying and public relations programs that were filed by the Department of Justice under the "Republic of Turkey." The most recurrent objectives of the lobbying and public relations work by the Turkish government were to create positive Turkish/U.S. relations and "counter the anti-Turkish lobbying" (Center for Security Studies, n.d.). The Turkish government stepped up its spending on lobbying in the last three years of the analysis period to counter the lobbying made by the Armenian government and the Armenian diaspora in the United States to persuade the U.S. Congress to recognize the Armenian genocide during World War I.

The Turkish nongovernmental lobbying and PR activities have been minimal compared to the governmental ones. In 2017, the governmental spending exceeded $7.3 million, whereas the nongovernmental spending was slightly over $500,000. During the analysis period, corporations from both the public and private sectors started to sponsor PR programs in the United States in 2011. The national military company, Teknolojileri Muhendislik ve Ticaret, sponsored several lobbying and public relations programs to maintain a beneficial relationship with the U.S. government and the exportation and importation of military products. Turkish Airlines, another national Turkish corporation, paid around $600,000 to publicize the Turkish presidency of the G20, in addition to sponsoring other public relations programs in 2016 to manage and monitor social media and communicate with customers.

The most numerous nongovernmental active clients from Turkey were political parties. FARA records show entries that were registered for two Turkish parties: the Peace and Democracy party (BDP) and the Republican People's Party of Turkey (CHP), in addition to the Istanbul-based Syrian Future Movement, which was registered as a political party. The BDP was more focused on extending relations with U.S. government and Congress members, whereas the CHP directed its U.S.-based public relations to coordinate grassroots campaigns and reach out to the Turkish diaspora. FARA records also show that some businessmen have sponsored lobbying activities on behalf of other beneficiaries. Such grassroots campaigning and sponsorship highlight two distinctive aspects of the lobbying and PR activities of the key Middle Eastern countries in the U.S.: diaspora PR and proxy lobbying/PR.

PROXY LOBBYING/PR

FARA entries of all four Middle Eastern key players reveal indirect practices of lobbying and public relations. Between 2007 and 2008, Ahmed Ezz, a businessman and leading figure from the then-ruling National Democratic Party (NDP) in Egypt, used personal funds to pay Qorvis Communications $204,000 to publicize the political and economic reforms in Egypt and advertise the annual convention of the NDP. The address of the client cited in the registration form was not the address of any of the Egyptian consulates in the United States nor the headquarters of the NDP in Tahrir, Cairo. It is well known that Ezz was a friend and close ally of Gamal Mubarak, son of Egypt's former president Hosni Mubarak, who was elevated to be at the helm of the NDP. Susan Crabtree, from the left-leaning website Talking Points Memo (TPM), commented that the work done "was to promote Egypt as a country" and raised concerns about who paid for the contract (Crabtree 2011). The FARA entry and contract for this deal indicate that Ezz was conducting proxy international public relations for the NDP.

FARA records show similar practices of businesspeople conducting proxy public relations for the benefit of political leaders or regimes. Cairo-based Challenger Limited, a Libyan oil company, signed five contracts with the public relations firm Brown Lloyd James (BLJ) between 2008 and 2010 to help the Libyan government reach the international community. The foreign principal cited in the registration forms was Hassan Tatanaki, a Libyan-born businessman and then chairman of Challenger Limited; the nationality of this principal in the form was "Egypt." According to FARA records, BLJ assisted the Libyan government, under Tatanaki's directive, to reach out to the international political community through the United Nations. The firm also coordinated the speeches of the Libyan president Qaddafi at Georgetown University and the United Nations.

A similar practice of proxy lobbying/PR is found in the Turkish FARA entries. Ekim Alptekin, the Turkish-Dutch businessman and owner of the Dutch oil company Inovo BV, authorized Flynn Intel Group, Inc., in 2016 to conduct research about Fethullah Gülen, a Muslim Turkish cleric residing in the United States. Gülen is also designated by the Turkish government as a leader of an armed terrorist group. The FARA records show that the research conducted by Flynn Intel focused on the charter schools that are associated with Gülen and shared the results with members of Congress with the aim of passing a vote to extradite Gülen, a demand that has been advocated by the Turkish government. This lobbying endeavor initiated by a private foreign company was deemed conspiratorial by a grand jury. According to the global news agency Reuters, "An ex-business partner of former U.S. national security adviser Michael Flynn and a businessman with ties to Turkish government officials have been charged with undisclosed lobbying aimed at the extradition of a Muslim cleric living in the U.S." (Layne 2018).

DIASPORA PR

Both the Jerusalem and America sections of the World Zionist Organization, along with the Jewish Agency of Israel, targeted the Jewish diaspora in the United States. These nonprofit clients introduced cultural and educational programs to encourage the immigration of Jews to Israel, foster the study of the Hebrew language, and maintain relations with the American Jewish community. They engage the Jewish community in educational and cultural programs, such as conferences, seminars, and camps. They also reach out to high school and college students and organize trips for them to Israel during either the summer or the school year.

The Republic of Turkey has also performed similar diaspora outreach to both Jewish and Turkish communities in the United States. These outreach programs were recurrent throughout the period of analysis, showing that a consistent effort was made to highlight Turkey's historical relationship with the Jewish people and strengthen the relations between the Turkish and Jewish communities in the United States. The Turkish diaspora in the United States was also targeted by the Republican People's Party of Turkey (CHP). This party established an office in D.C. (CHP Representation to the United States, LLC) and registered it as its U.S.-based agent. This in-house agent spent $887,000 on the coordination of several grassroots activities during the analysis period in order to target the Turkish diaspora in the United States.

ROLE FOR DEMOCRACY/TRANSPARENCY?

Saudi Arabia had the highest scores on the dictatorship/democracy scale (the higher the score, the lower the level of democracy and transparency), whereas Israel was the least dictatorial with the lowest score, followed by Turkey and Egypt. In order to answer RQ1 about whether the level of democracy/transparency in any of those countries is related to whom they target by their U.S.-based PR work, their activities were coded into several categories. The categories identified were government, media personalities, media watch, diaspora, business leaders, and others.

If a PR program included activities that targeted several types of audiences, it was coded as GOV if one or more activities in the program targeted legislative or executive members of

Table 6.3. Logistic regression estimates for level of democracy as a predictor of GOV and POL

Democracy	GOV (1)	POL (1)
Observations	727	686
Overall percentage	64%	61%
Coefficient	.057*	.051*
S.E.	.061	.061
Odds ratio	1.531	1.748
Constant	.558*	.426*
Log likelihood	1448.4	1465.5
Chi square	82.5*	49.2*

* p < .01

the government. This category was re-coded as a dummy variable into two codes: 1 (GOV) and 0 (all others). A binary logistic regression was used to test the relationship between these two variables: level of democracy (continuous) and type of target audience (dummy/nominal). According to table 6.3, targeting GOV with PR activities is significantly regressed on the level of democracy of the foreign client (odds ratio = 1.531, constant = .558, p < 0.01). The odds ratio is greater than 1, which indicates a positive relationship. When the score of the predictor variable (democracy/transparency) increases (the higher the score, the lower the level of democracy), the dependent variable (GOV) increases.

The third research question was about whether less democratic foreign clients will have a politics-dominated agenda for their PR activities (POL). Table 6.1 shows that Israel (the most democratic of all four countries) had the least emphasis on POL, whereas the majority of the U.S.-based PR activities of the less democratic foreign clients were focused on POL. Israel had a diverse agenda of PR objectives, such as seeking counseling about finance and banking regulations, lobbying for regulations about taxation and international trade, seeking advice on negotiating the terms of real estate leases, promoting tourism to Israel, conducting fund-raising for its cultural centers in Israel, and coordinating with U.S. research centers in order to open them up for Israeli scientists.

A substantial amount of Israel's U.S.-based PR activities were business-oriented. Israel also had a special emphasis on science and technology. The bulk of the Israeli PR budget was spent on an annual PR program organized by the World Zionist Organization for educational, cultural, and religious goals. In the year following the 9/11 attacks, Israel spent $240,000 on an anti-violence campaign in the United States.

The main political goals of Turkey's PR strategies were to promote Turkish–U.S. relations and to maintain a positive environment for Turkey. A second major aim of Turkish PR was to use mass media and interpersonal channels to disseminate a positive image of Turkey in the United States and to bolster trade, defense, aid, and bilateral talks. Some Turkish PR activities in the United States during the period of analysis were conducted by Turkish opposition parties and leaders. Almost 7% of Turkey's PR was conducted by the BDP (Peace and Democracy Party) for the purpose of meeting with U.S. governmental officials and other organizations interested in the history of Turkey. The BDP also showcased its role in promoting democracy in Turkey.

The FARA reports also show that Turkey participated in a 2014 campaign that aimed to restructure the United Nations and increase the number of permanent seats on the Security Council to more than just the five countries that have veto power. The motto of this campaign was "The World Is Bigger than Five." Turkey was unique among the four countries in inviting

American travel writers and editors and personal escorts on free trips to Turkey in 2010 and 2011.

Saudi Arabia directed its efforts toward lobbying the executive and legislative branches of the government. It also sought advice about the congressional communication regarding oil and energy. In 2002, Saudi Arabia spent almost $19.5 million on a media campaign to analyze mainstream media and increase awareness about its commitment to fighting terrorism. During the period of analysis, Saudi Arabia focused also on the war on terror and the kingdom's role in fighting violence. In 2013 and 2014, Saudi Arabia also sponsored a campaign, launched by the Organization of Islamic Cooperation (OIC), that aimed at countering Islamophobia in the United States. More importantly, the kingdom had the second-largest business-related PR agenda, with a special emphasis on oil agreements and marketing.

In 2017, Saudi Arabia celebrated its National Day by setting up a photography exhibit in Texas to showcase the work of some Saudi artists. It also hired LAPANA Films to produce a movie about Saudi Arabia's contemporary art scene. This was a significant shift in the U.S.-based PR activities conducted by Saudi Arabia.

Egypt mainly used its PR expenditures to contact U.S. government officials, maintain bilateral relations, and enlist U.S. military and financial aid. The agenda of Egypt's PR activities in the United States began to be more personalized in 2009–2010, promoting the planned visits of the former Egyptian president Hosni Mubarak and his son, in addition to promoting the visit of a prominent journalist who had a close relationship with the ruling political party then in power in Egypt. In 2004, Saudi Arabia also had a specific interest in the visit of one Saudi reporter to the United States. The FARA reports show that Saudi Arabia paid $250,000 for lobbying and legal counseling in order to acquire a visa for this reporter.

Egypt did not have any FARA-required entries in the second half of 2012 and the first half of 2013 (during the rule of the Muslim Brotherhood). After the Muslim Brotherhood government was toppled in July 2013, the new government spent nearly $3 million on reestablishing relations with the U.S. government and promoting its "Road Map" for building democratic institutions in Egypt.

Table 6.3 shows that the level of democracy of a foreign client significantly predicts the dominance of politics within its international PR agenda. The coefficient is highly significant ($p < .01$) and the odds ratio shows that pursuing a political agenda through PR activities varies according to the level of democracy.

DISCUSSION

The results of the present study show that the level of democracy of the main Middle Eastern allies of the United States has an impact on shaping their international PR strategies. Less democratic regimes have a more centralized approach. The notion of centralism in managing politics was first theorized by Karl Marx and later applied in a practical setting by Vladimir Lenin, who coined the somewhat oxymoronic term "democratic centralism" to describe the phenomenon (Bay Area Socialist Organizing Committee, n.d.). This centrality was reflected in the level of emphasis on targeting political elites and pursuing a political agenda in managing international public relations.

The results indicate that international public relations can be best understood in terms of both political and economic perspectives, rather than by the narrowly defined organizational function (Holtzhausen 2000). According to L'Etang (1996, 24), public relations has become "fossilized at the systems theory stage." Public relations is a communication function that carries the political, economic, and cultural imprints of the communicators, even if they communicate overseas. In this line of thought, Curtin and Gaither (2005) identified "regulation," or the cultural values that underlie the production of PR campaigns, as a major component of their "Circuit of Culture" (COC) Model. Similarly, Culbertson and Jeffers (1992, 5) identified SPE (social, political, and economic contexts) as a crucial factor in understanding the practice of PR.

The four countries analyzed in this study displayed differences in designing their PR strategies based on their political culture. Less democratic nations seemed to be practicing PR with the same mindset that prevails domestically: one that looks upon a government as the center of power and decision-making. Such nations tended to identify U.S. policy makers and lawmakers as the principal target audience for their PR tactics. This political culture, in which power sharing is minimal, if not totally lacking, was represented also when practicing public relations overseas.

In an analysis of how Curtin and Gaither's COC Model applies to Arab countries, the authors concluded that the production of PR strategies "is imbued by cultural considerations that include acquiescence to authority or individuals of social prestige" (Al-Kandari and Gaither 2011, 269). Symmetrical communication in such regimes is not feasible, as the government is heard, but is hardly a listener. Taylor and Kent (1999, 139) studied PR activities in Malaysia and reported that the secret of corporate success is to have "close relationships with government officials and bureaucrats [in order] to win lucrative projects." The results of the present study show that less democratic countries practice international PR while under the influence of this all-powerful image of a government. The most frequent PR activity sponsored by Turkey, Saudi Arabia, and Egypt was lobbying and seeking counsel on U.S. laws and regulations. Less democratic governments do not claim power based on contested elections; therefore, they are less accustomed to catering to public opinion, and more familiar with exercising the dominance of the central government.

For Israel, PR was used to shape public opinion and support its own Jewish lobby as much as it was used to target legislative and executive leaders. In the same vein, Israel conducted media monitoring and pitching more than the other countries. Israel's PR in the United States during the period of analysis was more pragmatic in terms of coordinating programs to raise funds and seek advice about pursuing various financing possibilities.

The present study also showed that less democratic countries were more focused on hitting political targets, rather than economic and cultural ones. More legitimate, stable regimes tend to employ a wider economic and cultural agenda for their international public relations endeavors. In his analysis of the PR contracts of 151 countries in the United States, Lee found that about 51% of those contracts had economic purposes, mainly related to trade and investment. Israel had a more salient economic/cultural PR agenda. It sought to promote tourism, boost U.S. aid to Israel, market their own high-tech products in the United States, and enhance technological assistance and cooperation.

In most cases, less democratic nations used international PR to maintain relations with the United States and to lobby the holders of executive and legislative power. Not only did Egypt and Saudi Arabia serve their own national political interests through their PR activities, but they also served the personal interests of non-official figures, such as the son of the former Egyptian president Hosni Mubarak and the Saudi reporter who was favored by the Saudi government. This reveals another objective that less democratic countries have for conducting PR in the United States: the "legitimization" objective. Political elites who do not hold official positions in their government sometimes seek both public exposure in U.S. media and relations with political leaders.

By the same token, most of the PR activities that Egypt paid for in the United States after the army ousted the democratically elected government in 2013 were devoted to communicating with the American government about the implementation of a "Road Map" for the establishment of democratic institutions in Egypt. Although those objectives sound like they would be more fitting in an internal PR campaign, the Egyptian government chose to target the U.S. officials. This is another aspect of the legitimization function of international PR.

The results of the present study provide an empirical basis for a cultural/political theory of international PR, one that positions the practice as a contextual function, in addition to having an organizational function. International PR activities are the product of the political context of foreign clients and their political culture. Looking at them this way also adds a new dimension for evaluating international PR according to the target audience and the objectives of the practice. Finally, the results of the present study can assist foreign clients in recognizing the importance of adjusting the practice of their international PR to the political culture of the host nation, rather than that of the client nation, unless the two cultures resonate.

REFERENCES

Bay Area Socialist Organizing Committee. n.d. "Democratic Centralism." *Encyclopedia of Anti-Revisionism On-Line.* Accessed February 5, 2016. https://www.marxists.org/history/erol/ncm-7/basoc/ch-5.htm.

Center for Security Studies. n.d. "Turkish Americans lobby Washington." Accessed February 22, 2020. https://css.ethz.ch/en/services/digital-library/articles/article.html/88724.

Center of Responsive Politics. 2020. "Foreign lobby watch." Accessed February 9, 2020. https://www.opensecrets.org/fara.

Crabtree, S. 2011. "Did DC public relations firm fully disclose its work for Egyptian steel tycoon?" Talking Points Memo (TPM), February 8, 2011. https://talkingpointsmemo.com/muckraker/did-dc-public-relations-firm-fully-disclose-its-work-for-egyptian-steel-tycoon.

Culbertson, H. M., and D. W. Jeffers. 1992. "The social, political, and economic contexts: Keys in educating true public relations professionals." *Public Relations Review* 11 (1): 5–21.

Curtin, P. A., and T. K. Gaither. 2005. "Privileging identity, difference, and power: The circuit of culture as a basis for public relations theory." *Journal of Public Relations Research* 17 (2): 91–115.

———. 2007. *International Public Relations: Negotiating Culture, Identity, and Power.* Thousand Oaks, CA: Sage Publications.

Davis, M. 1977. *Interpreters for Nigeria: The Third World and International Public Relations.* Champaign: University of Illinois Press.

Duncan, B. 2005. "PR firms burnish Arab image in US." Al Jazeera, September 2, 2005. http://www.aljazeera.com/archive/2005/09/200841011522162867.html.

Freedom House. 2016. "Methodology: Freedom in the world 2016." Accessed May 20, 2016. https://freedomhouse.org/report/freedom-world-2016/methodology.

Grunig, J. 1993. "Public relations and international affairs: Effects, ethics, and responsibility." *Journal of International Affairs* 47 (1): 137–62.

Holtzhausen, D. R. 2000. "Postmodern values in public relations." *Public Relations Research* 12 (1): 93–114.

Itkowitz, C. 2014. "Which foreign countries spent the most to influence U.S. politics?" *Washington Post*, May 14, 2014. https://www.washingtonpost.com/blogs/in-the-loop/wp/2014/05/14/which-foreign-countries-spent-the-most-to-influence-u-s-politics.

Johnson, M. A. 2005. "Five decades of Mexican public relations in the United States: From propaganda to strategic counsel." *Public Relations Review* 31 (1): 11–20.

Al-Kandari, A., and T. K. Gaither. 2011. "Arabs, the West and public relations: A critical/cultural study of Arab cultural values." *Public Relations Review* 37 (3): 266–73.

Kostyaev, S. 2013. "Regime change and Arab countries lobbying in the United States." *Arab Studies Quarterly* 35 (1): 54–72.

Kurlantzick, J. 2010. "When lobbyists work for authoritarian nations." *Newsweek*, July 27, 2010. http://www.newsweek.com/when-lobbyists-work-authoritarian-nations-74781.

Layne, N. 2018. "Flynn's former business partner charged with secret lobbying for Turkey." Reuters, December 17, 2018. https://www.reuters.com/article/us-turkey-usa-gulen/flynns-former-business-partner-charged-with-secret-lobbying-for-turkey-idUSKBN1OG1T3.

Lee, S. 2006. "An analysis of other countries' international public relations in the U.S." *Public Relations Review* 32 (2): 97–103.

Lee, S., and H. Hong. 2012. "International public relations' influence on media coverage and public perceptions of foreign countries." *Public Relations Review* 38 (3): 491–93.

Lee, S., and Y. Kim. 2010. "Return on investment (ROI) of international public relations: A country-level analysis." *Public Relations Review* 36 (1): 15–20.

———. 2018. "A time-series analysis of international public relations expenditure and economic outcome." *Communication Research* 45 (7): 1012–30.

L'Etang, J. 1996. "Public Relations as Diplomacy." In *Critical Perspectives in Public Relations*, edited by J. L'Etang and M. Pieczka, 14–34. London: International Thomson Business Press.

Manheim, J. B., and R. B. Albritton. 1984. "Changing national images: International public relations and media agenda setting." *American Political Science Review* 78 (3): 641–57.

Marcum, J. 1969. *The Angolan Revolution.* Vol. 1. Cambridge, MA: MIT Press.

Mickey, T. J. 1997. "A postmodern view of public relations: Sign and reality." *Public Relations Review* 23 (3): 271–84.

Page, B. I., and M. M. Bouton. 2006. *The Foreign Policy Disconnect: What Americans Want from Our Leaders but Don't Get*. Chicago: University of Chicago Press.

Sheafer, T., and I. Gabay. 2009. "Mediated public diplomacy: A strategic contest over international agenda building and frame building." *Political Communication* 26 (4): 447–67.

Taylor, M., and M. I. Kent. 1999. "Challenging assumptions of international public relations: When government is the most important public." *Public Relations Review* 25 (2): 131–44.

Transparency International. 2015. "Corruption perceptions index." Accessed January 30, 2019. http://www.transparency.org/research/cpi/overview.

U.S. Census. 2015. "Top Trading Partners—October 2015." Accessed January 30, 2016. https://www.census.gov/foreign-trade/statistics/highlights/top/top1510yr.html.

U.S. Department of Justice. 2007. Registration statement, Ahmed Ezz. Accessed February 21, 2020. https://efile.fara.gov/docs/5483-Exhibit-AB-20071130-12.pdf.

———. 2016. "Audit of the National Security Division's Enforcement and Administration of the Foreign Agents Registration Act." September 2016. https://oig.justice.gov/reports/2016/a1624.pdf.

U.S. Department of State. 2020. "U.S. relations with Saudi Arabia." December 15, 2020. https://www.state.gov/u-s-relations-with-saudi-arabia.

Uysal, N., J. Schroeder, and M. Taylor. 2012. "Social media and soft power: Positioning Turkey's image on Twitter." *Middle East Journal of Culture & Communication* 5 (3): 338–59.

Verčič, D., L. A. Grunig, and J. E. Grunig. 1996. "Global and Specific Principles of Public Relations: Evidence from Slovenia." In *International Public Relations: A Comparative Analysis*, edited by H. M. Culbertson and N. Chen, 31–66. Mahwah, NJ: Lawrence Erlbaum Associates.

White, C., and D. Radic. 2014. "Comparative public diplomacy: Message strategies of countries in transition." *Public Relations Review* 40 (3): 459–65.

Windrich, E. 1989. "South Africa's propaganda war." *Africa Today* 36 (1): 51–60.

Zaharna, R. S. 2000. "Intercultural communication and international public relations: Exploring parallels." *Communication Quarterly* 48 (1): 85–100.

Zhang, J., and G. T. Cameron. 2003. "China's agenda building and image polishing in the U.S.: Assessing an international public relations campaign." *Public Relations Review* 29 (1): 13–28.

7

Radio Sawa

Is Anyone in the Middle East Listening?

Fran Hassencahl

In January 2013, Hillary Clinton, U.S. Secretary of State and ex officio member of the Broadcast Board of Governors (BBG), testified before Congress that the BBG, which oversees the operations of Radio Sawa, "is practically defunct in terms of its ability to be able to tell a message around the world. So, we are abdicating the ideological arena, and we need to get back into it" (Reilly 2014). However, she did not speak to what the results are from the increased spending on broadcast satellites, building websites, establishing Twitter feed and Facebook pages, and developing programming for Radio Sawa along with Al Hurrah Television, developed by Voice of America (VOA) in the wake of 9/11. Matthew Weed noted in a 2016 report, "U.S. International Broadcasting: Background and Issues for Reform," prepared for the Congressional Research Service, that the audiences for the Middle East Broadcasting Network, which includes Radio Sawa, TV Al Hurrah, and Radio Afia Darfur, are on the decline.

Since its inception in 2002, Radio Sawa has encountered numerous problems. There is substantial evidence for the wisdom of choosing a commercial U.S. model of broadcasting. There are also obvious management issues incurred by its overseeing body, the BBG, who are unable to produce credible data about audience numbers or determine the impact of its programming. Other challenges include problems with achieving industry standards in the production of news and fending off the increased competition from local radio stations in the Middle East. In a 2007 summary of a Rand Corporation study, the Islamic Research Institute in Islamabad concluded that Muslims "are overwhelmed by a vast amount of often inaccurate and biased information" (Islamic Research Institute 2007, 276). Broadcasters no longer compete for frequencies because they can cheaply broadcast on the web using minimal equipment. In Amman, Jordan, alone there are thirty-two Arabic-speaking radio stations. With the advent of podcasting, anyone can be a journalist, thus compounding news choices.

RESEARCH QUESTIONS

Three significant components will be looked at during this research: chronicling the events leading up to the establishment of Radio Sawa, examining the arguments made by the supporters and opponents of Radio Sawa as to whether the research studies conducted for the BBG provide good data for decision making, and investigating whether the station's news meets currently accepted standards for broadcast news.

Sources for analysis include annual reports, budget requests, and press releases from the BBG; studies done by the Government Accounting Office (GAO); testimonies before the U.S. Senate Foreign Relations Committee; and publications from the American University in Cairo's Center for Electronic Journalism. Most of the discussion of the news broadcasts comes from former VOA employees who are now retired or working at universities and nonprofit organizations that focus on the Middle East. All are unhappy about the BBG's decision to drop VOA Arabic programming and the switch to the new format.

Events Leading to the Establishment of Radio Sawa

In March 2002, Radio Sawa (colloquial Lebanese Arabic meaning "together") replaced the VOA Arabic Service (1942–1945, 1950–2002) as the radio broadcast component of America's public diplomacy effort in the Middle East. Many veteran journalists and staff from the VOA and senior staff in the public diplomacy community did not support the format changes. They argued that the BBG's decision to focus on the under-30 age group abandoned the elites, the opinion and decision makers, who were longtime listeners of the VOA (Dizard 2004, Rugh 2006, Lord 2006, Muravchik 2003). The BBG's rationale was that 60% of the population in the Middle East are under the age of 30 and do not listen to the VOA Arabic Service. Consequently, the BBG closed down the VOA Arabic Service and changed the station's format from news and cultural programming to a Top 40 music format with current popular music in Arabic and English and minimal news.

Radio Sawa broadcasts 24/7. However, due to budget cutbacks in 2019, the station will only be heard on AM and FM radio in Iraq. Country-centric feeds, both online and over the air, for the Gulf, Egypt, Lebanon, Jordan, Morocco, Sudan, and Mauritania ended in 2019. Sawa will go digital, but at the expense of some seven million, or 60%, of the audience, who will no longer be able to listen via their home or car radios. Chris Greenway, assistant editor with the BBC Monitoring, states, "Clearly not everyone in the Arab world is willing or able to receive radio broadcasts via non-traditional means" (Careless 2018). By moving to web-based broadcasting, Radio Sawa opens itself up to possible blockages of its website by Middle Eastern governments.

The Evolution of Sawa as Public Diplomacy

Radio Sawa, like its counterparts VOA, Radio Free Europe / Radio Liberty, Radio Farda, Radio and TV Martí, Radio Free Asia, and TV Al Hurrah, is public diplomacy. Some might label it propaganda. Semantics aside, the goal is to persuade others, to shape public opinion, and to get listeners/viewers to believe the United States' story of events. Nancy Snow, a former employee of the U.S. Information Agency and editor of the book *War, Media, and Propaganda*, indicates, "We didn't call what we did then, propaganda, which was too loaded a term and one associated with dastardly regimes, such as Stalin and Hitler. Our euphemism was public diplomacy" (Snow 2004, 17). The new term now is "soft power," but the goal to persuade remains the same (Melissen 2005).

The BBG, a nonpartisan but politically appointed board, consists of eight individuals who oversee Radio Sawa. The Secretary of State is the ninth member ex officio. Appointments are often a reward for election campaign contributions. Board members do not need a journalism background. Currently, none of the members of the BBG are journalists. Kenneth Y. Tomlinson, chair of the BBG, in an address at Princeton University, characterized their mission as a "firewall to protect international broadcasting from becoming a mouthpiece for government officials," and to tell the truth and broadcast the news whether it is favorable or unfavorable to the United States (BBG 2004).

Choice of a Format That Works for American Commercial Radio without Consideration of Other Models

In November of 2000, President Clinton appointed Norman Pattiz to the BBG. Pattiz became the primary force behind the programming changes at the VOA Arabic Service. He is the founder and chair of Westwood One, which currently provides programming to over 8,000 affiliated radio stations (Nielsen 2019). Pattiz is politically well connected. He was an overnight guest in the Clinton White House (Broder and Van Natta 2000) and a contributor to Joe Biden's aspirations for the presidency in 1988. Biden, before becoming vice president under Obama, chaired the Senate Foreign Relations Committee, which oversees and recommends funding for U.S. broadcasting overseas.

Building commercial radio is a different project from creating a radio station to influence public opinion. Commercial radio lives and dies by the ratings, but these ratings only give information about audience share and do not measure attitudes or intentions to purchase a given product or service. Pattiz modeled Radio Sawa after commercial radio, not only in programming but in seeking to measure its success by numbers of listeners, without investigating whether they were buying into the message.

After a revolutionary trip to Qatar, Israel, Jordan, Egypt, and the West Bank in June of 2002, Pattiz told the Senate Foreign Relations Committee that he learned of "a media war going on and the weapons of that war include disinformation, incitement to violence, hate radio, Government censorship and journalistic self-censorship, and the United States didn't have a horse in this race" (BBG 2002). He also noticed that approximately 60% of the population was under the age of 30. Even though he does not speak Arabic, he found the local radio to be "dull," "drab," and sounding like "government radio." Pattiz also feared that Arab youth were "ripe for exploitation by radical Islamic fundamentalist ideology." It was crucial that the United States reached them (Pattiz 2004, 76).

Pattiz arranged for Edison Media Research, a company that he had worked with in the past, to survey Middle Eastern audiences in Amman, Cairo, and Bahrain. He also arranged for Edison to run focus groups in Amman and Kuwait City. The goal was "to find out what young people in the Arab world were looking for in a radio station" and then to give "the people what they want." Edison determined that there was a market for a new type of programming, a Top 40 mix, which would focus on pop music and alternate between Western and Arabic songs. Pattiz hired the same producer who helped Casey Kasem launch a successful and syndicated U.S. Top 40 radio show, to put together the programming format (Mayer 2002). Since media research, when conducted by a private company, is proprietary information, no information is available as to how Edison chose the interview sample or the process by which they chose and trained the local interviewers (Webster 2004).The view held by communications professionals that the mission was to change hearts and minds by presenting information and news about America while adhering to accepted standards of journalism was no longer accepted. As a result, in came models from commercial radio, which focus upon providing entertainment, not information, to capture audiences. Robert Reilly, the former VOA director, wrote in the

Washington Post that the BBG turned "the 'war of ideas' into the battle of the bands" (Reilly 2007).

Some accuse the BBG of wanting to substitute commercial programming for government programming (Whitworth 2004; Garfinkle 2004), but it seems more likely that the BBG turned to models of broadcasting and to resources that they had successfully used in the past. Taking his cues from the American radio stations that he sells programming to, Pattiz decided to go from news and cultural programs to a Top 40 format. Contemporary American and Arab music would comprise 75% of the programming. Long programming blocks were out. Short, fast-paced segments were in. News would thus follow the American model of headline-type news in three-minute segments.

The BBG Struggles to Provide Credible Audience Research

The Board of Governors has major management issues. Reilly (2014), director of the Voice of America in 2001–2002, notes that the BBG "doesn't report to anyone; it is outside the executive branch of command . . . with a $750 million budget." The BBG reports great success. The chair of the BBG, Kenneth Tomlinson, told the U.S. Senate Foreign Relations Committee on February 27, 2003, that Sawa was a "success story" and that there is "a real hunger for such information" (U.S. Senate 2003).

Tomlinson casts Sawa into the Cold War model by quoting the Polish leader Lech Walesa and emphasizing the role of radio in the collapse of the Soviet empire. He predicts a similar success "with the new war of ideas as we offer democracy, tolerance, and self-government as the positive alternative to tyranny, fanaticism and terror." This analogy is a weak argument. Nowhere in his extensive testimony does he offer any concrete data about the numbers of listeners and their opinions about Radio Sawa's programming, let alone any indication that the programming has enhanced America's public diplomacy efforts. He does claim that "informal survey data" show that Radio Sawa has gained "a significant audience in Baghdad." Skeptics would argue that since the Coalition Provisional Authority closed and regulated Iraqi media, Radio Sawa did not have local competition. Tomlinson also does not report that the Iraqis saw Radio Sawa as "state media" and that Sawa-Iraq's first director, Ahmed Rikabi, quit in 2003 in protest over coalition interference (Lynch 2005, 217).

Since 2003, the U.S. Senate Committee on Foreign Relations has not looked at Radio Sawa. The committee did briefly check in on it one time on November 17, 2015. In that 2015 hearing, Enders Wimbush, BBG board member from 2010 to 2012 and former director of Radio Liberty, criticized the BBG for ethical lapses and for a lack of strategy and oversight of broadcasting activities. "Largely absent are serious discussions by experts about content, audience, and impact: What should we be broadcasting, to whom, and to what end? What audiences do we seek to influence? How should we measure impact? Do numbers matter? And how does all of this contribute to advancing our foreign policy objectives?" (Wimbush 2015). Wimbush grants that these are difficult issues to resolve because BBG members often lack foreign policy experience and knowledge about broadcasting.

The Government Accounting Office watches over the governmental purse and seeks to determine the results obtained from an appropriation of funds. Starting in 2004, they began asking for data to support the BBG claims about audience numbers and effectiveness. In August 2006 the GAO noted that the BBG had developed performance indicators and targets for the size of the audience and programming credibility. "However, it is not clear whether the Radio Sawa and Al Hurrah performance targets have actually been met because of weaknesses in MBN's methodology and documentation" (GAO 2007, 33). They found problems with the lack of transparency about sample collection, the training for the data collectors, and the margin of error for the surveys. They found no quality-control mechanisms in place to verify that policies and procedures for data collection were consistently followed. In the budget projections for 2015, the BBG reported that they were still working on solving these problems (BBG 2014, 110–12). The GAO's 2007 report characterizes the BBG's research efforts as "little more than educated guesses" (5).

The response to the GAO's criticisms in 2006 by BBG chair Kenneth Y. Tomlinson (GAO 2006, appendix V) can be summarized in his disclaimer that they did not follow "textbook" survey methods, but they know that they are reaching a "very large" audience and that is what matters. Tomlinson rationalizes that, in the corporate world, good faith and not-too-expensive effort is enough to provide at least some data to justify a decision. He argues that "the aim of these studies is not to produce academic work, but to provide decision makers with data they can use" (GAO 2006, 61).

The measurements of program credibility are uncertain. In the BBG's 2008 budget request, data on news credibility for 2006, 2007, and 2008 are presented as targets and estimates. The budget request for 2011 provides no information on the numbers of listeners or their opinions about Sawa's programming. By 2013, the reported program credibility had risen to 85% of weekly listeners. By 2018, this number had fallen to 80%. The numbers combine both radio and TV data, which makes it impossible to evaluate Sawa's success in creating trustworthy information.

The U.S. Agency for Global Media (formerly BBG) budget request for 2019 indicates that contractors, who do not reveal their research methods, did phone surveys and face-to-face interviews (BBG 2018, 124). Data show that the Middle East Broadcasting Network experienced an audience drop from 27.5 million in 2016 to 24.7 million in 2018. It is important to note that these data combine listeners from Radio Sawa and TV Al Hurrah. My examination of information given by the BBG to Congress in their budget requests in 2007, 2008, 2011, 2019, and 2020 shows that claims of success are broadly made and usually focus upon the numbers of listeners rather than answering the more difficult questions of whether these broadcasts are changing any hearts and minds, or even whether the news and information is seen as credible.

Consequently, the BBG reports have been largely a public relations effort to convince Congress to continue and to increase their appropriations. Cole (2005) described the numbers as "smoke and mirrors." For example, the BBG claimed that 39.5% of the Kuwaitis listened, but failed to mention that the base number of Arabic speakers is exceptionally low because the majority of the population are international guest workers (Cole 2005).

Are we meeting public diplomacy goals in the Middle East? This question remains unanswered, and social scientists will attest that persuasion is a long and difficult process. They would state, however, that it is possible to do some measurement and gain some insights into what is working or not working.

Is Sawa Winning Hearts and Minds or Simply Entertaining Audiences?

Agha (2005) concludes that Radio Sawa is not "winning the hearts and minds" of radio audiences in Jordan. In face-to-face surveys of forty-eight listeners in Amman during the summer of 2004, she found that 50% listened to Sawa daily for an average of about one hour. Sixty percent also listened to the competition, Radio Fann, run by the Jordanian Armed Forces, which also offers a programming mix of Arabic and American pop music. Forty-one percent listened to Radio Jordan. Only 37% reported that they listened most of the time to Radio Sawa.

Agha also investigated whether audiences listen for music or for news. BBG reports do not differentiate whether the listeners listen to news in addition to the music. Agha found that only one respondent described Sawa as presenting "good and recent news." The rest of the sample either did not listen to Sawa's news broadcasts or voiced negative opinions about its news coverage. Eighty-nine percent listed Al Jazeera television as their preferred source of news. This finding is confirmed by Mahmoud Galander (2012), who surveyed students at Qatar University and concluded that Radio Sawa "is widely used as a music channel but it does not seem to succeed in selling U.S. foreign policy to the Arab youth."

Mohammed el-Nawawy (2007) surveyed 394 college students in Jordan, Kuwait, Morocco, Palestine, and the United Arab Emirates and found that 43.1% listened "often" or "very often" to the music on Radio Sawa, but only 13.5% listened "often" or "very often" to the news. In their responses to open-ended questions about their likes and dislikes about the programming, it was clear that the students perceived the news as manipulation. Answers to another question about what the United States needed to do to win the hearts and minds of the students showed that they wanted changes in U.S. policies toward Iraq and the Palestinian–Israeli conflict. Placing these findings in the context of the research on credibility, el-Nawawy concludes that until the United States changes its foreign policies, there is little likelihood of trust for American media or any other forms of public diplomacy.

The issue of Palestine remains a large factor in the acceptance of Sawa's news credibility. Telhami (2004a), in his statement before the U.S. Senate Subcommittee on International Operations and Terrorism, and Agha, in her thesis (2005), emphasized that without U.S. policy changes on the Middle East, and more specifically on Iraq and on the Israeli–Palestinian conflict, media efforts will have little success. Telhami pointed out that polling data that he gathered with Zogby International show that American policies, not public diplomacy efforts, determine the Middle Eastern attitudes about the United States. Snow (2007, 162) predicted that anti-Americanism and "an unfinished roadmap to peace in the Middle East" do not bode well for changing Arab public opinion.

Data show that the target audience of Arabic speakers under 30 do listen to the music, but when it comes to news or political programming, they either tune out or look elsewhere (Sharp 2004, Abunimah 2002, Dove 2002, Agha 2005). Hayden (2004) interviewed students in Saudi Arabia and found them to be dismissive of the news, accepting it as just "government propaganda." Kassman (2007) found that listeners to the old VOA believed that Sawa's news "focused on pronouncements out of Washington." Christie and Clark (2011) randomly sampled 503 listeners and non-listeners to Radio Sawa, ages 15–34, in the United Arab Emirates. They concluded that the listeners perceive "they are not getting the complete picture from Radio Sawa" (369). None of the research considers that young adults in the Middle East get most of their news from television (Telhami 2004b, Mellor 2005).

Radio Sawa has gained an unknown market share despite some obstacles. The major obstacle not addressed by the BBG is that the Middle East is a media-rich environment. Heil (2007) characterizes it as "an ocean of channels" containing 280 Arabic TV channels and predicts that more are on the way. Robin (2005) noted that U.S. public diplomacy still holds to the idea of information paucity in the Middle East. Although state-run television and radio stations dominate over-the-air broadcasting, access to satellite and Internet broadcasting has increased listening options.

The Absence of Good News Practices

Sawa's first news director was Mouafac Harb, a journalist who worked for al-Hayat and *Newsweek* and served as the general manager of radio and television at the National Broadcasting Network in Lebanon. The BBG hired new news personnel rather than drawing upon veteran journalists at the VOA. Harb hired some 400 Lebanese journalists who worked as stringers rather than full-time staffers. Fandy (2007) characterizes them as either "rejects" or "squatters" who have taken a leave of absence to work in the United States. He portrays them as paying "lip service to the promotion of America while serving their own parochial causes at the same time" (103). Fandy suggests that many needed a crash course in American politics, culture, and values (103–104) and lacked journalism training (109). Most of the staff were Maronite Christians, which did not enhance their credibility among Muslims (112). Pein (2005) accused Radio Sawa of giving the news "a heavy Lebanese tilt that turned off listeners in other countries." Charges of cronyism in hiring, mismanagement, and irregularities in the awarding of contracts for Radio Sawa and Television Al Hurrah contributed to Harb's resignation in 2006.

Despite Arabic being the fifth-most-spoken language in the world, it is not a uniform oral language, but rather a "macro language." Scholars recognize that Arabic is a group of spoken dialects and that people from other regions, such as Egypt, struggle to understand Mesopotamian Arabic (Greene 2018). Dialects matter. Mohammed al-Azdee's (2010) interviews with Iraqi students attending summer journalism classes at Indiana University in 2009 found that the Iraqis wanted news in the Iraqi dialect and not news broadcast by Jordanian speakers. They were offended not only by factual inaccuracies but also by the fact that the newsreaders had difficulties pronouncing the names of people and places in Iraq. The professional quality of the presenters varies greatly. Some are highly effective, and others, with awkward and halting voices, sound like amateurs. Two independent panels of Arab language experts hired by the State Department's inspector general found poor Arabic grammar and learned that some parents refuse to let their children listen because of the bad grammar (Kessler 2004).

The GAO (2006) criticizes the BBG for not providing any quality controls for hiring and training journalists. Ironically, many of the reporters do not know English, which makes it difficult for them to be interviewed or trained by their English-speaking counterparts. Iskandar (2005) reports that Sawa dropped the two-source rule that required that reporters had to seek at least two independent sources for their stories. Some news was directly copied from aljazeera .net (Fandy 2007, 109).

Sam Hilmy (2007), a veteran journalist retired from the VOA, monitored Sawa news and found problems with consistency and organization of the news stories. A newscaster might read three or four headlines, but the story order did not follow the headlines' order. Sometimes a big news event was used as a closer, and at other times a light routine story or a less important story would be the lead story. Major stories would not necessarily be repeated, added to, and rebroadcast or freshened in the next hour; they often just disappeared. Usually no more than 10 minutes of news occurs per hour, which brings the total news time to 240 minutes a day, far short of the 600 minutes per day claimed by the BBG.

Most of the news stories focus on events in the Arab world. Only one part-time reporter covers the State Department and the White House. The station does not cover the U.S. Congress or cultural and economic news stories that originate in the United States. Hilmy (2007) believes that the goal is to attract youth with pop music and not to broadcast anything but "parochial backyard Arab news."

Washington Post reporter Glenn Kessler (2004) discovered that some reporters quoted biased news stories that appeared in local Arab newspapers and Middle East news services.

Hilmy (2007) found duplicated material, poor or contradictory sourcing, unprofessional language, and outdated information. There appeared to be little planning or attention to timing. If it was time for the news and a song was playing, the song would abruptly end, rather than fade to make way for the news. A lack of preplanning and control permitted some news programs to be "a platform for emotional unrestrained views." Harb, in an interview with the *Washington Post*, denies such accusations and states, "We try to de-emotionalize the news. . . . We don't use adjectives" (Dobbs 2003).

R. S. Zaharna testified before the Senate Foreign Relations Committee in 2003 that she concluded the American radio model does not consider intercultural differences. For Arabs, building relationships is more persuasive than amassing facts and figures to support arguments. Americans may value direct communication, but the Arab public values indirectness. Zaharna recommended that the BBG hire a communication strategist and a polling company to better measure the needs of listeners and to plan future programming (Committee on Foreign Relations 2003, 73–74).

CONCLUSION

The important unanswered question is whether Radio Sawa is or can be effective public diplomacy. There are problems with audience research methodology. Sanford Unger (2005b), former director of the VOA, observed that the BBG "continue to play games about the size and nature of the audience." The audience numbers games continue, since the BBG budget request for 2020 does not give breakout numbers of Sawa's audience or base numbers for their conclusions. The budget request indicates that 97% of the weekly audience find the information broadcast to be "very or somewhat credible," which seems contrary to studies by academicians (Unger 2005a, 97).

Kalupa (2011) points out that more research is vital even though there are difficulties conducting opinion studies in authoritarian states. He recommends that the BBG develop new models for research instead of clinging to old models of audience research, because the "principles, theories, and results developed for traditional media might or might not be adequate in understanding and explaining audiences' attitudes, opinions, and behaviors" in the age of the Internet (16). Currently, we do not know who is listening and whether they perceive the programming as credible. Reilly (2007) argues that we do not teach civics to American teenagers by asking them to listen to pop music; thus, there is no rationale for teaching teens in the Middle East about democracy and America by broadcasting an MTV message.

Changes are not likely for Radio Sawa, because it gets little U.S. press attention. It has no constituency inside the United States and a vote for or against appropriations "never affects a member of Congress' prospects for reelection" (Unger 2005a). Rugh (2005) reports that when Senator Biden and others on the Senate Foreign Relations Committee visited the studios in Springfield, Virginia, they "were dazzled" by the up-to-date equipment and staff members, who were native speakers of Arabic, and concluded that the programs "must be good." The members of Congress did not ask whether we are reaching those goals of "changing hearts and minds."

The founders of Radio Sawa used the model of American commercial radio where audience share dictates the prices that stations can charge for advertising. Numbers do not necessarily translate into product acceptance or attitude change. In the case of Radio Sawa, we lack evidence as to whether the listeners are purchasing our version of the news or even have a better opinion of America after listening to the mix of pop music and "news light."

REFERENCES

Abunimah, A. 2002. "Radio Sawa: All dressed up with nowhere to go." The Electronic Intifada. August 20, 2002. http://electronicintifada.net/v2/article494.shtml.

Agha, S. 2005. "Radio Sawa's Reception in Amman, Jordan: Exploratory Research into Audience Effects." Master's thesis, University of Texas, Austin.

al-Azdee, M. 2010. "Investigation of U.S. Public Diplomacy in Iraq and Cuba in Terms of Sawa and Martí." Paper presented at the meeting of International Communication Association, Singapore, June 22–26, 2010.

BBG (Broadcasting Board of Governors; now U.S. Agency for Global Media). 2002. Testimony of Norman J. Pattiz, Broadcasting Board of Governors, before the Committee on Foreign Relations of the Senate, June 11, 2002. https://www.usagm.gov/2002/06/11/testimony-of-norman-j-pattiz-broadcasting-board-of-governors-before-the-committee-on-foreign-relations-of-the-united-states-senate. See also University of California at Los Angeles, Latin American Institute, "Al Jazeera, Radio Sawa Founders Report on Media in the Middle East," November 4, 2003, https://www.international.ucla.edu/lai/article/5087.

———. 2004. Remarks by Kenneth Y. Tomlinson, Chairman of the Broadcasting Board of Governors, to Princeton University's Woodrow Wilson School of Public and International Affairs, September 30, 2004. National Archives, Washington, D.C., Record Group 517, Records of the Broadcasting Board of Governors.

———. 2007. "Fiscal Year 2008 Budget Request." https://www.usagm.gov/wp-content/uploads/2011/12/bbg_fy08_budget_request.pdf.

———. 2010. "Fiscal Year 2011 Budget Request." National Archives, Washington, D.C., Record Group 517, Records of the Broadcasting Board of Governors.

———. 2014. "Fiscal Year 2015 Congressional Budget Request." https://www.usagm.gov/wp-content/uploads/2014/03/FY-2015-BBG-Congressional-Budget-Request-FINAL-21-March-2014.pdf.

———. 2018. "2019 Congressional Budget Justification." https://www.usagm.gov/wp-content/uploads/2018/02/BBGBudget_FY19_CBJ_2-7-18_Final.pdf.

Broder, J. M., and D. Van Natta Jr. 2000. "Senate donors among guests at White House." *New York Times*, September 23, 2000. https://www.nytimes.com/2000/09/23/nyregion/senate-donors-among-guests-at-white-house.html.

Careless, J. 2018. "Radio Sawa to scale back regional broadcasts." Radio World, March 28, 2018. https://www.radioworld.com/news-and-business/radio-sawa-to.

Christie, T. B., and A. M. Clark. 2011. "Believe it or not: Understanding the credibility and effectiveness of Radio Sawa in the UAE." *International Communication Gazette* 73 (4): 359–71.

Cole, J. 2005. "The disaster of destroying the Voice of America Arabic service." Informed Comment, May 3, 2005. http://www.juancole.com/2005/05/disaster-of-destroying-voice-of.html.

Committee on Foreign Relations, United States Senate. 2003. Testimony of R. S. Zaharna, American University, February 27, 2003. *American Public Diplomacy and Islam*. Publication No. YA.F67/2:HRg.108-21. Washington, DC: U.S. Government Printing Office.

Dizard, W. P., Jr. 2004. *Inventing Public Diplomacy: The Story of the U.S. Information Agency*. Boulder, CO: Lynne Rienner.

Dobbs, M. 2003. "America's Arabic voice: Radio Sawa struggles to make itself heard." *Washington Post*, March 24, 2003.

Dove, F., host. 2002. *Outlook* (radio broadcast), September 24, 2002. BBC World Service.

Fandy, M. 2007. *(Un)civil War of Words: Media and Politics in the Arab World*. Westport, CT: Praeger Security International.

Galander, M. M. 2012. "Radio Sawa and the U.S. public diplomacy in the Middle East: Entertaining the Arab youth or 'winning hearts and minds'?" *International Journal of Arab Culture, Management and Sustainable Development* 2 (4): 344–53. https://www.inderscienceonline.com/doi/abs/10.1504/IJACMSD.2012.053399.

Garfinkle, A., ed. 2004. *A Practical Guide to Winning the War on Terrorism*. Hoover Institution Press Publication No. 53. Stanford University, Hoover Institution Press.

GAO (Government Accounting Office). 2006. *U.S. International Broadcasting: Management of Middle East Broadcasting Services Could be Improved*. Report to the Chairman, Subcommittee on National Security, Emerging Threats and International Relations, Committee on Government Reform, House of Representatives, August 2006. http://www.gao.gov/new.items/d06762.pdf.

———. 2007. *U.S. Diplomacy: Actions Needed to Improve Strategic Use and Coordination of Research*. Report to the Ranking Member, Committee on Foreign Relations, U.S. Senate, July 2007. http://www.gao.gov/new.items/d07904.pdf.

Greene, L. 2018. "Out of one, many." *The Economist*, October 20, 2018, 78.

Hayden, C. 2004. "Looking for public diplomacy in Saudi Arabia: Finding proxies and suggestions for new strategies." University of Southern California Center for Public Diplomacy, April 1, 2004. https://www.researchgate.net/publication/265221101.

Heil, A. L., Jr. 2007. "Rate of Arabic language TV start-ups shows no sign of abating." *Arab Media & Society* 2 (Summer 2007). https://www.arabmediasociety.com/wp-content/uploads/2017/12/20070513132640_AMS2_Alan_Heil.pdf.

Hilmy, S. 2007. "Radio Sawa: America's new adventure in radio broadcasting." *Arab Media & Society*, May 21, 2007. https://www.arabmediasociety.com/radio-sawa-americas-new-adventure-in-radio-broadcasting.

Iskandar, A. 2005. "Speaking to the Enemy: U.S. Government Public Diplomacy and Discourses of Cultural Hybridity." Paper presented at the annual meeting of the International Communication Association, New York City, May 26–30, 2005. Retrieved from EBSCO database.

Islamic Research Institute. 2007. "Building moderate Muslim networks." *Islamic Studies* 46 (2): 265–76.

Kalupa, F. B. 2011. "International Broadcasting: Policies, Practices, and Perceptions of America's Middle East Broadcasting." Paper presented at Workshop on Media in the GCC at the University of Cambridge, United Kingdom, July 6–9, 2011.

Kassman, L. 2007. "Voice of America versus Radio Sawa in the Middle East: A personal perspective." *Arab Media & Society*, May 21, 2007. https://www.arabmediasociety.com/voice-of-america-versus-radio-sawa-in-the-middle-east-a-personal-perspective.

Kessler, G. 2004. "The role of Radio Sawa in Mideast questioned." *Washington Post*, October 13, 2004. https://www.washingtonpost.com/archive/politics/2004/10/13/the-role-of-radio-sawa-in-mideast-questioned/d7f0e399-f6b6-4305-a085-c9f9ce5139c5.

Lord, C. 2006. *Losing Hearts and Minds? Public Diplomacy and Strategic Influence in the Age of Terror*. Westport, CT: Praeger Security International.

Lynch, M. 2005. *Voices of the New Arab Public: Iraq, al-Jazeera and Middle East Politics Today*. New York: Columbia University Press.

Mayer, J. 2002. "The sound of America." *New Yorker*, Dept. of Propaganda, February 18, 2002. http://www.newyorker.com/archive/2002/02/18/020218ta_talk_mayer?printable=true.

Melissen, J. 2005. "The New Public Diplomacy: Between Theory and Practice." In *The New Public Diplomacy: Soft Power in International Relations*, edited by J. Melissen, 3–27. London: Palgrave Macmillan.

Mellor, N. 2005. *The Making of Arab News*. Lanham, MD: Rowman & Littlefield.

Muravchik, J. 2003. "America loses its voice." *Weekly Standard*, June 9, 2003. Retrieved from https://www.aei.org/articles/america-loses-its-voice.

el-Nawawy, M. 2007. "U.S. Public Diplomacy and the News Credibility of Radio Sawa and Television Al Hurrah in the Arab World." In *New Media and the New Middle East*, edited by P. Seib, 119–27. New York: Palgrave Macmillan.

Nielsen. 2019. "Westwood One adds Nielsen's national media impact to its audio insights platform." March 18, 2019. https://www.nielsen.com/us/en/press-releases/2019/westwood-one-adds-nielsens-national-media-impact-to-its-audio-insights-platform.

Pattiz, N. J. 2004. "Radio Sawa and Alhurrah TV: Opening Channels of Mass Communication in the Middle East." In *Engaging the Arab and Islamic Worlds through Public Diplomacy: A Report and Action Recommendations*, edited by W. A. Rugh, 69–89. Washington, DC: Public Diplomacy Council at George Washington University.

Pein, C. 2005. "The new wave: The Voice of America is being drowned out by a mix of pop-flavored propaganda." *Columbia Journalism Review* 44 (1). Retrieved from Galegroup database.

Reilly, R. R. 2007. "Brittany vs. the terrorists." *Washington Post*, February 9, 2007. http://www.washingtonpost.com/wp-dyn/content/article/2007/02/08/AR2007020801679.html.

———. 2014. "Unmuffling the Voice of America." *Wall Street Journal*, June 5, 2014. https://www.wsj.com/articles/robert-reilly-congress-needs-to-reinvigorate-the-voice-of-america-1402010377.

Robin, R. T. 2005. "Requiem for public diplomacy." *American Quarterly* 57: 309–33. Retrieved from Project Muse database.

Rugh, W. A. 2005. "Broadcasting and American public diplomacy." *Arab Media & Society*, March 1, 2005. https://www.arabmediasociety.com/broadcasting-and-american-public-diplomacy.

———. 2006. *American Encounters with Arabs: The "Soft Power" of U.S. Public Diplomacy in the Middle East*. Westport, CT: Praeger Security International.

Sharp, J. M. 2004. "The Middle East Television Network: An Overview." Congressional Research Service Report for Congress, October 15, 2004. https://www.google.com/url?q=https://congressional-proquest-com.proxy.lib.odu.edu/congressional/result/congresultpage:pdfevent?rsId%3D17B79E7C10D%26pdf%3D/app-bin/gis-congresearch/1/4/5/7/crs-2004-fdt-0270_from_1_to_6.pdf%26uri%3D/app-gis/congresearch/crs-2004-fdt-0270&sa=D&source=editors&ust=1632941701251000&usg=AOvVaw0fTrItXzaX-VguUhux8qvh.

Snow, N. 2004. "From Bombs and Bullets to Hearts and Minds: U.S. Public Diplomacy in an Age of Propaganda." In *War, Media, and Propaganda: A Global Perspective*, edited by Y. R. Kamalipour and N. Snow, 17–24. Lanham, MD: Rowman & Littlefield.

———. 2007. *The Arrogance of American Power*. Lanham, MD: Rowman & Littlefield.

Telhami, S. 2004a. Statement before the Subcommittee on International Operations and Terrorism Committee of Senate Foreign Relations Committee, April 29, 2004. https://congressional-proquest-com.proxy.lib.odu.edu/congressional/result/congressional/congdocumentview?accountid=12967&groupid=99683&parmId=17B80ED1C41&rsId=17B80EBB88F.

———. 2004b. "Reaching the Public in the Middle East." In *Engaging the Arab and Islamic Worlds through Public Diplomacy: A Report and Action Recommendations*, edited by W. A. Rugh, 4–10. Washington, DC: Public Diplomacy Council at George Washington University.

Unger, S. J. 2005a. "Pitch imperfect: The trouble at the Voice of America." *Foreign Affairs* 84 (3). http://www.jstor.org/stable/20034344.

———. 2005b. "Responses: His master's voice? Is the Voice of America a source of responsible journalism?" *Foreign Affairs* 84 (4). https://www.jstor.org/stable/i20034414.

USAGM (U.S. Agency for Global Media; formerly Broadcasting Board of Governors). 2019. "FY 2020 Congressional Budget Justification." https://www.usagm.gov/wp-content/uploads/2019/03/USAGM Budget_FY20_CBJ_3-15-19.pdf.

U.S. Senate. Committee on Foreign Relations. 2003. "American Public Diplomacy and Islam." Hearing before the Committee on Foreign Relations, United States Senate, One Hundred Eighth Congress, First Session, February 27, 2003. https://purl.fdlp.gov/GPO/LPS32659.

Webster, T. 2004. "Radio Sawa." Edison Research, October 12, 2004. https://www.edisonresearch.com/radio_sawa.

Weed, M. C. 2016. "U.S. International Broadcasting: Background and Issues for Reform." Congressional Research Service, December 15, 2016. www.crs.gov. https://congressional.proquest.com/congressional/result/congresultpage:pdfevent?rsId=17B75D5DDCF&pdf=/app-bin/gis-congresearch/3/a/d/f/crs-2016-fdt-0784_from_1_to_29.pdf&uri=/app-gis/congresearch/crs-2016-fdt-0784.

Whitworth, M. 2004. "Speaking out." *Foreign Service Journal*, January 2004: 13–15. https://afsa.org/sites/default/files/flipping_book/0104/index.html.

Wimbush, S. E. 2015. "Former BBG member S. Enders Wimbush testimony on options for reform-ing U.S. overseas broadcasting." BBG-USAGM Watch, November 15, 2015. http://bbgwatch.com/bbgwatch/former-bbg-member-s-enders-wimbush-testimony-on-Options-for-reforming-u-s-overseas-broadcasting.

IV

THE PENDULUM OF PROGRESS

Top-Down and Participatory Media's Role
in Development Communication

8

Sustainability Communication

The Evolving Landscape of Development Communication

Abeer Salem

Communication is indispensable for effecting social change. Development communication is a field that emphasizes the centrality of communication to development and focuses on how to best use media and their content to effect social change. Globally, the focus of the development field has shifted to sustainable development, emphasizing the importance of sustainability to future life on earth. All countries across the world are adjusting their present and planning for their future in accordance with the main common goal of achieving a sustainable future for life on earth. Arab countries are no exception; a major shift in focus from an economic-oriented view of the future to a sustainability-oriented view is becoming an urgent requirement.

The global transition to the ideas and goals of sustainability calls for a different understanding of world challenges and novel ways to approach them. While the world is shifting from a development paradigm to a sustainable development paradigm, the mediascape is simultaneously evolving, which reframes the role of the media in tandem. This calls for creating new roles for media and new forms of communication that facilitate the pursuit of solutions to world problems from a sustainability perspective.

This chapter will examine the field of development communication, its complexity, and the main theories that governed its evolution, providing examples from the experiences of Arab countries and drawing on the lessons learned worldwide from experiences in development communication efforts. We will also take a look at the digitization phenomenon and its possible impact on Arab countries, highlighting the need to optimize its options and understand its limitations. Finally, we will discuss what must constitute the next evolutionary stage for media and communication in light of the emerging global sustainability issues and their looming adverse consequences: sustainability communication.

FORCES OF CHANGE IN AN INTERCONNECTED WORLD

Among the many changes occurring in our fast-paced world, two are particularly significant to the present discussion. One is the transition from the development paradigm to sustainability. The second is the digitization phenomenon, which has increasingly affected all aspects of life, including communication. These two changes, whether separately or combined, have a considerable effect on the world in which the Arab region is embedded. This section briefly discusses these changes and highlights how Arab countries are affected.

Transitions from Development to Sustainability

The Millennium Development Goals (MDGs) are eight broad benchmarks for development adopted by the international development community at the beginning of the millennium. These benchmarks include goals for developing countries, such as eradicating poverty and hunger, achieving universal primary education, achieving gender equality, and ensuring environmental sustainability, among others (McPhail 2009). The MDGs are supposed to guide the process of development and measure the progress of developing countries toward achieving success on several development-related fronts. Progress toward the state of development is gauged through measuring each country's achievement of these goals.

Although these specifically defined goals governed the field of development for decades and have been constantly quantitatively measured and pursued against specific deadlines, they were heavily criticized. Some of the criticism relates to the difficulty of achieving these goals, as they are designed according to Western thought. Another criticism is that developing countries did not take part in planning these goals and that they were mandated in a top-down manner. This resulted in lack of ownership and absence of clear accountability on the part of developing countries (Fehling et al. 2013, McAnany 2012, McPhail 2009). The MDGs are also viewed as too generic to adequately address the specific needs of individual developing countries.

As issues of sustainability gained salience, the focus of the development field shifted from development to sustainable development, thus shifting the global focus from an economic deterministic perspective to a focus on environmental and sustainability concerns. The basic premise of sustainability is a healthy balance among the environment, the society, and the economy. Its ideals include intergenerational equity, ecological sustainability, and fair distribution of wealth and access to resources (Tilbury and Wortman 2004). A global call for sustainable development was thus articulated in the Sustainable Development Goals (SDGs), highlighting the importance of balancing current local realities and needs with the needs and prospects of future generations.

In 2015, the SDGs were adopted by the United Nations, replacing the MDGs. The SDGs are distinctly different from the MDGs in many aspects. Most notably, the SDGs carry the potential for a transformative agenda (Fukuda-Parr 2016), and its issues require action from all countries, not only the developing ones. This current transition to the ideas of sustainability and the goals of sustainable development derives lessons from decades of development and demands a different understanding of world challenges and novel ways to approach them. This, in turn, calls for reframing the role of development communication in pursuit of solutions from a sustainability perspective.

In Arab countries, planning for the SDGs may start with taking stock of the level of achievement of the MDGs. Considerable, albeit uneven, progress was reached by Arab countries in achieving the MDGs during the period 1990 to 2012. There are some notable differences among countries in the region, as well as inadequate achievement on some important targets like combating hunger (Saab and Sadik 2016) and achieving universal primary education in some countries. The ultimate achievement of all the MDGs will be a considerable challenge for Arab countries, especially while managing natural resources in a sustainable manner. Meanwhile, the Arab region is among the most vulnerable to the potential impacts of climate change because of its existing vulnerabilities, notably water scarcity and recurrent droughts (Saab and Sadik 2016, Elasha 2010, Hatjian 2011).

Digitization and the Emergence of Networked Communication

While the world was turning from a development perspective to a sustainability-oriented perspective, an era of shifting communicative power was emerging. The evolution from institution-based to network-based communication created a new form and repositioned its power in the hands of citizens. While digitization does not totally obviate the power of institutions, it has clearly highlighted not only the possibility but also the importance of citizens' voices. Online and social media have clearly influenced communication patterns and shifted the focus from traditional top-down approaches to communication to bottom-up approaches through networked citizens (Deane 2014) and through citizen-generated content.

The Arab networked public sphere is primarily country-based. Arab bloggers are predominantly young males, with the highest proportion of female bloggers in Egypt (Etling et al. 2014). A 2010 study of the blogosphere in Lebanon, Egypt, and Kuwait revealed the contextual differences among bloggers in these countries while maintaining a unique cross-cutting Arab character (Riegert 2015). Arabs have adopted blogging technologies to produce content that is beyond controlling, regulating, or censoring (Hamdy 2009). Arab bloggers mainly discuss controversial issues in areas of politics, culture, and social issues and norms, as well as local and personal issues (Etling et al. 2014). Blogging specifically for the purpose of mobilizing development and social change does not seem to be one of the main objectives of Arab bloggers.

The opportunities for contribution and engagement in societal and public affairs offered by the new media technologies cannot be considered pervasive. A study conducted in Jordan, Lebanon, and the UAE revealed that while youth are highly adept at using new media, they are mostly consumers, not producers, of content. It also shows that youth predominantly use new media for entertainment, to connect with others, and/or for studying and work-related purposes, not necessarily for blogging or for voicing their opinions. Meanwhile, those who blog use a foreign language (English) rather than Arabic, their native language (Melki 2010).

New media technologies, nonetheless, allowed for the emergence of social media, which can enable a participatory culture. They are characterized by openness, participation, connectedness, and community. They can potentially play a great role in the area of development through facilitating connections and collaborations among people, creating and sharing content, and locating content and information. Social media serve the function that development players have struggled with for decades: building effective participation mechanisms. Social media can offer people in the developing world enhanced tools to make their voices heard and seek their preferred development paths (Sheombar 2017).

DEVELOPMENT COMMUNICATION: COMPLEXITIES AND CONTROVERSIES

The development communication field is laden with complexities. One of these complexities is that it represents a merging of two multidisciplinary fields, communication and development, while aiming at facilitating the complicated process of social change. Adding to the complexity is the dynamic nature of the development communication field, which is in continuous evolution and flux, where new ideas are continually added to a canvas of already known ideas, often in contradiction. Hence, the field is guided by a multitude of ideas that are often contradictory and are both simultaneously workable and unworkable, depending on the specific setting, context, culture, and numerous other variables that affect peoples and societies.

Despite this complexity, however, communication is indispensable for development and for effecting social change. More specifically, the interdisciplinary nature of development communication is essential and most fitting for facilitating development, as it is also a multidisciplinary field that involves a multitude of factors and sectors that define the process of social change. Social change is dependent on a multitude of variables and contextual varieties. While each sector is specialized in its particulars, the interdisciplinarity of the field of development communication provides the connection needed for the overall representation of the situation (Mefalopulos 2008).

Development communication is described as a social intervention. It aims to achieve positive social change through media and education (McPhail 2009). Other definitions of development communication highlight and revolve around its main functions, such as the imparting and sharing of knowledge and achieving a common base of understating or consensus, among different actors in the process of social change (Mefalopulos 2008, Servaes and Malikhao 2008). These two functions of development communication may also contribute a certain amount of complexity, as they are often applied as contradictory opposites. Imparting information and knowledge sharing are considered prerequisites to people's acceptance. These are mostly practiced as top-down processes, relayed from experts to the people who are targeted for development. They also achieve acceptability and a common understanding regarding development that requires participation and ownership by the people.

Hence, these two functions represent two different views on development communication: a mechanistic versus an organic view (Servaes and Malikhao 2008). Taken separately, these two distinctive views can be aptly considered one of the main dilemmas of the field—one that adds to its many layers of complexity. Theoretically, the function of imparting knowledge can be attributed to the communication models that emerge from the modernization theory, which is mainly a top-down approach to communication and development. On the other hand, a greater degree of consensus is attributed to the participatory approach, which advocates ownership of a people's development through their active participation. It is quite difficult to combine knowledge and information sharing with achieving acceptability and understanding through participation and engagement. This is particularly challenging in light of questions about what can be considered positive change and from whose perspective social change should be viewed as positive, which are quite pertinent.

MODERNIZATION-INSPIRED DEVELOPMENT COMMUNICATION

Development communication theories provided a multitude of ideas that dominated the field for decades. These ideas have contributed much to our understanding of the scope of the role of media and communication in developing societies. These ideas range from top-down, diffusion, and behavioral change approaches to participatory, entertainment-education, and social marketing approaches, among others.

Early development communication efforts were inspired by the modernization theory that focused on economic growth and the acquisition of technology as essential means to achieving economic growth. Development was equivalent to modernization, which was characteristic of Western countries. Hence, development as modernization and Westernization became the goal to be pursued, and deviation from the Western model was not considered development. In Egypt, television programming, especially Egyptian melodrama, as well as motion pictures, helped to promote the ideals of modernization (Abu-Lughod 2002, Armbrust 1995).

Development communication inspired by the modernization theory includes two models known as "behavioral change" and "diffusion of innovations." These models posited that development can be attained by non-developed societies when they receive the right information. Information considered relevant to development was transmitted from developed countries in a top-down approach characteristic of the magic bullet theory. The recipients of this information were expected to change their traditional behavior and adopt new behaviors that are consistent with modernization. Development, therefore, was seen as a top-down and linear process, and so was the communication model that promoted it, known as the behavioral change model. The behavioral change model dominated the field of development communication for decades, supported by the logic of the diffusion-of-innovations theory (Rogers 2010, McPhail 2009, Thomas 2014).

Edutainment: The Entertainment-Education Nexus

Entertainment-education (EE), or edutainment, is a behavioral change strategy that employs mass media entertainment to transmit social change ideas and messages. Entertainment is seen as the most preferred approach for most people, and is becoming an integral part of people's lives (Singhal and Rogers 2002). This strategy tries to overcome the limitations of degraded entertainment content and the boredom-inducing types of programs and produce programs that are socially responsible, entertaining, and educational (Brown and Singhal 1999). The unique feature of this strategy is the intentional placement of educational or developmental messages in entertainment programming.

EE is essentially about knowledge dissemination and is based on the assumption that by acquiring the necessary and correct knowledge in an entertaining way, the audience will adopt behaviors that are consistent with development (Singhal and Rogers 2002). To appeal to their audience, EE programs must compete with other programming in production and entertainment values (Adams 2006). To be effective, however, EE should respond to the viewer's frame of reference, and messages should be crafted in a way that abides by the particulars of this frame of reference, not the frame of reference of the message developer. This is a difficult dimension of EE since probing into the particulars of the frame of reference of the audience is quite challenging.

Entertainment-education interventions, whether radio or television serials, aim at triggering intrapersonal, interpersonal, and group conversations that catapult societies into the process of social change at the individual, community, and societal levels. They have been implemented in many countries across the world through entertainment genres including radio and television soap operas, popular music, and comic books, among others (Khalid and Ahmed 2014). EE can take many different shapes and forms and can be provided in varying degrees of intensity based on different factors, such as the context, the audience, the message, and the topic (Singhal and Rogers 2002, 2003).

Prominent examples of EE in the Arab region include the television show *Ana Zanana* (Lane 1997, Brown and Singhal 1999), which promoted family planning to Egyptian audiences. The title role was played by a well-liked and famous comedian who offered inaccurate medical and family planning advice to her daughter and son-in-law based on popular misconceptions regarding family planning ideas and methods. When she is corrected by other family members and the physician, the episode relays accurate information to counter the misinformation and misconceptions held by community members (Lane 1997, Abdulla 2004).

Another example of successful EE content in Egypt is the series *Secret of the Land*, which offered farmers agricultural and irrigation information. It started in 1989, lasted for several years, and was rebroadcast on Egyptian and Arab television stations for a long time. The episodes featured a peasant whose agricultural decisions and daily work in the field are critiqued and corrected by others, including an agricultural engineer. This show created trust in the government-appointed agricultural engineers who are available to give information to peasants in Egypt (Abdulla 2004).

Social Marketing: Bridging the Social and the Commercial Worlds

Social marketing is an approach extensively used under the premises of the diffusion-of-innovation and the behavioral change models (Waisbord 2001, Adams 2006, Andreasen 1994). It is the adaptation of commercial marketing techniques to programs designed to influence the target audiences for social change through the dissemination of socially beneficial ideas (Andreason 1994, Fine 1981). The main influence of social marketing on the field of development communication is helping to bridge the social and commercial worlds and to create a connection between two things that are usually seen as opposites (Hastings and Saren 2003). Social change and development issues are usually seen and dealt with as not-for-profit goals and activities, while marketing campaigns are planned and executed with the intent of making profit out of people's purchasing decisions. The contribution of social marketing is to transfer the basics of the success of profit-seeking marketing campaigns to the non-profit-seeking social change and development campaigns.

An example of a social change campaign that employed social marketing in an Arab country is the oral rehydration campaign (ORC) in Egypt. The campaign included a televised public education campaign and public service announcements to address infant mortality in Egypt and was implemented successfully from 1983 to 1991. It contributed immensely to decreasing infant mortality rates in Egypt (Abdulla 2004, El Kamel 1995). Egypt experienced a reduction of 65.4% in infant mortality rates and a reduction of 72.9% in diarrhea-related child mortality between 1983 and 1989. This decrease is widely attributed to the success of this campaign (El Kamel 1995).

Social marketing, however, is criticized for various reasons. Short-term social marketing campaigns are often viewed as ineffective, since social change requires time. Meanwhile, long-term campaigns lose effectiveness over time, as evidenced by anti-smoking and HIV/AIDS campaigns in various parts of the world (Adams 2006). In Egypt, campaigns promoting family planning were successful on a short-term basis (El Kamel 1995). In the long run, however, Egypt still suffers from high birth rates. Moreover, social marketing is also criticized as a top-down strategy involving no audience participation in the formulation of the message. Focusing on individual behavior and failing to address the larger social, political, and economic factors is considered a drawback of social marketing (Adams 2006).

Issues in Modernization-Based/Inspired Development Communication

Development communication strategies emerging from the top-down model of behavioral change communication were successful in several cases. The edutainment or entertainment-education (EE) model and the social marketing models are examples of communication theories and strategies that succeeded in raising awareness and mobilizing action through imparting knowledge in a top-down approach in accordance with the behavioral change model. Several campaigns stand out as particularly successful examples of edutainment and social marketing campaigns. In Egypt, for example, most drama presented on TV was seen at some point as attempting to contribute to social learning, ranging from general social affairs to more focused and elaborated EE content (Abdulla 2004).

Despite this success, the top-down approach characteristic of the behavioral change model of communication was largely criticized for assuming the effectiveness of the development messages transmitted. Messages designed by specialists and experts, foreign and local, were assumed to be suitable and appropriate for local communities. These communities are not included in the formulation of the development plans or the development communication messages espousing them. Other points of criticism included overlooking traditional knowledge and considering it irrelevant to development, and disempowering communities by considering them passive recipients who should act on the received information without real ownership of the ideas of development or the messages reflecting these ideas, and with no ability to reject, modify, or adjust the development programs that were being directed at them (Waisbord 2001, McPhail 2009).

Another point to consider is that public education through EE or social marketing cannot work alone, since imparting knowledge is only one of many components. The successful examples demonstrate that imparting knowledge should be complemented by other sociocultural and structural factors, such as improved services and more affordable costs. The contribution of each factor to the overall outcome should not be overlooked or underestimated (El Kamel 1995). This idea closely relates to the ecological model of behavioral and social change, which posits that focusing solely on the individual and on intrapersonal-level change strategies often overlooks the larger context surrounding and reinforcing these behaviors. Change requires addressing the multiple levels of influence within which this behavior is embedded, and which allow it to persist (Robinson 2008, Golden et al. 2015).

PARTICIPATORY DEVELOPMENT COMMUNICATION

The effectiveness of one-way communication was ultimately questioned, and the failures of development projects were largely attributed to ineffective communication and lack of participation from those who are affected by development (Mefalopulos 2008, Brown and Singhal 1999). In opposition to one-way communication inspired by diffusion and modernization theories, participatory communication started to gain popularity as the most effective method of communication to bring about agreement and consensus on change from the community.

The logic of participatory communication rested on ideas that contrast with the main ideas of one-way communication inspired by diffusion and modernization theories. These ideas promote the right of societies to decide their own future, that they should be able to use their traditional knowledge in their development, and that their ownership of their vision of the future will maximize the success of development (McPhail 2009). Hence, development should be responsive to diversity and plurality, and specific development goals should be elicited from the individuals and societies in deciding their own future and responding to their needs (Huesca 2008, McPhail 2009).

Despite the benefits expected from participatory communication approaches, it has its own challenges to proper implementation. These include how to ensure the neutrality of the development communication message that elicits participation from society in the first place. It may also be difficult to obtain balanced participation from everyone involved, since some people prefer not to take part while others may want to dominate. The pressures of time and finances may make it difficult to include everyone's opinion and voice. There is also the problem of pseudo-participation, where participants may refrain from offering their opinion in favor of the mainstream or more approved opinion, so that their participation does not truly represent their voice or their viewpoint.

Participatory Development Communication in Arab Countries

Experience in participatory communication in Arab countries was found to be successful, though challenging. One example is the participatory video training in Egypt, a project that aimed at communicating basic life skills and reproductive health information while strengthening the voices of local women in discussing these issues. Women from Cairo and Minya were trained in making simple videos about culturally embedded community issues using a home video camcorder. The issues included local environmental pollution, girls' education, and the high costs of marriage. Besides being a grassroots communication activity, which depicts reality and works toward effecting change, the project created female role models and community leaders who served their community and affected others (Gumicio Dagron 2001).

In Lebanon, a participatory communication strategy was implemented in a pastoral community that suffered from conflict over natural resources. This strategy included participatory video making and production, alongside the traditional *majlis* setting (meetings of the elders to discuss problems through face-to-face communication) and participatory workshops (Hamadeh et al. 2006).

Experiences in participatory communication in Arab countries include those that integrate entertainment-education and social marketing. In Egypt, an initiative that integrated EE and social marketing strategies with participatory communication was considered successful in reaching several target groups. The initiative combined family planning with maternal and child health messages, thus achieving multiple levels of awareness of the relevant issues (Hess et al. 2012).

DIGITIZATION AND DEVELOPMENT COMMUNICATION

Technological advances and digitization have affected the field of communication in many ways. New digital media provide development communication with a new linear model that is neither one-way nor top-down. It offers endless possibilities for dynamic, interactive, and multidirectional communication, and for multiple forms of citizen engagement (Tufte 2013). New media can provide opportunities to disadvantaged communities to become active partners in their country's development (Rodrigues 2010). It has also enhanced the ability of citizens and NGOs to engage in media advocacy (Guo and Saxton 2014).

Although digital media can support development communication efforts, they are not the main or only factor that determines the success of these efforts. The impact of digitization and information and communication technologies (ICT) is determined by the quality of the communication work and research conducted prior to implementing them (Mefalopulos 2008). The impact of digitization and ICT on development communication is, therefore, controversial, and this persistent two-sided argument is inherent to any discussion of the impact of digitalization on development communication.

The Dilemma of the Digital Divide

One of the main hurdles to the effective use of ICT in development communication is the digital divide. This term describes a state of discrepancy in benefiting from technology among people and nations. It refers to the difference in access to, and purposeful use of, information systems and technologies by people, societies, or countries. The digital divide is not a static phenomenon. It evolves and changes over time along its different dimensions: access, usage, and inequalities in outcomes. Hence, the digital divide is often a reflection of economic, social, and technological divides (Skaletsky et al. 2017). Using ICT for development in digitally divided populations means that the groups who can reap the benefits of digitization are those who have the financial, physical, and even geographical ability to access ICT and digital technologies. This is hardly fair to those who have limited or no access.

In Arab countries overall, digitization has undoubtedly broadened the scope of what media and communication can do. It has enhanced the ability of citizens to engage in news writing and reporting through citizen journalism (Hamdy 2009, Khamis and Vaughn 2011, Khamis 2011) via online platforms. Some bloggers have also specifically targeted their blogs to effect social change (Hamdy 2009), although these are fewer than those who use blogging for political issues.

Digitization has set new rules for media production. Citizen journalism, for example, is mostly viewed by some citizen journalists in the Emirates as having its own rules that are not related to those that govern traditional journalism. They assert that the main premise of citizen journalism is to reflect the truth, which is the logic behind presenting raw news videos in order not to manipulate the news coverage in any way (El Semary and Al Khaja 2013). This also applies in other Arab countries where bloggers are not journalists and do not wish to follow the guidelines, laws, or codes of ethics that apply to journalists (Hamdy 2009).

It is interesting to note, however, that although Internet use in Arab countries is intensifying, the Arabic language content is extremely limited (Abubaker et al. 2015) and there is no distinctive Arab cyber identity (Eid 2009). Meanwhile, the pervasive use of the Internet has resulted in a mix of signals reflecting positive as well as negative social change. Research has shown that in Saudi Arabia, the Internet and social media had a positive impact in terms of allowing space for Saudi women to engage in intellectual discussions (Al-Saggaf 2004), but had a negative impact on inter-family interaction (El Khouli 2013, Elshenawy 2017). Moreover, Saudi women have found social media, including Twitter, a safe space for them to express their views (Al-Jabri et al. 2015). In Kuwait, during the early years of the Internet, young people used it to challenge the socially conservative environment in terms of social relations (Wheeler 2001), a situation that is highly likely to be similar in other Arab countries as well.

SUSTAINABILITY COMMUNICATION

Although the participatory and the top-down approaches to communication are mostly viewed as contradictory opposites, they both continue to be used in development communication efforts, as each of them provides complementary functions to development projects. The main two functions of communication, providing information and rallying communities to participate, are crucial to the success of social change and development efforts. Efforts to effectively contribute to development and sustainability should not consider these two functions of communication as mutually exclusive opposites, but rather ways to reconcile them.

Meanwhile, as the vision of sustainability becomes the core of the future of societies, sustainability communication emerges as an essential process. This process provides a much-needed understanding of a range of sustainability issues that are not usually included in media content and are possibly difficult to communicate to and/or be understood by laypeople and non-scientists. While communication about sustainability issues is a challenging task, it is an absolute necessity. Viewed from an evolutionary perspective, this new role should build on the lessons learned from decades of development communication research and practice, which can be described as sustainability communication. In order to meet the SDGs and face the sustainability challenges that confront the world, communication should take on a new role that maximizes the engagement of societies in the formation of knowledge and science while utilizing new ways to engage scientists with society at large.

Ultimately, the aim of sustainability communication is to introduce a different understanding of the world, one that is centered on the relationship between people and the environment and how this relationship is connected to social values and norms (Godemann and Michelsen 2011). Sustainability communication is thus an alternative paradigm of communication that seeks to combine behavioral change and participatory communication strategies to achieve maximum effectiveness. It is mainly concerned with the range of sustainability issues that face the world, including global warming, climate change, deforestation, and water scarcity, among others.

The logic underlying sustainability communication is the necessary engagement of people at large through real participation in mitigating sustainability issues or adapting to the implications or consequences. This will require a considerable shift in the purpose and functions of communication. It capitalizes on and aims to reinstate the value of communication and media as a highly influential socialization and culturalization tool that is still underutilized.

Citizen Engagement and Participation

The participatory culture created by digitized media (Jenkins 2004) allows the general public to create content and disseminate it in various ways. It can also provide opportunities for engagement in communication endeavors that seek to understand as well as find ways to adapt or mitigate the range of sustainability issues that confront the world.

Citizen engagement and participation are emerging concepts that are considered increasingly important in advancing science and technology (Powell and Colin 2008). Meanwhile, citizen participation is increasingly recognized as a most necessary, albeit often missing, link to effectively address climate change, which is one of the most crucial sustainability concerns (Ockwell et al. 2009, Spence and Pidgeon 2010) and is one of the sustainability threats facing the Arab region. Experience in addressing climate change more specifically reveals that providing information to citizens may help them properly understand that the phenomenon is of crucial importance, and that their participation is essential (Moser 2010).

Technological developments are providing new ways to support citizen engagement and participation in locally based science issues (Mazumdar et al. 2018). One area where new media can be used by citizens to address sustainability issues is citizen science. Citizen science is any process in which scientists and volunteers from the general public work together to answer real-world scientific questions (Toomey and Domroese 2013, West 2017). Citizen science is increasingly being used in environmental research studies that would otherwise be too difficult to conduct due to costs (Toomey and Domroese 2013) or inaccessibility. With the prevalence of the Internet and digital technologies, and the ubiquity of information and communication technology, opportunities for public participation in science have greatly increased, not only in the form of data collection but also for initiating locally inspired science projects (Mazumdar et al. 2018, West 2017). When the public participates in scientific studies, they find it easier to understand environmental issues and are more motivated toward behaviors that are conducive to conservation (Toomey and Domroese 2013).

Convergence and the Question of Participation

Media convergence is a phenomenon that describes the evolution of media production as it emerged with the advancement of digital technologies. The idea of convergence incorporates two overlapping and interdependent trends: the convergence of media industries and the convergence of media production and consumption. This reflects the enlargement of the scope of the media consumer, who can now become a media source and a co-creator of media content (Deuze 2008), creating a convergence culture (Jenkins 2004). Convergence therefore represents a combination of top-down and bottom-up communication.

Media industries and media consumers are engaging with each other in new ways that can be reinforcing or challenging. The process effectively redefines media consumers from passive to active, and from isolated to belonging to a collective (Jenkins 2004). The possibilities of citizen engagement and participation that are made available through the convergence phenomenon are unprecedented in the history of development communication and can provide the answer to the question of participation that has puzzled the field for many years.

While convergence does not have a clear definition in Arab countries (Hamdy and Auter 2011), it has occurred in ways that elicited strong interactions and alliances between Arab media and citizen journalists. However, the transition from discrediting citizen-generated content to embracing it took place at different speeds in different Arab countries (Hamdy 2010). Building on the example of citizen journalism, citizen engagement in addressing sustainability issues in Arab countries can be anticipated where media institutions can work with citizens to highlight and portray local issues through citizen-generated content.

CONCLUSION

The current transition to ideas of sustainable development highlights the importance of balancing current local realities and needs with the future needs and prospects of all countries, regardless of their development status. It derives lessons from decades of development and works toward a different understanding of world challenges, while reframing the role of communication in pursuit of solutions from a sustainability perspective. This brings to the fore the concept of sustainability communication, which offers a much-needed framework for understanding a wide variety of social systems and actors, including the environment, science, media, business, and education, and their interrelatedness as a prerequisite for ensuring the sustainability of society and earth.

It is therefore useful to reflect on how these ideas can be used to inform the role that media can play in the Arab world for sustainability. Novel phenomena can shed light on the area of development and sustainability. This chapter argues that in order to align with the goals of sustainability, the full potential of the new developments in the field of communication should be utilized. These developments should enable the media to take on a new role that maximizes effective citizen participation in knowledge making and knowledge sharing.

Digitization, as a novel phenomenon, and its effect on the power of citizens to participate can be a perfect solution to the drawbacks of early development communication efforts, which relied mainly on top-down communication to effect change. A culture of media convergence can be viewed as enabling a culture that can play a big role in providing a platform for participation from locally rooted citizens that is bound to gain wider support for ideas of sustainability. It also can effect a wider and more lasting change of ideas, values, and perspectives in favor of actions that can contribute to sustainability.

REFERENCES

Abdulla, R. A. 2004. "Entertainment-Education in the Middle East: Lessons from the Egyptian Oral Rehydration Therapy Campaign." In *Entertainment-Education and Social Change: History, Research, and Practice*, edited by A. Singhal and E. M. Rogers, 301–20. New York: Routledge.

Abubaker, H., K. Salah, H. Al-Muhairi, and A. Bentiba. 2015. "Digital Arabic Content: Challenges and Opportunities." In *2015 International Conference on Information and Communication Technology Research (ICTRC)*, 330–33. New York: IEEE.

Abu-Lughod, L. 2002. "Egyptian Melodrama: Technology of the Modern." In *Media Worlds: Anthropology on New Terrain*, edited by F. D. Ginsburg, L. Abu-Lughod, and Brian Larkin, 115–33. Berkeley: University of California Press.

Adams, D. M. 2006. "Media and development in the Middle East." *Transformation* 23 (3): 170–86.

Andreasen, A. R. 1994. "Social marketing: Its definition and domain." *Journal of Public Policy & Marketing* 13 (1): 108–14.

Armbrust, W. 1995. "New cinema, commercial cinema, and the modernist tradition in Egypt." *Alif: Journal of Comparative Poetics* 15: 81–129.

Brown, W. J., and A. Singhal. 1999. "Entertainment-Education Media Strategies for Social Change: Promises and Problems." In *Mass Media, Social Control, and Social Change: A Macrosocial Perspective*, edited by D. Demers and K. Viswanath, 263–80. Ames: Iowa State University Press.

Deane, J. 2014. "Media Development." In *The Handbook of Development Communication and Social Change*, edited by K. Wilkins, T. Tufte, and R. Obregon, 226–41. Hoboken, NJ: John Wiley & Sons.

Deuze, M. 2008. "The professional identity of journalists in the context of convergence culture." *Observatorio (Obs*) Journal* 2 (4): 103–17.

Eid, M. 2009. "On the Way to the Cyber-Arab-Culture: International Communication, Telecommunications Policies, and Democracy." In *Cyberculture and New Media*, edited by F. J. Ricardo, 69–98. Amsterdam and New York: Rodopi.

Elasha, B. O. 2010. *Mapping of Climate Change Threats and Human Development Impacts in the Arab Region*. UNDP Arab Development Report–Research Paper Series. UNDP Regional Bureau for the Arab States.

Elshenawy, A. A. 2017. "Globalization's effect on Qatari culture." *Journal of Cultural Studies* 2 (1): 6–17.

Etling, B., J. Kelly, R. Faris, and J. Palfrey. 2014. "Mapping the Arabic Blogosphere: Politics, Culture, and Dissent." In *Media Evolution on the Eve of the Arab Spring*, edited by L. Hudson, A. Iskandar, and M. Kirk, 49–74. New York: Palgrave Macmillan.

Fehling, M., B. D. Nelson, and S. Venkatapuram. 2013. "Limitations of the Millennium Development Goals: A literature review." *Global Public Health* 8 (10): 1109–22.

Fine, S. H. 1981. *The Marketing of Ideas and Social Issues*. Westport, CT: Praeger.

Fukuda-Parr, S. 2016. "From the Millennium Development Goals to the Sustainable Development Goals: Shifts in purpose, concept, and politics of global goal setting for development." *Gender & Development* 24 (1): 43–52.

Godemann, J., and G. Michelsen. 2011. "Sustainability Communication: An Introduction." In *Sustainability Communication: Interdisciplinary Perspectives and Theoretical Foundation*, edited by J. Godemann and G. Michelsen, 3–11. New York: Springer.

Golden, S. D., K. R. McLeroy, L. W. Green, J. A. L. Earp, and L. D. Lieberman. 2015. "Upending the social ecological model to guide health promotion efforts toward policy and environmental change." *Health Education & Behavior* 42 (1S): 8S–14S. Society for Public Health Education: SAGE.

Gumicio Dagron, A. 2001. *Making Waves: Stories of Participatory Communication for Social Change; A Report to the Rockefeller Foundation.* New York: Rockefeller Foundation.

Guo, C., and G. D. Saxton. 2014. "Tweeting social change: How social media are changing nonprofit advocacy." *Nonprofit and Voluntary Sector Quarterly* 43 (1): 57–79.

Hamadeh, S., M. Haidar, R. Zurayk, M. Obeid, and C. Dick. 2006. "Goats, Cherry Trees and Videotapes: Participatory Development Communication for Natural Resource Management in Semi-arid Lebanon." In *People, Land, and Water: Participatory Development Communication for Natural Resource Management*, edited by G. Bessette, 62–67. London: Earthscan and IDRC.

Hamdy, N. 2009. "Arab citizen journalism in action: Challenging mainstream media, authorities and media laws." *Westminster Papers in Communication & Culture* 6 (1): 92–112.

———. 2010. "Arab media adopt citizen journalism to change the dynamics of conflict coverage." *Global Media Journal: Arabian Edition* 1 (1): 3–15.

Hamdy, N., and P. Auter. 2011. "Divergence on convergence: U.S. and Egyptian journalism professionals and educators respond." *Journal of Middle East Media* 7 (1): 62–91.

Hastings, G., and M. Saren. 2003. "The critical contribution of social marketing: Theory and application." *Marketing Theory* 3 (3): 305–22.

Hatjian, B. 2011. "2010 Report of the Arab Forum for Environment and Development on Water." *Climate Change and Environment in the Arab World* (May 2011), Issam Fares Institute for Public Policy and International Affairs.

Hess, R., D. Meekers, and J. D. Storey. 2012. "Egypt's Mabrouk! Initiative: A Communication Strategy for Maternal/Child Health and Family Planning Integration." In *The Handbook of Global Health Communication*, edited by R. Obregon and S. Waisbord, 374–407. Chichester, UK: Wiley-Blackwell.

Huesca, R. 2008. "Tracing the History of Participatory Communication Approaches to Development: A Critical Appraisal." In *Communication for Development and Social Change*, edited by J. Servaes, 180–98. New Delhi: Sage Publications India.

Al-Jabri, I. M., M. S. Sohail, and N. O. Ndubisi. 2015. "Understanding the usage of global social networking sites by Arabs through the lens of uses and gratifications theory." *Journal of Service Management* 26 (4): 662–80.

Jenkins, H. 2004. "The cultural logic of media convergence." *International Journal of Cultural Studies* 7 (1): 33–43.

El Kamel. 1995. "The use of television series in health education." *Health Education Research* 10 (2): 225–32.

Khalid, M. Z., and A. Ahmed. 2014. "Entertainment-education media strategies for social change: Opportunities and emerging trends." *Review of Journalism and Mass Communication* 2 (1): 69–89.

Khamis, S. 2011. "The transformative Egyptian media landscape: Changes, challenges and comparative perspectives." *International Journal of Communication* 5 (19): 1159–77.

Khamis, S., and K. Vaughn. 2011. "Cyberactivism in the Egyptian revolution: How civic engagement and citizen journalism tilted the balance." *Arab Media & Society* 14 (3): 1–25.

El Khouli, M. 2013. "The most important negative aspects of using social networking affecting the family stability in Abu Dhabi: A pilot study." *International Journal of Engineering and Technology* 5 (1): 85.

Lane, S. D. 1997. "Television minidramas: Social marketing and evaluation in Egypt." *Medical Anthropology Quarterly* 11 (2): 164–82.

Mazumdar, S., L. Ceccaroni, J. Piera, F. Hölker, A. Berre, R. Arlinghaus, and A. Bowser. 2018. *Citizen Science Technologies and New Opportunities for Participation.* London: UCL Press.

McAnany, E. G. 2012. "Social entrepreneurship and communication for development and social change." *Nordicom Review* 33 (special issue): 205–17.

McPhail, T. L., ed. 2009. *Development Communication: Reframing the Role of the Media.* Hoboken, NJ: John Wiley & Sons.

Mefalopulos, P. 2008. *Development Communication Sourcebook: Broadening the Boundaries of Communication.* Washington, DC: World Bank.

Melki, J. 2010. "Media habits of MENA youth: A three-country survey." *Youth in the Arab World.* Working Paper Series, No. 4. Issam Fares Institute for Public Policy and International Affairs (IFI), American University of Beirut.

Moser, S. C. 2010. "Communicating climate change: History, challenges, process and future directions." *Wiley Interdisciplinary Reviews: Climate Change* 1 (1): 31–53.

Obregon, R., and S. R. Waisbord, eds. 2012. *The Handbook of Global Health Communication.* Vol. 29. Chichester, UK: Wiley-Blackwell.

Ockwell, D., L. Whitmarsh, and S. O'Neill. 2009. "Reorienting climate change communication for effective mitigation: Forcing people to be green or fostering grass-roots engagement?" *Science Communication* 30 (3): 305–27.

Powell, M. C., and M. Colin. 2008. "Meaningful citizen engagement in science and technology: What would it really take?" *Science Communication* 30 (1): 126–36.

Riegert, K. 2015. "Understanding popular Arab bloggers: From public spheres to cultural citizens." *International Journal of Communication* 9: 20.

Robinson, T. 2008. "Applying the socio-ecological model to improving fruit and vegetable intake among low-income African Americans." *Journal of Community Health* 33 (6): 395–406.

Rodrigues, U. M. 2010. "The promise of a new media and development agenda." *Media International Australia* 137 (1): 36–46.

Rogers, E. M. 2010. *Diffusion of Innovations.* New York: Simon & Schuster.

Saab, N., and A. Sadik, eds. 2016. "Arab Environment: Sustainable Development in a Changing Arab Climate." In *Annual Report of Arab Forum for Environment and Development (AFED).* Beirut: Technical Publications.

Al-Saggaf, Y. 2004. "The effect of online community on offline community in Saudi Arabia." *Electronic Journal of Information Systems in Developing Countries* 16 (1): 1–16.

El Semary, H., and M. Al Khaja. 2013. "The credibility of citizen journalism and traditional TV journalism among Emirati youth: Comparative study." *American International Journal of Contemporary Research* 3 (11): 53–62.

Servaes, J., ed. 2007. *Communication for Development and Social Change.* New Delhi: Sage Publications India.

Servaes, J., and P. Malikhao. 2008. "Development Communication Approaches in an International Perspective." In *Communication for Development and Social Change,* edited by J. Servaes, 158–79. New Delhi: Sage Publications India.

Sheombar, A. 2017. "Constructing an Applicability Framework for Organisational Social Media Use by Development NGOs." Paper presented at ICIS: Thirty-Eighth International Conference on Information Systems, South Korea, December 10–13, 2017. Association for Information Systems (AIS). https://aisel.aisnet.org/icis2017/SocialMedia/Presentations/14.

Singhal, A., and E. M. Rogers. 2002. "A theoretical agenda for entertainment-education." *Communication Theory* 12 (2): 117–35.

———. 2003. "The Status of Entertainment-Education Worldwide." In *Entertainment-Education and Social Change History, Research, and Practice,* edited by A. Singhal and E. M. Rogers, 25–42. New York: Routledge.

Skaletsky, M., J. B. Pick, A. Sarkar, and D. Yates. 2017. "Digital Divides: Past, Present, and Future." In *The Routledge Companion to Management Information Systems*, edited by R. D. Galliers and M. K. Stein, 416–43. New York: Routledge.

Spence, A., and N. Pidgeon. 2010. "Framing and communicating climate change: The effects of distance and outcome frame manipulations." *Global Environmental Change* 20 (4): 656–67.

Thomas, P. N. 2014. "Development Communication and Social Change in Historical Context." In *The Handbook of Development Communication and Social Change*, edited by K. G. Wilkins, T. Tufte, and R. Obregon, 5–19. Hoboken, NJ: John Wiley & Sons.

Tilbury, D., and D. Wortman. 2004. *Engaging People in Sustainability*. Gland, Switzerland: IUCN.

Toomey, A. H., and M. C. Domroese. 2013. "Can citizen science lead to positive conservation attitudes and behaviors?" *Human Ecology Review* 20 (1): 50–62.

Tufte, T. 2013. "Towards a Renaissance in Communication for Social Change Redefining the Discipline and Practice in the Post 'Arab Spring' Era." In *Speaking Up and Talking Back? Media, Empowerment and Civic Engagement among East and Southern African Youth*, edited by Tufte et al., 19–36. Gothenburg, Sweden: Nordicom.

Waisbord, S. 2001. "Family Tree of Theories, Methodologies and Strategies in Development Communication." Prepared for the Rockefeller Foundation. http://archive.cfsc.org/pdf/familytree.pdf.

West, S. 2017. *How Could Citizen Science Support the Sustainable Development Goals?* Stockholm: Stockholm Environment Institute.

Wheeler, D. L. 2001. "The Internet and public culture in Kuwait." *Gazette* (Leiden, Netherlands) 63 (2–3): 187–201.

Wilkins, K. G., T. Tufte, and R. Obregon. 2014. *The Handbook of Development Communication and Social Change*. Hoboken, NJ: John Wiley & Sons.

9

Toward Happiness, Accountability, and Transparency

ICTs in the E-Governance of the United Arab Emirates

Oshane Thorpe

The United Arab Emirates (UAE) is located on the west coast of the Arabian Gulf, with a land area of 83,600 square kilometers. According to the government's portal,[1] the population is around nine million. Unlike many other Gulf countries, expatriates outnumber locals in the UAE by several million: according to studies, fewer than 20% of the population are local Emiratis (Gallacher 2009, 13). Like the United States of America, the UAE is a federation, but it is made up of seven emirates instead of states. Unlike the United States, the political system is not a constitutional democracy, but a federal presidential absolute monarchy. The 2010–2011 Global Information Technology Report indicates that the UAE is at the forefront of innovation in the Middle East and North African (MENA) region, particularly in the context of leveraging information and communication technology (ICT) for increased economic diversification and competitiveness (Al Athmay 2015). To this end, the UAE has an active Internet culture.

Many residents of the UAE occasionally follow important political figures on Twitter and other social media platforms; these media are the fastest way to become aware of various policy developments. Thus, it is apparent that the government considers the value of ICTs in reaching its publics, as opposed to reliance on traditional media. This study examines data sets collected by the UAE Ministry of Happiness, and measures them in critical discourse analysis alongside textual analysis of essential works on the subject. At first glance, the UAE seems to be the only country attempting to quantify its residents' "happiness" via national initiatives. The initiatives used by the government are extensive; e-governance is essential in this discourse because it provides the Ministry of Happiness a platform and capacity to study and implement the happiness matrix. E-governance initiatives have been formed on three fronts: the community (local government), government (federal), and international levels.

Each emirate currently has autonomy in determining its e-governance future to fulfill the community-level initiatives. Therefore, each has an e-government portal with its own initiatives and strategies. At the same time, at the federal government level, there is a unified federal portal. Even though work is being done at these two levels, a noticeable disparity exists in the effort put forth by the different emirates to bolster ICT use in governance; this is deduced from government services applications developed for users with or without mobile phones. Notably, there is an apparent disparity among Dubai, Abu Dhabi, and Umm al-Quwain, which gives the impression of slow progress and little federal government intervention (Hamid 2013), even though e-government was officially launched in the UAE at the federal level in 2001 with the principal mandate to make the government accessible and open for business for the convenience of end-users. According to Al-Khouri (2012), the UAE's e-government strategy at the federal level can be broken down into three categories: e-service, e-readiness, and an ICT environment. E-services are characterized by providing high-quality services to meet customer needs. E-readiness expresses the ability of governments to organize and deliver services effectively. Finally, ICT covers the physical infrastructure and regulations needed to achieve successful e-governance.

This research aims to assess the extent to which the UAE uses smart governance (e-government, m-government) to foster happiness, accountability, and transparency. The study will chronicle the development of e-governance inside and outside the UAE, as well as its implications in terms of transparency and accountability. Finally, the practicality and achievability of national happiness at the community or individual level will be discussed.

The main objective of this study is to provide a comprehensive overview of e-governance in the UAE context, while highlighting the landmark Happiness Initiative e-governance projects and the impact the initiative has on society. In addition, the article will look at the effect of the Happiness Initiative on citizens through case studies and examples, and it will ascertain the effect of the e-governance on residents' perceptions of accountability and transparency. Finally, challenges and hurdles in the implementation of the e-governance services will be discussed in light of potential implementation in other Gulf states.

A HISTORY OF E-GOVERNANCE

Governance is described as a process whereby a society determines its future through decision making. This process requires two crucial steps. The first is to determine the relevant stakeholders, and the second is to determine a method by which they can provide input into the decision-making process. Therefore, governance is not only primarily the idea of interaction between a government and its publics in a traditional sense (Graham et al. 2003). Many governments were reluctant to accept the early forms of e-governance, which was then referred to as "new public management" (NPM) (Hughes 2012).

Ott (2011) argues that a lack of customer-centered focus, which is a central theme in the NPM school of thought, can be attributed to a lack of government enthusiasm. Most importantly, a customer-centered system would require governments to improve the quantity and quality of their interactions with the public. Furthermore, systems would have to be in place to create and analyze the data. Finally, action would have to follow the results of such data collection. Therefore, for e-governance to grow, the first hurdle, the amount of interaction, had to be overcome. In its early stages, the system was used solely to increase interaction between a government and its publics, with less focus on improving services (Ott 2011).

Hughes (2012) asserted that the shift toward e-governance began in the 1990s. Several developed nations led the move, none of which were in the Middle East or North Africa. The quality focus did not develop during these years when governments were restructuring themselves like businesses in the NPM model (Andrews and Van de Walle 2013). However, it paved the way for the development of modern-day e-governance (Dunleavy et al. 2006). The death of the NPM structure did not indicate a failure of the government's customer or end-user focus. However, it heralded a new era in which digitizing services on the newly popularized Internet would help governments reach a broader cross section of their populations (Chen 2003).

Khosla (2016) agreed that the growth of e-governance started with the computerization of services, but believed other factors were instrumental in driving adaptation. One such factor is the rapid growth of ICTs that changed the landscape over time, promoting progress and development in the field. Therefore, Khosla argued that continued innovation in the tech space is the primary catalyst that prompted governments to keep up with the growing technology to introduce the new era of social and economic progress. Thus, e-governance is an area that has expanded solely as a result of ICTs. It is agreed that ICTs ultimately lead to greater citizen participation in governance. It should be noted that private enterprises were utilizing ICTs to maximize profits and customer interaction long before governments adopted it.

Hazlett and Hill (2003) posit that an intermediary period occurred between NPM and the current form of e-governance. This period was characterized by an environment in which the strengths of private agencies' information systems were reflected in the expectations of public bodies. Thus, certain fundamental private-sector principles, such as faster delivery and high demand, were applied to government agencies. The nature of the new government–public relationship included improved public services, as well as more efficient information sharing (Ongaro 2004). Though a definite improvement from NPM, in its early implementation, buzz-words such as "citizen-centric" and "governance-centric" were used to mask poorly planned e-governance efforts that lacked a clear focus (Saxena 2005). In this model, there was a wide disparity between the idea of e-governance and the computerization of services. In other words, merely digitizing services is not adequate for e-governance.

Ultimately, in the current dispensation, e-governance is not merely a buzzword used by governments to highlight a commitment to technological development. It is now a viable tool in the battle against corruption because it removes bureaucracy and directly and uninterruptedly allows communication with citizens (Mansa 2016). The focused administrative leadership provided by e-governance is essential in making governments more approachable and increases engagement in the new dispensation. According to Mimicopoulos et al. (2007), governance should fulfill three dimensions of need: efficiency, transparency, and participation. They further argue that of the three, efficiency is the most essential feature. They emphasize that the government must be attuned to the needs of the citizens.

ICT'S IMPACT ON TRANSPARENCY AND ACCOUNTABILITY

To combat corruption, a significant number of the analytical frameworks emphasize that accountability and transparency are the two key factors. Accountability is acknowledged as an essential foundation of good governance; it refers explicitly to the capacity of the public to assess governmental performance. Transparency and accountability are closely related, as access to information is directly linked to the ability to assess the effectiveness of performance (Graham et al. 2009). However, they are not the same thing. Public access to information is at the core of accountability, specifically in the realm of public-sector accountability. Therefore, accountability is bolstered if strict consequences follow from the lack of effective dissemination, or from poorly executed performance, outcomes, or policies. Here accountability refers to the uninhibited public access to information and the measures in place to punish the withholding of such access.

Alternatively, transparency is realized as a result of the implementation of formalized procedures, in addition to accurate documentation or record keeping of decision making and procedures. Tillema et al. (2010) reviewed the performance index of the public sector in developing

nations. Public sectors in these nations were found to be underfunded, corrupt, lacking structure and formality, characterized by low institutional capacity, and receiving limited input from
stakeholders. It was deduced that the regulatory practice coupled with low public accountability and the absence of transparency are the factors that lead to the institutionalization of corruption. Hence, transparency is not likely to be achieved without clear procedural development
and inclusion of stakeholders in the decision-making process.

Cain (2001) argues that in the literature, two factors, public-sector accounting and effective
financial management, are believed to be paramount in achieving transparency and accountability. He argues that the literature purports an assumed cause-and-effect relationship between
transparency and accountability that he cannot verify. On this note, he asserts that the literature
oversimplifies the matter. It is essential to understand that despite one's leanings on Cain's
analysis, one thing is irrefutable—that is, corruption *is* antithetical to the development of the
public's access to goods and services, and that therefore public transparency and accountability are desirable and should be ensured. Whether they share a cause-and-effect relationship
remains to be seen. Nevertheless, being accountable to the citizenry does ensure that public
services meet an acceptable standard.

Thus, to have a fair and equitable society, public accountability and transparency must be
enabled. Graham et al. (2009) and Iyoha and Oyerinde (2010) agree that ICT must play a critically important role in this endeavor. It can be inferred that if ICTs and e-governance can support transparency and accountability, the recent UAE drive toward ICT development and better
access to public service shows the government's commitment to a more transparent society.
Notably, the UAE not only ensures transparency and accountability through its websites and
official portals, but also creates a forum for residents to help the government improve through
constructive criticism. As an example of this commitment, the Happiness Initiative is one of
the UAE's achievements on the e-governance front in the last decade.

THE BIRTH OF UAE E-GOVERNANCE

The UAE has accomplished several things in developing e-governance and improving access
to smartphones and the Internet. In 2010, the United Nations Public Administration Program
undertook an extensive study (United Nations 2010) to rank the most e-government-friendly
states in the world. At the time, the UAE was ranked 40th in e-government usability and success. In 2012, the UAE improved its ranking to 28th, placing it among the most elite e-governed
states in the world. More recently, in 2018, the UAE ranked 21st. Even more notably, the UAE
leaped from 25th to 2nd in the Telecommunications Infrastructure Index. Therefore, since its
introduction of e-governance, the UAE has made major strides and garnered recognition on
the global stage, which is significant, as it has been suggested that the international level is the
ultimate indicator of e-governance excellence.

According to the official government portal for the UAE,[2] the country's move into the
m-governance sphere began on May 22, 2013. The initiative was introduced under the patron-
age of H. H. Sheikh Mohammed bin Rashid Al Maktoum, vice president and prime minister of
the UAE and the ruler of Dubai. The rationale behind the initiative was to provide government
services to the people, with no limits as to time and location. Since then, the UAE has made
very rapid progress in implementing e-government nationwide. Its growth can also be seen at
the regional level, especially in terms of the e-government index and the online service index
(table 9.1).

Table 9.1. Government app distribution across the UAE in 2019

Locale	IOS Apps	Android Apps	TOTAL
Federal government	55	33	88
Abu Dhabi	27	12	39
Dubai	56	57	113
Sharjah	12	10	22
Ajman	5	6	11
Fujairah	5	2	7
Ras al-Khaima	6	5	11
Umm al-Quwain	1	0	1
Learning institutes	4	3	7
Media institutions	9	10	19
Total	180	138	318

Source: https://u.ae/en/about-the-uae/digital-uae/uae-mgovernment-initiative

Initially, the UAE ranked 2nd behind Bahrain in 2012–2013 (Al Athmay 2013). On the global stage, the UAE ranked 28th and 25th in 2012 and 2013, respectively, according to the UN E-Government Readiness Report. The ranking is a significant achievement, as 190 other nations competed for top spots. More impressively, the young country ranked 12th in the online service index against the same group of countries. These early victories are proof of the renewed efforts of the UAE government to develop and improve its service agenda. However, more work needs to be done; the UAE is currently aiming for better unification of its services under the federal government umbrella in 2019. However, it was observed that the government portals of three of the emirates (Dubai, Abu Dhabi, and Sharjah) included many apps that were unique and independent of the federal government. As can be seen in table 9.1, these three emirates skewed the data significantly. The UAE is now trying to develop a unified, cohesive system that will optimize data and services across the country (Hamid 2013).

The movement to unify the country's electronic efforts is interlinked with the development of mobile services (m-services). H. H. Sheik Mohammed's goal was to ensure the initiative made all government customer services available on mobile phones. The m-service focus can strengthen the e-governance of the UAE and move the country up the ranks on the global indices. The ambitious initiative was part of the UAE's Vision 2021, and part of the ongoing program to build a thriving world-class government. It aims to build "world-leading public infrastructure, government services, and a rich recreational environment." The program implementation timeframe was set at two years. As of 2019, 180 IOS and 138 Android mobile apps were available in various app stores or directly through the government's website (UAE, n.d.).

For the goals of the UAE to be achieved, there should be simultaneous implementation of app services in all emirates. However, the biggest challenge to effective national m-service integration is the federal organization of the country. Each emirate is still endowed with the autonomy to develop rapidly or to stagnate. To remedy this situation, a single app called "One App" will merge more than 4,000 local and federal services under one application. One App will effectively reduce or eliminate the disparities among the emirates in the adoption of m-governance. It was announced on government websites that the app, which was still under development as of 2019, will use location-based services as well as intuitive user data collection to streamline the 4,000-plus services down to the essentials for an individual user.

One App is a critical part of the National E-Governance Plan (NeGP). If this app were to be developed and released to the public, it would be a significant step toward effective m-governance. However, with an initiative of this magnitude, several potential issues can be expected, such as runtime of the app, lag, crashes, and security of user data, among others.

E-GOVERNANCE VS. M-GOVERNANCE

The research for this study indicates that the UAE is a pioneer in the use of ICT in governance. Although it is by no means today's preeminent smart country, it aims to be so by 2021. In several UAE government white papers and road maps for the e-government initiative, e-governance and m-governance are often used interchangeably. Although they are comparable in terms of scope, each requires a different kind of ICT integration to be achieved.

According to eGov Noida, m-governance and e-governance, though they complement each other, are not the same. E-governance requires structural development and investments in IT and Internet; m-governance uses mobile or wireless devices that are equipped with wireless Internet capabilities to improve the delivery of government services in an anytime/anywhere fashion (Elets News Network 2015). According to the government's official portal, the objective is to make government services accessible through mobile portals and apps, which is an essential step in fixing the last-mile problem. In this research, both terms are used interchangeably to represent the ICT adaptation of the UAE, as they are cogs in the same machine. They may be slightly differentiated, but they work toward the same purpose, which is to increase the ICT usage in e-governance.

ICT INITIATIVES IN THE UAE

In recent years, the UAE's government has instituted a few important initiatives that reflect its commitment to ICT development and adaptation.[3] The initiatives are interconnected, but most of them can operate on a standalone basis.

One such initiative is the National Customer Relations Management (NCRM), which unifies all government services under one phone number. The goal is to reduce the likelihood of a customer of government services misplacing an important government agency's phone number. The digital switchboard provided by the NCRM will provide peace of mind and increase customer happiness. In theory, this initiative is both innovative and practical; however, it is possible that the network could become congested, increasing wait times substantially, with an adverse effect on customer satisfaction and on the promotion of happiness.

Another innovative ICT initiative is the SmartPass system, which aims to streamline the login process to government services. Currently, the UAE has successfully placed all government services online. Before the SmartPass system, residents had to memorize a separate login and password for each service. Under the new SmartPass initiative, all government systems will be on a secure network accessible with a unique identifier that will be given to residents and visitors upon request. This system will allow users of government services in the UAE to manage their online identity more efficiently: the SmartPass security features avoid the need to repeatedly upload documents each time a user wishes to interact with the government. The SmartPass system's single login credential is proof that consolidation is a step toward e-governance excellence.

In consideration of possible consolidation, the Government Service Bus (GSB) initiative provides e-government services with a centralized interconnectivity platform. It facilitates protocols for accessing services and enhances the integration and quality of government services in a safe electronic environment. The GSB is part of the Federal Network (FedNet), which seeks to consolidate the IT systems of forty-two federal bodies within the UAE. The network is characterized by security and efficiency. The servers will host all government data that is held electronically and facilitate the sharing of information between these bodies. The aim is to reduce the time spent requesting information from customers and to serve them better. Most importantly, it will lead to a truly digital government. It should be noted that the changes mentioned above do not include m-services, which will be provided by the final initiative.

Finally, the Center of Digital Innovation (CoDI) is an innovative idea that gives government entities the ability to contribute to the continuous development of apps, to benchmark them continuously to global standards, and to create and test apps using state-of-the-art technology. Under the CoDI initiative, the UAE has signed memorandums of understanding and agreements with Apple, Android, Blackberry, and Microsoft to train its development teams. The UAE also provides training to other GCC nations through this initiative. The cross-platform application of all government services is guaranteed with this initiative. The services fall into four main categories: consultation, technical training, laboratory for testing mobile applications, and finally the Innovation Center.

IS HAPPINESS MEASURABLE?

Freedom in the pursuit of happiness is a fundamental right that is traditionally interpreted as the individual's ability to self-actualize. Securing the happiness of the citizenry has not always been a central goal of governments. However, it should be, because happiness can boost productivity in many sectors. In the UAE, happiness is the government's expressed desire for its residents. Some mainstream media have described the government's desire to measure the happiness of residents as frightening, and as evidence of the insecurity of the nation (Gambrell 2015). Many pundits are not aware of the reasoning behind the UAE's concern with quantifying and assuring happiness. This section will briefly discuss the reasons for it. The main difficulty is to determine the feasibility of measuring the happiness of individuals on a mass scale and what variables are needed in such a measurement. The question then becomes: Is the UAE utilizing any of these variables in its Happiness Initiative?

Yaghi and Al-Jenaibi (2018) posit that smart government is tied to a public policy aimed at improving people's happiness by using ICT to deliver public services. They believe that happiness and ICT service delivery are interrelated. Their thirty-four interviews with the managers of government agencies in the UAE suggest that smart government does contribute to making people happy, and that the policy improves not only public-sector services but also the relationship between people and government. The improvement of this relationship is linked to happiness. Though the reasoning may seem linear, there are far too many complexities to make such a deduction. It can be concluded that there are gaps in correlating happiness to service received. Yaghi and Al-Jenaibi's study conducted interviews with various users of government services, and found that efficiency and connectivity did not increase happiness. The opposite, however, turned out to be true: poor and slow service had a significant effect on unhappiness. Thus, it is fair to conclude that excellent service may not increase happiness, but poor service has an absolute effect on unhappiness.

Yaghi and Al-Jenaibi (2017) found the correlation between efficient service and happiness to be inconclusive in an absolute sense. To measure happiness effectively, other variables must also be examined. The variables utilized by the UN's World Happiness Report (2017) indicate the UAE ranks 20th among 156 countries. The determining variables in this ranking were: GDP per capita, social support, healthy life expectancy, freedom to make life choices, generosity, perception of corruption, and dystopia. While this list is not exhaustive, it does set an unofficial benchmark for the factors that should be included in measurements of happiness. Consequently, this study will ask how well the UAE's initiative meets these variables.

Policymakers have pointed out the state-level process of reforming the public sector in two stages; as previously mentioned, the initial step took place between 2009 and 2014. At this stage, agencies were encouraged to deploy smart services to supplement regular operations. The second stage began in 2015 and will last until 2020–2021; during this time, government entities have been instructed to be fully upgraded and efficient in the customer-centered model. A well-developed modus operandi, which includes customer-focused strategies, operations, and finally service delivery methods including smart services, should also accompany this (*al-Bayan* 2015a, 2015b; Sharefa 2013; Dubai Smart Government 2013). This is similar to the initial expectation that happiness will be closely tied to improving services, which has since been found not to be sufficient in increasing happiness with any degree of certainty.

However, the unique vision in the UAE, which is echoed in speeches and press releases, is that the reform of public agencies is paramount in mobilizing the public sector to be more competitive, as streamlining the operation will lead to happiness. Incidentally, this also bolsters transparency, which is the most important result of the e-governance program. The ideology of happiness is expressly included in the UAE Vision 2021 and the Abu Dhabi Vision 2030. Therefore, investments, plans, activities, and operations are all directed toward achieving this goal (Abu Nemeh 2013, Al Zarooni 2014). As previously mentioned, Yaghi and Al-Jenaibi (2018) argue that the pursuit of happiness is not practical. Although it is a legitimate and moral policy goal, it is too idealistic and is not achievable. They also argue that the government should use the current momentum to continue its growth and focus instead on open-governance indicators such as responsiveness, efficiency, and competitiveness.

Other writers suggest that despite the lack of a clear correlation, mobile development and e-governance do boost transparency and accountability, both of which are good for governance. *Al-Bayan* (2015a, 2015b) urges the UAE government to continue to take advantage of the current rapid rate of infrastructure and mobile technology development (Helbig et al. 2009, Al-Khouri 2014, Al-Khouri and Bal 2007, Sabri 2009, Osman 2013, *al-Bayan* 2015a). Branding happiness as an absolute creates a challenge: although improved services will invariably lead to customer service happiness, a holistic achievement of happiness is impossible to achieve or measure. One crucial question to ask is: How will efficient e-service increase personal happiness? Since it is impossible to correlate services with personal happiness, it would be more pertinent to focus on aspects of e-governance such as transparency and accountability. These could lead to greater ease and peace of mind, while also being testable variables that play a vital role in assessing a government's efficacy and how it is perceived by its citizens.

Despite the apparent shortfalls of the initiative, several aspects of it show that it has not yet reached its full potential in the UAE. The project is still under development, and like many things in the UAE, it is being approached through an ingrained belief that nothing is impossible. The following section will focus on the steps[4] that have been taken so far. They are known as the Happiness Meter, National Survey for Happiness and Well-Being, Happiness Journey, Happiness and Well-Being Policy Bundle, Well School Network, Project Purpose National, School of Life Community Initiative, and Child Digital Safety. These are the backbone of the developing happiness movement in the UAE.

THE UAE'S FIRST STEPS TOWARD HAPPINESS[5]

The Happiness Meter is the UAE's take on a customer service survey. It asks visitors and residents of Dubai to rate services using the traditional happy, neutral, and sad emoticons. The services that can be rated include government agencies and airports. The captured data are shared with the government. This survey shows the government the areas in which it is deficient, and thus where to emphasize training in customer service.

The National Survey for Happiness and Well-Being captured the response of 16,000 individuals in the UAE. The survey sought to obtain more comprehensive data that the Happiness Meter could not capture. To help the government identify the areas of society that were most likely to influence happiness and well-being, it focused on the suggestions of individuals based on experience. The undertaking was useful in that it demonstrated that the government is committed to utilizing the voice of those it truly wants to serve as the sounding board for its policies. This will reduce the gap between the general public and the policies that will affect them.

The Happiness Journey is a community event designed to merge entertainment with the awareness of the happiness and wellness drive. At this event, people who have inspirational stories of triumph and bravery are brought in as speakers to inspire their peers.

The Happiness and Well-Being Policy Bundle is a combination of several policies that will benefit UAE society generally. One of them is the back-to-school policy, which is different from the others in that it focuses specifically on the happiness of government employees. With this policy, government employees can accompany their children on their first day at school. This allows government workers to be part of essential milestones in their child's development and allows children to have the support of their parents on an important day in their lives.

A related program, the Well School Network, provides schools with a number of programs and mechanisms that students and teachers can use to encourage the principles of well-being and happiness that the government is trying to promote at the institutional level.

A similar program, Project Purpose National, is aimed specifically at university-level Emirati students. It helps students to set life goals and shows them ways in which these goals can intersect with national service.

The School of Life Community Initiative is designed to foster better life skills based on the national agenda. This initiative was a product of the Government Annual Meetings held in November 2018.

Finally, the Child Digital Safety program works in collaboration with the National Program for Happiness & Wellbeing to protect the digital safety of children.

CONCLUSION

This chapter has assessed the readiness of the UAE to measure happiness effectively. Though this is a noble cause, much more needs to be done, and more variables must be considered, in order for there to be any level of confidence in the project. There is still room to improve and add variables as time progresses. Alternatively, it is possible for the UAE to abandon the pursuit of happiness, and instead concentrate on easing unhappiness. Although the two appear similar, the semantics entrenched in the language of the former invite impossibility.

The most significant result of the e-governance drive is the transparency and accountability that is a byproduct of the ICT integration of the government and its publics. Although this may not be a high priority of the UAE at the moment, the increasing level of transparency that it provides is a model not only to other countries in the Gulf but also globally. Countries in the Gulf that seek to improve their image on the world stage, and make a meaningful impact on the development of alternative forms of government to the mainstream ideology of democracy, should take the UAE's example as a benchmark for success.

NOTES

1. https://u.ae/en/information-and-services/social-affairs/preserving-the-emirati-national-identity/population-and-demographic-mix.
2. https://u.ae/en/about-the-uae/digital-uae/uae-mgovernment-initiative.
3. https://u.ae/en/about-the-uae/digital-uae/uae-mgovernment-initiative.
4. https://u.ae/en/about-the-uae/digital-uae/uae-mgovernment-initiative.
5. https://www.hw.gov.ae.

REFERENCES

Abu Nemeh, H. 2013. "Good government goes to people and does not wait for them to come to her" (in Arabic). *Al-Emarat al-Youm*, May 23, 2013. http://www.emaratalyoum.com/local-section/other/2013-05-23-1.577420.

Andrews, R., and S. Van de Walle. 2013. "New public management and citizens' perceptions of local service efficiency, responsiveness, equity and effectiveness." *Public Management Review* 15 (5): 762–83.

Al Athmay, A. 2013. "E-governance in Arab countries: status and challenges." *Global Journal of Business Research* 7 (5): 79–98.

———. 2015. "Demographic factors as determinants of e-governance adoption: A field study in the United Arab Emirates (UAE)." *Transforming Government: People, Process and Policy* 9 (2): 159–80. https://doi.org/10.1108/TG-07-2014-0028.

al-Bayan. 2015a. "Ministries and federal bodies adopting smart technologies: One-month grace period for those lagging behind" (in Arabic). April 23, 2015. http://www.albayan.ae/across-the-uae/news-and-reports/2015-04-23-1.2359794.

———. 2015b. "Mohamed ben Rashid: The measure of people's happiness is to make their life easier" (in Arabic). May 24, 2015.

Cain, K. B. P. 2001. "Information, not technology, is essential to accountability: Electronic records and public-sector financial management." *Information Society* 17 (4): 247–58.

Chen, H. 2003. "Digital government: Technologies and practices." *Decision Support Systems*, 34 (3): 223–27. doi:10.1016/s0167-9236(02)00118-5.

Dubai Smart Government. 2013. *E-Visions* 118 (August 2013): 1–8. www.dsg.gov.ae/SiteCollection Images/Content/DeG%20Documents/August-2013-en.pdf.

Dunleavy, P., H. Margetts, S. Bastow, and J. Tinkler. 2006. "New public management is dead—long live digital-era governance." *Journal of Public Administration Research and Theory* 16 (3): 467–94.

Elets News Network. 2015. "We serve masses anytime, anywhere, anyhow." eGov, May 7, 2015. https://egov.eletsonline.com/2015/05/we-serve-masses-anytime-anywhere.

Gallacher, D. 2009. "The Emirati Workforce: Tables, Figures and Thoughts." Accessed January 1, 2019. https://www.academia.edu/5813970/The_Emirati_Workforce_Tables_figures_and_thoughts.

Gambrell, J. 2015. "If you're unhappy in Dubai, the police may call you." *Independent*, October 26, 2015. https://www.independent.co.uk/news/world/middle-east/if-youre-unhappy-in-dubai-the-police-may-call-you-a6709876.html.

Graham, C., T. Hopper, M. Tsamenyi, S. Uddin, and D. Wickramasinghe. 2009. "Management account-ing in less developed countries: What is known and needs knowing." *Accounting, Auditing & Accountability Journal* 22 (3): 469–514. https://doi.org/10.1108/09513570910945697.

Graham, J., T. W. Plumptre, and B. Amos. 2003. *Principles for Good Governance in the 21st Century.* Ottawa: Institute on Governance.

Hamid, T. 2013. "Lagging e-government portals prove burden for UAE competitiveness." *The National,* July 8, 2013.

Hazlett, S. A., and F. Hill. 2003. "E-government: The realities of using IT to transform the pub-lic sector." *Managing Service Quality: An International Journal* 13 (6): 445–52. https://doi.org/10.1108/09604520310506504.

Helbig, N., J. R. Gil-García, and E. Ferro. 2009. "Understanding the complexity of electronic govern-ment: Implications from the digital divide literature." *Government Information Quarterly* 26 (1): 89–97.

Hughes, O. E. 2012. *Public Management and Administration.* Basingstoke, UK: Palgrave Macmillan.

Iyoha, F. O., and D. Oyerinde. 2010. "Accounting infrastructure and accountability in the management of public expenditure in developing countries: A focus on Nigeria." *Critical Perspectives on Account-ing* 21 (5): 361–73.

Khosla, C. 2016. "E-governance in India: Initiatives and issues." *Journal of Governance & Public Policy* 6 (1): 47–58. https://www.proquest.com/docview/1858086840?accountid=145382&forcedol=true.

Al-Khouri, A. M. 2012. "E-government strategies: The case of the United Arab Emirates (UAE)." *Euro-pean Journal of ePractice* 17 (September 2012): 126–50.

———. 2014. "Identity management in the age of mobilification." *Internet Technologies and Applica-tions Research* 2 (1): 1–15.

Al-Khouri, A. M., and J. Bal. 2007. "Electronic government in the GCC countries." *International Jour-nal of Social Sciences* 1 (2): 83–98.

Mansa, D. 2016. "Innovative tool for new and change government of India: E-governance." *Interna-tional Journal of Advanced Research in Computer Science* 7 (6): 172–6.

Mimicopoulos, M., L. Kyj, N. Sormani, G. Bertucci, and H. Qian. 2007. *Public Governance Indicators: A Literature Review.* New York: United Nations Department of Economic and Social Affairs.

Ongaro, E. 2004. "Process management in the public sector." *International Journal of Public Sector Management* 17 (1): 81–107. https://doi.org/10.1108/09513550410515592.

Osman, M. 2013. "Development toward smart government requires development of smart ser-vices" (in Arabic). *Emirates Today,* July 26, 2013. http://www.emaratalyoum.com/local-section/other/2013-07-26-1.594049.

Ott, J. C. 2011. "Government and happiness in 130 nations: Good governance fosters higher level and more equality of happiness." *Social Indicators Research* 102 (1): 3–22.

Sabri, A. 2009. "After e-government: Toward knowledge-based society" (in Arabic). *Social Affairs* 26 (101): 191–99.

Saxena, K. B. C. 2005. "Towards excellence in e-governance." *International Journal of Public Sector Management* 18 (6): 498–513. https://doi.org/10.1108/09513550510616733.

Sharefa, S. 2013. "Role of Communication and Public Relations in Electronic Government" (in Arabic). Publication of the Authority of Social Affairs.

Tillema, S., N. P. S. Mimba, and G. J. Van Helden. 2010. "Understanding the changing role of public sector performance measurement in less developed countries." *Public Administration and Develop-ment* 30 (3): 203–14.

UAE. n.d. "UAE mGovernment Initiative." Accessed February 10, 2019. https://u.ae/en/about-the-uae/digital-uae/uae-mgovernment-initiative.

United Nations. 2010. *United Nations E-Government Survey 2010.* New York: United Nations. https://publicadministration.un.org/egovkb/portals/egovkb/documents/un/2010-survey/complete-survey.pdf.

Yaghi, A., and B. Al-Jenaibi. 2017. "Organizational readiness for e-governance: A study of public agen-cies in the United Arab Emirates." *South Asian Journal of Management* 24 (1): 203–14.

———. 2018. "Happiness, morality, rationality, and challenges in implementing smart government policy." *Public Integrity* 20 (3): 284–99.

Al Zarooni, M. 2014. "Plan to use quadcopters to deliver ID cards, driving licenses." *Khaleej Times*, February 12, 2014. http://www.khaleejtimes.com/article/20140211/ARTICLE/302119913/1002.

10

Community Media and Development in Upper Egypt

A Case Study of *Nagaawya* Newspaper in Nag Hammadi

Hend El-Taher

Arab publics, having been repressed by dictators and absolute monarchs for more than 30 years, have rarely seen public service ideals applied in media practice. Yet the astonishing events that unfolded in the region at the start of 2011, with the eruption of mass youth-led protests against corruption, unemployment and police brutality, opened a new horizon for media reform. (Sakr 2012)

In 1789, Napoleon introduced the first newspaper printed in French in Egypt. Later, the Arabic language was introduced as a medium for the press, which created a challenge to illiteracy. However, the management of the press was dominated by elitists and politicians. At the beginning of the nineteenth century, the press (sponsored by government) covered issues such as agriculture, the economy, or judicial information. Toward the end of that century, the press could be characterized as a tool to serve the political agenda of its owners.

Fortunately, the following century witnessed greater press freedom and there was an exponential rise in the number of journals published, which culminated in a diversification of news and an increasing readership. Nonetheless, once the Free Officers took control of Egypt in 1953 after a military coup, media once again served as propaganda for the regime (Hamada 2002).

In the late 1990s the al Jazeera channel was introduced by Qatar, providing greater access to information and opening the gate for political debates. This coincided with the emergence of political communication studies and their influence on the public. Moreover, changes within the community were strongly linked with social media. For example, after a call on Facebook for solidarity with textile workers, a strike was organized on April 6, 2008. The strike and its associated "Stay at Home" campaign were successful and are thought to have been the impetus for the January 25 revolution in 2011. The strike and the 2011 revolution are regarded as cornerstones in the history of the news in Egypt, because they introduced a different type of news and because of their influence on the community (Leihs and Roeder-Tzellos 2015).

There is no doubt that, compared to the situation prior to the revolution, the political transition that occurred in Egypt after the January 2011 revolution had a positive effect on the media (Leihs and Roeder-Tzellos 2015). During Mubarak's regime, independent media had no place because of the government's dominance over land-based channels; thus, independent and community media could only function online or through private channels. Like other countries during the Arab Spring, Egypt relied mainly on regular citizen reporting from the street, as well as on individuals posting reports on social media to cover the ongoing situation. These reports were considered more reliable and were sometimes an alternative to the state media (Leihs and Roeder-Tzellos 2015). Since then, Egyptians have become accustomed to new media concepts such as "citizen journalism," "independent media," and "community media." Having clear legal frameworks and policies to help journalists do their jobs smoothly was supposed to bring transformation. Nonetheless, the media encountered a struggle for freedom, independence, and sometimes legitimacy for people's acceptance and approval.

In the Arab region, a few community media models operated after the Arab Spring, although a few minimal models had been operating before that. These mainly consisted of community radio such as Radio6 Tunis and Radio Kalima in Tunisia, established in 2007 and 2008 respectively. Their shows were broadcast online, and because they opposed the regime, they struggled fiercely against the state. Restrictions were imposed, but they managed to operate as underground stations and were sometimes broadcast from abroad. After the revolution, those stations and eight others were given licenses (Groth 2017).

Jordan had AmmanNet2 and Al-Balad; the latter was launched in 2000 and began its land-based transmission in 2005. It is considered the pioneer of online radio in the region and the very first community radio in Jordan. The radio was managed by an independent team of journalists and was supported by the municipality of Amman and UNESCO. Even though it faced challenges in broadcasting political news, the radio persisted in informing the public, steadily increasing in popularity (Buckley 2013). A survey conducted in 2009 revealed that Al-Balad was among the most highly rated stations in Jordan. It still broadcasts a vast array of programs related to women's issues, entertainment, art, sports, youth programs, and education. It sustains a feedback-based policy to ensure contribution of its audience to the content (Buckley 2013).

In Egypt, Horyatna and Hoqook are examples of community radios. In Alexandria, Radio Tram—even though it focused more on underground music—also broadcast several revolution-related topics. In the realm of newspapers, *Welad El Balad* is prominent as the most unique and sustainable newspaper experiment in Egypt. It played a significant role in bringing attention to marginalized regions in Upper Egypt, the Delta, and the West of Egypt, where Bedouins live. Research affirms how community radios have contributed to the developmental processes of civic engagement, social change, sustainable development, and preserving heritage. This chapter will examine the definition of community media, its characteristics, its function, and the challenges it encounters through a case study of the *Nagaawya* newspaper.

COMMUNITY MEDIA AND RESEARCH PROBLEMS

Because community media is a relatively new branch of media, it receives less attention from scholars in both the theoretical and practical fields. It lacks a thorough analysis of its content, audience, and institutions. Currently, community media is considered an interdisciplinary field with indigenous, cultural, and political studies in the public sphere. This leads to a wealth of definitions for "community media"; Howley (2013) counts ninety-four. This means that choices must be made among many possible approaches to the subject, with the result that a number of related studies seem very similar to one another (Howley 2013). This can lead to gaps in the conceptualization and the theorization of community media. Furthermore, in most cases, mass communication intersects with other disciplines; therefore, for rigorous research, an interdisciplinary approach must be considered.

Jankowski (2003) states that in the late 1990s there was not much interest in community media research. Fortunately, beginning around that time, digitization enabled researchers to uncover new aspects of media usage (Howley 2013). However, community media, and community radio in particular, still suffered marginalization from scholars and in cultural studies in general (Groth 2017). Howley's thinking is in alignment with Groth, as he believes that cultural studies failed to produce methodological and theoretical studies in mass communication (Howley 2013). The lack of research in this area is due in large part to the minimal presence of independent media compared to the dominance of the mainstream, as well as to political oppression (Groth 2017).

Research on community media in Egypt is confronted with the same problems, since most of the available research comes from the West. Unlike in the West, the problem of centralization is very important. Centralization is manifested in metropolitan cities not only with regard to public services, but also in the fact that media studies are heavily concentrated in the larger cities. Upper Egypt—the geographical area that extends from Giza to Aswan governorate and actually constitutes the majority of the Egyptian territory—receives less attention. More specifically, this huge area suffers from a lack of research on the use of media for sustainable development.

WHAT IS COMMUNITY MEDIA?

All of the many definition of community media reflect nearly the same meaning, function, and characteristics. Community media is characterized by content different from the mainstream, since it focuses on the groups with less representation. It is also defined as "media which originates, circulates, and resonates from the sphere of civil society" (Howley 2013). A more traditional definition of community media refers to community participation, such as the one Joy Elizabeth Hayes presents in her study of the Latin American model. According to her, they are "the places where people negotiate the push and pull between local and global, traditional and modern, and rootedness and transience that shapes everyday life" (Hayes 2018, 268).

In this sense, community media is founded to serve a particular group or local community, providing a fresh and more relevant perspective on the news. Community media can be geographically based, but not always. It can serve several geographical areas, or it can go beyond geography, as in the case of Internet-based communication, allowing it to disseminate its message to a much larger audience (Bailey et al. 2007). It is well adapted to covering small, underprivileged, or marginalized groups. According to a UNESCO report in 2013, community media strives to empower citizens through advocating civic engagement and the right to freely express themselves without political or commercial sophistication. It is also accountable to the communities it serves. "Therefore, it is in the community, for the community, about the community and by the community" (Short and Rice 2002). In the literature, it can be referred to as "alternative media," "grassroots media," and "local media" (Forde 2011).

Community media is an alternative to state-based and profit-based platforms. It promotes social and political activism by sharing information with its public, thereby allowing them freedom of expression. Hence, community media plays a part in community development and in promoting social or political change. As it informs the audience and allows them to express their views freely, people are given the opportunity to practice citizen media—as well as to directly affect the decision-making process (Buckley 2013).

COMMUNITY MEDIA PRINCIPLES

Three principles form the pillars of community media: (1) independence, (2) democracy, and (3) participation. These three characteristics are what distinguish community media from the state, private, or mainstream media.

First, community media is not privately or publicly owned. It is instead based on nonprofit principles to serve a community, and it is known for its independence in administration and management. This independence determines the agenda, which will be biased toward the people it serves, as it concerns their economic well-being, right to access information, freedom of expression, and involvement in the decision-making process (Bailey et al. 2007). Unlike the mainstream media, the main source of funding is not advertising. It may enhance its sustainability through advertising, but to avoid biases or dependency, it does not depend upon it as a sole source of revenue (Mojaye and Lamidi 2015).

Second, community media keeps people informed by dispersing knowledge, while at the same time maintaining a keen awareness of what is untold and a healthy skepticism about what is told. Creating, criticizing, and suggesting content are shared responsibilities. When people possess a "shared consciousness" and when their interests, disappointments, and needs are communicated and acknowledged, they feel that they are treated as citizens (Howley 2002). Community media bridges the gap between what happens on the ground and what is unspoken, while providing a fresh perspective on the topics presented. It works in alignment with and complementary to the role of traditional media. Consequently, it acts as a watchdog to the state, not only at the political, social, or economic level but also because its scrutiny of the official media is based on professional and ethical principles. Essentially, community media challenges, verifies, and questions the content of traditional media (Forde 2011). This, in essence and practice, is the democratic process of sharing knowledge, and it is what differentiates community media from other, traditional types.

According to the Independent Broadcast Authority Act (IBA) in 1994, community media is described as follows: (1) fully controlled by a nonprofit entity and carried on for non-profitable purposes; (2) serve a particular community; (3) encourage members of the community served, or persons associated with or promoting the interests of such community, to participate in the selection and provision of programs to be broadcast; and (4) may be funded by donations, grants, sponsorships, or advertising or membership fees, or by any combination of these (Tacchi 2003).

Because of this orientation, in some countries community radio is given special attention and even priority over commercial media (Buckley 2013). It is even considered a fourth broadcasting channel in addition to the public, commercial, and subscription broadcasting channels (Jurriëns 2013). As a partner in the development process, it was entrusted with the dissemination of information in order to boost the economy and to raise awareness regarding certain topics (Cerbino and Belotti 2018).

Regardless, licenses can be difficult to obtain. It may take months to get the required approvals. Rather than waiting forlornly, and in order to maintain their connection with their audience, community media channels resort to "special event licenses" and recorded programs on CDs, which are then broadcast on other radio stations (Tacchi 2003).

Third, participatory media is designed to engage audiences in the whole process: managing the broadcast entity, selecting the topics, setting the agenda, and producing the content. Allowing people to contribute by being actively involved in the creation of the content is something that has not been offered by the mainstream media (Nassanga 2009). Unlike most traditional media, the structural organization of community media is flexible. Rather than relying solely on professional staff, it is dependent on volunteer members as well as professional journalists (Forde 2011).

Forde states that community media emerges in response to political regimes, yet it is not limited to politics. Community media covers stories related to the community it serves and gives voice to the voiceless. It reflects the things that occur in these areas and asks, "What are the concerns of the indigenous groups?" It can also be a catalyst to incite citizens' participation in discussions and debates, and encourages their contributions to future broadcasting content. In brief, it aims at promoting active citizenship (Forde 2011).

Interestingly, community media creates an active audience who, by volunteering to be part of the production process, are able to voice opinions, engage in discussions, and create their own meaning by selecting what contents are to be discussed and what issues concern them. This, in return, sustains civic engagement and social solidarity among different clusters of people. It challenges the existing models and offers an opportunity for social transformation (Jurriëns 2013). By selecting the content, the audience consistently seeks to present something different, resulting in diverse and creative content (Mojaye and Lamidi 2015).

GLOBALIZATION VERSUS LOCALIZATION: IDENTITY, SENSE OF BELONGING, AND HERITAGE

According to Shahzalal and Hassan (2019), cultural sustainability is concerned with identity, values, norms, and traditions. It requires people to embrace sustainable behavior and community media that facilitate and manifest social change. Shahzalal and Hassan consider community radio in rural and less developed areas to be an effective communication tool because of its low cost, and because its programs are suitable for both the literate and illiterate. Modern technology has given people the chance to be trained on information and communication technology (ICT) to produce programs.

Notably, changing behavior also involves a change of mindset. People need to have access to information, but also to knowledge-based programs that compel their brains to think. This can only occur if the people concerned accept change, so that they can align their behavior with these new expectations. Self-efficacy models can also be a factor in effecting change. Change can be enhanced by presenting role models, positive messages, and success stories through community media (Shahzalal and Hassan 2019).

Globalization absorbs small identities by regarding unique cultures as "isolated," but community media enhances people's identity (Howley 2013). To this end, some types of community media have offered minority groups the opportunity to voice their own opinions and to confront the pervasive discrimination they encountered in the mainstream media (Dreher 2010).

At a certain point in this process, the group's "self-definition" is strengthened. This is done either by providing content in their indigenous language or by covering news about their original homeland; thus, those groups feel a greater connection to each other and to their origins. At another point, their sense of belonging and patriotism within the larger community is enhanced by demonstrating that the smaller groups are part of the host country, contributing both diversity and unity (Adoni et al. 2006).

COMMUNITY MEDIA IN UPPER EGYPT: *NAGAAWYA* NEWSPAPER

The whole experience is a source of pride for us; we wish other cities would apply it, and other countries know we have such a good model in Egypt. (Amir Elsaraf, *Nagaawya* editor in chief, 2019)

Nagaawya newspaper is one of the media services of *Welad El Balad*,[1] established in Nag Hammadi[2] in 2011 and named after the town. During its first years, the staff worked tirelessly with a team of well-trained young journalists and amateurs in different governorates, constantly seeking to improve on the services provided. Currently, the *Nagaawya* team includes six journalists, an editor in chief, and a legal representative. The newspaper is an independent local publication that represents the community, empowers the marginalized, and creates media products that address the heritage, concerns, complaints, and local events of its people. In brief, it enables their voices to be heard and to reach the appropriate persons. On many occasions, it has influenced and even provoked public opinion. Because of this active role, it is considered a partner in the process of development.

From its inception, *Nagaawya* has not been identified as a "community newspaper" because of people's unfamiliarity with the term. It simply discussed the positive and negative aspects of Nag Hammadi, surpassing other media by focusing on the local people and valuing their customs and traditions. Weekly meetings were held to discuss events and decide on the topics for each issue. However, some years after its formation, the print newspaper ceased its production due to increasing costs which, despite all efforts, it was unable to accommodate. Switching to digital journalism, *Nagaawya* now uses media arts and provides content that is differentiated from other publications. Even though there is tough competition, it maintains its own high standards.

Nagaawya's Values

Teamwork, credibility, access to information, and protecting people's privacy are indispensable for community media. According to Abul Maaref al-Hefnawi, a journalist for *Nagaawya*, speed and accuracy are also essential; however, this may pose a risk for the journalist. For example, when a Christian was killed on a farm, the newspaper needed to cover the story quickly, before religious sensitivity had time to become inflamed. This is because of a history of religious strife between Muslims and Christians in Nag Hammadi. "People know where we live, so when we cover sensitive or debatable stories, we expect some risk," said al-Hefnawi.

Furthermore, mistaken information is rare, because local journalists are expected to have a thorough knowledge of the community they serve. The team is always present in the streets. They have sources in offices, as well as the "citizen journalists" who provide them with photos, videos, and notification as soon as an incident takes place. All of this community support contributes to *Nagaawya*'s ability to cover events quickly and efficiently. As described by Bassam Abdelhamid, another journalist for *Nagaawya*: "We report with people's eyes; we consider the tribal, social, and humanitarian side of the story we cover. This explains why people cooperate by giving us information when incidents take place; we have been building trust for eight years."

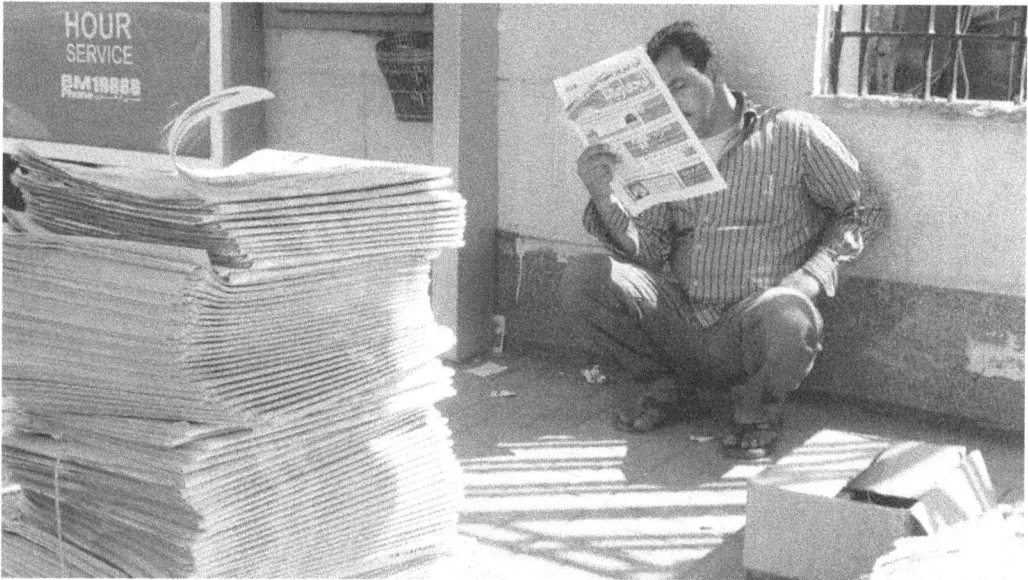

Figure 10.1. *Nagaawya* rural community newspapers.

Community Media and Development in Nag Hammadi: Civic Engagement, Social Change, and Sustainable Development

As described by its editor in chief, *Nagaawya* has introduced a new medium to the city, where the reader is the hero, the citizen is the speaker, and the official is there to answer the questions and concerns of the citizen. This orientation has enabled the paper to gain popularity and the trust of the people.

For example, stories about temporary jobs for cleaning persons and the laborers at an aluminum factory expressed the workers' dissatisfaction over the workload, the low wages, and the deteriorating quality of products. Notably, the factory administration worked alongside the newspaper to find out people's opinions about the problem, and sought government subsidies for electricity expenses by publishing the stories in *Nagaawya*. The newspaper reported on two villages famous for drug and weapons trade, Hamra Dom and Abu Hizam, telling the other side of the story by directing attention to the residents' pursuit of services and developmental projects. It is worth noting that the first female journalist to enter those villages for a news story was from *Nagaawya*.

As an Upper Egyptian community, Nag Hammadi is challenged by outmoded traditions such as retaliation, child marriage, deprivation of females' liberty and inheritance, and tribalism. Nonetheless, *Nagaawya*'s team do their best to empower women socially, economically, and politically. *Nagaawya* is considered a partner in the development process. It publicizes local crafts, women's homemade products, and natural resources, and stimulates tourism by promoting the local archaeological sites. These steps raise awareness about specific areas of development, and also provide the impetus for the decision makers to take action.

Covering Stories in a Time of Crisis

Nag Hammadi saw a spate of child kidnapping in the years after the 2011 revolution. Thanks to *Nagaawya*, two children were returned to their families. In this conservative community, the

Figure 10.2.   Female journalist.

first reported rape incident aroused public opinion, especially because the accused belonged to a notable tribe. While adhering to journalistic ethics, *Nagaawya* was extremely cautious about how they handled information from conflicting sources, such as reports of retaliation on either side of the case. Instead, they relied on the syndicate of lawyers and other official sources. When the journalists proved trustworthy, the victim approached them for an interview via video. In order to protect her identity, her interview was produced in a written format only. In the end, their coverage of the story enabled her to stand up for her right to sue the wrongdoers and wait for the decision of the court.

Social change needs time, but as *Nagaawya* gives access to information and disperses knowledge, this will give people the options to think about so they can choose what is best for them. In light of this, Nag Hammadi's municipality asked *Nagaawya* to help establish a financial plan for developing the city and its surrounding villages.

Preserving Heritage and Reviving Old Traditions

Nagaawya has become a trusted partner of South Valley University in Qena. The university has relied on it several times for documenting important events and stories on heritage. The research of some of its graduate students has reported the newspaper as the most popular in the city, having played a vital role in putting an end to retaliation between some tribes. It also documented the tradition of tribal marriage.[3] At another level, *Nagaawya* used to have a weekly cultural seminar that introduced new talents and different art forms.

The paper's staff has contributed to rediscovering the city's heritage by dedicating a space on its website to Nag Hammadi's culture and heritage. "Nis'na fi-l-qura," or "Our People in Villages," is a feature that rediscovers the hidden gems of the villages from several angles: history, traditions, and inherited customs, such as infertile women crossing canals in the hope of becoming pregnant, and "Isbu' al-alam," the Holy Week preceding Easter that Christians celebrate with certain rituals. The online show "Rahlat arba' banat" (Four Girls' Trips) follows four women traveling between villages to discover archaeological sites and customs. They document their visits with a selfie mobile camera; the films exceed 30,000 views within a month. At first, viewers were critical of women traveling alone, but as the show gained popularity and its audience began giving positive feedback on social media, the women sometimes received invitations to visit specific villages.

Challenges Facing *Nagaawya*

Even with all its success, *Nagaawya* is still burdened with financial challenges, which affect the journalists' salaries. Likewise, recruiting skilled journalists who can commit to long-term contracts is a challenge, especially for female journalists, who eventually marry and get a "more secure job" in a government office or become homemakers. According to Mariam Elromihy, a female journalist, "The administration system here is too flexible, so we work for long hours and this is exhausting sometimes." Her colleague Mary Katan adds, "It is inhumane to put too big a load on the journalists because the number of hired journalists is less than the workload."

Nonetheless, despite the challenges, *Nagaawya* stands as a successful community media model that promotes civic engagement and social change and works to revitalize its local heritage. In accordance with self-efficacy models, *Nagaawya*'s diligence in presenting good role models through their reporting motivates people to believe in themselves and to accept their roles in social responsibility (Bryant and Oliver 2009). Specifically, it has transformed the way the community perceives working women. As Elromihy and Katan say, it was difficult at the

Figure 10.3. Reporting on community problems.

beginning for a conservative community in Upper Egypt to accept female journalists staying for long hours in the office, working in the streets, and traveling for training. Sometimes they were perceived as "too open" or "easy girls," but they have gained people's respect and trust.

In Egypt, community media is, arguably, still a new concept, and this justifies the struggle to sustain its reputation and presence. According to social identity theory, when people obtain knowledge, they understand both their own characteristics and those of others, and can then discover what their common characteristics are. In this way, they develop "self-identification," which augments their sense of belonging (Baker 2012). It is no wonder, then, that *Nagaawya* has enhanced people's pride and sense of belonging in Nag Hammadi. Some shops in the city have even taken on the newspaper's name, and the journalists identify themselves as *Nagaawya*'s team. Although some of them have other jobs, they prefer to be identified as a journalist for *Nagaawya*.

CONCLUSION

It is clear from the example of *Nagaawya* that community media is an effective tool, not only to enhance positive qualities in a community and challenge long-held and damaging traditions, but also to pave the way for social transformation. Thus, community media needs to be seen as a catalyst or a stakeholder in the development process for sustainable results that impact grassroots transformation. Such models of success deserve every support from governmental and nongovernmental entities to develop and sustain comfortable, convenient, and progressive working conditions.

ACKNOWLEDGMENTS

This work has been made possible by the support of my family, colleagues, and influential educators throughout the process. I very much appreciate the valuable contribution and cooperation of *Nagaawya*'s team and *Welad El Balad*'s owner, Mrs. Fatma Farag.

Nagaawya journalists interviewed:

1. Amir al-Sarf (2019), editor in chief, Nag Hammadi
2. Mariam al-Romihy (2019), journalist, Nag Hammadi
3. Mary Katan (2019), news desk and journalist, Nag Hammadi
4. Abul Maaref al-Hefnawi (2019), journalist, Nag Hammadi
5. Bassam Abdelhamid (2019), journalist, Nag Hammadi
6. Ayman al-Wakil (2019), journalist, Nag Hammadi
7. Islam Nabil (2019), journalist, Nag Hammadi

Interviews were conducted after obtaining written consent from the *Nagaawya* team. *Nagaawya* website: https://nagaawya.weladelbalad.com.

NOTES

1. *Welad El Balad* is an independent integrated network of local newsrooms and products serving local communities in Egypt: Marsa Matruh, Fayoum, Beni Suef, Asyut, Abu Tisht, Nag Hammadi, Dishna, Qena, Qus, and Luxor. It has an online platform that supports a social media service, along with up-to-the-minute videos that are displayed in partnership with YouTube and Masrawy.com, one of the most popular websites in Egypt. One of its distinctive features is a website devoted to citizen media. It was founded in order to promote local community media with up-to-date, decentralized news. At its start, it covered ten areas with an overall circulation of 900,000 copies of its printed newspaper.

2. Nag Hammadi is a city in Upper Egypt (the southern part of Egypt), located on the west bank of the Nile in Qena governorate, a few kilometers away from Luxor. It is famous for manufacturing sugar, as it has extensive agricultural lands devoted to sugar, and also processing aluminum. Nag Hammadi also has historical significance, as it includes several archaeological sites from the early Muslim conquest and the Ottoman period as well as palaces for Prince Youssef Kamal, who is a descendant of Mohammed Ali's royal family. In 1945, a collection of early Christian documents written in the Coptic language was discovered near Nag Hammadi.

3. Some tribes in Nag Hammadi, such as the Howara and the Ashraf, are strict about their marriage traditions. Their members are obliged to marry within family in order to maintain a pure lineage.

REFERENCES

Adoni, H., D. Caspi, and A. Cohen. 2006. *Media, Minorities, and Hybrid Identities: The Arab and Russian Communities in Israel.* New York: Hampton Press.

Bailey, O., B. Cammaert, and N. Carpentier. 2007. *Understanding Alternative Media.* New York: McGraw-Hill Education.

Baker, C. A. 2012. "Social identity theory and biblical interpretation." *Biblical Theology Bulletin* 42 (3): 129–38.

Bryant, J., and M. B. Oliver. 2009. *Media Effects: Advances in Theory and Research.* 3rd ed. New York: Routledge.

Buckley, S. 2013. *Community Media: A Good Practice Handbook.* Paris: UNESCO Publishing.

Cerbino, M., and F. Belotti. 2018. "Between public and private media: Toward a definition of 'community media.'" *Latin American Perspectives* 45 (3): 30–43.

Dreher, T. 2010. "Speaking up or being heard? Community media interventions and the politics of listening." *Media, Culture & Society* 32 (1): 85–103.

Forde, S. 2011. *Challenging the News: The Journalism of Alternative and Community Media.* Basingstoke, UK: Palgrave Macmillan.

Groth, S. 2017. "Citizens' radio in North Africa and the Middle East: Meaningful change through citizen empowerment? An experience from Tunis." *Global Media Journal–German Edition* 3 (2): 1–19.

Hamada, B. I. 2002. "Historical and political analysis of mass media in Egypt." *Egyptian Journal for Communication Research* 9 (2): 1–31.

Hayes, J. E. 2018. "Community media and trans-localism in Latin America: Cultural production at a Mexican community radio station." *Media, Culture & Society* 40 (2): 267–84.

Howley, K. 2002. "Communication, culture and community: Towards a cultural analysis of community media." *Qualitative Report* 7 (3): 1–24.

———. 2013. "Community media studies: An overview." *Sociology Compass* 7 (10): 818–28.

Jankowski, N. 2003. "Community media research: A quest for theoretically grounded models." *Javnost—The Public* 10 (1): 5–14.

Jurriëns, E. 2013. "Social participation in Indonesian media and art: Echoes from the past, visions for the future." *Bijdragen tot de taal-, land- en volkenkunde / Journal of the Humanities and Social Sciences of Southeast Asia* 169 (1): 7–36.

Leihs, N., and M. Roeder-Tzellos. 2015. "Political Communication Research in the Middle East." In *International Encyclopedia of Political Communication*, edited by G. Mazzoleni, 1–8. Chichester, UK: Wiley-Blackwell.

Mojaye, E., and I. Lamidi. 2015. "The role of community media in building democratic values in Nigeria." *European Journal of Research and Reflection in Arts and Humanities* 3 (1): 63–74.

Nassanga, G. L. 2009. "An assessment of the changing community media parameters in East Africa." *Ecquid Novi* 30 (1): 42–57.

Sakr, N. 2012. "Public Service Initiatives in Arab Media Today." In *Regaining the Initiative for Public Service Media*, vol. 1, edited by G. F. Lowe and J. Steemers, 183–98. Gothenburg, Sweden: Nordicom.

Shahzalal, M., and A. Hassan. 2019. "Communicating sustainability: Using community media to influence rural people's intention to adopt sustainable behaviour." *Sustainability* 11 (3): 1–28.

Short, G., and D. Rice. 2002. *UNESCO Community Media Sustainability*. UNESCO. https://en.unesco.org/themes/community-media-sustainability.

Tacchi, J. 2003. "Promise of citizens' media: Lessons from community radio in Australia and South Africa." *Economic and Political Weekly* 38 (22): 2183–87.

11

Internet and Social Media in Algeria

Saddek Rabah

Arab countries in general are different, but they share common political characteristics, including the privatization of the state and very low participation of the population in institutions. This dual characteristic inevitably leads to corruption, arbitrariness, mismanagement of state resources, and obstruction of economic development (Addi 2011). Thus, the social discontent that has accumulated over the years has exploded throughout the region to reject a mode of state management that has led to a deadlock.

In this perspective, the Algerian regime is threatened by a deep discontent fueled by its economic and social record and by the deterioration of the image of the leaders in the eyes of the public. Faced with this situation, the regime had developed "its capacity to neutralize everything that could threaten its survival" (Hamadouche 2012, 65). The thirst for profound change has brandished the fear of chaos. Demands for political reform are granted windows of freedom of expression and criticism. Persistent social protest is neutralized by redistributions of oil rent in all directions. But in the long term, neutralization was all the more difficult because it was almost impossible to carry out equally. The Algerian regime's resources in terms of response and resilience are threatened not only by extinction (revolutionary legitimacy) but also by non-renewability (oil).

In the Arab world, Algeria was the country most exposed to the wind of revolt that had blown over its neighbors. But it was also the country that resisted it best. So is there an Algerian exception? Algeria is a living society and its history is marked by many forms of struggle: struggle for independence (1956–1962); workers' strikes of 1977; Amazigh movement (April 1980); popular revolts of October 1988; call for democratic openness (1989); appearance in 2001 of the popular movement of Kabylia and insurrectional riots of April 2001; march of Kabylia of June 14, 2001; interrupted legislative elections (1992); and war between the army and Islamist movements between 1992 and 1999 (Bichara 2012).

The year 2010, for example, has been described by some as the year of a thousand and one riots. During the first eleven months, according to the police services, there were 112,878 law enforcement interventions at the request of local administrative authorities in several *wilaya*s (provinces). During the first half of the year, there were 81,565 law enforcement interventions, and in the third quarter alone the national police had to intervene 31,313 times. This latest review does not include the interventions of the security forces in December, which was marked by violent riots in Algiers (Bennadji 2011). However, these movements revealed that mobilizations are fragmented, corporatist, and dispersed. These individual protests failed to develop into political demands at the national level, let alone become an alternative to the regime (Ammour 2012).

Algeria has continued, until recently, to give the impression of a relatively peaceful oasis in the midst of revolutions. But this impression is false and does not reflect reality. "The instinct for freedom," according to Meddeb Abdelwahab (De Saint Perier 2011), is contagious, because it is at the heart of the most entrenched popular aspirations. These aspirations have root causes: a general fatigue of the worn-out, elderly, repressive, and predatory regime; a sense of shame and humiliation of being governed by men of no stature; and the impatience of young people in the face of a blocked situation. This is why Algerian protests, also known as the "smile revolution," are experienced as a newfound pride, a "revolution" of dignity. Algerians' perception of themselves has changed. Suddenly, even the perceptions of others became more attentive, more tender, almost empathetic.

The spread of the Internet, social networks, urbanization, and education have changed the situation. Young Algerians are now more aware of the world around them than older generations. The trade-off between (partial) redistribution of wealth and political acquiescence is becoming increasingly obsolete, especially when the resources to support it are in decline (Cristiani 2017). In recent years, Algerians have witnessed a resurgence of online debate on the country's political situation, the authoritarian nature of the regime, and, in particular, corruption scandals involving people close to the administration. People of all ages have begun to relay information, more or less verified, on the ill-gotten achievements of Algerian political figures, and political discussion forums have exploded in popularity, especially among young people.

This chapter presents a historical and critical perspective on the Internet and social media in Algeria as they evolved in the context of totalitarianism that characterized the Algerian regime until recently. It surveys milestones in Internet and social media history, laws and regulations, and their social and political functions in Algeria. The chapter shows that the Internet and social media in Algeria experienced steady expansion in terms of users and functions in the last few years, with a telecommunications market that has very strong development potential. The telecommunications sector in Algeria has undergone a major transformation. It went from a situation where the state held the monopoly to one where several operators (public and private) positioned themselves and tried to impose themselves. The chapter concludes that the rapid breakthrough of social media and, in general, the Internet in the country is therefore less synonymous with the democratization of public space than with the fragmentation of authority, which, surprisingly, can contribute to creating a unitary dynamic in a context of protest emulation.

HISTORICAL BACKGROUND

Algeria's population was estimated at 42 million in 2018 according to the National Statistics Office (ONS). According to the same center, nearly 54% of the population is under 30 years of age and more than 70% is urban (ONS 2019).

Despite its wealth, youth, and particularly strategic geographical location, Algeria is still lagging behind in the development of the Internet. The Internet has been slower to reach Algeria than its North African neighbors. Perhaps this is because of its historical links with France, a country that has itself been slow to engage in the adoption of the Internet, and partly because of the general shutdown of investments in technology and infrastructure during the civil war. The low Internet penetration is partly related to the low number of fixed telephone lines available; in 2010, for example, there were about 4.5 million active fixed telephone lines compared to about 35 million active mobile lines (International Media Support 2013).

In the early 1990s, Algeria developed X.25 networks based on the DPS 2500 system developed by Alcatel. The Algerian X.25 network, DZ-pack, includes four routers that serve the majority of the country's urban areas. The total capacity of this network was about 4,000 lines with international connections to Euronet and Europac (ERCIM, n.d.).

In 1989, RCSTI/CERIST (Research Centre on Scientific and Technical Information) was entrusted with the establishment of the Algerian research network and the development of a global network policy. At the time, there were only two networks, the Postal Cheques network and the Air Algeria network. The Algerian Academic and Research Network (ARN) was implemented in three successive steps: selection and connection of regional nodes, selection of university and research institutes to be connected to regional nodes, and connection of regional nodes to the main node and development of services. RCSTI was the only access provider in Algeria, where about 420 institutions use the Internet, which should correspond to an average of 2,000 regular users. The communication kit cost $2,300 (ERCIM, n.d.).

Algeria had an international capacity of 476Kb, which had increased to 1Mb in January 1998. A 64Kb fiber optic cable had connected Algiers to Paris. Algiers was also connected to Washington by a satellite link with a capacity of 512Kb, and an additional 256Kb line had been planned.

Subsequently, the implementation and management of Algeria's national information and communication technology (ICT) policy was mandated to the Ministry of Posts, Information, and Communication Technologies (MPTIC). The first major policy was developed in 2000 with the creation of regulatory authority for post and telecommunications (ARPT) and the split of Algeria Posts and Telecommunications into two companies, one of which became the incumbent telecom operator Algérie Télécom (AT). The ARPT is in charge of regulating postal services and the telecommunications sector. This includes promoting competition in the latter. It is also responsible for the procedures for the allocation of operating licenses and defines the rules on pricing for the services provided to the public. It ensures that the license conditions are implemented and that the telecommunications infrastructure is shared.

In addition to the MPTIC and the ARPT, the Ministry of Higher Education has also played an important role in the ICT field, especially through RCSTI/CERIST, which functioned as the only Internet service provider (ISP) before market liberalization. However, in 1994, Algeria still had only 70 users registered with CERIST (Renaud 2007).

In 2006, Algeria scored only 0.35 on the UN E-Government Readiness Index, with a mere 1.1 personal computers and 0.59 broadband subscribers per 100 people. Since then, however, liberalization has created a competitive market in Algeria, increasing the total number of telephone subscribers (mobile and fixed telephony) to more than 30 million from 1.4 million in 2002. There are now 71 ISPs and 11 providers of Voice over Internet Protocol (VoIP) services (APC and Hivos 2009).

In 2012, the Internet in Algeria had low speed, frequent interruptions, and excessive subscription fees, classifying it as "elitist" according to a ranking of Netindex. It was also not very lively and the penetration rate was low, with only 1.6 million individual subscribers to the various ADSL networks for 36 million inhabitants, and only 20% of companies connected to the Net. Across the board, the problem is not technical; it is human. One need only consult the website of any ministry to realize that the most recent information is three months old, and the available indicators and statistics are three years old (Amari 2012).

By 2015, Algeria was considered one of the slowest countries in terms of Internet connectivity, ranking 174th out of 189, with 2.69 megabits per second (Mbps) and a loading speed of 1.2 Mbps. The corresponding figures for mobile connection are 2.5 Mbps for connectivity and 1 Mbps for uploading (Hamada 2015). This ranking was confirmed in 2018 by the Worldwide Broadband Speed League, where Algeria, with a download speed of 1.25 Mbps, found itself in 175th place. According to this report, it would take 9 hours and 7 minutes for an Algerian Internet user to download a 5 GB (gigabit) film, whereas this time is only 11 minutes and 18 seconds in Singapore, which is first in the ranking at a speed of 60.39 Mbps. In the previous year, Algeria was 161st out of a total of 189 countries (Nour 2018). Its Moroccan and Tunisian neighbors, according to Speedtest Global Index, are respectively ranked 101st and 119th, with an average connection speed of 13.59 Mbps for Morocco and 8.19 Mbps for Tunisia. Libya, which has been affected by armed conflict since 2011, also outranks Algeria, in 126th place, with an average connection speed of 6.50 Mbps (Rek 2018).

This situation can be explained mainly by the absence of strategy, and of general planning for installation and access to the Internet in the country. To further complicate the situation, several private operators have accused the sector's regulatory authority of blocking the development of the Internet, in particular through absurd regulations and prohibitive fees, which give individual connection tariffs the highest prices, in some cases representing 1/10th of the minimum wage (Abderrahim 2013). In this field, as in many other sectors of economic activity, the lack of a plan and an overall vision hinders Algeria's improvement. The country's enormous financial resources do not amount to a policy. Relying too much on the idea that you can buy everything, the Algerian leaders have destroyed creativity and innovation.

The country had 34.5 million fixed and mobile Internet subscribers in 2017, compared to 28.5 million in 2016, which was an increase of more than 6 million subscribers, according to the French Post and Telecommunications Regulatory Authority (ARPT). But these figures include a significant share of 3G and 4G, since of the 34.625 million Internet subscribers, 31.460 million are mobile Internet subscribers and only 3.168 million are fixed Internet subscribers. Of this customer base, 90.85% are on mobile networks, while 9.15% are on fixed networks (Bey 2018).

The proportion of households with Internet access at the end of 2017 (45.04%) increased by 3.5% compared to 2016 (41.54%). This is mainly due to the increase in the number of ADSL Internet and 4G LTE subscribers, which recorded the same trend, with 163,804 and 143,576 new subscribers respectively. In 2017, mobile Internet reached 74.55%, an increase of more than 12% compared to 2016. The mobile Internet market remains dominated by the 3G segment (69%), despite strong growth in the 4G segment (Bey 2018).

As of January 2019, 58% of the population (24.48 million) are active Internet users, with 53% (22.36 million) also being active mobile Internet users. Fifty-four percent (23 million) are active social media users, and more specifically, 50% (21 million) are mobile social media users. There are also more than 49.53 million mobile subscriptions in Algeria, the equivalent of 117% of the population (HootSuite 2019).

The annual digital growth occurring in Algeria between January 2018 and January 2019 has been, on average, greater than global growth (+2%). Mobile subscriptions have increased by 4%, Internet users have increased by 17%, active social media users have increased by 9.5%, and mobile social media users have increased by 11% (HootSuite 2019).

At present, the telecommunications market has very strong development potential. Algeria Telecom, the current operator, holds a monopoly on fixed telephony. Three operators hold a mobile license: Algeria Telecom's Mobilis (public), Orascom's Djezzy (51% public and 49% Veon, a Dutch company), and Wataniya's Ooredoo Algeria (private).

Coverage performance is important, but even more important is network quality because it defines the ability of each operator to provide the best connection and services. The deployment obligations for fourth-generation mobile telephony are very different from one operator to another. They are the result of the commitments made by each party in accordance with specifications drawn up by the Post and Telecommunications Regulatory Authority, which is responsible for close supervision of the service. As it happens, the same authority takes care of measuring the coverage rate, but not the quality of the network. In any case, operators have a strong interest in providing a quality network. First of all, it ensures smooth and constant traffic for users, without slowdown or interruption. In addition, it allows the quantity and price of mobile data to be justified in the rate offers made to potential customers (Saidoun 2017).

Although Algeria's fixed-line penetration has been steadily reduced over the years, the government has continued to ensure that the fixed-line infrastructure is extended to underserved areas. This infrastructure developed on the national level includes the national fiber optic backbone, which was increased with the new undersea link to Valencia in April 2017. Algeria is now part of the 4,500 kilometers of the overland trans-Saharan backbone network that will link the national network to other fiber optic networks in the region.

Competition among the three mobile network operators (MNOs) has intensified. Combined with the increase in taxes on voice and data services, competition has affected the operators' revenues. The development of the Algerian market for the sale of fixed broadband lines has been hampered by the limited scope of the fixed network as well as by the capacity of the infrastructure to offer broadband services. The success of Universal Service Telecommunications (UST) authorizations since 2016 also meant that by 2018, mobile Internet would represent nearly 92% of all Internet connections (ISP Today 2019).

Algeria offers a top-level domain in Latin characters. Domains are administered by the Network Internet Center, and have very few restrictions. The only restriction to apply for a domain name is that the applicant organization must have a presence in Algeria itself. A domain name costs about 1,000 Algerian dinars, or 14 U.S. dollars, per year. The top-level domain is .dz; the second-level domains are:

- .asso.dz
- .art.dz
- .com.dz
- .edu.dz
- .org.dz
- .gov.dz
- .net.dz

The use of the Internet continues to grow rapidly in Algeria, affecting society, economy, and government. In 2006, a study (Nabil 2006) on Internet use among young people in Algeria was carried out on a sample of 210 young Algerians aged 15 to 30. It included the different socio-professional categories such as academics, employees, senior managers, and the unemployed. Nabil noted that most respondents (40.2%) spend between 30 minutes and one hour on the Internet, while 35.5% connect to the Internet for one to two hours a day. The study showed that only 32.2% of the young people surveyed have an Internet connection at home, compared to the 74.3% of users who connect in Internet cafés. The study pointed out that 61.3% use the Internet for information research, 43.3% for communication, 32.3% for friendship, 29.5% for games, and 12.1% are looking for romantic relationships. Concerning the most visited websites, the study revealed that 75.3% use the Google search engine, compared to 53.3% and 51.3%, respectively, who prefer the MSN and Yahoo sites.

In 2009, a study titled WebDialn@ (meaning "our web" in Algerian Arabic), which surveyed about 6,000 Algerian Internet users on ADSL, mobile Internet, online advertising, and e-commerce, estimated that 4.5 million people (12.8% of the Algerian population) use the Internet, and that they rely heavily on it for their information, research, and activities such as social networks. The study also showed a gender gap and regional disparities in Internet use. The typical Algerian web user is described as male (72.2%), aged between 20 and 29 (29.2%), educated at least to the secondary-school level +1 (66.2%), and living in Algiers (29.28%). Women represent just 25.8% of Algerian web users.

Online media are the main destinations for Algerian Internet users: 80.8% read online newspapers, 19.9% listen to the radio, and 11.4% watch TV programs. The Internet is also used for research (80.7%) and business contacts (22.9%). Social networks also seem to be very popular, with 40% of respondents having a Facebook profile (Meddah 2009).

Another study conducted in 2012 to investigate the use of social networks by Algerian youth aged 8 to 24 years revealed that 84% of the population surveyed used Facebook, 8% Twitter, and only 4% MySpace. Thirty-seven percent of respondents indicated that making new friends was the main reason for using social networks, 40% mentioned their usefulness in acquiring new knowledge, 11% mentioned effective communication, and 18% mentioned networking. The results of the study also showed that 65% of the surveyed population benefited from social networks to improve their foreign language skills, 25% to strengthen national identity and belonging, and 11% to acquire the ability to convince in debates (Boumarafi 2015).

In March 2016, another study found that the four most popular social networks among adults in Algeria are Facebook (99%), YouTube (97%), and Skype and Viber (both 93%). Facebook (97%), Skype (85%), Viber (80%), and YouTube (75%) are the networks with the highest number of subscribers in Algeria. Facebook (84%) is the social network most used by Algerian adults. Consulting content (96%), sharing content (81%), and interacting with others (75%) are the three activities that are practiced by the largest proportion of Algerian adults on Facebook. In terms of professional social networks, LinkedIn seems to be better known (59%) and has more registrations (44%) than Viadeo, which stands at 29% in terms of popularity and 14% in registrations (Kouaci 2016).

The seventh edition of the Arab Social Media Report (2017) reported that Algeria witnessed an increase of more than 20 percentage points in Facebook account penetration over a 30-month period between June 2014 and January 2017. At the beginning of 2017, the rising star in terms of increase in share was Algeria, which gained 4% of the total share of Facebook users in the region. In terms of gender balance, the gender gap in social media in Algeria has persisted. By 2017, women represented 38.2% of all Facebook users across the country, while men represented 61.8% (Salem 2017).

In 2016, the top five *wilaya*s of the country according to the number of users were:

1. Algiers: The capital has 5,200,000 users, more than 1/3 of all Algerian Facebook users; 88% of these users connect via mobile.

2. Oran: This *wilaya* alone has more than 1/15th of the number of Algerian users, more than 1,300,000; the rate of mobile usage is 77%, the lowest rate in the country.
3. Sétif: This *wilaya* has 740,000 users, a considerable number, 86% of whom tend to use their mobiles to connect.
4. Constantine: This *wilaya* has 690,000 users, a substantial number, with a rate of 83% of use via mobile.
5. Batna: This *wilaya* has more than 550,000 users, a significant population, 82% of whom choose to connect via mobile. (Beji 2016)

In 2015–2016, Algeria was one of the countries with the largest increase in the percentage of users interacting in Arabic on Facebook (43%), after Tunisia (50%) and before Morocco (37%), Lebanon (33%), and Somalia (22%). Algeria also experienced the strongest growth in terms of new active Twitter users in the region, with about 774,000 new users. The estimated number of tweets produced monthly by active Twitter users in Algeria was approximately 71 million in March 2016. On average, active Algerian Twitter users send about 2.3 million tweets per day (Salem 2017).

Of all LinkedIn users in the Arab world, 8.4% are based in Algeria. The top seven countries in the region in terms of gender balance remained the same from 2014 to 2017, including Algeria. Algeria has one of the highest rates of younger LinkedIn users in North Africa, with nearly 79.5% of users under 35 years of age.

Algeria also has one of the highest rates of Instagram use among the Arab countries, with 3.25% of all Instagram accounts in the Arab region. Five countries exceed the regional average in terms of the number of active users, including Algeria with 230,000. The others are Saudi Arabia with 2.1 million, followed by the UAE with 1.2 million, Egypt with 800,000, and Lebanon with 570,000.

The digital advertising market has been evolving in Algeria since its beginnings in 2006. After the first few years with double- or triple-digit increases, the market stabilized in 2014–2015. In 2016, due to the crisis in the automotive sector, the market slowed down, but then resumed its development in early 2017, with the emergence of new players from the agri-food sector and smartphone and household appliance manufacturers (Benali 2017).

Many Algerian companies have discovered the advertising services offered by the web giant Google. Little by little, Google is becoming an advertising agency that captures and manages part of the digital advertising of Algeria. Almost a dozen Algerian companies, including major advertisers, have entrusted part of their digital advertising to Google AdWords (now Google Ads). They include the Algerian subsidiaries of Jumia, Coca-Cola, Renault, Kia, Total, and Peugeot, as well as Condor Electronics, Trust Bank Algeria, and the juice brand Tchina, a subsidiary of Cevital Agro-Industrie. Others, such as Iris, another Algerian brand of electronics and household appliances, have used AdWords for limited-time advertising campaigns.

In addition to Algerian companies, foreign entities also target Algerian Internet users with the services offered by Google through its subsidiary Google Ads. We can mention smartphone brands such as Samsung, Huawei, and Apple, and major commercial companies such as the Chinese Alibaba and the American giant Amazon, as well as Tunisian and Turkish travel agencies and other air transport companies. At first, only one Algerian car dealership, Renault Algeria, advertised using Google Ads, but now there are three: Renault Algeria, Kia Algeria, and Peugeot Algeria (Saadi 2018).

Communication and advertising agencies are still looking for a solution to offer to other Algerian companies wishing to make themselves known on the Internet. More than ten years after its appearance in Algeria, Internet advertising investment is not really known, but we know that the automotive sector is undoubtedly the most present on the web (32%), followed very closely by ICT (telephony, IT, consumer electronics) with a rate of 25%. Other sectors are beginning to invest in Internet media: real estate, airlines, food, and tourism (Azzouzi, 2019).

Looking at different social media platforms, the total addressable advertising audiences in Algeria can be deduced and compared. In January 2019, the monthly number of active Facebook users was 22 million, 62% male and 38% female. Snapchat had about 2.35 million monthly users, 59% of whom were women and 36% men. Instagram had 4.4 million active monthly users, 59% male and 41% female. On Twitter, there were 483,000 monthly users, 79% male and 21% female. On LinkedIn, of the 1.8 million users, 70% were male and 30% female (HootSuite 2019).

LAWS AND REGULATIONS

The telecommunications sector in Algeria has undergone a major transformation. It went from a situation where the state held the monopoly to one where several operators, public and private, positioned themselves and tried to obtain market share. The ARPT has been publishing annual activity reports for years, presenting major developments in the sector. Through these reports and statistics published by other bodies, such as the ITU (International Telecommunication Union), it is clear that the effects of the opening of telecommunications are significant in quantitative terms. This is reflected in the increase in Internet and mobile phone penetration rates, improved network coverage, increased investment, and job creation in this sector.

Before the 2000 law, the information and communication technology sector in Algeria was governed by provisions based on a state monopoly, both for postal services and for telecommunications. This system has created certain constraints, including a rather cumbersome procedure management system, the absence of competition, and insufficient self-financing capacities. This has led to a significant delay in the dissemination of Internet services. Law 2000-03 of August 5, 2000, introduced institutional reform: separating post and telecommunications; creating a postal company and a telecommunications company; distinguishing between telecommunications infrastructure and services; opening the capital of the existing operator, Algeria Telecom (AT), to the private sector with a view to privatization; introducing and gradually opening up all segments to competition; creating a postal and telecommunications regulatory authority (ARPT) to ensure the proper functioning of the market and competition and to protect the interests of users; and finally the establishment of a ministerial department responsible in particular for defining sectoral policy. The aim is to open up the market to competition, promote the participation of private investment, and preserve the development of universal service throughout the country. New players were introduced in the telephone and Internet services (Kherbachi and Gani 2016).

For fixed telephony, the Algerian government has been determined to give private operators access to public infrastructure in order to put an end to the public operator's monopoly. The opening to competition was initiated in December 2004 with the granting of a license to operate the fixed long-distance, international, and local loop telephone network to an Egyptian consortium, Orascom Egypt Telecom, already established and holding a GSM license, worth $65 million. This duopoly was very short-lived as the operator filed for bankruptcy in 2009, ending competition from fixed-line operators (Kherbachi and Gani 2016).

Since then, the ARPT had begun its administrative and technical transformation to better respond to the realities of the current communications market. The telecoms regulator had already officially changed its name to the Regulatory Authority for the Post and Electronic Communications (ARPCE). This new title reflected the expansion of the telecoms regulator's competencies in all segments of electronic communications: fixed and mobile telephony, computer programming, cybersecurity, and so on. Indeed, unlike the ARPT, which was limited to the management of the postal sector and telephony, the ARPCE now controls postal activities and any emission, transmission, or reception of signs, signals, writings, images or sounds, data, or information of any kind by wire, optical, or electromagnetic means (Agence Ecofin 2018).

Since 2004, Algeria has set up a system to combat cybercrime through the promulgation of Act No. 04-15 of November 10, 2004, on infringements of automated data processing systems (STAD). The country also launched a program to combat cybercrime and established the National Gendarmerie's center for the fighting and prevention of cybercrime, as well as other specialized laboratories and brigades within the National Security Directorate. There is also Act 09-04 of August 5, 2009, on special rules for the prevention and combating of offenses related to information and communication technologies (Benelkadi 2018).

Before 2004, with regard to online content, Decree 98-257 of August 25, 1998, stipulated that Internet service providers are responsible for all published content hosted on their servers, and are also responsible for monitoring content considered to be "contrary to public order and morality." Algerian legislation has even incorporated the notion of "digital content" through an amendment to the penal code. It considers insult or defamation to include writings, drawings, speeches, radio and television broadcasts, or any other electronic means (including computers and the Internet) (APC and Hivos 2009).

By law, ISPs are subject to criminal sanctions for the material and websites they host, particularly if the topics covered are "incompatible with morality or public opinion." The Ministries of Justice, Interior, and Posts, Information Technology, and Communications have supervisory responsibilities in this matter. The law provides for prison sentences of six months to five years and fines ranging from DZD 50,000 to 500,000 (US$625 to $6,252) for users who do not comply with the law, including the obligation to cooperate with law enforcement authorities against cybercrime (U.S. State Department 2014).

Cybercrime is a constantly increasing practice in Algeria, in line with the growth in the number of Internet users. To track down criminals, the national gendarmerie created the Center for the Prevention and Fight against Computer Crime and Cybercrime (CPLCIC) in 2008. It has handled thousands of cybercrime cases and has already built a good reputation. The creation of this body was enacted by Act No. 09-04 of August 5, 2009.

In 2017, the CPLCIC processed some 1,000 cybercrimes, a 68% increase over the previous year. Also in 2017, 2,130 cybercrime cases were recorded by the General Directorate of National Security (DGNS), compared to 1,055 in 2016, representing an annual increase of almost 102% (F. L. 2018). This evolution of cybersurveillance activity is mainly due to the expansion of Internet use in Algerian society, particularly with the advent of 3G and 4G, and the resulting consequences in terms of fraudulent and malicious use of this technology. Another important factor that has contributed to this change in the number of cases is the emergence of a culture of denunciation among Algerian citizens.

Among the famous offenses that have been identified by the center's patrols was the video showing a sub-Saharan child slapped violently by a man from whom he was asking for alms. The perpetrators of the attack were located and arrested. The CPLCIC also managed to find the man who suspended a baby from the balcony of a high-rise apartment in a city in Bab-Ezzouar (Algiers). A similar process led to an identification and arrest in the city of Oran (West). An instigator on Facebook was making threats against women who posted in solidarity with a young woman who was abused during her jog in Algiers, by encouraging people to spray acid on the faces of women who were not properly dressed, in order to "educate" them.

In terms of international cooperation, Algeria became a member of the Egmont Group in July 2013 and has signed 17 memoranda of understanding and information exchange agreements with its counterparts in Africa, the Middle East, and Europe. Algeria has also adhered to the Arab Convention on Combating Cybercrime, ratified by Presidential Decree No. 14-252 of September 8, 2014 (Hammadi 2018).

SOCIAL AND POLITICAL FUNCTIONS OF SOCIAL MEDIA

According to the 2013 Civil Society Barometer, Algeria is last in the ranking (3.65 out of 10), not because civil society is nonexistent, but because of the difficulties faced by actors, particularly organizations involved in human rights, memory, or the social movement, in influencing the country's future in a context of aborted revolution (IRIS 2014). Civil society has struggled to raise its head since the civil war of the 1990s and appears exhausted, unstructured, and controlled by the state, despite bastions of resistance demanding change, thus defying the widespread fear of falling back into chaos. But the unease is palpable: immolations, riots, repeated strikes.

In 2011, the National Coordination for Change and Democracy was created. Unfortunately, this platform bringing together both political opposition and civil society disappeared without succeeding in overcoming the divisions or building a credible alternative, because it was perceived by the population, from the outset, as a "partisan gathering" controlled by particular interests and therefore far from unanimously accepted within the protest space (Geisser 2012). In 2014, the Barakat ("Enough") movement, a fierce opponent of former President Abdelaziz Bouteflika's fourth term, tried to rely on social networks to get their messages across. But it suffered the same fate as the other "informal movements" of young people such as the MJIC, Algeria Pacific, and others. On the other hand, in some instances, the emergence of civil groups on social networks has activated a range of Internet-based projects, such as cleaning campaigns, environmental initiatives, book swaps, and fund-raising. Social media–guided campaigns, like the one launched on Facebook in 2017 calling for the boycott of the car market in Algeria, have proven very successful.

A symbol of the weight of social media, particularly Facebook, in the protest movement was a viral publication inciting Algerians to "harass" the university hospitals in the capital of Switzerland, where the former Algerian president was hospitalized (February 24, 2019). This resulted in a flood of messages and phone calls—a collective action which, as noted by *Jeune Afrique* magazine (Alilat and Attia 2019), overwhelmed the Geneva telephone switchboard. One more example of the impact of social networks on mobilization.

Social mobilization has taken on a new dimension by structuring itself around autonomous unions and collectives of unemployed and precarious workers. In 2013, the "March for Dignity" organized in the south of the country symbolized the shift from the epicenter of the protest, hitherto confined to the capital, to a region still marginalized. The regime has responded to these demands with front-line institutional reforms and piecemeal economic measures to ensure social peace.

All these forms of accumulated activism have joined a common goal and spontaneously contributed to a form of protest that mostly rejects participation in formal politics. Indeed, political parties, whether linked to the regime or to the opposition forces, are discredited because of their fragmentation, inconsistent discourse, and participation in clientelist networks closely linked to the regime itself (Casati 2019). On February 26, 2019, the militant networks that had been mobilized for several decades, even during the civil war of the 1990s, finally saw the fruits of their ceaseless efforts to bring criticism to life in the public space, with thanks also to the web, which broke the "wall of fear" that had long held the opposition.

According to Dalia Ghanem-Yazbeck, a resident scholar at the Carnegie Middle East Center, social media have made a huge impact in Algeria. She focused on Facebook, which is very popular in Algeria. Facebook and other platforms, such as Twitter, are used as vehicles of expression for millions of Algerians who are dissatisfied and frustrated by the administration. They connect people to each other and are valuable tools for organizing local initiatives such as demonstrations and strikes, suggesting slogans, providing guidelines, sharing photos, and live-streaming videos (Bessadi 2019).

In the absence of political alternatives to the system, Algerians have found in social networks spaces for exchange and major levers for citizen mobilization. Everything that is difficult to achieve in real life due to the strong police presence on the street becomes possible thanks to the Internet, even if the cyber police are on standby. In a country where the government has done everything possible to silence and weaken the press, networks are also becoming sources of information for millions of readers. Shared videos, for example, give notoriety to their authors and help to gradually break down the wall of fear erected by years of authoritarian social control. This is reflected in the welcome given here and there to candidates such as Rachid Nekkaz, an Algerian businessman and political activist. Today, a wide range of social actors regularly use social media to denounce the status quo and the widespread feeling of *hogra*, a word used in Algeria to express a mixture of anger and humiliation caused by exposure to social injustice.

The Algerian state has repeatedly shown that it will not hesitate to use digital censorship to repress and stifle popular movements capable of questioning its authority or sovereignty. In 2011, Internet access was blocked in parts of Algeria and Facebook accounts were reportedly deleted. Thousands of pro-democracy demonstrators were also arrested during violent street demonstrations (Ramdani 2011). The most recent example is the day before the protest movement of February 22, 2019. While rumors of an impending disconnection were spreading on social networks, the national telecommunications company Algeria Telecom was quick to deny it to reassure its customers. But the truth was quite different. On the evening of February 21, Algerian Internet users noticed a spectacular drop in connection speed, followed by intermittent outages and finally a general outage. This was observed among all Algerian Internet service providers—Ooredoo, Djezzy, and Mobilis (Jahus 2019).

Previous cases of Internet censorship in Algeria reveal a filtering of messaging platforms and social networks, which became completely inaccessible. Thus, Facebook Messenger, Instagram, WhatsApp, Discord, Twitter, and many others are filtered through the Internet addresses of their servers. Other popular platforms, such as Google and its services (Gmail, Google Play, and YouTube), Outlook, and live services (Skype and Yahoo), have been blocked to prevent civil-society members from finding an alternate way to communicate.

In general, Algerian censorship laws are both vague and strict, which resulted in a low average score of 35/100 for freedom of expression in the media in 2018 (Freedom House 2018). The government monitors some email and social media sites. Internet users regularly exercise their right to freedom of expression and association online, including through online forums, social media, and email. Activists reported that some social media postings could lead to arrests and interrogations; observers widely understood that intelligence services were closely monitoring the activities of political activists and human-rights defenders on social media sites, including Facebook.

The expression of dissent on social media platforms may be punishable under defamation laws. The 2009 Cybercrime Act gives authorities the right to block websites that are "contrary to public order or morality," and a centralized system monitors Internet traffic. To cite just two examples among many others, in 2015, activist Zoulikha Belarbi was convicted of undermining Bouteflika by posting satirical online photos of the head of state on her Facebook page (El-Issawi 2017). Similarly, in 2019, activist Hadj Ghermoul was sentenced to six months in prison and fined for "offending public institutions" after a photo on Facebook was posted showing him holding a poster opposing a fifth term for former president Abdelaziz Bouteflika (*HuffPost Algérie* 2019). In short, when citizens criticize government officials or policies, or when they write something that is considered to exceed the limits set by the regime, they are liable to fines or arrest.

On March 4, 2019, a court in Skikda (East) reduced the prison sentence of blogger Merzoug Touati and released him. Touati was arrested and charged with "encouraging civil unrest." He was sentenced to ten years in prison in May 2018 after being convicted of providing "information to agents of a foreign power likely to harm Algeria's military or diplomatic position or its essential economic interests" (Netizen Report Team 2019). His release came as part of an ongoing protest movement in the country.

Like other countries in the Maghreb and the Arab world, "Algeria experienced a particular and unfinished episode in the controversial series of 'Arab Spring' revolts" (Merah 2016). Just like other countries of the region, Algeria was not spared by the "springizing" wave of 2011, in the expression of Bensaada (2019). Nevertheless, the "spring" did not have any impact on the Algerian population because of the painful memory of a certain black and bloody decade (1991–2002) that plunged the entire nation into mourning. However, the actors of the revolt were at work.

Many years after the "Arab uprisings," the Algerian regime showed remarkable stability and continuity. It adapted to new local, regional, and international realities. To preserve itself while managing demands for democratization, the regime opened the political arena, allowed greater freedom of association and expression, and (selectively) liberalized the economy while continuing to co-opt important and diverse interest groups and personalities and to use coercion to avoid social unrest (Ghanem 2017).

Faced with this situation, society did not give up, but adopted a culture of abstention already well established in the Algerian political landscape. In recent years, abstention from voting has become a constant feature of the country's elections: there was a 57.10% abstention rate for the 2012 legislative elections and 65% for the 2007 legislative elections (Ouchiha 2018). The boycott campaign of the 2017 parliamentary elections conducted on social media and particularly Facebook influenced the turnout in this election, which was historically very low (38.25%, according to the Algerian Ministry of the Interior).

Social media have given young people a virtual space to protest, and platforms like Facebook have become important safety valves to ease social pressure. Even if the Internet is not restricted, the state monitors Internet activity and electronic communications (Ghanem 2017). The use of cyberspace makes it possible to coordinate efforts, organize actions on the ground, share information, and transmit instructions so that demonstrations comply with the basic principles of nonviolent struggle.

In an atmosphere of multiple restrictions, opposition to the former president's fifth term, known as the "term of shame," undeniably became a common and open "text." Thanks to social networks, the indignation that had hitherto been silent or circumscribed became audible to as many people as possible, on a national scale. Avoiding the controlled environment of television and radio information, it spreads from one category to another, from one generation to another, from one city to another (Fabbiano 2019).

The instantaneous means of communication were extremely effective at the beginning of this movement, in the relay, if not the emulation, of events which themselves were often planned on the web. Since then, events have echoed, images and slogans have circulated almost instantaneously, and demonstrations have spread and responded, becoming more and more massive and more and more regular. By February 2019, not only Algiers and the main coastal cities (Oran, Bejaia, Annaba) were involved, but also Constantine, Touggourt, Adrar, Tiaret, Relizane, Tizi Ouzou, Bouira, and Sétif. Others, including Tlemcen, Skikda, Bordj Bou Arreridj, Tébessa, and Ghardaia, were mobilized over the next few days and actions were carried out there.

On Friday, February 22, 2019, millions of people from different social classes took to the streets in a momentous uprising, reappropriating a public space that had long been confiscated. The demonstrations were triggered by anonymous calls on the Internet, which snowballed across the country. They were peaceful ("peaceful" was one of the many songs that resonated in Algerian cities) and civilized, politically conscious and responsible. Mahdi Khelfaoui, a University of Ottawa researcher, argued that the people's anger took root in the stands of football stadiums. He noted that the songs of supporters "reflecting distress and oppression" were massively posted on social networks (Sideris 2019). Hasni Abidi, a professor at the University of Geneva, explained that "in a totally locked country, sports fields are the only places where young Algerians can meet and let off steam. For lack of space for democratic expression, they have become real political forums" (Gouëset 2019).

Calls to write songs, slogans, and signs, and to manage security, were circulating on social media, especially Facebook. Many feared that the regime would be tempted to send thugs to attack demonstrators or that it would order the police to cause chaos and smear the image of the peaceful protest movement (Ghanem 2019). Algeria had not seen such a broad, diversified, and widespread movement since 1962, when Algerians took to the streets to celebrate their hard-won independence from French colonial rule (Hamouchene 2019). The national and international press was full of praise for the political maturity of Algerian youth, their high sense of humor, and their exemplary organization.

The slogans and songs were funny, but sharp. The two emblematic slogans of this peaceful protest movement, "They must all go" and "The country is ours and we'll do what we want," symbolize the radical evolution of this popular movement that was triggered by the octogenarian president's announcement to run for a fifth term despite serious health problems. Other slogans were also present, such as "Proud to be Algerian" and "One hero, the people," which was an old revolutionary slogan. The demonstrators marched toward Algiers's landmark, the Grande Poste. Algerian flags were carried on shoulders and around necks. The crowd would sing a leader's name, such as "Bouteflika," "Ben Salah," or "Said," or the name of a party—"FLN," "RND"—and the answer would come back: "*Dégage!*" ("Get out!").

A cyberspace of political discourse is taking shape in Algeria, coinciding with widespread access to the Internet through 3G and then 4G technologies, the rise of social networks, and the massive use of smartphones. Fueled by the nascent energy of a mobile population, this discourse of cyberspace potentially has the capacity to influence Algeria's political trajectory and to question the legitimacy of the state.

Algeria has been through a lot, especially over the past three decades. The country has not yet grieved or healed from the trauma of the 1990s, triggered by the army's cancellation of the electoral process in 1992, which led to a brutal civil war, but Algerians have developed a keen sense of humor to laugh at themselves and their situation. Political experts and the media have long described Algerians as politically passive or unable to protest without violence (Souames 2019). This recent protest movement has shown the opposite. The demonstrations were extraordinarily well organized. Demonstrators avoided clashes with the police and even cleaned the streets after the protests.

However, this Algeria, which manifested in joy and communion for weeks, is not necessarily the one that was present in social media. Facebook and Twitter have become territories where no holds are barred in the anonymity of the pseudonym and the fake profile. While some debated on the basis of arguments and ideas, others used filthy language that had nothing to do with the serene debate required by the current political situation (Métaoui 2019). Political articles and videos cause a lot of irritation on social media, which is understandable in times of instability, but the least understandable kind of communication is abusive language and baseless criticism that targets everyone without any nuance, questioning, or restraint. Thus, the real society is more advanced and courageous than the virtual society in Algeria, aspiring to live together in plurality.

Certainly, it is obvious that the protests in Algeria would not have evolved in the same way without the Internet and Facebook, Twitter, YouTube, and other social media. But it is nevertheless necessary to qualify their impact somewhat, as an explanatory factor of the conditions of birth and functioning of the social movement. For several years now, major physical public spaces, such as sports competitions and the groups of supporters of the clubs concerned, have become privileged places of expression. On the other hand, within civil society, among others, a Mouwatana ("citizenship") citizen movement has appeared since June 2018, totally opposed to the political elite in power and systematically challenging the very foundations that have long ensured its legitimacy.

"Internet, Facebook, or Twitter, these words now serve as totems for a whole tribe of commentators who are discovering the democratic virtues of Arab peoples after those of the Internet," says Yves Gonzalez-Quijano (2011), ironically. It is true that the role of the Internet and social media should not be overestimated and must be put into proper perspective in order to understand the meaning of the protest movements in Algeria. These protests are not so much social media revolutions as they are revolutions in the age of social media. The nuance is not simply a language game, but a necessary relativization of the role of NICTs (new information and communication technologies) in social movements.

The precise evaluation of NICTs' role in the current protest cycle cannot be satisfied with a global discourse with exotic accents on the subversive charms of the "Arab web" (orientalism in the Internet age in a way) (Gonzalez-Quijano 2011). It is clear that the "success story" of social media in the Arab world, including Algeria, is a lesser factor than the symptom of the emergence of new forms of activism and, more deeply, of the relationship to authority (Gonzalez-Quijano 2011). As a result, their use is symptomatic of the crisis of centralized leadership modes, and of the top-down movements that characterized the sociopolitical mobilizations of previous decades. "The famous 'get out!' reflects a shift in the perception of power relations between rulers and governed" (Camau 2011, 27). The rapid breakthrough of social media and, in general, the Internet in the country is therefore less synonymous with the democratization of public space than with the fragmentation of authority, which, surprisingly, can contribute to creating a unitary dynamic in a context of protest emulation (Geisser 2012).

REFERENCES

Abderrahim, K. 2013. "Les problèmes d'accès à Internet en Algérie." *HuffPost Maghreb*, July 15, 2013.

Addi, L. 2011. "Le régime algérien après les révoltes arabes." *Mouvements* 2 (66): 89–97. https://www .cairn.info/revue-mouvements-2011-2-page-89.htm#xd_co_f=NzE2NjllMzktYmExOC00Y2ExLTg4 NDYtNDQxZTI5YzAzNTEz.

Agence Ecofin. 2018. "Algérie: l'ARPT a mué pour devenir l'ARPCE." *Osiris*, July 19, 2018. http:// www.osiris.sn/Algerie-l-ARPT-a-mue-pour-devenir.html.

Alilat, F., and S. Attia. 2019. "Bouteflika en Suisse: Quand les Algériens appellent l'hôpital où est soigné leur président." *Jeune Afrique*, March 5, 2019. https://www.jeuneafrique.com/745020/politique/ bouteflika-en-suisse-quand-les-algeriens-appellent-lhopital-ou-est-soigne-leur-president.

Amari, C. 2012. "En Algérie, l'Internet est encore à l'âge de pierre." *Slate Afrique*, September 11, 2012. http://www.slateafrique.com/94309/internet-et-communication-la-traine-alger.

Ammour, L.-A. 2012. "The Legislative Environment of the Algerian Civil Society." In *Governing the Public Sphere: Civil Society Regulation in North Africa*, edited by B. Moyo, 1–56. Dakar: Trustafrica. https://www.academia.edu/9589029/The_Legal_Environment_of_Civil_Society_in_Algeria_2012.

APC and Hivos. 2009. *Global Information Society Watch 2009*. Association for Progressive Communication (APC) and Humanist Institute for Cooperation with Developing Countries (Hivos). https:// giswatch.org/sites/default/files/algeria.pdf.

Azzouzi, H. 2019. "Abdenour Boussaba, Docteur en sciences de l'information et de la communication: Le marché de la publicité en ligne n'est pas encore mature." *El Watan*, January 2, 2019. https://www .elwatan.com/pages-hebdo/etudiant/abdenour-boussaba-docteur-en-sciences-de-linformation-et-de-la -communication-le-marche-de-la-publicite-en-ligne-nest-pas-encore-mature-02-01-2019.

Beji, I. 2016. "Chiffres clés de Facebook en Algérie." *MediaNet Blog*, October 25, 2016. http://blog .medianet.tn/blog/chiffres-cles-de-facebook-en-algerie-0.

Benali, A. 2017. "Publicité digitale en Algérie: Seulement 500 millions de dinars investis en 2016." *Algérie Eco*, June 6, 2017. https://www.algerie-eco.com/2017/06/06/publicite-digitale-algerie-500 -millions-de-dinars-investis-2016.

Benelkadi, K. 2018. "Entre liberté d'expression et abus réseaux sociaux: La controverse." *El Watan*, October 30, 2018. https://www.elwatan.com/a-la-une/entre-liberte-dexpression-et-abus-reseaux -sociaux-la-controverse-30-10-2018.

Bennadji, C. 2011. "Algérie 2010: L'année des mille et une émeutes." *L'Année du Maghreb* 7: 263–69. https://journals.openedition.org/anneemaghreb/1254.

Bensaada, A. 2019. "Huit ans après: La 'printanisation' de l'Algérie." *Mondialisation*, April 8, 2019. https://www.mondialisation.ca/huit-ans-apres-la-printanisation-de-lalgerie/5632556.

Bessadi, N. 2019. "Algerians riding a cyberspace wave." *Qantara*, March 27, 2019. https://en.qantara.de/ content/government-by-consensus-post-bouteflika-algerians-riding-a-cyberspace-wave?nopaging=1.

Bey, S. 2018. "La 3G et la 4G boostent l'internet en Algérie avec 31,460 millions d'abonnés." DIA (Dernières infos d'Algérie), April 24, 2018. http://dia-algerie.com/3g-4g-boostent-linternet-31-460 -millions-dabonnes.

Bichara, K. 2012. "Le 'printemps arabe': Un premier bilan." *Alternatives South* 19 (March 2012). https:// www.cetri.be/Le-printemps-arabe-un-premier-2644?lang=fr.

Boumarafi, B. 2015. "Social media use in Algerian universities: University of Constantine 2 case study." *IAFOR Journal of Education* 3 (SE): 31–41. https://files.eric.ed.gov/fulltext/EJ1100620.pdf.

Camau, M. 2011. "La disgrâce du chef: Mobilisations populaires arabes et crise du leadership." *Mouvements* 2011/2 (66): 22–29. https://www.cairn.info/revue-mouvements-2011-2-page-22.htm.

Casati, C. 2019. "When Algiers reminds Cairo." Fifth Estate, March 8, 2019. http://wpmu.mah.se/nmict 191group5/when-algiers-reminds-cairo/#.XNKNx44zY2w.

Cristiani, D. 2017. "Fears of a new Arab Spring: The Algerian riots in context." Jamestown Foundation, January 24, 2017. https://jamestown.org/program/hot-issue-fears-new-arab-spring-algerian-riots -context.

De Saint Perier, L. 2011. "Abdelwahab Meddeb: 'C'est surprenant qu'en Tunisie la révolution n'ait pas eu lieu plus tôt.'" *Jeune Afrique*, May 6, 2011. https://www.jeuneafrique.com/191893/politique/abdel wahab-meddeb-c-est-surprenant-qu-en-tunisie-la-r-volution-n-ait-pas-eu-lieu-plus-t-t.

ERCIM (European Research Consortium for Informatics and Mathematics). n.d. "Le développement d'Internet dans les pays méditerranéens et la coopération avec l'Union européenne." https://www .ercim.eu/publication/policy/Internet-med.pdf.

Fabbiano, G. 2019. "À l'écoute de l'Algérie insurgée." La Vie des idées, Collège de France, March 29, 2019. https://laviedesidees.fr/A-l-ecoute-de-l-Algerie-insurgee.html.

F. L. 2018. "Lutte contre la cybercriminalité: Le visible et l'invisible." *El Moudjahid*, June 30, 2018.

Freedom House. 2018. "Freedom in the World 2018: Algeria." Accessed March 23, 2019. https:// freedomhouse.org/country/algeria/freedom-world/2018.

Geisser, V. 2012. "Les protestations populaires à l'assaut des régimes autoritaires: Une 'révolution' pour les sciences sociales?" *L'Année du Maghreb* 8: 7–26. https://journals.openedition.org/ anneemaghreb/1373.

Ghanem, D. 2017. "The Algerian enigma." Carnegie Middle East Center, May 2, 2017. https://carnegie -mec.org/2017/05/02/algerian-enigma-pub-69845.

———. 2019. "A protest made in Algeria." Carnegie Middle East Center, April 2, 2019. https://carnegie -mec.org/2019/04/02/protest-made-in-algeria-pub-78748.

Gonzalez-Quijano, Y. 2011. "Les 'origines culturelles numériques' des révolutions arabes." *Le Monde*, March 22, 2011. https://halshs.archives-ouvertes.fr/halshs-00615005/document.

Gouëset, C. 2019. "En Algérie, l'étincelle de la contestation est née dans les stades de football." *L'Express*, March 3, 2019. https://www.lexpress.fr/actualite/monde/afrique/en-algerie-l-etincelle-de -la-contestation-est-nee-dans-les-stades-de-football_2065850.html.

Hamada, W. 2015. "L'Algérie est l'un des pays les moins rapides en matière de connexion internet." *HuffPost Maghreb*, February 16, 2015.

Hamadouche, L. D.-A. 2012. "L'Algérie face au 'printemps arabe': L'équilibre par la neutralisation des contestations." *Confluences Méditerranée* 2 (81): 55–67. https://www.cairn.info/revue-confluences -mediterranee-2012-2-page-55.htm.

Hammadi, S. 2018. "Luttes contre les violences sociales: Les réseaux sociaux, sources d'alerte." *Liberté*, August 6, 2018. https://www.liberte-algerie.com/actualite/les-reseaux-sociaux-sources-dalerte -297773.

Hamouchene, H. 2019. "Algeria in revolt: 'We woke up and you will pay!'" Open Democracy, April 12, 2019. https://www.opendemocracy.net/en/north-africa-west-asia/algeria-in-revolt-we-woke-up-and -you-will-pay.

HootSuite. 2019. *Digital 2019 Algeria*. January 2019. Retrieved from https://wearesocial.com/global -digital-report-2019.

HuffPost Algérie. 2019. "Hadj Ghermoul condamné à 6 mois de prison ferme pour 'outrage à corps constitué.'" *HuffPost Algérie*, February 2, 2019.

International Media Support. 2013. "Authoritarianism and media in Algeria." July 2013. https://www .mediasupport.org/wp-content/uploads/2013/07/authoritarianism-media-algeria-ims-20131.pdf.

IRIS. 2014. "Le baromètre 2013 des sociétés civiles: L'autre visage de la mondialisation." February 2014. https://ccfd-terresolidaire.org/IMG/pdf/barometre-des-societes-civiles.pdf.

ISP Today. 2019. "The telecommunications market in Algeria." Accessed March 13, 2019. https://isp .today/en/list-of-all-services/ALGERIA,telecommunications-market.

El-Issawi, F. 2017. "Algerian national media: Freedom at a cost." LSE Middle East Centre Report. http:// eprints.lse.ac.uk/69567/1/AlgerianNationalMedia.pdf.

Jahus. 2019. "Algérie: Telegram, ou comment contourner la censure." ObservAlgerie, March 18, 2019. Retrieved from https://www.observalgerie.com/actualite-algerie/algerie-telegram-comment -contourner-censure-internet.

Kherbachi, H., and N. Gani. 2016. "Déréglementation des télécommunications en Algérie: Evaluation de l'impact qualitatif basée sur la perception des utilisateurs." *Revue d'économie et de statistique appliquée* 25: 141–68. http://www.enssea.net/enssea/majalat/2511.pdf.

Kouaci, H. 2016. "Les réseaux sociaux en Algérie: Une adoption massive par les internautes et une grande opportunité pour les entreprises." *Revue des réformes économiques et intégration dans l'économie mondiale* 11 (22): 87–114. https://www.asjp.cerist.dz/en/article/10554.

Meddah, M. M. 2009. "WebDialn@ study of Algerian Internet users results." StartUpArabia, September 26, 2009. http://www.startuparabia.com/2009/09/webdialn-internet-study-of-algerian-internet -users/comment-page-1.

Merah, A. 2016. "Nouvelles formes de participation en ligne des jeunes en Algérie: Entre démarches stratégiques et impensées pour le changement." *REFSICOM* 2. http://www.refsicom.org/177.

Métaoui, F. 2019. "L'Algérie, pacifique et exemplaire dans la rue, agressive et vulgaire sur les réseaux sociaux." TSA, March 30, 2019. https://www.tsa-algerie.com/lalgerie-pacifique-et-exemplaire-dans -la-rue-agressive-et-vulgaire-sur-les-reseaux-sociaux.

Nabil. 2006. "Étude sur l'usage de l'internet en Algérie." N'tic Web, October 31, 2006. http://www .nticweb.com/it/210-etude-sur-lusage-de-linternet-en-algerie-.html.

Netizen Report Team. 2019. "Netizen report: Activists reject EU plans to pre-censor copyright violations, 'terrorist' content." Advox Global Voices, March 9, 2019. https://advox.globalvoices.org/2019/03/08/ netizen-report-activists-reject-eu-plans-to-pre-censor-copyright-violations-terrorist-content.

Nour, E. 2018. "Internet/L'Algérie à la 175e place dans le classement mondial du débit." Algérie Focus, July 22, 2018. https://www.algerie-focus.com/2018/07/internet-lalgerie-a-la-175e-place-dans -le-classement-mondial-du-debit.

ONS (Office national des statistiques). 2019. "Démographie." June 6, 2019. http://www.ons.dz/-Demog raphie-.html.

Ouchiha, T. 2018. "Les réseaux sociaux et la participation politique en Algérie." *Communication* 35 (2). https://journals.openedition.org/communication/8846.

Ramdani, N. 2011. "Algeria tried to block Internet and Facebook as protest mounted." *Telegraph*, February 11, 2011. https://www.telegraph.co.uk/news/worldnews/africaandindianocean/algeria/8320772/ Algeria-tried-to-block-internet-and-Facebook-as-protest-mounted.html.

Rek, K. 2018. "Débit Internet: l'Algérie deuxième pire pays du monde." ObservAlgerie, December 10, 2018. https://www.observalgerie.com/actualite-algerie/debit-internet-lalgerie-deuxieme-pire-pays-du -monde.

Renaud, P. 2007. "Internet au Maghreb et au Machrek: De la 'recherche et développement' à l'appropriation sociale." In *Le Maghreb dans l'économie numérique*, edited by M. Mezouaghi, 55–70. Tunis: Institut de recherche sur le Maghreb contemporain. https://books.openedition.org/ irmc/374?lang=en.

Saadi, Y. 2018. "Publicité sur Internet: Google AdWords fait ses premiers pas en Algérie." *HuffPost Maghreb*, October 5, 2018.

Saidoun, N. 2017. "La qualité réseau des trois opérateurs testée pour vous." *Liberté*, September 24, 2017. https://www.liberte-algerie.com/actualite/la-qualite-reseau-des-trois-operateurs-testee-pour -vous-277926.

Salem, F. 2017. *Social Media and the Internet of Things*. Seventh Arab Social Media Report 2017. Dubai: Mohammed Bin Rashid School of Government. https://www.mbrsg.ae/getattachment/1383b88a-6eb9 -476a-bae4-61903688099b/Arab-Social-Media-Report-2017.

Sideris, F. 2019. "Manifestations en Algérie: Les réseaux sociaux au cœur de la contestation." LCI, March 3, 2019. https://www.lci.fr/international/manifestations-en-algerie-contre-le-5e-mandat -d-abdelaziz-bouteflika-les-reseaux-sociaux-au-coeur-de-la-contestation-facebook-youtube-twitter -2114983.html.

Souames, F. 2019. "Indignity and solidarity are being televised in Algeria." *Africa Is a Country*, April 3, 2019. https://africasacountry.com/2019/03/indignity-and-solidarity-are-being-televised-in-algeria.

U.S. State Department. 2014. *Algeria 2013 Human Rights Report*. April 14, 2014. https://www.justice .gov/sites/default/files/eoir/legacy/2014/04/09/Algeria.pdf.

V

MAJOR MOVES
Convergence, Globalization, and Technological Change

12

Digital Disruptions in Traditional Arab Media Industries

An Analysis of Key Sectors Impacted by the Communications Transitions

Mohammad Ayish

Since their independence from European colonial rule, Arab states have always seen the media as central drivers of socioeconomic and cultural development. During the three postcolonial decades, media development in the Arab world was often high on national agendas, leading to the launch of nationwide state broadcasting services and the expansion of press institutions with mixed ownership features. Successive Arab governments invested hugely in building up national media capacities in order to keep their publics informed about socioeconomic development. In mostly authoritarian Arab countries, the media were viewed as a credible tool of political legitimization and cultural assertiveness that warranted such massive support. While state subsidies were instrumental in keeping government-owned and -operated Arab media afloat, private publications were always struggling under varying economic constraints defined by both limited advertising and readership. In the Gulf region in particular, economic prosperity, as induced by rising oil prices, has positively reflected on media economics, giving rise to advanced media infrastructures and high employee incentives.

By the end of the 1980s, every Arab country had at least one land-based TV channel, several radio stations, and a range of print media publications. Across the region, the undeclared missions of national media systems may be summarized as follows: to support leadership decisions and policies, promote state ideologies, communicate developmental achievements to national audiences, engage populations with state-initiated projects, foster cultural identity and affiliation, and raise public awareness of issues relating to health, education, and the environment. All media activities were regulated through press and publication legislation, broadcast policies, and general communication guidelines.

In the early years of the 1990s in the Arab world, it was clear that the above-described mass media systems were showing signs of serious ruptures not only in their regulatory regimes, but also in their missions, functions, and relations with publics. In the emerging age of satellite television and the web, it became extremely difficult for states to maintain total media monopolies in a digital environment of limitless media choices, empowered audiences, and transnational mobile-enabled communications. For media organizations, declining advertising dollars, changing work practices, rising competition, and digital migration of their audiences seem to have generated critical existential threats. Practitioners also had to grapple in significant ways with issues relating to their roles as professional communicators in a new working environment marked by multitasked assignments, digitally based tools, more sophisticated workflows, and more symmetrical relations with audiences. Arab audiences, as key stakeholders in the media industry, viewed the digital revolution as a huge opportunity to tap into for greater access, empowerment, and social impact. For advertisers, the choices seemed equally challenging, with uncertainty surrounding the online/digital sphere in terms of Internet penetration, computer and mobile proliferation, and, far more important, quality content that sells.

As the Arab world continues to embrace digitization in all sectors (including communications), this chapter aims to discuss how the region's traditional media systems are faring under a range of digital disruptive innovations that are critically detrimental to their existence. In this chapter, "disruptive innovation" is defined as an innovation that "creates a new market and value network and eventually disrupts an existing market and value network, displacing established market-leading firms, products, and alliances" (Airini et al. 2017). Areas impacted by digital disruptions in the region include state monopoly and control, finances, organizational structures and professional roles, media education, and relations with publics.

DISRUPTIVE INNOVATION THEORY

Christensen's notion of disruption (1997) has informed much of our thinking of how technological innovations are redefining the concept and practice of business in a range of industries, including media. His theory was originally applied to shifting corporate management practices in the context of information technology innovations. As conceived by Christensen, technology denotes "the processes by which an organization transforms labor, capital, materials, and information into products and services of greater value" (9).

In his seminal work *The Innovator's Dilemma*, Christensen describes how large, successful organizations were toppled by much smaller startups, despite adopting sound management practices. He observed that products based on disruptive technologies are typically cheaper, simpler, smaller, and, frequently, more convenient to use. Examples he used to support his thesis of technological disruption included the personal desktop computer, discount retailing, and off-road motorcycles introduced by Honda, Kawasaki, and Yamaha. In the motorcycle examples, Christensen conceived of the disruptive impact of those machines relative to the powerful, over-the-road cycles made by Harley-Davidson and BMW. The dilemma of innovators, according to Christensen, derives from three key factors: the distinction between sustaining and disruptive technologies, the observation that technologies can progress faster than market demand, and the conclusion by established companies that investing aggressively in disruptive technologies is not a rational financial decision for them to make (Christensen 1997, 10–12).

The disruptive impact of digital and cyberspace technologies on traditional media structures and practices has always fueled discussions of the future of mass communications. The basic tenets of such debates have generally been based on the shifting paradigm of mass communications as based on one-way flow of information, static content, and a highly passive audience. In the declining mass media age, the all-powerful media theory metaphorically spoke of media messages as bullets or hypodermic needles with immediate and direct effects. Audiences were seen as highly vulnerable subjects who could be easily manipulated (McQuail 2013).

In the late 1930s, the limited-media-effects paradigm was gaining popularity in the context of Paul Lazarsfeld's research on the 1940 presidential election that revealed the limited power of media to affect public opinion (McQuail 2013). Further shifts in the communication paradigm were noted in the 1970s and 1980s with the rise of the moderate-effects perspective that accounted for numerous socioeconomic and psychological mediating factors in defining media effects. McQuail (2013) noted that by the end of the twentieth century, public communication was being better represented by a new paradigm, although no single name has been coined. He observed that nearly all the features highlighted by the idea of mass communication "have been modified or reversed" (218). In the area of networked communications, McQuail views open access to the Internet as a driver of a myriad of new entrants as communicators who have published personal weblogs, along with a range of other possible motivations.

The emerging digital mediascape has been characterized as manifestly transnational, highly interactive, and more multi-mediated and individualized, with hugely empowered users who no longer are referred to as audiences. The promise of the Internet as a new frontier of more free and symmetrical communications accessible to all has sparked high hopes on the part of communities, corporations, and governments for greater empowerment to advance social, commercial, political, and personal goals. In the emerging digital era, it is knowledge companies such as Google, Facebook, Apple, and Microsoft that seem to define the scope and substance of the new business models. According to a KPMG Industry Innovation Survey (KPMG 2019, 1), global tech industry leaders ranked social networking as the second-most-disruptive business model after e-commerce. Results from KPMG 2019 global surveys show over three billion people around the world were using social media on mobile devices, with an annual 10% increase expected in the coming years. Further research done by the Boston Consulting Group (2018, 13) noted that social media's five-year annual total shareholder returns (TSR) of 28% surpassed that of a host of more traditional segments, including movie studios (17%), publishing (16%), advertising (15%), and broadcast TV, cable, and satellite (10%). The report noted that these numbers reflected the continued and growing dominance of Facebook, Alphabet, Amazon, and Netflix.

The rise of the smartphone as the prime web access point has been a major feature of ongoing media disruptions. Research findings around the world show mobile phones outperforming desktop and laptop computers and tablets in accessing online information and engaging in social space. The Reuters Institute for the Study of Journalism Digital Report (Newman et al. 2016) noted three trends in digital news industries: the growth of distributed (offsite) news consumption, a sharpening move to mobile, and rising ad-blocking practices worldwide. These three trends in combination are putting further severe pressure on the business models of traditional publishers and new digital-born players—as well as changing the way in which news is packaged and distributed (7). In a study of twenty-six countries in North America and Europe, the report noted that smartphone usage for news is sharply up, reaching half of our global sample (53%), while computer use is falling and tablet growth is flattening out. The report also observed that the biggest change in digital media has been the growth of news accessed via social media sites like Facebook, Twitter, Instagram, and Snapchat. In the United States, for example, the percentage of people saying they use social media as a source of news has risen to 46% of the sample—almost doubling since 2013 (9).

A significant feature of media industries affected by digital disruptions has been the business model. In its basic configuration, a business model is defined as a high-level plan for profitably operating a particular business in a specific marketplace (Kopp 2019). Peckham (2018) identifies five overarching business models relevant to media industries: transactions (buy to own/unlock), subscriptions, licensing, content marketing, and advertising. ESCWA (2013) reports additional content-creation business models such as brokerage (bringing buyers and sellers together), infomediary (information intermediaries), utility, and community.

Traditionally, business models in Western media industries were limited to advertising, sponsorship, subscriptions, and license fees (for TV). In the United States, advertising has been the driver of the media's financial survival, with television maintaining the lion's share of revenue. In some countries such as the United Kingdom, a fee is levied on TV sets to support the BBC budget, while sponsorships from corporate and non-corporate bodies for media content remain a key source of income. In countries with dominant government control over media operations, state financing and subsidization of media activities represent a distinct model of media economics.

The same ESCWA report notes several factors contributing to the rise of business models in content creation. They include infrastructure and cloud, online utilities, social networks, and mobility. In significant ways, the digital revolution has created a rupture in those business models, with continuing shifts toward digital advertising, individualized communications, value-added innovation, and social analytics. The entry of new players into the media market with a subscription business model, such as Netflix and Spotify, in addition to the integration of digital advertising into the major social networking platforms, has created a major transition in the traditional business models. The cases of Amazon and the Apple and Play stores present striking examples of the depth and scope of change taking place in media business models.

THE ARAB WORLD'S DIGITAL/ONLINE MEDIASCAPE

It is clear that the digital communications revolution of the 1990s triggered successive waves of disruption in the MENA region's mass media industries. As previously mentioned, satellite television was the earliest disruptor of state-controlled broadcasting, which for decades had defined the region's radio and television arena. By the end of 2019, over 1,500 free-to-air satellite TV channels were operating on numerous satellite systems such as ARABSAT and NILESAT, carrying a wide array of channels with national and international affiliations. The main seismic effects, however, were coming from the digital web and social media transitions, which not only revolutionized our communication style and format, but also empowered private individuals on the social, cultural, political, and economic frontiers.

The mobile boom and an accelerating Internet penetration have been the key drivers of the digital revolution. Radcliffe et al. (2019) provide updated statistics on social media proliferation in the Arab world that show Facebook enjoying 164 million active monthly users, up from 56 million just five years earlier. Egypt remains the biggest national market for Facebook in the region, with 24 million daily users and nearly 37 million monthly mobile users. While less than 30% of Twitter users in MENA post original content, there are about 12 million daily users of Snapchat in the GCC region. The number of YouTube channels in MENA rose by 160% between 2017 and 2020, with more than 200 YouTube channels in the region having over one million subscribers and over 30,000 channels having more than 10,000 subscribers. In the Arab World Online report issued by the Mohammed Bin Rashid School of Government (Salem 2017), growth in the Arab world's digital landscape between 2010 and 2020 included 40.7% in mobile subscriptions, 148.9% in Internet users, 308.7% in fixed broadband, 886.4% in Internet of things (IoT) devices, 1132.9% in mobile broadband, and 1373.2% in social media usage.

The MENA region's digital social revolution is presenting traditional media with both opportunities and challenges as they struggle to enhance engagement with their audience (Ayish and Mellor 2015). While a social/online media-rich MENA region would beef up traditional media engagement with audiences, it also constitutes a viable communication alternative for the millions of people disenchanted with state-controlled media. In this chapter, I argue that the majority of MENA media seem to see emerging social/online outlets more as supportive tools rather than as rivals. All traditional media organizations have thus chosen to maintain their existing functionality and business models while drawing on digital/social tools to expand their reach and optimize engagement with audiences. This has been most conspicuous in their own websites/portals and social media accounts on different platforms.

Ayish and Mellor (2015) analyzed social media practices in ten pan-Arab media organizations and found substantive social integrations in their operations. It was noted that media practitioners in those organizations are also involved in the social sphere. Some of those organizations have established their own social media departments to coordinate communications with audiences in social space and to divert social traffic to their websites. Interviews with practitioners in those organizations revealed a profound belief in the power of social media to enhance traditional media work and bolster their competitive standing in the public sphere. By creating a virtual structure to support physical operations, media organizations are hybridizing their work practices and outputs to account for new audiences with clear online engagement.

The convergence of young demographics and social media has been a key feature of the digital disruptions in the MENA region's communications. A number of research works have demonstrated a growing number of Arab millennials strongly engaging with social media as user-generated content creators, social influencers, and professional startup entrepreneurs. According to one report (Booz & Co. 2013), an Arab digital generation (ADG) is emerging with a strong attachment to digital mediascapes. The report notes that advances in information and communications technology (ICT) are shaping ADGs, who use digital technology to socialize with their friends, to browse online for products and services, and to upload YouTube videos to express themselves, voice their social and political beliefs, and broadcast local events for the entire world to watch (4).

The 2018 Arab Youth Survey revealed that almost two-thirds (63%) of Arab youth look first to Facebook and Twitter for news. More widely, nearly half of young Arabs (49%) say they get their news on Facebook daily, up from 35% the previous year, and 61% of Arab youth say they use Facebook more frequently than a year ago (ASDA'A-BCW 2018). The 2019 Youth Survey shows Arab youth calling for religious reforms in the region (ASAA'A-BCW 2019). Al Shoaibi (2018, 11) notes that social media are acting as the harbinger of change. With a majority of the Middle Eastern population consisting of younger people, technology and social networking sites have quickly gained influence on the accessibility and sharing of information.

HOW DIGITAL DISRUPTIONS IMPACTED ARAB WORLD MEDIA INDUSTRIES

It is unfair to claim that the digital communications revolution took traditional Arab media industries by surprise. By the late 1990s, the magnitude of digital technology–induced change was clear to all media stakeholders in the region; however, transition into the emerging landscape was highly problematic, as it implied sweeping revamps of all structures, work practices, content formats, delivery methods, finances, and consumption patterns. More importantly, the uncertainty surrounding the emerging digital environment did much to restrain faster transitions. But as digital/online technologies came to prove themselves as effective platforms for doing business, learning, communicating, marketing, and socializing, it became increasingly impossible to imagine doing business as usual without grappling with these ongoing disruptions. This section will identify the challenges presented by digital disruptions and how different stakeholders met them.

State Monopoly over National Communications

In the traditional mass media environment, Arab states exercised full control over communication flows within their national frontiers. Land-based television from neighboring countries barely reached populated areas, and hostile foreign radio transmissions were often subject to jamming. Publications such as books, newspapers, and magazines were also subject to censorship if their content was perceived to be harmful. Press and publication laws and broadcast policies were enforced to ensure all messages were complying with state policies.

In most of the Arab countries, ministries of information were entrusted with enforcing censorship regulations and journalists' licensure. By law, broadcasting was limited to the state, and licensure was required for all publications. Of course, the strictness of state controls varied across the region, and some countries with diverse press systems, such as Lebanon and Kuwait (Rugh 1979), enjoyed considerable freedom in their print publications. In broadcasting, all Arab countries, with the slight exception of Lebanon, had state-controlled radio and television services that were envisioned as voices of the nation's political outlook and cultural identity. As Ayish (2002) noted, broadcasting was viewed as too sacred to be left to private-sector actors. In most Arab countries, chief editors and media leaders were appointed by governments to ensure full compliance with existing regulations.

With the advent of satellite television and the web, Arab states lost much of their traditional control over communications. Digital developments in satellite broadcasting enabled high-quality regional transmission of hundreds of television channels with wide-ranging contents that were not always compatible with existing state policies and orientations. Free-to-air television in the Arab states increased its audiences' exposure to more competitive Western-style television content in news and public affairs, entertainment, sports, and other subjects. The states were completely unable to take action against possibly hostile programming that might negatively affect public opinion. It is true that the Arab States Broadcasting Union has issued a code of ethics regarding the use of ARABSAT by member states, but no country seems to comply when tensions arise with another country in the region.

On the web frontier, state loss of control seems to be far greater than in the satellite television broadcasting arena. Thanks to the Internet's convenience of access and information sharing, the problems facing governments in the region have become more complicated, as seen in the so-called Arab Spring upheavals of 2011. Recent advances in social networking have made it possible to integrate artificial intelligence features into social media communications that promote fake news and the spread of rumors. The immediate and global reach of social media sharing has made it difficult to exercise any control over information flows or to contain their effects. In recent years, inter-state tensions in the Arab world have generated huge spouts of hate speech, warmongering, sectarian incitement, and character assassination that served to aggravate conflicts.

To deal with their declining control over communications in the disruptive cyberspace environment, Arab states have passed cybercrime laws that apply to online forms of misconduct. Cyber legislation has surfaced in countries such as Saudi Arabia, Egypt, Jordan, Kuwait, and the United Arab Emirates. Although those laws diverge on some issues relating to online communications, they seem to target common violations relating to state security, privacy, financial practices, cyberbullying, and copyright. Over the past few years, some countries in the region have prosecuted citizens under those laws for violations ranging from insulting the state to hacking computer systems to invading other people's privacy to carrying out cyber extortion and bullying. Penalties imposed on convicted persons range from imprisonment to hefty fines. Arab states have also been proactive in the online fight by tracking criminals through collaboration with some international authorities such as the Virtual Global Taskforce.

Media Finances

Another critical area of digital disruption in Arab media industries relates to their finances. Traditionally, media economics in the Arab region has been defined by state finances (for government-owned newspapers and broadcasting services), state subsidies for nongovernmental publications, and political party support for affiliated publications. Advertising has been a key source of media financing in countries with commercial media interests as well as those with affluent populations, such as the Gulf region. Another source of funding has been subscription by readers.

Advertising spending has been a key factor of economic survival for many Arab media. A 2016 study from Northwestern University–Qatar on Arab media industries (NU-Q 2016, 12) reported that the size of the advertising market in the Arab region in the 1990s, at the beginning of the digital revolution, was approximately US\$5.5 billion, with television and newspapers as the most important advertising platforms. In fact, television and online advertising have grown—the former at a much lower level than the latter. Newspapers have lost market share but remain the most important platform for national advertising, often paid for by governments and other noncommercial organizations. The study also found that pan-Arab advertising has increased significantly since 2015. Most advertising agencies are located in Egypt and the UAE. While the subscription business model represents only a negligible portion of traditional Arab print media, it too seems to have taken a hard beating in recent years. Arab youth, who constitute 65% of the region's population, are turning to social media for news and entertainment more than ever.

But as TV and newspapers continue to dominate the Arab world market, digital and mobile advertising seems to be on the rise. Market research estimates put the digital and mobile advertising market size at \$3.1 billion in 2016, with agencies such as AdFalcon, Plu7.me, MAddict, InTarget, AdZouk, MENA Marketplace, and Eronat Online Media taking the lead on this front (Thalamus 2018). Though it is difficult to make any statement about the actual digital/mobile advertising market as of 2020, it is clear that social media platforms and knowledge companies are working hard to enhance the monetization potential of the Arab market. Efforts to tap the region's digital/mobile resources started immediately after the so-called Arab Spring, based on compelling evidence of rising public engagement with social media networks.

Curely (2013) reported that YouTube opened its Partner Program in Egypt, the United Arab Emirates, and Saudi Arabia to enable casual users to monetize their YouTube streams by adding in-video or pre-video advertisements. In 2018, Facebook introduced ad breaks in the UAE, Saudi Arabia, and Jordan to allow publishers and creators from the region to monetize the video content they share on Facebook (Mahmud 2018). Whenever an ad break is shown, the publisher or creator earns a share of the resulting ad revenue. A significant aspect of online/digital advertising is social influencer marketing, where advertisers find sales through publishers like social media stars and bloggers. In the United Arab Emirates, this profit-making feature of social influencer engagement has prompted a new law that requires their licensure.

Digital disruptions in the Arab region have already begun to reflect on the region's conventional media operations, especially those in the print sector. Changing demographics seem to have converged with digital technologies and liberal market economics to bring about significant changes in the media landscape. Generally speaking, digital disruptions have been manifested in the media sector in three ways: media extinction, media survival through hybridization, and media birth. Media extinction refers to the weakening or disappearance of conventional media organizations because of inadequate finances resulting from dwindling advertising or subsidies. Examples of this process include *al-Hayat* newspaper, *al-Safir* newspaper, and al-Moustaqbal TV channel. Media survival through hybridization refers to media being kept afloat by merging with the online environment while retaining conventional business models based on advertising, state subsidies, or subscriptions. The hybridization trend, embraced by the majority of conventional mass media organizations, involves an extension of operations into virtual space to expand their reach and enhance their engagement with audiences (Ayish 2016). Media birth refers to the creation of new media outlets that are digitally native and function entirely in an online environment. Examples include media websites such as Elaph and Erem news, Mada Masr, 7hbr, and Daraj.

Shifting patterns of media usage in the region provide good evidence of the changing face of media. The expansion of online and on-demand media subscriptions in the Arab region has marked a drastic shift from the traditional free-to-air access to TV entertainment and radio broadcasts. Historically, the region's entertainment landscape was generally limited to cinema, radio, and television. But the advent of the Internet and digital communications has brought about new methods of delivering and consuming entertainment. They include video on demand, subscription television, video streaming services, and open video access. Music has also been hugely affected by the digital revolution, with the entry of international music streaming services such as Spotify Arabia. Netflix, the U.S.-based film streaming service, has also been a major player in cinema entertainment in the region. On-demand TV and video are delivered mainly by telecommunications services such as Etisalat (UAE) and Zain (Kuwait, Jordan, and Saudi Arabia).

According to a study from Northwestern University–Qatar on entertainment in the Arab region (NU-Q 2014, 23), half of the respondents were likely to stream or download at least one form of content (49%), ranging from 23% for television shows to 35% for video games. Internet users in the Arab region are more likely to pay for video games, films, and sports events online (35%, 33%, and 31% respectively) and less likely to pay for music and television series (28% and 23% respectively). In its 2018 media use study, Northwestern University–Qatar found that more Arab nationals are paying for online media content. More people in 2018 than in 2016 said they paid for online music, sports, or film content in the past year, though the figures for each are below 10%. The study also found that the percentage of Arab nationals who said they watched TV content on an actual television in the past six months dropped to 81% from 89% in 2016. However, the share of people who had watched TV content on a phone in the last six months rose to 13% from 4% in the same period (NU-Q 2018).

Television remains the most popular medium in the geographical area covered in the 2018 NU-Q media study. Virtually every household watches TV. Typically, adults spend just over three hours a day in front of a television. The Internet is a close second, though, with Internet users spending just under three hours a day online at home. The study notes that Internet use is ubiquitous in the Gulf, even rivaling TV in those states, but lags far behind in Egypt and Jordan. It also notes that the generation gap in Internet use is wide, with 82% of people under the age of 25 using the Internet, compared to only 37% of those over 45.

Media Organizational Structures and the Role of Practitioners

Convergence has been a key feature of the digital disruptions in the Arab media scene. As media organizations partially migrate to online environments, they tend to readjust their structures and functions and prioritize their development needs. The United Arab Emirates presents the clearest case of media convergence, with media organizations arranging their operations around one centralized hub that manages multiple types of media content and format.

Under Abu Dhabi Media (https://www.admedia.ae/ar) there are four major publications: *al-Ittihad* newspaper, *Zahrat al-Khaleej* magazine, *Majid* magazine for children, and *National Geographic al-Arabeya* magazine. TV channels include al-Emarat TV, Abu Dhabi TV, Abu Dhabi Sports 1, Abu Dhabi Sports 2, Yas, Majid TV, National Geographic Abu Dhabi, and Abu Dhabi Drama. Radio stations include Quran Karim, Emarat FM, Abu Dhabi FM, Star FM, Abu Dhabi Classic FM, Radio Mirchi, Radio 1, and Radio 2. Digital media platforms include Ana Zahra (https://www.admedia.ae/en/DigitalMedia/2/anaZahra), Zayed Digital TV (https://www.admedia.ae/en/DigitalMedia/10/Zayed-Digital-TV), and Mohtawa (https://www.admedia.ae/en/DigitalMedia/11/Mohtawa).

Dubai Media Incorporated (http://www.dmi.gov.ae/content/corporate/en-ae/home.html) is an umbrella organization housing a range of outlets that include five television channels, two newspapers, five radio stations, two online outlets, and two printing and distribution services. In 2019, Dubai was declared Media Capital of the Arab World in recognition of its role as a regional and global media center. The Sharjah Media Corporation also houses four TV channels, four radio stations, and one online news service. UAE-based media free zones also apply convergence practices, as they operate in highly advanced networked and digital communications infrastructures.

Business models have also been shaped by the digital transition, as evident in the rise of media free zones across the region. Jordan and Egypt have media zones that host media organizations with multiple functions catering to a wide range of clients in video production, advertising, publishing, print newspapers, digital marketing, and TV broadcasting. But the biggest example of media free zones is in the United Arab Emirates, which houses at least five of them. By June 2019, there were about 1,500 companies with over 25,000 workers from 142 nationalities operating from Dubai Media City, which was launched in January 2001. Two-Four54, an Abu Dhabi–based media free zone, aims to cultivate Abu Dhabi's media free zone and provide products and services to attract local, regional, and international media businesses to Abu Dhabi. SHAMS, Sharjah's media free zone, was launched in 2017 to attract small and medium-sized businesses (SMEs), entrepreneurs, and larger companies to start and grow their businesses in a world-class, innovative, and creative Free Zone Hub in Sharjah. Other media facilities include Dubai Production City, Dubai Studio City, Ajman Media Free Zone, Fujairah Creative City, and RAK Media City.

International media organizations such as CNN International, Bloomberg, Reuters, Middle East Broadcasting Center Network, Sky News Arabia, Al-Arabiya TV Network, and many others carry out their operations from UAE media free zones, attracted by unique business opportunities. Dubai Media City, for example, offers media investors 100% foreign ownership, full repatriation of profits and capital, a fifty-year exemption from personal income and corporate taxes, exemption from customs duty for goods and services, world-class infrastructure to help support the growth of the cluster, and a twenty-four-hour visa service.

The changing face of the Arab region's media has also affected the practitioners' roles and functions. The traditional divisions of labor are becoming blurred as journalists and media staff in general are expected to perform tasks beyond their normal roles. In the age of online, mobile, and digital transitions, it has become quite difficult to maintain single-task assignments for writers, photographers, videographers, editors, translators, producers, directors, designers, and presenters. Digital media convergence has also brought with it new skill sets to support content creation in the form of text, audio, video, infographics, animation, and others. As media organizations in the Arab region move closer to the digital/online frontiers, their need for a digitally enabled workforce has never been more critical. Across the region, traditional print and broadcast organizations have initiated digital capacity-building programs to enable a smooth transition into the new digital era. In many respects, Google's News Initiative in the Arab region has helped to provide journalists with key digital skills in content creation, fact checking, and social analytics. In some organizations, layoffs were necessary. The need for multitasking practitioners with comprehensive, up-to-date digital competencies is now conspicuous in job advertisements.

Media Education Programs

Just as the digital communications revolution has impacted media industries at the organizational and professional levels, it has changed the face of media education across the Arab region, albeit slowly. Universities in the Arab world have become aware of a widening gap between what students learn in the classroom and what practitioners do in the professional field. At the end of the 1990s, most universities in the Arab world were offering media education based on old conceptions and practices that depended on analog technologies, propaganda studies, the idea of a passive audience, single-task media assignments, and—far more important—less exposure to liberal arts education. A survey of media education programs at Arab universities found concentrations in print journalism, broadcasting, and public relations dominating the curricula.

Though it was possible in the late 1990s to see some courses in online journalism and multimedia, most universities were slow to pick up on the digital transformation. But by 2017, the digital face of media education in the Arab world became brighter, with more programs offering training in digital tools and practices. Ayish (2019) noted that state universities in the Arab world continued to maintain some of the old curriculum features, but have also been open to digital developments. The introduction of international media education models and accreditation features, such as those introduced by UNESCO and the U.S.-based Accrediting Council for Education in Journalism and Mass Communication, has helped to accelerate the digital transformation in curricular contents across the region.

Audience Relations

As elsewhere, audiences in the traditional Arab media environment were viewed as helpless and passive subjects who were vulnerable to media manipulations and effects. For many years, the Arab region was the battleground for a fierce psychological warfare that involved nations from the region and beyond. As noted earlier, it was quite possible for states to control media flows within their national boundaries through strict censorship and radio jamming systems to undermine potential impacts on public opinion in their nations.

With the arrival of satellite television in the region in the early 1990s, audiences were the prime beneficiaries of this technological development, as they obtained access to literally hundreds of TV outlets with a wide range of perspectives and contents. The expansion of choices led people to take a more critical look at the ideas offered by their national state broadcasters.

They were exposed to social, cultural, and political views and perspectives that were not necessarily congruent with those promoted by their governments. The rise of political talk shows and Western-style drama underscored the need for greater diversity and artistic talent in order for the region to move forward in its development.

But while satellite television expanded choices and allowed exposure to diverse formats and perspectives, Arab audiences were still viewed in terms of the same passive model that had characterized mass communications in the twentieth century. It was the introduction of the Internet, social media, and the mobile phone that transformed the concept and role of the audience. In the online/digital/mobile environment, Arabs were no longer passive audiences targeted by media messages. They turned into active users who are able to communicate and express their views to a global audience in the channels and formats of their choice.

The notion of citizen journalism came into vogue in the region during and after the so-called Arab Spring upheavals. Arab citizens wanted to tell their own stories that mainstream media were not willing to carry. Their voices were becoming louder and their role in defining public conversations was becoming more powerful. The recent upheavals in Iraq, Lebanon, and Sudan spoke to an empowered media activism that is capable of making a difference in people's efforts to support justice and freedom. There is no reason to think that social media trigger social upheavals, but there is a strong reason to believe that social media and cyber communications are powerful tools of coordination and communication in times of crisis.

The emergence of a digitally empowered citizenry in the region has presented media organizations with serious challenges. Media outlets, whether government or private, are no longer the sole sources of information about national and international issues and events. Arabs, especially youth, with a mobile phone and Internet connectivity are now able to access and engage with knowledge online from a limitless number of media outlets. Research has shown that there are more social media users than newspaper readers in the region, and this trend is continuing. This disruption in how audiences relate to traditional media has been costly not only in advertising terms, but also in moral, political, social, and cultural terms. With an expanding digital/online media landscape in the region, it has become difficult to speak of a mass media effect on a public opinion that is continually shaped by digital spaces. Instead, the media need to approach audiences in a way based more on engagement than on manipulation. The opening up of media spaces for user engagement in the form of comments and sharing suggests more symmetrical relations with the public, based on respect, fairness, and responsibility.

CONCLUSION

It is clear that the face of mass communication in the Arab world, as we knew it in the mid-1990s, is constantly changing, thanks to innovations in digital and mobile technology. As elsewhere around the world, this transformation is a critical disruption not only of conventional practices, structures, and tools, but also of a long-standing mindset about media as a powerful force that can be harnessed to bring about state-desired results. The scale of disruption has had different implications for different stakeholders, who found themselves with no choice but to see transitions as opportunities to capitalize on. While digital disruptions deprived states of their ability to control the flow of communication, and thus to control public opinion within their national frontiers, they have also offered those same states greater opportunities to expand communications and exercise control. By the same token, while digital media disruptions have caused enduring fractures in media practices and structures, they have also presented opportunities to enhance communications and engagements in cyberspace.

In significant ways, digital disruptions have induced media organizations to be more innovative by considering alternative models for monetization, management, and professional practice. Advertisers in the region, prompted by digital expertise from outside the region, are paying more attention to cyberspace as the new marketing frontier, especially in view of shifting demographic and economic priorities. Arab citizens themselves have found empowerment in digital disruptions by freeing themselves from the bondage of a strictly controlled mass media system with limited choices and low-quality content. They are now able to share views and contest government stories, in addition to creating innovative online projects of their own. Finally, media education programs have revised their offerings to meet the changing demands of a digital market.

But it would be wrong to view digital disruptions in the Arab region as a total boon. As much as those transitions have generated opportunities for larger, freer, more global, more interactive, and faster communications, they have also presented states and societies in the region with challenges. Limited Internet penetration across the region, strict cybercrime regulations, the uncertainty of monetization, and the huge lack of digital literacy all make the transition painful. It is true that cybercrime laws are necessary to check online violations such as privacy invasions, cyberbullying, fake news circulation, extortion, and financial abuses, but their sweeping application to all types of online conduct could have a chilling effect on the future of the web as a democratic public sphere. The availability of Internet services across the region shows critical gaps, with over 75% of Arab populations still lacking online access. If the region is unable to bring cyberspace within its citizens' reach, radio broadcasting and satellite television using conventional transmission systems would be the next-best choices. By the same token, if advertisers are not yet convinced of the value of digital/online media as marketing tools, any advances toward the digital frontiers will be slow. And finally, if media organizations lack vision for how they should evolve in the short term within continuing disruptions, their ability to survive will be highly compromised. The key to weaving all those threads into a coherent framework of transition is a media strategy that sees digital disruptions as technologically deterministic, and the management of them as socially informed.

REFERENCES

Airini, A. R., U. Z. Abdul Hamid, and T. A. Chin. 2017. "Emerging technologies with disruptive effects: A review." *PERINTIS eJournal* 7 (2): 111–28.

ASDA'A-BCW. 2018. "Arab Youth Survey: Investing in Arab youth—fostering responsible leadership." Tenth Annual ASDA'A-BCW Youth Survey. https://www.arabyouthsurvey.com/pdf/white paper/en/2018-AYS-White-Paper.pdf.

———. 2019. "Arab Youth Survey: A call for reform." Eleventh Annual ASDA'A-BCW Youth Survey. https://www.arabyouthsurvey.com/pdf/downloadwhitepaper/download-whitepaper.pdf.

Ayish, M. 2002. *Arab World Television in the Age of Globalization: Emerging Trends*. Hamburg: Center for Middle Eastern Studies.

———. 2016. "Media hybridization in the MENA region: How traditional media harness online/social transitions for survival." *International Journal of Media, Journalism and Mass Communications (IJMJMC)* 2 (1): 28–38.

———. 2019. "Journalism education at state universities in the Arab region: The search for identity." World Journalism Education Congress, Paris, July 9–11, 2019.

Ayish, M., and N. Mellor. 2015. *Reporting in the MENA Region: Cyber Engagement and Pan-Arab Social Media.* Lanham, MD: Rowman & Littlefield.

Booz & Co. 2013. "Understanding the Arab Digital Generation." Accessed December 12, 2019. https://www.investinlebanon.gov.lb/Content/uploads/Understanding_the_Arab_Digital_Generation.pdf.

Boston Consulting Group. 2018. "Hardwiring Digital Transformation." Accessed November 15, 2019. http://image-src.bcg.com/Images/BCG-Hardwiring-Digital-Transformation-Feb-2018_tcm9-184713.pdf.

Christensen, C. 1997. *The Innovator's Dilemma: When New Technologies Cause Great Firms to Fail.* Boston: Harvard Business School Press.

Curely, N. 2013. "YouTube enables monetization for Egypt, the UAE, and Saudi Arabia: What it means for entrepreneurs." Wamda, March 18, 2013. https://www.wamda.com/2013/03/youtube-enables-video-advertising-for-egypt-the-uae-and-saudi-arabia-what-it-means-for-entrepreneurs.

ESCWA (Economic and Social Commission for Western Asia). 2013. "Business Models for Digital Arabic Content." E/ESCWA/ICTD/2013/Technical Paper 1, June 20, 2013.

Kopp, C. 2019. "What is a business model?" Investopedia. Accessed December 13, 2019. https://www.investopedia.com/terms/b/businessmodel.asp.

KPMG. 2019. "Disruptive companies and business models." October 8, 2019. https://home.kpmg/us/en/home/insights/2019/09/disruptive-companies.html.

Mahmud, S. 2018. "Facebook launches ad breaks in UAE, Saudi Arabia & Jordan." *Arabian Marketer*, October 28, 2018. https://arabianmarketer.ae/facebook-launches-ad-breaks-in-uae-saudi-arabia-jordan.

McQuail, D. 2013. *Mass Communication Theory.* London: Sage.

Newman, N., R. Fletcher, D. Levy, and R. Kleis Nielsen. 2016. *Reuters Institute Digital News Report.* Oxford: Reuters Institute for the Study of Journalism.

NU-Q (Northwestern University–Qatar). 2014. "Entertainment Media Use in the Middle East, 2014: A Six-Nation Survey." Accessed October 15, 2019. http://www.mideastmedia.org/survey/2014.

———. 2016. "Media Use in the Middle East, 2016: A Six-Nation Survey." Accessed October 15, 2019. http://mideastmedia.org/survey/2016.

———. 2018. "Media Use in the Middle East, 2018: A Seven-Nation Survey." Accessed October 15, 2019. http://www.mideastmedia.org/survey/2018.

Peckham, E. 2018. "Business models for media companies." Monetizing Media. Accessed December 17, 2019. https://monetizingmedia.com/business-models-for-media-companies.

Radcliffe, D., P. Bruni, and C. Gedrose. 2019. "State of Social Media: Middle East 2018." Accessed December 26, 2019. https://scholarsbank.uoregon.edu/xmlui/bitstream/handle/1794/24301/social_media_middle_east_2018_final02.pdf?sequence=4&isAllowed=y.

Rugh, W. 1979. *The Arab Press: News Media and Political Process in the Arab World.* Syracuse, NY: Syracuse University Press.

Salem, F. 2017. *The Arab World Online 2017: Digital Transformations and Societal Trends in the Age of the Fourth Industrial Revolution.* Vol. 3. Dubai: Mohammed Bin Rashid School of Government.

Al Shoaibi, M. 2018. "Social media and its impact on Arab youth identity." *Review of European Studies* 11 (1): 1–13.

Thalamus. 2018. "The top 25 Middle Eastern mobile ad networks." Accessed December 20, 2019. https://www.thalamus.co/blog/middle-east-mobile-ad-network.

13

Global Gaming in the Arab World

Karin Wilkins and Kyung Sun Lee

In Jamil Jan Kochai's (2020) recent story "Playing Metal Gear Solid V: The Phantom Pain" in the *New Yorker*, he deftly characterizes the complex alienation and attraction an adolescent boy feels while acquiring and playing an interactive video game. This video game sets the stage for conflict in Afghanistan: his own father's stories of his experience of violence and dread in that region compel our protagonist to make distinct choices in this game and to become overwhelmed through this play. This fictional narrative raises a central concern with how players experience stereotyped conflict through designated heroes and villains, and how landscapes are featured in ways that may connect to familial and cultural histories. Given the dominance of a particular approach to video game narratives, which privilege Northern and Western, whiter masculinities, the shifts in global industries toward more regional production demands our attention, considering the potential room for competing narratives and characterizations.

Video game production has become an increasingly profitable global media industry, surpassing that of global film. According to Price Waterhouse Cooper's Global Entertainment and Media Outlook, the video games and electronic sports (e-sports) sector constituted US$118 billion in 2019, predicted to comprise 14% of the total entertainment media market share in the Middle East North Africa (MENA) region compared to a 9% share globally. This particular market segment exceeds even that of television and home videos, at 8% of the market share. Within the MENA region, reflecting broad trends, most video game and e-sport users (68%) are under the age of 34. And while currently this population accounts for only 3.6% of the global games market, this is the region with the highest growth rate (Sharma 2020); the annual growth in MENA is estimated at 25%, higher than that of Latin America (13.9%), Asia Pacific (9.2%), North America (4%), or Western Europe (4.8%) (Newzoo 2019).

The rapid growth of interactive gaming and sports within MENA has important consequences not only for the economic industry of the region, but also for the potential for creative contribution to narratives that compete against problematic characterizations in video games based in the West. Contrasting video game narratives across origins of production promises to be a critical investigation for future work. Given that this trend is only recently emerging, we must first explore contemporary trends in video game production and distribution, focusing on the MENA context.

This chapter will focus on preliminary work that needs to be done to position this as an industry within the MENA region, leaving interests in content and reception to supplementary studies. Similar to other trends toward regional production in media industries, video game production has emerged in several regions with varying degrees of penetration in the international market, including pockets of Asia, Latin America, and Eastern Europe (Hjorth and Chan 2009, Mezihorak 2004, Penix-Tadsen 2016). In this chapter, we highlight the Arab Middle East, given its growth in this global industry and the relative lack of attention to MENA in regional studies of media. First, we situate this study within critical communication scholarship on global media industries.

GLOBAL MEDIA INDUSTRY

The political economy of media examines the nature of the relationship between media industries and the broader sociopolitical structure of society. This approach "endeavors to connect how media and communication systems and content are shaped by ownership, market structures, commercial support, technologies and government policies" (McChesney 2008, 12). Accordingly, media are conceptualized as embedded within the larger structure of political and economic power; the purpose, then, of critical media scholarship in this area is to study the power relations that contribute to the production, distribution, and consumption of communication resources (Mosco 2009). Within the study of global media, political economy approaches consider how commercial media, supported through public policies and regulation, structure the circulation of messages, images, and values in ways that reinforce the elite ambitions of military and industrial agents (Herman and Chomsky 1988, Kellner 2004, Schiller 1991).

Although scholars tend to agree that global media production has historically been dominated by global political powers, and that over time media industries have become more regional in their origin and distribution, their disagreement lies with the potential consequences of asymmetrical production and distribution. Global communication scholars have raised concerns about cultural homogenization and imperialism enacted when some centers of production dominate networks of distribution. The essence of this concern is with the direction and the dominance of a few actors in shaping media across cultural and national boundaries. Kraidy (2003) situates these networks as "dialectical because it simultaneously recognizes the role of material forces such as economics, technology and politics, and dialogical because it also focuses on issues of culture, textuality and meaning construction" (40). Foregrounding the processes engaged in production and distribution as both dialectical and dialogical allows us to problematize simplistic visions of global media flows as unidimensional.

Similarly, Thussu (2006) explains that although "the Northern conglomerates continue to shape the global media landscape, the flow of global media products is not just one way from the media-rich North (and within it the Anglo-American axis) to the media-poor South" (2). Other competing flows across the global landscape include films (e.g., Korean and Indian), soap operas (e.g., *telenovelas*), and news (e.g., Al Jazeera). Since Thussu's publication referenced above, regional production of media has strengthened even more, though still within the parameters of global capitalist networks that structure these media industries. Straubhaar (1991) describes a nuanced approach to understanding power dynamics given these flows as "asymmetrical," recognizing that at that time regional production was growing, but the global prevalence of particular actors, rooted in Northern, wealthier nations, persisted.

GLOBAL GAMING INDUSTRY

Corporate producers focused on interactive games as an industry are headquartered in a few select countries: the United States, China, Japan, and South Korea. Therefore, it is essential to recognize the importance of East Asia as a host to major game development and production centers. The rise of the Chinese game industry represents a contra-flow of content on a global scale. According to Peichi Chung and Anthony Fung (2013), Chinese gamers identify with national branding that promotes indigenous content through the policies of "healthy online games." "These policies enforce an anti-addiction, antigambling, and real-name registration rule to 'naturalize' the state's intervention into the operation of online games in China" (236).

In the last decade, these transnational game corporations have increasingly established branch offices in Canada, Eastern Europe, and China, and have acquired successful production studios in dispersed locations (Kerr 2017). Accordingly, the global video game culture is said to be "inherently asymmetrical" (Šisler et al. 2017, 3857) with games produced in particular regional centers dominating the diverse global markets. This is a key feature in the contemporary global media economy, with East Asia contributing significant gaming products for global export.

To capture the complexity of global media flows, Thussu (2006) differentiates between "dominant flows," largely emanating from the United States toward global audiences against contra-flows, which cross national boundaries with a strong regional presence, and geo-cultural flows. The latter serve "linguistic audiences" across global settings (13). Given this insightful framework, we recognize both the origin of production and the network of distribution, in order to understand the potential power and reach of regional media production. While Thussu offers a valuable complexity to these categorizations, we find that an additional path is needed to account for significant new flows of game distribution, given the emergence of East Asia as a dominant agent of production with global distribution.

Along with the intensive growth of the gaming industry, communication scholarship on this subject has also accelerated in the past two decades. Studies that examine the game industry from political economy and globalization perspectives have contributed to decentering gaming as a monolithic enterprise in order to capture the complexity of the stages that comprise it, including game development, publishing, distribution, and consumption. Within this process are multiple layers of power relationships between game developers and publishers, creative labor and manufacturing labor, as well as the role of governments and the industry. As Aphra Kerr (2006) states:

> Online gaming is a socially constructed artifact that emerges from a complex process of negotiation between various human and non-human actors within the context of a particular historical formation. Online gaming cannot be understood without paying attention to the late capitalist economic systems from which it emerged and the changing political, social and cultural contexts in which its commodities are produced and consumed. (4)

GLOBAL GAME PRODUCTION

Global gaming industries engage labor and financing, as well as material and other capital, in the design and production of games for purchase and consumption. Emerging trends include attention to the role of creative labor in this process, given economic conditions and political regulations that accentuate inequities in pay and benefits, as well as gendered participation in the workforce[1] (Dyer-Witheford 1999, Dyer-Witheford and De Peuter 2009, Kerr and Flynn 2003, Kerr 2006; Miller 2008). These studies, grounded in critical political economy, reveal how the global capitalist system shapes the ownership structure of the gaming industry, which resembles major transnational corporations—the software and hardware manufactured around the world for a relatively small, privileged few in the wealthiest markets—as embodied examples of existing social relations.

While most gaming hardware and software is sold in North America, the majority of hardware production takes place in countries where console gaming is not as popular, such as China, India, and Taiwan. Many of the raw materials required for production include minerals that come from countries like Congo, Rwanda, and South Africa. By relying on multiple levels of outsourcing, corporations, such as Microsoft and Sony, are less able or likely to monitor how these minerals are procured, thus avoiding accountability for the labor conditions grounding the manufacturing of these products (Dyer-Witheford and De Peuter 2009).

Studies that position gaming in a globalization framework have aimed to analyze the dynamics of gaming, considering the tensions between global and local flows. The scholarship situates the interests of various stakeholders, including developers, governments, publishers, and players, in contributing to gaming as a social, cultural, and economic enterprise (Huntemann and Aslinger 2013). The growing power of the game industry lobby capitalizes on this as a political power base, with consequences to regulations and policies that govern new media industries.

The global game industry closely resembles the global supply chain of media companies: a few vertically integrated conglomerates dominate a majority of revenues. In order to set the stage for understanding gaming within MENA, we describe the specific companies that dominate corporate production, highlighting their bases of operation.

Table 13.1. Global gaming industry

Rank	Company	Revenue 2018 ($Million)	Headquarters
	Top 20 Public Companies by Game Revenue		
1	Tencent	19,733	Shenzen, China
2	Sony	14,218	Tokyo, Japan
3	Microsoft	9,754	Washington, USA
4	Apple	9,453	California, USA
5	Activision Blizzard	6,892	California, USA
6	Google	6,497	California, USA
7	NetEase	6,177	Guangzhou, China
8	EA	5,294	California, USA
9	Nintendo	4,288	Kyoto, Japan
10	Bandai Namco	2,741	Tokyo, Japan
11	TakeTwo Interactive	2,580	New York, USA
12	Nexon	2,252	Tokyo, Japan
13	Ubisoft	2,221	Montreuil, France
14	Netmarble	1,893	Seoul, South Korea
15	Warner Bros	1,835	California, USA
16	Square Enix	1,583	Tokyo, Japan
17	NCSoft	1,343	Seoul, South Korea
18	Cyber Agent	1,324	Tokyo, Japan
19	Mixi	1,222	Tokyo, Japan
20	Konami	1,210	Tokyo, Japan

Source: Adapted from Newzoo, *Global Games Market Report 2019*.

In table 13.1, the top 20 companies in terms of 2019 revenue are charted, demonstrating heavy concentrations both vertically and horizontally. Moreover, the top 35 companies account for 82% of the global games market revenues. The top five companies alone account for almost half (43%) of global games revenue (Newzoo 2019). Out of these top 20 companies, eight (40%) are based in Japan and seven (35%) in the United States. Another two are based in South Korea and one in France. While China serves as the headquarters for two of the top 20 game companies, Tencent accounts for a hefty amount of the total gaming revenues, outstripping top global telecommunications companies, double the amount of Microsoft, the third in rank. How, then, are these global corporations distributing their games to the Arab Middle East? Next we explore this process, considering the sales as well as the adaptive strategies used to promote game consumption across cultural contexts.

GAMING IN THE ARAB MIDDLE EAST

Despite the rapidly growing body of research on gaming industries more broadly, there is a dearth of research concerning the Arab context in particular. Notable exceptions are two edited works: Wolf's *Video Games around the World* (2015) and Penix-Tadsen's *Video Games and the Global South* (2019), both including chapters on gaming in the Arab world.

Within MENA, governments and the industry are increasingly supporting the growth of the gaming market by hosting gaming conventions. Such conventions work to make one's mark in the global market, to invigorate the network of industry agents, and to foster a culture among gamers. Sony PlayStation Middle East, Microsoft Gulf, Red Entertainment, and Pluto Games co-host GAMES, provide fans and gamers access to upcoming games and technology, and host various tournaments, events, and e-sports competitions. In addition to a host of game-related international conventions, Dubai hosts Girl Gamer E-sports Festival, an all-female gaming competition that aims to make gaming competition more inclusive for both genders. Such events are not only highly profitable,[2] but attract global gaming industry companies into the region.

In the region, mobile and tablet games make up 58% of the market, console games 20%, and downloaded/boxed PC 20%, while traditional PC games account for just 3% (McFarlane 2019). In the Gulf, the console is the preferred device, but the Sony PlayStation (PS) models far outweigh the Microsoft Xbox. A survey measuring consumer preference for electronic brands found that about 38% prefer Sony PlayStation 4, which was four times higher than the percentage of gamers who prefer Microsoft Xbox 360 (18%) (McBride 2015).

Since the second generation of Sony PlayStation (PS) was first released in the Middle East in 2000, the platform has remained the best-selling console in the region. In the UAE, for example, the PS4 has outsold Microsoft's console by 17.59 million to 4.69 million (Krish 2019). The overwhelming popularity of Sony's console may be due to the international gaming conglomerate's business strategy: Penix-Tadsen (2019) notes that in India, Microsoft marketed the Xbox but did not provide development licenses for Indian developers, which, according to the author, reflects "a general tendency of game corporations who manufacture but do not develop games in the global south" (20). On the other hand, Sony encouraged development of original titles from local developers. In MENA, local developers also release their original games on Sony's console (Al Otaibi 2020), and many more titles are available in Arabic versions compared to Microsoft Xbox.

A notable change is the increase in the popularity of mobile gaming over console gaming. According to a Media Use in the Middle East survey conducted by Northwestern University in Qatar, 75% of all smartphone users in MENA play games on their phones (Dennis et al. 2018). In countries like the UAE and Qatar, where smartphone penetration is close to 100%, the demographic of mobile gamers has skewed more toward older and female users. Globally, video games for smartphones comprise over 50% of all game sales at US$70.3 billion. Smartphone games are designed to be less competitive, more completion-based, and less time-intensive, which makes these games more appealing to casual gamers compared to console-based games, which are more competitive and time-intensive.

At US$250 per person, players in Saudi Arabia spend the most on gaming compared to other countries globally. This figure is nearly eight times the average amount spent by Chinese players (US$32), for example. Contributing to such high amounts of spending may be the fact that other popular entertainment venues, such as cinemas, were banned until recently, leading young people to turn to video games as an outlet (Amos 2015).

Next, we consider the ways in which global corporations attempt to create games that will appeal to consumers in the Arab Middle East, given the growth of this market. We describe production processes of localization and co-production as ways of seeing different ends of a more complicated spectrum of design and manufacturing.

Localization

The global game industry's reaction to the rapidly growing Middle Eastern market is perhaps best seen through the localization strategies of game development and publishing companies. Localization is the process of modifying a video game in order to make it accessible, usable, and culturally suitable to a target audience. There are multiple levels in which localization takes place in order to make the games suitable for international distribution. They are both translated and adapted for national regulatory boards and regional software requirements (Carlson and Corliss 2011). Along with game content, design aesthetics such as images, animations, and game mechanics, as well as user interface and narrative, all of which are instrumental to providing immersive user experience, are modified to accommodate the perceived differences between regional markets.

Given the growing market for gaming in MENA, localization among global game companies has been a growing trend, based on numerous market data in part as a response to production capacity and in part as a way to generate profit with more locally appreciated content. The costs of production are managed within global structures of corporate interests, raising the competitive tension between asserting cultural products and tailoring to meet local conditions. This reflects an asymmetrical interdependence (Straubhaar 1991) in the gaming industry, whereby localization allows a few predominant international gaming companies to further penetrate regional markets, depending on their ability to tailor their products to local conditions.

In MENA, localization is demonstrated in two types of business operation models. First, international game developers set up studios in the region. The company sets up a localization team and employs local talent. South Korean Netmarble's move to localize its games into Arabic and Turkish was instrumental to its rapid increase in rank to eighth worldwide (LAI Global Game Services 2018). Netmarble's studio in Istanbul also invests in startup mobile game developers in Turkey by providing financial support and mentoring opportunities (Baghdadi 2016). Ubisoft, the first international game company to set up a studio in the GCC, has expanded the scope of localization beyond translation to creating an immersive user interface that compares quite favorably to the games' English-language versions.

Localization is preceded by "internationalization," which means that from the early stages of design and development, it is taken into consideration that the game will be targeted to audiences of different languages and cultures. As localization is increasingly integrated into the production process, and as companies set up local studios, developers have taken more direct, even reflexive, interest in the process. An interview with the localization manager and user interface manager of Ubisoft in developing voice-over of *The Division* illustrates the process of localization.

> Taking into consideration Arabic from its early stages of development, we are able to prepare our tech for the challenges we would face. Things like changing alignment or re-ordering UI [user interface] elements became a basic part of how we develop our UI, so making these changes for Arabic became a simple process. The game UI is initially designed to support left to right alignment and later on adapted to Arabic reading flow. This process is part of the internationalization stage and, as soon as the final design is reviewed and approved, the UI translation starts. (Jisr 2016)

In MENA, another key element of localization is navigating regulation of content. Although the situation varies across countries in MENA, some countries regulate nudity, sexual explicitness, and violence, with implications for accessibility across countries within the region. Navigating regulations and content guidelines results in negotiation over modifying visuals while trying to leave the gaming experience of players intact (Demmig 2018).

Localization is complemented by marketing that reaches directly out to regional gamers in other ways. For example, Ubisoft has partnered with a theme park in Dubai, IMG World, to showcase games such as *Assassin's Creed*, *Rabbids*, and *Just Dance* brands. Games thus become part of a more comprehensive entertainment industry, with characters and themes contributing to brands that transcend one particular commodification.

Although MENA is the fastest-growing gaming region worldwide, game developers there find it a challenge to attract funding, because investment in gaming is perceived as high risk. Game developers must often rely on their own sources of funding. "We know so much about the American culture because we grew up with those mediums but the rest of the world doesn't know much about us as Emiratis, Arabs or Muslims," says an Emirati game developer, Al Mansouri (Euronews 2019). One of the ways in which local game developers have navigated the financial side of the industry is through co-production.

Co-production

Co-production is a trend in media globalization. It refers to joint development of games with a partner that is equipped with technical, financial, and/or cultural capital. Co-production is said to enable a moving up in the value chain of the industry as the transfer of knowledge and movement of human capital closes the technological gap. It allows values and ideas from the margin to gain presence through partnership with established, "willing collaborators" (Yecies et al. 2016, 8). The potential of co-production to move creativity from the "margins to the center of economic activity" (Jin and Otmazgin 2014, 43) has led some scholars to ask whether co-production offers the potential to change the structure of the global cultural market (Su 2017).

For Middle Eastern game developers, co-production offers an opportunity to take advantage of established resources; to make up for a lack of skills, know-how, and funds; and to build global networks to export Arab culture. Financial pooling is an important benefit for smaller, independent game developers, and talent exchange is a valuable asset. Young, independent game developers acquire the technical resources and skills of each stage of game development and production, resulting in high-quality games that integrate game narratives from the perspective of the game developer. Quirkat, a Dubai-based startup with a studio in Jordan, co-produced a US$5 million game with U.S.-based Breakaway Games. Called *Arabian Lords*, it is a disk-based PC strategy game that allows players to become merchant lords during the time of the rise of Islam. The game sold about 20,000 copies on the PC. Despite the relatively small number, the game was a best seller in the region at the time. Quirkat, like other locally based studios in the region, strategizes to produce an "art style [that] is distinctive and identifiably Arabic" (Takahashi 2011).

In Saudi Arabia, co-production is a government-led strategy to introduce locally developed cultural content to the international audience. A subsidiary of the Prince Mohammed bin Salman Foundation, Manga Productions, has partnered with a Japanese company, Toei Animations, to develop a series of animations and games. The two companies signed an agreement of partnership one month before Saudi Arabia lifted its thirty-five-year ban on cinemas. For the Saudi government, the purpose is to "promote Saudi ideas and messages internationally through unique and professional productions" (Manga Productions 2020). The company has branches in Riyadh and Tokyo, and Saudi designers and programmers have been trained in creating animation and games at Digital Hollywood University in Tokyo, Japan (Mateo 2020). The Saudi government's move reveals its perceived need to develop an entertainment industry that will reinforce its regional influence and promote its status globally.

Saudi's first-ever co-produced film, set to launch in 2021, is fully financed by Manga Productions and the company holds worldwide distribution rights (Abueish 2021). Demonstrating its connections with East Asia, the film is produced by prominent Japanese media professionals, including its director, writer, character designer, and musical composer (Hodgkins 2019). Its production team consists of some of the most prominent Japanese figures, reflecting the hybrid nature of this entertainment medium.

Co-production in film serves as a valuable example for how producers of gaming might also collaborate across regional lines. Co-production assumes more of a partnership status than a production process, in which the gaming content is produced in one place and then adapted through translation for use in another cultural community. Actually, contributing to the process of design and production signifies a different level of engagement from simple localization after the fact. Interest in co-production has been inspired by critiques of the representation of the Middle East in U.S.-based media.

Problematic Gaming Narratives

While critical analyses of media manufacturing raise concerns about the labor conditions of production, as well as the environmental consequences of discarded devices, media scholarship also questions the dominant narratives distributed along with the sales of devices and games. In this way, we understand games as a form of play conditioned through the structured choices embedded within the game, often featuring conflict in interaction and competition in goals. Video game play that features military conquest limits players' roles through structured choices, themselves stereotyping characters in terms of gender, ethnicity, and nationality. Fortunately, alternative narratives and more flexible characters in video game play are now starting to emerge.

Considering games as narratives calls attention to the importance of conflict being situated in particular landscapes, tied to existing places, and depending on the guided characterization of heroes saving victims from villains. These conquest and rescue narratives clearly resonate with broader U.S.-based media narratives concerning the Middle East. The images of Arabs and Muslims in games do not circulate in a vacuum but are tied into a wider matrix of media constructions. The body of literature exploring U.S. media demonstrates that the portrayals of Arab characters and the Middle East in games closely align with representations of the Middle East in other media such as film and television.

Research on video games in the Middle East tends to center analyses on the problematic representations in which players engage through structured play (Höglund 2008, Kavoori 2008, Reichmuth and Werning 2006, Šisler 2008). This body of work typically interrogates the representational politics of games that are produced outside the region, then distributed to and consumed by participants who do not identify with the heroes presented in the games.

Some scholarship examines how game production within the region offers alternative possibilities for players (Galloway 2004, Machin and Suleiman 2006, A. Shaw 2010, Šisler 2018, Tawil-Souri 2007). Recognizing that not all games follow similar genres or attract the same audiences, a point worth recognizing is the strategic design of games to educate, such as the re-creation of Islamic holy sites and rituals and the use of games to teach the basic tenets and values of Islam (Campbell 2010). Further research would provide a more comprehensive inventory of the types and appeal of games produced in the region.

The expanding literature on the representation and construction of gender, race, sexuality, and ethnicity in games has situated the conversations on representations in games in international and comparative contexts. Games originating from North America or Western Europe are noted for the ways in which Arab characters are simplified and vilified. Šisler (2008) notes that, particularly in games produced in the United States and Europe, the Middle East is construed as an exotic, timeless, and ahistorical entity. It is often conflated with Persian and Indian architectural characteristics. Arabs and Muslims are represented as the cultural other, either through vilification (e.g., terrorist, tyrant) or dehumanization, particularly in first-person shooter games, where the player is a hero destroying the enemy.

Clément (2019) confirms the importance of these narratives, particularly in terms of how "the world understands [Middle Eastern] culture and the way [Middle Easterners] understand themselves" (119). The dominant narrative constructions in mainstream games show that video games, like film, constitute a global cultural industry (Kerr 2006) whose hegemonic representations and narrative constructions cannot be separated from politics and racial relations (Leonard 2006), colonial and postcolonial conflicts (Mukherjee 2017), and military conquests (I. G. R. Shaw 2010), mediated through play.

The prevalence of hegemonic representations of Arabs and the Middle East in video games is due to several factors. First, the high production costs and the competitive nature of the game market encourage the creation of games with repetitive themes so as to avoid economic risk. The high degree of uncertainty associated with variation drives game developers to rely on overused hegemonic representational strategies (Šisler 2008). Second, a hegemonic representational strategy in video games may be attributed to the medium itself, which relies on readability that requires minimal interpretation by the player (Penix-Tadsen 2019, 180). Dehumanization of the enemy, within a familiar context, relies on the idea that this violence is necessary. These narratives then echo colonial and imperialistic agendas through their justification of this conflict. Finally, some scholars suggest that this particular industry lacks the critical analysis that media scholars apply to many other genres and technologies (Reichmuth and Werning 2006, 47), though clearly this is an important area for future research.

Some Arab and Muslim producers have sought to challenge the representational strategy in U.S. and European games (Šisler 2008). Outside of the scope of professional production, some amateurs and religious organizations have created projects referred to as "Islamogaming" (Halter 2006). These games were designed to replace an American or European action hero with a Muslim protagonist. Referring to his actions as "digital dignity," Radwan Kasmiya, a Syrian game developer, has sought to reclaim an Arab identity and religious and cultural relevance from others' focus on "the Crusades, oil and terrorism" (cited in Penix-Tadsen 2019, 117).

Innovative Minds, a game production company based in the United Kingdom, has created games intended to educate players about Islam and to engage them as participants in Hezbollah's Islamic Resistance in southern Lebanon. These first-person shooter games are strategically designed to counter other games that convey a distorted image about Arabs, and to provide alternative narratives of regional conflicts. Afkar Media's Radwan Kasmiya emphasizes that games like *Under Siege* are intended to reflect the experiences on the ground through the eyes of Palestinian families (Extreme Tech 2006). Referring to American military games that are used to recruit soldiers, Kasmiya states that the games were created "so players can tell the difference between a history game based on lives of real people trying to survive [the] ethnic cleansing and [the] political propaganda that is trying to inject morals in[to] future marines to justify their assaults on nations far away from their homeland" (Extreme Tech 2006).

While the perspective of the character engaged by the player offers one area for contrast, the structure of play remains one of conflict. These games are noted for their similarity to militaristic games produced by Western media companies (Galloway 2004, Machin and Suleiman 2006, Šisler 2008). Games such as *Under Ash* engage in a dichotomized "hero" and "victim" narrative with the glorified and the villainized parties reversed. Shaw points out that much of the literature on Arab gaming situates its characters as reactions to the images of Arabs in Anglo-produced games, which suggests that these games are "interesting only in their relation to American/European video games" (A. Shaw 2010).

Switching the cultural references without altering the simplified action-adventure approach sustains the problematic limitations of a narrative that does not allow for empathy across perspectives or tolerance across difference. Scholarship on gaming needs to understand embedded cultural texts within the context of their production and consumption. The economic conditions of the global gaming industry, along with political regulation of content and technologies, must be understood in relation to the cultural ideology in which texts are proposed, created, purchased, and engaged (Clément 2019).

FUTURE RESEARCH

Current conditions of global video game production complicate our theoretical frameworks and inspire potential research projects, particularly in terms of industry and reception within the MENA region. First, global communication tends to center on either Northern and Western sites of production or regional industries; however, our consideration of global gaming demonstrates the importance of East Asian production, particularly across regional markets. This newly emerging industrial link between centers of production in East Asia and sites of consumption in the Arab Middle East complicates previous conceptualizations of global flows that privilege North-to-South and West-to-East manufacturing and marketing pipelines. This linking of East Asia with MENA also suggests that drawing linguistic and cultural lines within regions and across diasporic audiences does not fully account for this significant trend between game production in China, Japan, and South Korea and its adaptations for Arab markets in the Middle East region.

Given the emerging demographics within MENA that suggest higher concentrations of youth, with access to interactive devices and games, a thorough understanding of the game content, in terms of narratives and characterizations, will be crucial. While the global flows may be more complex, what remains is a global capitalist enterprise in which marketing and adaptations, in language and text, are designed to meet profit incentives. Future research may need to contrast origins as well as processes of production in order to analyze potential effects on the narratives produced—particularly significant given the perspectives and experiences of players.

NOTES

1. While the game development sector is 24% women (Statista 2021), workers in manufacturing factories are predominantly female.

2. The e-sports industry is bigger than the physical sports industry: in 2018, the e-sports industry made US$140 billion, the sports industry US$93 billion, and the film industry roughly US$30–40 billion (Hammond 2019).

REFERENCES

Abueish, T. 2021. "Manga Production's first ever Saudi-Japanese anime film set to hit theaters in 2021." *Al Arabya News*, March 2, 2021. https://english.alarabiya.net/life-style/entertainment/2021/03/02/Manga-Production-s-first-ever-Saudi-Japanese-anime-film-set-to-hit-theaters-in-2021.

Amos, D. 2015. "As Saudi Arabia's love of online gaming grows, developers bloom." NPR, August 10, 2015. https://www.npr.org/sections/parallels/2015/08/10/431241078/saudi-arabias-passion-for-online-gaming.

Baghdadi, A. 2016. "The growth of the gaming industry in Turkey and the MENA." Arabnet, April 8, 2016. https://www.arabnet.me/english/editorials/technology/games/the-growth-of-the-gaming-industry-in-turkey-and-the-mena.

Campbell, H. 2010. "Islamogaming: Digital Dignity via Alternative Storytellers." In *Halos and Avatars: Playing Video Games with God*, edited by C. Detweiler, 63–74. Louisville, KY: Westminster John Knox Press.

Carlson, R., and J. Corliss. 2011. "Imagined commodities: Video game localization and mythologies of cultural difference." *Games and Culture* 6 (1): 61–82.

Chung, P., and A. Fung. 2013. "Internet Development and the Commercialization of Online Gaming in China." In *Gaming Globally*, edited by N. Huntemann and B. Aslinger, 233–50. New York: Palgrave Macmillan.

Clément, P. 2019. "Not Waiting for Other Players Anymore: Gaming in the Middle East between Assignation, Resistance and Normalization." In *Video Games and the Global South*, edited by P. Penix-Tadsen, 115–28. Pittsburgh, PA: Carnegie Mellon University, ETC Press.

Demmig, M. 2018. "Games localization for Arabic cultures: An interview with Malek Teffaha, head of localization and communication at Ubisoft Middle East—Part I." Altagram, November 15, 2018. https://altagram.com/interview-malek-teffaha-ubisoft-middle-east-part-1.

Dennis, E. E., Martin, J. D., & Hassan, F. 2018. *Media Use in the Middle East, 2018: A Seven-Nation Survey*. Northwestern University in Qatar. Retrieved from www.mideastmedia.org/survey/2018.

Dyer-Witheford, N. 1999. "The work in digital play: Video gaming's transnational and gendered division of labour." *Journal of International Communication* 6 (1): 69–93.

Dyer-Witheford, N., and G. De Peuter. 2009. *Games of Empire: Global Capitalism and Video Games*. Minneapolis: University of Minnesota Press.

Euronews. 2019. "Here's what is pushing the right buttons with MENA game developers." April 8, 2019. https://www.euronews.com/2019/08/02/here-s-what-is-pushing-the-right-buttons-with-mena-gaming-developers.

Extreme Tech. 2006. "Islamogaming: Looking for video games in the Muslim world." Fox News, September 11, 2006. https://www.foxnews.com/story/islamogaming-looking-for-video-games-in-the-muslim-world.

Galloway, A. 2004. "Social realism in gaming." *Game Studies* 4 (1). http://gamestudies.org/0401/galloway.

Halter, E. 2006. "Islamogaming: Looking for video games in the Muslim world." *Computer Gaming World* 266: 38–41.

Hammond, A. 2019. "Girl gaming world finals to be held in Dubai." *Gulf News*, August 27, 2019. https://gulfnews.com/uae/girl-gaming-world-finals-to-be-held-in-dubai-1.66039603.

Herman, E. S., and N. Chomsky. 1988. *Manufacturing Consent: The Political Economy of the Mass Media*. New York: Pantheon.

Hjorth, L., and D. Chan. 2009. *Gaming Cultures and Place in Asia-Pacific*. New York: Routledge.

Hodgkins, C. 2019. "Saudi Arabia's Manga Productions, Toei Animation reveal title, more staff, visual for upcoming collaboration film." Anime News Network, May 19, 2019. https://www.animenewsnetwork.com/news/2019-05-19/saudi-arabia-manga-productions-toei-animation-reveal-title-more-staff-visual-for-upcoming-collaboration-film/.146891#.

Höglund, J. 2008. "Electronic empire: Orientalism revisited in the military shooter." *Game Studies* 8 (1). http://gamestudies.org/0801/articles/hoeglund.

Huntemann, N., and B. Aslinger. 2013. *Gaming Globally: Production, Play, and Place*. Basingstoke, UK: Palgrave Macmillan.

Jin, D. Y., and N. Otmazgin. 2014. "Introduction: East Asian cultural industries: Policies, strategies and trajectories." *Pacific Affairs* 87 (1): 43–51.

Jisr, L. 2016. "How Ubisoft localized *The Division*." IGN Middle East, February 16, 2016. https://me.ign.com/en/xbox-one-gaming-hardware-xbox-one/115818/feature/how-ubisoft-localized-the-division.

Kavoori, A. 2008. "Gaming, terrorism and the right to communicate." *Global Media Journal* 7 (13): 1–16.

Kellner, D. 2004. "9/11, spectacles of terror, and media manipulation: A critique of Jihadist and Bush media politics." *Critical Discourse Studies* 1 (1): 41–64.

Kerr, A. 2006. *The Business and Culture of Digital Games: Gamework and Gameplay*. Los Angeles: Sage.

———. 2017. *Global Games: Production, Circulation and Policy in the Networked Era*. New York: Routledge.

Kerr, A., and R. Flynn. 2003. "Revisiting globalisation through the movie and digital games industries." *Convergence: The International Journal of Research into New Media Technologies* 9 (1): 91–113.

Kochai, J. J. 2020. "Playing Metal Gear Solid V: The phantom pain." *New Yorker*, January 6, 2020, 54–57.

Kraidy, M. M. 2003. "Glocalisation: An international communication framework?" *Journal of International Communication* 9 (2): 29–49.

Krish, D. 2019. "The influences on video game console popularity in the UAE." Guide2Dubai, September 12, 2019. https://www.guide2dubai.com/news/latest-news/2019/the-influences-on-video-game-console-popularity-in-the-uae.

LAI Global Game Services. 2018. "Middle East, North Africa (MENA) & Turkish game markets." Accessed January 15, 2020. http://www.laiggs.com/en/middle-east-north-africa-mena-turkey-turkish-game-markets.

Leonard, D. J. 2006. "Not a hater, just keepin' it real: The importance of race- and gender-based game studies." *Games and Culture* 1 (1): 83–88.

Machin, D., and U. Suleiman. 2006. "Arab and American computer war games: The influence of a global technology on discourse." *Critical Discourse Studies* 3 (1): 1–22.

Manga Productions. 2020. "About Manga Productions." Accessed January 15, 2020. http://manga.com .sa/#About.

Mateo, A. 2020. "Saudi Arabia's Manga Productions, Toei Animation finish the Journey film." Anime News Network, February 25, 2020. https://www.animenewsnetwork.com/news/2020-02-25/saudi -arabia-manga-productions-toei-animation-finish-the-journey-film/.156836.

McBride, S. 2015. "PS4 four times as popular in GCC as Xbox One." Arabian Business, May 27, 2015. https://www.arabianbusiness.com/ps4-four-times-as-popular-in-gcc-as-xbox-one-594175.html.

McChesney, R. W. 2008. *The Political Economy of Media: Enduring Issues, Emerging Dilemmas*. New York: Monthly Review Press.

McFarlane, N. 2019. "Gaming in the Middle East and Africa: The stats you need to know, from average spend to numbers of gamers." *The National*, November 23, 2019. https://www.thenational.ae/ arts-culture/gaming-in-the-middle-east-and-africa-the-stats-you-need-to-know-from-average-spend -to-numbers-of-gamers-1.940720.

Mezihorak, P. 2004. "The state of game development in Eastern Europe." Gamasutra, November 24, 2004. https://www.gamasutra.com/view/feature/130582/the_state_of_game_development_in_.php.

Miller, T. 2008. "Anyone for Games? Via the New International Division of Cultural Labor." In *The Cultural Economy*, edited by H. Anheier and Y. R. Isar, 227–40. Los Angeles: Sage.

Mosco, V. 2009. *The Political Economy of Communication*. 2nd ed. Los Angeles: Sage.

Mukherjee, S. 2017. *Videogames and Postcolonialism: Empire Plays Back*. Cham: Springer.

Newzoo. 2019. *Global Games Market Report 2019*. Light version. https://newzoo.com/insights/trend -reports/newzoo-global-games-market-report-2019-light-version.

Al Otaibi, W. 2020. "A brief history of gaming in the Middle East." Superjump, September 6, 2020. https://medium.com/super-jump/a-brief-history-of-gaming-in-the-middle-east-e45a97c2e63c.

Penix-Tadsen, P. 2016. *Cultural Code: Video Games and Latin America*. Cambridge, MA: MIT Press.

———, ed. 2019. *Video Games and the Global South*. Pittsburgh, PA: Carnegie Mellon University, ETC Press.

Reichmuth, P., and S. Werning. 2006. "Pixel pashas, digital djinns." *ISIM Review* 18: 46–47.

Schiller, H. I. 1991. *Culture, Inc.: The Corporate Takeover of Public Expression*. Oxford: Oxford University Press on Demand.

Sharma, A. 2020. "Middle East among the fastest growing gaming markets in the world." *The National*, November 2, 2020. https://www.thenationalnews.com/business/technology/middle-east-among-the -fastest-growing-gaming-markets-in-the-world-1.1103958.

Shaw, A. 2010. "Beyond comparison: Reframing analysis of video games produced in the Middle East." *Global Media Journal* 9 (16): 1–31.

Shaw, I. G. R. 2010. "Playing war." *Social & Cultural Geography* 11 (8): 789–803.

Šisler, V. 2008. "Digital Arabs: Representation in video games." *European Journal of Cultural Studies* 2 (11): 203–20.

———. 2018. "Virtual Worlds, Digital Dreams: Imaginary Spaces of Middle Eastern Video Games." In *Digital Middle East: State and Society in the Information Age*, edited by M. Zayani, 59–83. London: Hurst.

Šisler, V., J. Švelch, and J. Šlerka. 2017. "Global digital culture: Video games and the asymmetry of global cultural flows: The game industry and game culture in Iran and the Czech Republic." *International Journal of Communication* 11 (23): 3857–79.

Statista. 2021. "Distribution of game developers worldwide from 2014 to 2019, by gender." Accessed January 15, 2020. https://www.statista.com/statistics/453634/game-developer-gender -distribution-worldwide/#:~:text=The%20statistic%20shows%20the%20distribution,while%20 24%20percent%20were%20women.

Straubhaar, J. 1991. "Beyond media imperialism: Asymmetrical interdependence and cultural proximity." *Critical Studies in Mass Communication* 8 (1): 39–59.

Su, W. 2017. "A brave new world? Understanding U.S.–China coproductions: Collaboration, conflicts, and obstacles." *Critical Studies in Media Communication* 34 (5): 480–94.

Takahashi, D. 2011. "Quirkat to develop games for the Middle East market." *Venturebeat*, March 16, 2011. https://venturebeat.com/2011/03/16/quirkat-hopes-to-bring-fun-to-gamers-in-the-middle-east/.

Tawil-Souri, H. T. 2007. "The political battlefield of pro-Arab video games on Palestinian screens." *Comparative Studies of South Asia, Africa and the Middle East* 27 (3): 536–51.

Thussu, D. K. 2006. *Media on the Move: Global Flow and Contra-Flow*. New York: Routledge.

Wolf, M. J., ed. 2015. *Video Games around the World*. Cambridge, MA: MIT Press.

Yecies, B., M. Keane, and T. Flew. 2016. "East Asian audio-visual collaboration and the global expansion of Chinese media." *Media International Australia* 159 (1): 7–12.

14

Understanding Egyptian Television

The Audience Perspective

Tara Al-Kadi

The Egyptian broadcast landscape has been in a transitional state since the 2011 revolution. The 2014 constitution promised democratic changes for the broadcast system, particularly articles pertaining to differences between state and private channels. The focus was mainly on efforts to alleviate state channels' funding problems and to decrease viewership problems. However, there were still some areas of concern associated with the broadcast structure, such as the powerful role of the Ministry of Investment as an official regulator of satellite channels and the creation of new regulatory bodies such as the Supreme Council for Media Regulation and the National Bureau for Press and Media.

This chapter focuses on the Egyptian broadcast industry and audience perceptions of it in post-revolutionary Egypt. Although television is being superseded in many countries by smartphones and the web, it is still a very important part of mediated Egyptian culture. Egyptian television is still a main agent of socialization. It both reflects and contributes to the creation and preservation of cultural values and beliefs. Egyptians gather around television daily at home and in cafés. It is still the number one medium in Egypt, especially with free access to satellite channels (Broadcasting Board of Governors 2014).

The aim of this study is to understand the manner in which Egyptian audiences experience and perceive the Egyptian broadcast system. This includes an investigation of how Egyptian audiences view television in a normative sense—its objectives and role in society. The research also explores how audiences feel about the actual current state of Egyptian TV, and more specifically, how they evaluate current practices associated with it.

This study generally investigates television's overall role in society with respect to relevant critiques, providing a valuable source of information about viewer experiences, desires, and reactions. In assessing audience perspectives, the study stimulates discussion about broader themes such as critiques of excessive commercialization of television. The analysis of the focus group discussions offers insight into the types of regulation or change that audiences demand for the Egyptian broadcast system. This is considered to be of great importance, since television plays such a large role in shaping the opinions and attitudes of the public. The research is particularly timely, given the creation of the Supreme Council for Media Regulation (SCMR) in 2016. The findings could be of value in highlighting areas of concern from the viewer's perspective, which the council could further look into and remedy.

THE HISTORY AND ROLE OF EGYPTIAN TELEVISION
PRIOR TO THE 2011 REVOLUTION

For decades, Egyptian media, including television, were state-owned, funded by public money yet controlled by the government. Television has been recognized as an instrument for propaganda, functioning in a public service capacity. Under the state-owned model, Egyptian television supervised the nature of any content broadcast (Kamalipour 2007).

Egypt saw a tremendous proliferation of satellite channels in the late 1990s. These channels have gained more popularity and credibility than land-based ones. Egypt has more than 150 satellite channels (Abbassi 2013). This figure is significant because it relates to (a) funding of the Egyptian broadcast industry; (b) the ability, or inability, of the state to monitor and regulate television; and (c) the status of Egyptian media with respect to the rest of the region.

Before the 2011 revolution, three main themes characterized Egyptian television and were closely related to its content and the nature of its broadcasts: the political theme, the commercialism theme, and the religious theme.

The Political Theme

The first major broadcasting theme was related to the political aspect of the country and its influence on the media. Amin (2008) and Sakr (2007) agreed that the government heavily controlled Egypt's broadcast system, including NILESAT, even after the introduction of the competitive Saudi ARABSAT satellite system. Amin (2008) described the land-based system of channels as extensively controlled by the government, with a monopoly on Arabic series and a variety of programs produced by its studios.

Sakr (2007) noted that one way the government maintained indirect control was by dictating that companies operating in the free zone were subject to regulations by the Public Authority for Investment and Free Zones, which was authorized to suspend licenses. She gave a clear example of such control: the biased television coverage of the 2005 presidential elections. During that time, television gave the majority of the coverage to incumbent president Hosni Mubarak.

Because the government financially supported the state channels, it was easily able to strictly monitor and regulate content (Amin 2007). This directly threatens the principles of public service broadcasting, which advocates a democratic, free television system and values diversity in opinion.

Amin (2007) also discussed a more serious trend—self-censorship—particularly in the area of political coverage. He noted that, despite a 1971 constitutional law guaranteeing complete media freedom, except in times of war, strong media censorship and self-censorship continued to exist.

In 1975, stricter regulation was imposed when a specific law mandated that cinematic theatrical or musical works needed to obtain a license to air from the censorship unit. A similar law was enacted in 1983 governing Egyptian Radio and Television Union transmissions. The laws empowered censors to edit out scenes relating to national security, religion, or government activities (Amin 2007).

The Commercialism Theme

Although political influences persisted, advances in technology and the emergence of new, independent satellite channels led to more liberal media practices and a rise in commercialism (Hammond 2004, Sakr 2007, Tartoussieh 2009, Aly 2011).

With advertising becoming the main source of media funding (Herman and Chomsky 1988), there was a global trend toward a more commercial broadcast model. As commercialism and materialism grew, profit- and advertising-driven activities interfered with the Egyptian media's much-needed public service role.

The medium of television, in particular, did not represent all societal groups. It ignored the nation's ethnic, religious, economic, and social composition and focused only on the desires and interests of a small segment of the population (Aly 2011): those who can afford. The main aim of television became targeting the segments of society that had strong purchasing power, and the media were tailored according to their needs.

Various communication scholars criticized the global trend toward commercialization of media (Artz 2007; Hammond 2004; Herman and Chomsky 1988; Mullen 2010; Murdock and Golding 1999). Herman and Chomsky argued that the media had become alarmingly profit-oriented. Galician (2004) further noted that a major by-product of commercialism was that viewers had become skeptical of the media they were exposed to. Audiences became increasingly suspicious, looking for the media's "hidden agenda" and trying to uncover marketing manipulation. The result was a sense of distrust, questioning the credibility of the media.

Media credibility is highly important if the media are to act as a watchdog and support democracy. However, if media content is nothing more than a promotional vehicle, the media will no longer be credible. In this situation, reality is not presented accurately, as it is consistently biased in favor of glamorizing the advertised products. Hackley et al. (2008), Sung et al. (2008), Gutnik et al. (2007), Schejter (2004), and Wenner (2004) have all expressed similar concerns about the ethicality of excessive commercialism of the media.

The Religious Theme

The third broadcasting theme prior to the 2011 revolution relates to the role of Islamist thought. Although this thought had begun spreading in the 1990s, it became more prominent in the period that immediately followed the Egyptian revolution of 2011, as the Muslim Brotherhood gained political power.

Because Egypt has an overwhelming Muslim majority, Egyptian television programming and content are widely influenced by Islamic laws and traditions. Accordingly, Islamic religious teachings are also expected to influence and guide public service television and state-controlled broadcasting.

The power of Islamists represented by the Muslim Brotherhood on Egyptian media had been visible since the time when they were still an underground party. During the 1990s, the Muslim Brotherhood (a banned underground political party at the time) utilized successful communication strategies and benefited from the growth of satellite channels to spread its religious ideology (Richter 2008, Tartoussieh 2009). The term "clean cinema," which has been used since the 1990s to refer to a new mode of Islamic and morally acceptable film production, is an example of this influence. According to Tartoussieh, "'Clean cinema' rejects the explicit portrayal of sexuality, impropriety, or nudity and favours piety and social awareness" (177).

After the Revolution

In the wake of the January revolution, a new Egyptian constitution was instituted in 2014 following a public referendum (Sayah and Tawfeeq 2014). It stated clearly the right to freedom of thought and opinion. Of significance to this study is Article 211, which creates the Supreme Council for Media Regulation.

The SCMR's constitutionally assigned role is to oversee all state and private audiovisual media. The SCMR is to be actively involved in all discussions about any new laws relating to the media. Its other duties are to preserve the Arabic language, culture, and values, and protect media ethics (Egyptian Constitution 2014).

UNDERSTANDING THE AUDIENCE PERSPECTIVE

The main focus of the present research was to develop a better understanding of the Egyptian audience's perception and experience of television. Six focus group discussions were conducted in June 2014. The aim was to incorporate different demographic groups from Egyptian society, taking into account practical and risk factors such as safety. All participants were residents of Cairo. Table 14.1 describes the participants.

For ease of reference, table 14.2 contains a simple coding system developed to help identify and refer to the demographic information of focus group participants.

Because this was an exploratory, qualitative study, the discussions were based on open-ended questions to stimulate participants to provide feedback. The data gathered provided a wealth of information on general audience perceptions of Egyptian television.

Focus group analysis was guided by the grounded theory approach. Numerous themes emerged from focus group conversations. Overall, there was consensus about the main issues. However, differences were found—especially related to age, gender, and socioeconomic

Table 14.1. Focus group participant demographics

Focus Group	Age	Gender	Socioeconomic/Educational Background
1	18–25	4 males and 4 females	Moderate to high
2	35–50	4 males and 4 females	Moderate to high
3	18–25	6 males	Lower
4	18–25	6 females	Lower
5	35–50	6 males	Lower
6	35–50	6 females	Lower

Table 14.2. Participant coding guide

Participant Reference Code	Gender	Age	Socioeconomic/Educational Background
FYH	4 females	18–25	Moderate to high
MYH	4 males	18–25	Moderate to high
FOH	4 females	35–50	Moderate to high
MOH	4 males	35–50	Moderate to high
MYL	6 males	18–25	Lower
FYL	6 females	18–25	Lower
MOL	6 males	35–50	Lower
FOL	6 females	35–50	Lower

Table 14.3. Themes emerging from focus group discussion analysis

Main Themes	*Subtopics*
Overall criticisms of television	• Lack of objectivity and credibility in news reporting • Disapproval of increased indecent content • Nostalgia for television of the past
Demands of television	• Credibility in news reporting • Censorship of indecent and immoral content • Reexamination of certain religious programming • Improving children's programming • Improving quality, making content attractive and innovative

background. These instances are highlighted and analyzed in the following sections. Table 14.3 presents the relevant findings.

Prior to holding the main focus group discussions, a pilot session was conducted to allow for improvements to the original audience research design.

OVERALL PERCEPTIONS OF EGYPTIAN BROADCASTING

Generally, there was agreement among participants in all groups that television played an integral role in the daily life of Egyptians; it was considered an important source of news, information, and entertainment. "Egyptian channels" includes Egyptian land-based state channels as well as privately owned Egyptian satellite channels based in Egypt.

In this research, audience perceptions of television are considered an essential component in determining the expected role of television in Egyptian society. A rather surprising finding from the focus groups was that every participant had a negative overall perception of Egyptian television channels. The reasons for these perceptions are explored below.

Lack of Objectivity and Credibility in News Reporting

While participants provided several reasons for their negative attitudes toward Egyptian television channels, the one most frequently mentioned was the perceived bias in news reporting. Participants were unanimous in their condemnation of Egyptian channels (both ERTU and private commercial ones) because of what they perceived as a lack of credibility and distortion of the truth in the presentation of news. In their opinion, events were often exaggerated or underplayed to support preset agendas.

Participants did not hold back when it came to voicing their disapproval. They used terms such as "hypocritical" and "brainwash." They openly accused the channels of being cheerleaders for the government when it came to political issues. Many noted that information presented by Egyptian channels was less credible than non-Egyptian ones. For example, an MOL participant explained in frustration, "There are events that happen in front of my eyes. I am a first-hand witness! Yet the next day I find Wael El-Ebrashi [a well-known talk show host] saying something completely different. There is a great contradiction between what happens and what we are told." Similarly, an MYL added, "I feel that talk shows or political ones are all directed toward a certain goal. They all either praise someone or criticize someone simply to fit in with the trend and act in a politically acceptable way."

Several major trends emerged from the conversations. Firstly, this perception did not differ across age, religion, or socioeconomic background. Younger and older participants, Christians, Muslims, and upper and lower socioeconomic/educational groups were all very displeased with what they perceived as unprofessional and subjective news reporting on Egyptian television.

Secondly, focus group members did not hold back in elaborating on what, for Egyptians, could be seen as a sensitive issue. An FYL (female young participant from the lower socio-economic/educational group) boldly noted that censorship on Egyptian television was only applied to political and news content, but not in other areas, such as entertainment or advertising, where it was truly needed.

This outspokenness is an interesting and unanticipated finding because, in line with previously cited Arab audience research findings (Amin 2007, 2008), the expectation was that focus group members would be fearful and reluctant to express politically related views. This was hardly the case during the group discussions. On the contrary, participants had a strong desire to express their views and criticize television's news coverage and political content. Often, the groups had to be reminded that the focus of the discussion was not about politics or news, but rather the overall role of Egyptian television, including advertising and product placement.

Thirdly, during the focus group discussions, there were no verbal or visual cues that revealed any reluctance in the participants. This may also mean that Egyptian audiences have evolved and become more outspoken since Amin's (2007, 2008) articles were published and since the revolution. This could be a positive outcome of the Arab Spring revolutions, which sought to empower citizens and promote freedom of expression and democracy. It could mean that people were no longer as scared to express their views. On the contrary, these participants clearly had a desire to share their opinions. It also suggests that audiences want to be and should be heard in future broadcast policy decisions.

Disapproval of Increased Indecent Content Coupled with Nostalgia for Television of the Past

Beyond the issues of credibility, participants expressed dissatisfaction with the overall type of television content offered. Many yearned for "the old television of earlier times." Although this wistfulness may not be uncommon or unique to Egyptians (Havlena and Holak 1991, Holbrook and Schindler 2003, Scott and Zac 1993), in this particular case, the yearning was directed toward a different time when there was perceived to be less violence and chaos.

With the exception of the area of news reporting, all focus groups displayed this notable nostalgia and longing. Although participants decried state interference in television, at the same time they wanted more government regulation. Clearly, focus groups isolated political news coverage from other nonpolitical content and evaluated each of those categories differently. In areas that did not relate to politics, there were interesting and important insights to be shared.

There was a common perception that in the 1980s and the 1990s, Egyptian television was more family-friendly and respectful of culture and traditions. Almost all participants reminisced about more conservative, nonpolitical content and the stronger educational role television played in society. There was a clear longing by most members of all groups for times when Egypt was less commercial and less influenced by Western culture. An FYL added, "The female TV presenters did not wear too much makeup, as they do now. Actors and presenters were classier and more elegant. Their style and language on the screen were much more respectable." This young woman's observations were particularly interesting because she was only a child in the 1990s. Although feelings of nostalgia would logically be expected among older participants, it was striking that they were as strongly felt even by the 18- to 25-year-old males and females, irrespective of their socioeconomic background.

There seem to be many reasons for such strong sentiments of nostalgia shared by both younger and older focus group members. One of them relates to the common perception of participants that current television programming has become alarmingly "obscene and vulgar" in a manner that does not respect religion, culture, or traditions. Evidently, the concern here was not political interference, but the commercialization and Westernization of television.

Numerous scholars have criticized the Westernization of Arab television (Sakr 2007, Sabry 2006, Ayish 2014, Hammond 2004, Kraidy and Khalil 2007, Gouaaybess 2008). The perceptions of the focus group participants seemed to be in line with these scholarly critiques. There was also a reiterated concern about children being exposed to content that was not age appropriate. This was especially evident among females, yet males met their observations with nodding and approval. An FOH complained, "Children ask us questions we don't know how to answer. For example, once there was a scene in the Ramadan series *Kasserat* [Minors] about a young girl who had to undergo surgery to restore her virginity. My confused young daughter asked me what that was and whether it would happen to her." Interestingly, despite the fact that they were young and not yet parents, both MYL and FYL were concerned about younger viewers who were being exposed to indecent, vulgar, and sexual TV content. Here, there was clear evidence in support of the media's third-person effect theory.

The third-person effect suggests that people tend to believe that mass media messages have a greater effect on others than on themselves. Accordingly, viewers who often dismiss the potential danger to themselves of product placement for certain brands may do so because of this effect. They assume that they are not as naïve and vulnerable as others (Galician 2004). In their investigation, Shin and Kim (2011) conclude that college students favor regulation and censorship of alcohol product placements because they fear their negative impact on younger viewers. Such sentiments reflect a strong desire for a socially responsible broadcast system, which suggests the usefulness of a Public Service Broadcast model for Egyptian society.

There was also increasing discontent about inaccurate portrayals of Egyptian society through vulgar, indecent, and sexually charged content. According to participants, this was propagating a damaging image of Egypt by making misleading and sweeping generalizations about its customs and traditions.

The concern about sexual content, which was raised by participants in all groups, was not surprising, given the religious and conservative nature of Egyptians. However, what was unexpected was that, without prompting, the issue of "vulgarity" was raised by participants in lower socioeconomic groups. The degree of repulsion against "vulgar tastes and vulgar language" in TV content was overwhelming. Public discourse about this issue has often assumed that "vulgar" content was a result of strong demand for this by lower, less educated socioeconomic classes (*Daily News Egypt* 2011).

Still, these perceptions of focus group members raised a critical question: If current Egyptian television is perceived as cheap and vulgar by both upper and lower socioeconomic groups, then who are the audiences targeted by such programs? One possible explanation is that participants may pretend to shun vulgarity in order to appear more sophisticated. For example, some women from lower socioeconomic classes complained that their husbands actually enjoy watching the same "vulgar" belly dancing channels that they openly criticize. In short, people's unconscious desires may not always match what they believe to be moral or right and what they express in discussions with others.

As Barwise and Ehrenberg (1988) have noted, some viewers may express liking or dislike for certain programs "merely because this seems to be the socially acceptable response" (55). Thus, the lower socioeconomic classes may have been eager to reject and criticize such content only to show that they do not truly belong in a lower educational or socioeconomic classification.

Unfortunately, there has been very little audience research among Egyptians, and among Arabs in general, which makes it difficult to understand the reasons Egyptian audiences may be reluctant to admit watching those programs. As Sabry (2007) asserts, "There is a poverty of audience research in the Arab world, most of which is quantitative, commercially driven, and tells us hardly anything about who Arab audiences are or how they interact with and read media texts" (160).

Another explanation may be that the focus group members in this study, who were not statistically representative, do not include all Egyptian socioeconomic groups. Other, unrepresented Egyptian segments, such as those in distant geographic locations in Egypt, may indeed enjoy and admit to viewing this type of programming.

AUDIENCE EXPECTATIONS OF TELEVISION

The elaborate demands and expectations expressed by focus group participants reflect an audience that is actively interested and eager for a particular broadcast system. They want to see television playing a socially responsible role.

Specific demands called for by the focus group members included credibility in news reporting, censorship of nonpolitical content, monitoring of religious channels to prevent the spread of extremism, reforming children's programming through more appealing educational formats, and using modern, more visually appealing design in television programs. This list logically stems from the concerns voiced in the previous sections. For example, complaints about vulgarity and indecency culminated in a call for censorship of such content.

Credibility in News Reporting and Censorship of Indecent, Immoral Content

Participants strongly believed the widespread perception that Egyptian channels act as a mouthpiece for the government. This major flaw has cost the Egyptian broadcast industry a large market share, with people turning to pan-Arab channels instead. The finding is consistent with the argument presented by Sakr (2007) that Egyptian audiences perceived Egyptian channels to be the least credible. It is interesting that other Arab channels, such as Al Arabiya, or international channels, such as the BBC, were seen as more authentic. Further, since most participants had expressed disapproval of the excessive use of sexuality, drug abuse, violence, and vulgar language, they wanted more state involvement through direct government intervention in nonpolitical content. The majority within all groups agreed that such material must be censored to preserve values and protect culture and religious traditions.

However, not all participants agreed on this. Tension in this area was evident in the higher socioeconomic/education participants. One MOH rejected the call for more censorship or increased regulation, which he said might limit and control content and interfere with freedom. Despite his dissatisfaction with Egyptian television's current programming in all genres, he began to argue for freedom of choice and educating viewers as an alternative to censorship.

It was also clear that, generally, females were more conservative and demanded higher degrees of censorship than males. For example, all females in all groups were strongly in favor of censorship of "immoral content." However, the males were not so unanimous. Maybe maternal tendencies in females can explain their desire to "protect society" from immoral media. As noted above, there was clear support for the media's third-person effect among females, who were clearly concerned about potential harm to children.

It was interesting that the few respondents who completely rejected censorship tended to belong to the category of males in the older age groups, while the 18- to 25-year-olds found it more necessary. This was surprising because it was expected that younger generations would be more liberal than older ones. Perhaps the older males were more experienced and wiser and realized that, in the long run, education is more effective and preferable to censorship. They may have witnessed the negative effects of censorship on society. As an MOH noted, "The real control must come from the home."

Despite the few voices that rejected censorship with regard to certain programming contents, there was general agreement in all groups that the current private channel licensing system needed reforming and more control. The way participants saw it was that the current system lacked sufficient controls or filtering because anyone could launch a new channel. Focus group participants wanted the current system to be reevaluated to ensure that certain regulations were imposed before new channels were launched. Here again, there was a call for government regulation, to some degree, which should not be overlooked. The females in the younger groups pointed out the example of a belly dancer, Sama el-Masry, who launched a channel in which she danced and attacked the previous Muslim Brotherhood regime. They strongly believed that the government should not have licensed "petty" channels in the first place and that stricter measures had to be applied to control what is aired.

Similarly, participants alluded to the danger posed by the numerous religious channels that were launched after the 2011 revolution. Although some participants were aware that those channels had recently been shut down under the current president, Abdel Fattah al-Sisi, there was a consensus that the main problem was that such channels are easy to launch owing to ineffective licensing laws.

On a more general level, what also became clear from the concerns voiced by participants was that wider decisions are needed on the form that the Egyptian broadcast system and its regulation should take.

Reexamination of Religious Programming

The need to revisit religious programming was a major demand by the participants. However, it was different from the discussion of censorship and control of inappropriate television content in that participants deemed "religious censorship" necessary for reasons of national security and internal stability.

Participants unanimously felt that religious programs needed to be more closely monitored, because they were worried about the rise of religious fanatics and extremists launching new channels to serve as a communication and/or recruitment platform for terrorist groups. They also expected television to take a more proactive role to counteract the impact of misleading or extremist views. "Television should play a more effective role in terms of religious education," insisted an MOL.

This expectation for the broadcast industry is crucial because it suggests a strong audience desire for more educational and citizen-oriented programs—something that a purely commercially driven or entertainment-driven system is unlikely to provide. There is one problem with this control logic, though: it is very subjective. Who will determine how much religious programming is enough or too much? Who gets to speak, and which opinions get to be heard? What about minorities such as Coptic Christians? Would they get an equal share of religious programming in a Muslim country?

Improving Children's Programming

With respect to children's programs, participants had additional criticisms beyond the previously discussed concerns about vulgarity and inappropriate or obscene content. Many stressed the need to revolutionize children's programming in a manner that would take into account the new and powerful role of the Internet.

Current Egyptian television programs targeting younger viewers were perceived as "unattractive," "shallow," "dull," and "outdated." Although mothers were naturally eager to elaborate on this topic, even 18- to 25-year-olds seemed very interested in this issue. They were often nodding in agreement when another group member criticized children's programming. Many respondents from different demographic groups agreed that television was not living up to its potential in terms of educating younger generations and teaching them valuable behaviors and ethics. An MYL noted, "Egyptian TV channels do not take into account that younger viewers are now using the Internet and video games. They are more technically advanced than previous generations. Egyptian channels insist on using old, outdated formats that children find boring. They don't appeal to children."

This is an insightful comment, which should not be underestimated by the broadcast industry. Television must consider the "appeal" factor or else it will lose younger viewers to the Internet, which has become easily accessible to children in Egypt. Comparisons were also made to other, "superior quality" regional and international channels such as Disney, Nickelodeon, and Cartoon Network. It should be noted here that such channels are available in Arabic, which allows them to compete effectively with Egyptian programs. Disney and Nickelodeon are available for a monthly subscription fee, which may be a deterrent to the majority of Egyptians, who can access other satellite channels such as Cartoon Network at no cost.

Although no specific current Egyptian children's programs were criticized, there was a clear consensus about the lack of adequate educational content and appeal. There was also a sense of nostalgia for children's programs of the 1980s and 1990s, which contained the educational elements missing from today's shows. An FOL noted, "1980s and '90s children's television shows like Nagwa Ibrahim's *Mama Nagwa* (Mother Nagwa) or *Cinema al-Atfal* (Children's Cinema) used to have a purpose and teach children important values. Television now lacks such shows. Our parents even used to enjoy watching them with us."

This longing for an earlier time must be analyzed from many angles. Firstly, it might be nostalgia for a time when Egyptian television really did provide better children's programming. Participants may have been looking at the past and glamorizing it in an exaggerated way.

Secondly, although there seems to be a longing for programs of the 1980s and 1990s, it is probably unrealistic to assume that they will be popular today among children growing up with tablets, smartphones, video games, and so on. In the 1980s and early 1990s, such devices did not exist and children were not as technologically savvy as they are today. Television programs from that era might be viewed as too simple or boring.

Thirdly, entertaining programs are not always educational. Some are based purely on humor and entertainment. Children's entertainment programs are more popular in commercial broadcast systems such as Disney and Nickelodeon, whereas educational programs such as *Eftah ya Semsem* (Open Sesame) are a core component of a public service system. As confirmed by the focus groups, this is clearly the type of programming that they want Egyptian channels to provide. Here again, a public service–oriented broadcast system appears to be essential in meeting Egyptian audience demands.

Improved Quality, Attractive Content, and Innovative Approaches

In addition to changes in children's programming, audiences also demanded improved quality, attractive content, and innovative approaches. Compared to state channels, privately owned Egyptian channels fared better in terms of perceived quality and attractive content. Participants pointed out that government channels needed to be more competitive in comparison to Egyptian and non-Egyptian regional private channels such as MBC, CBC, al-Hayat, and Dream. They noted that government channels frequently air old series and films, and criticized the general lack of originality, variety, and visual appeal on these channels.

There was also a strong desire for improvement in national and international sports programs. At least one male in each group wanted an increase in sports coverage, highlighting this as a major failing in Egyptian channels, both government and private. Participants pointed out that Egyptian channels were not competitive in this domain, compared to other satellite channels such as Al Jazeera Sports and the private BeIn, major competitors in this area. Both channels offer exclusive coverage of various sports championships and football tournaments.

Gender differences were clear in this area, as females did not bring up sports and they displayed no nonverbal cues that might have suggested interest in this type of programming.

Although the interest of male participants in sports was anticipated, what was interesting and unexpected was a huge demand by males for documentaries. Males from all age groups and socioeconomic backgrounds complained about the low quality and number of documentaries. This was especially true for the younger participants, who mentioned National Geographic and Discovery and wondered why similar programs did not exist on Egyptian television. An MYH wondered, "Why don't [we] have channels like Animal Planet? We are part of Africa, a continent rich in animal diversity. We need to learn about North African animals and wildlife!" He continued, "We used to have on Friday a show called 'Animal World' and it was canceled!"

In all focus groups, there was a clear message that Egyptian television needed to offer viewers more choice through variety and diversity in programming.

WHAT DOES THIS MEAN?

In analyzing the overall viewer perceptions of television, the focus group discussions revealed some inconsistencies. While there was a call for less government control in news coverage and analysis, there was also a demand for more regulation and censorship in other areas. In particular, vulgarity and indecency of content were listed as drawbacks, which alarmed participants and required government intervention.

In addition, there was unanimous objection to current religious programming, a main threat posed by new satellite channels, which appear to lack regulation from the perspective of focus group members. This inconsistency in calling for both censorship and freedom of speech simultaneously can perhaps be explained by the recent rise of extremist channels that legitimize murder in the name of religion.

Religious programming may be viewed as a threat because it could endanger national unity and internal political stability between Egypt's Coptic Christian minority and the Muslim majority. The rise of extremist groups such as the Islamic State in Iraq and Syria (ISIS) and the Islamic State in Egypt and Libya (ISEL) may have led the public, at least under these particular circumstances, to favor peace and stability over freedom and democracy, the original triggers behind the 2011 revolution.

As for the interest in regulating overly sexual or vulgar content, this is nothing unusual and is common in many societies. Egyptians are no exception here.

Overall, the focus group discussions revealed a need for balanced regulation. A solution may come from a system similar to the PSB model, which allows for the democratic expression of differing opinions, but also sets necessary controls while offering variety and innovation in programming. Advertising and product placement practices must also fit in with the objectives and aims of such a system.

The recently formed SCMR, described in the literature review, may be a useful tool for implementing such regulations. For example, the SCMR already has a specialized committee for receiving audience complaints against media content in both state and satellite channels. In addition, the SCMR's monitoring committee reviews the content of the media programs and television drama. Through this monitoring committee the SCMR also surveys audience preferences and attitudes toward media outputs, and analyzes public opinion relating to the media (SCMR website).

The findings of this study regarding audience critiques, such as vulgarity and indecent content, could be further examined by the complaints and monitoring committees. Ultimately, a comprehensive and fair system of sanctions against violations could be set in place: one that takes into account viewer concerns, while continuing to protect freedom of expression and artistic creativity.

REFERENCES

Abbassi, J. 2013. "Free-to-air satellite TV channels in the Arab world: The growth in supply continues." Satellite Today, November 18, 2013. http://www.satellitetoday.com/publications/2013/11/18/free-to-air-satellite-tv-channels-in-the-arab-world-the-growth-in-supply-continues.

Aly, R. 2011. "Rebuilding Egyptian media for a democratic future." *Arab Media & Society* 11 (14): 1–7. http://www.arabmediasociety.com/?article=771.

Amin, H. 2007. "Strengthening the Rule of Law and Integrity in the Arab World: Report on the State of the Media in Egypt." Second draft. The Arab Centre for the Development of the Rule of Law and Integrity. http://www.arabruleoflaw.org/Files/PDF/Media/English/P2/Egypt_MediaReportP2_En.pdf.

———. 2008. "Arab Media Audience Research: Developments and Constraints." In *Arab Media: Power and Weakness*, edited by K. Hafez, 69–90. New York: Continuum.

Artz, L. 2007. "The Corporate Model from National to Transnational." In *The Media Globe: Trends in International Mass Media*, edited by L. Artz and Y. R. Kamalipour, 141–62. Lanham, MD: Rowman & Littlefield.

Ayish, M. 2014. "Political communication on Arab world television: Evolving patterns." *Political Communication* 19: 137–54.

Barwise, P., and A. Ehrenberg. 1988. *Television and Its Audience*. London: Sage.

Broadcasting Board of Governors. 2014. "Contemporary Media Use in Egypt." https://www.bbg.gov/wp-content/media/2014/03/Egypt-research-brief.pdf.

Daily News Egypt. 2011. "A question of morality in 'Haram Street.'" September 21, 2011. http://www.dailynewsegypt.com/2011/09/21/the-reel-estate-a-question-of-morality-in-haram-street.

Egyptian Constitution (official Arabic version). 2014. https://www.sis.gov.eg/Newvr/consttt%202014. pdf.

Galician, M. L. 2004. "Introduction: Product placements in the mass media: Unholy marketing marriages or realistic story-telling portrayals, unethical advertising messages or useful communication practices?" *Journal of Promotion Management* 10 (1/2), 1–8.

Gouaaybess, T. 2008. "Orientalism and the Economics of Arab Broadcasting." In *Arab Media: Power and Weakness*, edited by K. Hafez, 199–213. New York: Continuum.

Gutnik, L., T. Huang, J. B. Lin, and T. Schmidt. 2007. "New trends in product placement." *Strategic Computing and Communications Technology*, Spring 2007: 1–22. http://people.ischool.berkeley .edu/~hal/Courses/StratTech09/Tech/Preso/D-placement.doc.

Hackley, C., R. Tiwaskul, and L. Preuss. 2008. "An ethical evaluation of product placement: A deceptive practice?" *Business Ethics: A European Review* 17 (2): 109–19.

Hammond, A. 2004. *Pop Culture Arab World! Media, Arts, and Lifestyle*. Santa Barbara, CA: ABC-CLIO.

Havlena, W., and S. Holak. 1991. "The good old days: Observations on nostalgia and its role in consumer behaviour." *Advances in Consumer Research* 18: 323–29.

Herman, E., and N. Chomsky. 1988. *Manufacturing Consent: The Political Economy of the Mass Media*. New York: Pantheon.

Holbrook, M., and R. Schindler. 2003. "Nostalgic bonding: Exploring the role of nostalgia in the consumption experience." *Journal of Consumer Behaviour* 3: 107–27.

Kamalipour, Y. R. 2007. *Global Communication*. Belmont, CA: Wadsworth Publishing.

Kraidy, M. M., and J. F. Khalil. 2007. "The Middle East: Transnational Arab Television." In *The Media Globe: Trends in International Mass Media*, edited by L. Artz and Y. R. Kamalipour, 79–98. Lanham, MD: Rowman & Littlefield.

Mullen, A. 2010. "Twenty years on: The second-order predication of the Herman-Chomsky propaganda model." *Media, Culture & Society* 32 (4): 673–90.

Murdock, G., and P. Golding. 1999. "Common markets: Corporate ambitions and communication trends in the UK and Europe." *Journal of Media Economics* 12 (2): 117–32.

Richter, C. 2008. "The Effects of Islamist Media on the Mainstream Press in Egypt." In *Arab Media: Power and Weakness*, edited by K. Hafez, 46–65. New York: Continuum.

Sabry, T. 2006. "What is 'global' about Arab media?" *Global Media and Communication* 1 (1): 41–48.

———. 2007. "In Search of the Arab Present Cultural Tense." In *Arab Media and Political Renewal: Community, Legitimacy and Public Life*, edited by N. Sakr, 154–68. London: I. B. Tauris.

Sakr, N. 2007. *Arab Television Today*. London: I. B. Tauris.

Sayah, R., and M. Tawfeeq. 2014. "Egypt passes new constitution." CNN, January 18, 2014. http://edi tion.cnn.com/2014/01/18/world/africa/egypt-constitution.

Schejter, A. 2004. "Product Placement as an International Practice: Moral, Legal, Regulatory and Trade Implications." Paper presented at the 32nd Research Conference on Communication, Information and Internet Policy, October 1–3, 2004, Arlington, Virginia.

Scott, J., and L. Zac. 1993. "Collective memories in Britain and the United States." *Public Opinion Quarterly* 57 (3): 315–31.

Shin, D. H., and J. K. Kim. 2011. "Alcohol product placements and the third-person effect." *Television & New Media* 12 (5): 411–40.

Sung, Y., J. Choi, and F. De Gregorio. 2008. "Brand placements in Korean films, 1995–2003: A content analysis." *Journal of International Consumer Marketing* 20 (3/4): 39–53.

Tartoussieh, K. 2009. "Islam, media, and cultural policy: A preliminary investigation." *International Journal of Cultural Policy* 15 (2): 171–78.

Wenner, L. 2004. "On the ethics of product placement in the mass media entertainment." *Journal of Promotion Management* 1 (1–2): 101–32.

15

Network Journalism in Post-Revolution Egypt

Ahmed El Gody

News-making has always been influenced by the utilization of technological innovations inside newsrooms. Allan and Thorsen (2014) discussed how journalism has experienced significant changes during the past decade as an outcome of information communication technologies (ICTs). One major finding was the convergence of social media in the journalism process (Allan and Thorsen 2014). Social media offered news organizations the possibility of developing new types of journalism to help them connect and interact with their audiences (Quandt and Singer 2009).

The term "convergence" comes up all the time, and it means different things in different contexts. A more common approach to convergence of social media in news operation is journalists' move away from covering stories for a single medium to "manufacturing" a content pool and disseminating it in a variety of social media formats (figure 15.1). Thus, journalists must learn to communicate and network effectively using a more multifaceted vocabulary of media technologies than they have in the past. The end result is a convergence of journalists and various types of journalism that have been operating in separate spheres, such as television, radio, newspaper, magazine, and online, to provide news in all those different formats (Kolodzy 2006). It is a type of cross-newsroom cooperation that allows the news organization as a whole to cover more ground by dividing the aspects of the work among the different media (Beltrame 2001, Kolodzy 2006).

On another level, social media, at their core, form a social network where information circulates from one communicator node to many others without the help of an institutional medium. As a result, convergence affects not just the way journalists go about their jobs, but also the way they conceptualize those jobs and their roles within society (Salvatore 2013, Radsch 2018). The nature of public communication also is subject to change, with the potential for greater inclusion of individuals and communities (Allan and Thorsen 2014, Bruns 2005). The development of networks ultimately engendered a new form of journalism, called networked journalism, and thus created a conscious sense of how to reach citizens and listen to them, make them part of the news-making process, and enable them to listen back and forth to one another (Duffy 2011).

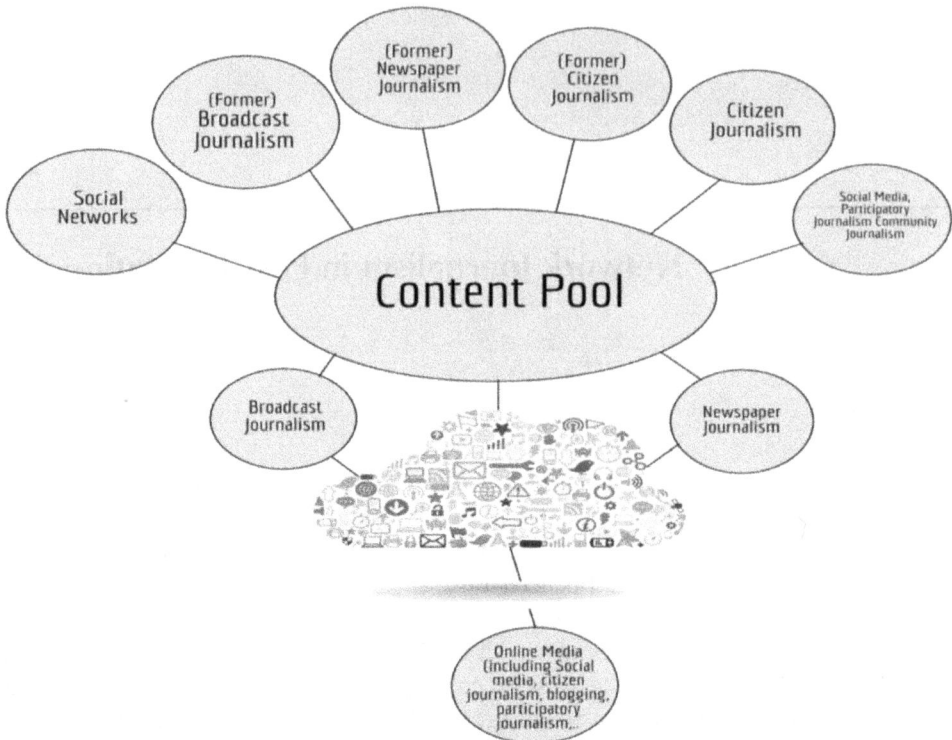

Figure 15.1. Content Pool Newsroom operation (Adapted from Quandt and Singer).

MEDIA DELIBERATION AND NETWORKED PUBLIC SPHERE

ICTs introduced alternative spaces for Egyptians to participate in discussions on issues of common concern. The more Egyptians that join cyberspace, the more people cluster into networks. Therefore, the more such active participation occurs, the more Egyptians come closer to reaching their sociopolitical development goals. These discussions are taking place in several online spaces, including Facebook, Twitter, chat rooms, mobile texts, and news websites (Radsch 2018, Anderson and Eickelman 2008).

The advent of ICTs offered news organizations the possibility of developing new types of journalism that are different from other traditional systems. Several studies (Atton 2010, Radsch 2018) discussed how ICTs could be used as a tool to escape government control and how journalists could be the agents for social change, engaging in public argument on sociopolitical reforms (Radsch 2018).

The role of the media in providing opportunities for democratic deliberation is explicit in Jürgen Habermas's discussions of his concept of the "public sphere," first outlined in *Strukturwandel der Öffentlichkeit* in 1962. The Habermasian public sphere can be defined as "an arena in which people participate in discussions about matters of common concern, in an atmosphere free of coercion or dependencies that would incline individuals toward acquiescence or silence" (Warren 1995). Through informed and critical discussion, the public can create and/or influence the public opinion process, applying pressure to the political class (Dahlberg 2001, Murphy 2011).

For Habermas, the press (journalism) plays an essential role in the public sphere, enlightening people by building a healthy and progressive society. The media in an "ideal" public sphere help to increase the audience's willingness to learn and its capacity to be critical, away from political and market pressure (Fraser 1990, Habermas 2006). However, as time has passed, the press has come to be inextricably linked to the capitalist system. The emergence of a "mass" press has resulted in the public sphere losing much of its original character in favor of commercialism and entertainment (Volkmer 2003, Murphy 2011).

The rise of commercialization forced the press to lose its autonomy, impeding freedom and rational debate. The media incorporated ideological positions, pandered to popular opinion as shaped by authority or ruling-party politics, and became increasingly reliant on government subsidies and advertising revenues to sustain its existence (Murphy 2011, Habermas 1997, Castells 2015). Many theorists discussed the emergence of ICTs and social media applications as foundations for a new form of public sphere that takes into account social structure and a communication system that binds them—a networked space providing tools and setting the dynamics of a new mediated arena.

Revisiting his model, Habermas came to view the public sphere as "a network for communicating information and points of view . . . the streams of communication are, in the process, filtered and synthesized in such a way that they coalesce into bundles of topically specified public opinions" (Habermas 1997, 29). The public sphere, as described by Habermas, helps us to understand the networked society and the conditions that facilitate its discourse. Castells further argued that if the communication of networks of any kind forms the public sphere, then the network society organizes its public sphere into different networks, on the basis of media communication network (Castells 2008). ICTs network online spaces, allowing new forms of interactivity, enabling users to communicate in real time away from state and economic power and to exchange and critique issues of common concern (Dahlberg 2001, Castells 2015).

According to Castells, the networked public sphere constitutes the social morphology of societies' communication and information. In other words, the sphere focuses on social networks that process and manage information (Castells 2008, 2015). The diffusion of a networking logic substantially modifies the operation and outcomes in processes of production, experience, power, and culture. Networks have therefore become the basic units of modern society. These units include individuals, groups, organizations, and communities linked by information processes between and among them (Castells 2008, 2015; Van Dijk 2012).

As in a traditional public sphere, the media in general and a journalism process in particular are at the center of the networked public sphere and are the reason for its continuation (Castells 2008). For Castells, a strong network is an active network in which news and information travel between different actors/stakeholders, opening whole new lines of connection between journalists and their audience. Further, the development of Web 2.0 social media, blogs, vlogs, podcasts, streaming, and other forms of interactive, computer-to-computer communication set up even more communication networks that allowed individuals, groups, and activists to communicate with each other without going through the usual channels set up by the institutions of society for socialized communication. This new form of media constitutes what Castells (2008) conceptualizes as mass self-communication: networks of communication that relate many to many in the sending and receiving of messages in a multi-modal form of communication that bypasses traditional mass media and often escapes government control. This latter characteristic is of particular interest with regard to the role of social media in developing a networked public sphere in nondemocratic societies.

Although several theorists have postulated that the public sphere, in its true sense, exists only in established democratic societies, others, such as Volkmer (2003) and Castells (2008, 2015), have stated that the emergence of new media networks in a globalized context changed the nature of the public sphere, widening its scope to include groups, segments, and geographical territories that were not included earlier. The function of the public sphere in the democratization process is a focal point of audience desire for "the good society" where popular political will takes shape and citizens are able to constitute themselves as active agents in the political process. The introduction of Internet technologies in geographical territories beyond the Western democracies has had an impact on their democratization process, with Internet technology mobilizing and facilitating new patterns of political participation and creating new forms of sphere(s), such as networked spheres (Dahlgren and Sparks 1992, Van Dijk 2012). New publics, especially marginalized groups, diasporas, and ethnic, religious, and political minorities, became active actors/nodes by utilizing social media to join the network sphere, creating new forms of online advocacy and new approaches toward democracy to attract an audience (Arquilla and Ronfeldt 2001, Anderson 2003).

In Egypt, ICTs, especially Internet technologies, were integrated as a medium for public deliberation that created a networked sphere(s). Many banned groups found a new avenue to reach audiences. Issues that had been considered closed for discussion thus came to be discussed (Radsch 2018). Salvatore examined the role of ICTs, especially social media, in promoting a democratic public sphere. Discussing Egypt, the author stated that new media liberalized the public, allowing them to participate in active discussions and thus promoting the process of democratization (Salvatore 2013). Egypt at that time was governed by a strict regime where many opposition parties and political groups were denied access to communicate with society. New media technologies offered Egyptians a space separate from the customary cultural authorities and historical framework of engagement, particularly between the elite and the subaltern.

A new class of interpreters, facilitated by this medium, addressed and reframed political and social authority and gave a voice to those like themselves and others who visited the sphere (Anderson and Eickelman 2008). Internet communication networks, which were subject to minimal censorship but close government monitoring, placed no limitations on the free flow of public information, providing a genuine public space for processing, synthesizing, and filtering information and debate. This led to discursive public dialogue in an entirely new public sphere (Radsch 2016).

This shift in audience participation presented a challenge to journalists, as it necessitated a fundamental shift in their agenda-setting role. It was a new and different type of journalism, requiring a conscious sense of how journalism initiatives can make a deliberate attempt to reach out to citizens, to listen to them, and to have citizens listen and talk to each other. The future of an information society in Egypt seemed promising, as online news communities began to deepen and enhance political participation in the democratic process, creating an active parallel communication and information system. By paying due attention to public affairs, the web provided a true democratization infrastructure, which seemed to promise that the contemporary process of constitutional representative democracy would develop through the utilization of social media.

SOCIAL MEDIA AND THE EGYPTIAN NETWORK SOCIETY

Whenever new media are introduced into a society, they play a role in reshaping the fabric of that society and, if properly utilized, create a new environment. McLuhan (1994) argues that new media—satellite television and radio at that time—re-created the world in the image of a global village, an extension of the human nervous system abolishing both time and space.

Jenkins discussed how countries beyond the Western Hemisphere viewed new technologies, mainly the Internet, as a means to escape from traditional information and communication systems to a new time and space, thus creating a reality of their own where news is interactively produced and reproduced by journalists and their audiences. Therefore, it created an agenda for development that could then be implemented offline. Jenkins's thesis considers development as a type of social change resulting from the introduction and utilization of technology in the social system (Ingraham and Moynihan 2000, Jenkins 2003).

Castells considered that one of the most important factors making online networks an alternative medium that fosters knowledge in a society is its ability to create free expression in all its forms. It is purpose-oriented communication: with open sources, free posting, decentralized broadcasting, interaction, and shared creation. The configuration of social networks as an interactive, participatory medium of communication and information makes it a "pull" technology, in contrast to the "push" technology of other forms of mass media. These technologies have dominated the Internet and had a decisive impact on individuals and society, ultimately obscuring the social life and the sociological network of the actors that shape its development and implementation. Interactivity is a crucial characteristic in networked media. It allows journalists and users to become involved in the communication process, regardless of distance and time, with more control over the information exchange process (Sicilia et al. 2005; Castells 2008, 2015).

In Egypt, the introduction of the Internet in news media production extended the media space beyond the local realm. As the number of online media outlets increased, the public space widened, with more actors being introduced in public discussion and more taboo issues being tackled. This new sphere did not confine itself to local or regional boundaries. It merged with the global public sphere, especially after 9/11, as Egypt became a battleground in the new war on terror. Global calls for modernizing Egypt and intensifying democratic governance coincided with national debates on political reform, opening the door for new political players to use new technologies. These new media spaces were used to attract audiences to their causes and programs (El Gody 2008).

To some researchers the Egyptian public sphere is not an atypical form, as most of the media outlets in Egypt do not have a global reach and only a few are financially and editorially independent. Most of them do not reflect a genuine public space, since they are still under government control. Nonetheless, the existence of the public sphere lies in the presence of multiple media outlets, especially new independent media. They create a mass-mediated arena and encourage citizens to become actively involved in the making of media content, as well as in the discussions created online and then pursued offline in other forums, including the government media (Ayish 2008, 2018).

Hence, the Egyptian public sphere could be seen through the lens of mediated space associated with the development of media, old and new: an arena where local/global and state/non-state actors, including media, exist, all utilizing new ICTs to debate issues of concern to local citizens. Despite skepticism, there is an Egyptian/Arab public sphere where discussions are centered on the analysis of genuine sociopolitical issues. These arguments are derived from global, regional, and local discussions on development and democracy and are then adopted mainly by Egyptian new media, especially independent and nonpartisan opposition journalists, to become issues in the Egyptian sociopolitical discourse. As a result, these issues are made present through genuine citizens' discussions (Lynch 2007, Ayish 2018).

Applying the Egyptian networked environment to the public sphere from subsystems of communication loops has more fluidity and increasingly greater mutuality of influences (Pepe

2011). The Egyptian networked sphere reflects Castells's (2008) definition of the "networked public sphere" as a set of interconnected nodes, representing audience, groups, activists, and others, expressing points at which a curve intersects itself. Networks are dynamic, innovative, open structures that are infinitely expandable and integrate new nodes as long as they share the same communication codes. New "networks" and "groups" started interpreting the news provided over the Internet and shaping/reshaping them according to their ideologies. It is not difficult, then, to argue that online news in Egypt started to operate on different terms from the state-controlled media, especially on sensitive and taboo issues (Fahmy 2010).

New media, especially the Internet, can be seen as agents for the representation of ideas. Those ideas divide the audience into organized, diverse social groups, which are then able to express their views. In that sense, Egypt created an early version of a virtual knowledge-networked communitarian society that clustered around different ideologies of development and freedom (Fahmy 2010, Ayish 2018). Online discussions in authoritarian regimes like Egypt can encourage people to participate in public issues: they talk to their peers or other segments of society, and their voices are then heard by the authorities and policy makers. Their interactive discussion is considered by Internet users to be more truthful, reliable, and revealing than the mainstream government media (Teel 2007).

Examining the role of ICTs in media as a source of political information and a sphere for public expression shows that online communication regarding politics has allowed citizens to gain knowledge about certain issues and coordinate certain actions to address joint concerns: "Newspaper reading and broadcast news viewing have repeatedly been linked with civic engagement, likewise, online information seeking appears to influence participation" (Shah et al. 2005). News websites, especially independent media, started extending their communication space from the real to the virtual world to explore realms that lie beyond the existing social, political, and physical constraints. This new realm promoted intra-cultural dialogue among different political parties, civil societies, networks, groups, and individuals to create or extend their physical presence into cyberspace. The elimination of physical distance encouraged citizens to increase their presence in active online participation. Using this approach, problems in Egypt were analyzed at different levels, from international to local, and development began to be perceived as need-oriented, endogenous, contributive, self-reliant, equitable, and promoting local cultures (Amin 2010).

Within a few years, new forms of interactive media, including social media, compensated for the inability of the weak and rigid political system to establish and mobilize links with Egyptian society. The increase in market competition among websites led to even more media liberalization and more citizen deliberation. New forms of citizen journalism started to develop (Hofheinz 2009). Citizens started using interactive features to fill the void created by traditional media's ignorance of important events and issues. More people joined the wired world for news and information, asking questions, offering comments, stating their opinions, engaging in political debates, and communicating with other readers. These are all features that make social media appealing to readers. Online news on social media became an alternative urban hub and acts as an interface between events in the streets and the Internet, facilitating a sense of network communities connecting the real and the virtual worlds (Salah-Fahmi 2009).

Social media transformed communication in Egypt from a mouthpiece for the Egyptian government to a tool that teaches citizens about their rights by breaking all traditional taboos and exposing the hypocrisy of the Egyptian political system (Salah-Fahmi 2009). Social media became the alternative to political systems, allowing the average person to actively participate in discussions and debate issues that affect their daily life. News networks succeeded in using the Internet as an active public sphere, putting pressure on rigid Arab systems and creating new realities out of virtual politics (El Gody 2008). Toulouse and Luke described the network cybersphere as a "transnational realm of society where transformation of societies takes place." They further explained that the new network sphere "became the locus of a new politics that spills out of the computer screen and revitalizes citizenship and democracy" (Toulouse and Luke 1998, 49).

NETWORKED JOURNALISM

In an increasingly interactive environment, media organizations need to fit themselves into the audience information flow. The time when news was pushed by media organizations to citizens has long gone. The public has become more active in the news production process (Heinrich 2012, El Gody 2013). The task for journalism organizations now is to figure out how to include their traditional and alternative content in the information nodes that their audiences are involved in every day (Deuze 2008).

"Networked journalism" is a type of journalism that includes active journalists and audience working together beyond time and space in news production (Salvatore 2013). Reporters and editors embracing networked journalism understand that audiences can and do get their news from a variety of outlets, so connecting their message to the audience network is important if they want to survive (Duffy 2011, Ardic 2012, Rosen 2011). Traditional news outlets have historically avoided linking with their audience, in the belief that professional journalism belongs to the elite class of journalists and that audiences need to be "passive recipients" of the news that is presented to them (Rosen 2011). However, the rising wave of online activism opened the door for a new form of journalism where active activists, citizens, and journalists meet to produce a type of journalism that needs to send information fast and across different platforms (El Gody 2013, Rosen 2011).

In addition to embracing a culture of linking to other sources, networked journalism also welcomes the audience as contributors to the news. Networked journalism creates platforms of interactivity to the public, taking into account the collaborative nature of journalism among professionals, amateurs, and citizens. At its core, networked journalism uses new technologies to include the citizen in every aspect of news gathering, production, and publication, using techniques like crowdsourcing, social networking, wikis, and Twitter (Beckett and Mansell 2008, Russell 2011). Many of these techniques build on existing journalism methods. It also requires a revolution in the way we make the news, in terms of audience participation: both working together to get the real story and linking together to share information and perspectives (Beckett and Mansell 2008, 205).

The use of social media by citizens and independent journalists created a new type of professional who functions as a node in the complex environment between technology and society, news and analysis, annotation and selection, and orientation and investigation (Deuze 2008). Journalists can no longer work in "splinted isolation," thanks to the abundance of information and the facts that, first, the public are perfectly capable of accessing news and information for themselves, and second, the institutional players (for-profit, governmental, non-profit, activist) are increasingly geared toward addressing their constituencies directly instead of using the news media as a go-between (Russell 2011, Heinrich 2012). The utilization of social media in journalism has added a new dimension to the production and the consumption of news journalism in Egypt, and has enabled the creation of new communication spaces where diverse voices engage in conversation about matters affecting people's daily lives.

In democratizing societies such as Egypt in particular, journalists need to be active in the network society, seeing different publics as creators, (re)actors, (re)makers, and redistributors of news. Journalists need to be bridge builders, distributing information from and among different political activists and networks and their audience(s) and providing citizens with vital and unadulterated news and information (Radsch 2018, Hamdy 2009, Russell 2016).

EGYPTIAN NETWORK SOCIETY AND THE EGYPTIAN REVOLUTION

Until the beginning of the twenty-first century, Egyptian print media organizations and journalists did not understand the use of ICTs. An organization's online presence was seen as merely an extension to expand the organization's geographical footprint so as to increase its popularity and circulation. Content remained static. Meanwhile, the traditional Egyptian news organizations, especially government ones, were losing ground to alternative and regional media (Teel 2007), as they failed to serve, interact with, or develop their citizens (Ayish 2008). Garrison (2004) added that the diffusion of social media in the making of news was finally seen as the missing link in the new journalism formula.

More and more Egyptians began communicating in cyberspace, not only to access information, but also to create a reality of their own. And it soon became clear that even a virtual reality can cross the boundary into the real world (El Gody 2013). Several newspapers, especially independent and opposition media, started expanding toward their audience's agenda and aligning themselves with civil movements like Kefaya and April 6th. News organizations started investing in ICT infrastructure and creating social media portals to encourage the communities of online activists to exchange ideas (Hamdy 2009, Ardic 2012).

News became more vibrant, more liquid, when content was customized, edited, and retransmitted via various platforms (Deuze 2008, El Gody 2013). Independent and opposition newspapers started creating posts that became weapons against the restricted flow of information enforced by the Egyptian government. This process reflected a shift in the media's influence in society, as people began to take information from alternative sources rather than traditional ones (Salah-Fahmi 2009). Egyptians started utilizing social media platforms to debate current events; criticize the government, public officials, and political parties; share personal experiences; propose solutions to sociopolitical problems; and construct different visions of the country's future (El Gody 2016).

Between 2006 and 2011, online sociopolitical discussions reached an all-time high. Citizens quickly created news sites, blogs, video blogs, YouTube videos, podcasts, SMS text messages, mobile phone websites, and accounts on social networks. Social media platforms, especially Facebook and YouTube, became the most visited sites in Egypt (El Gody 2013). Journalism and advocacy were produced and disseminated more quickly than the government controls could keep up with (Abbott 2016, Ayish 2018). Facebook and YouTube exploded in 2008 with the group protests of April 6th. For example, the April 6th call for the 2008 strike garnered 70,000 followers in a few days (Faris 2008, Salah-Fahmi 2009, El Gody 2013). Activists saw in social media an opportunity to elude government pressure, creating a space to discuss matters of common concern, enabling people to bypass the controlled regime and traditional mass media, and allowing the society to create a developmental agenda of its own (Salah-Fahmi 2009, El Gody 2016).

People continued to utilize social media to expose government scandals, delegitimize the government narrative, and analyze government figures and announcements. Journalists and activists started to echo social media content in their coverage, linking their own content to social media accounts (Faris 2008, El Gody 2013). During the 2010 parliamentary elections, people used their mobile phones to capture pictures and videos that showed fraud. News organizations, especially independent and opposition media, circulated them in an effort to call for change (El Gody 2016).

Before the 2011 revolution, over 80,000 social news websites evolved. They became the playground for activists, political parties, and other groups to cater to their audience's emerging needs. During the protests that led to the January 2011 revolution, activists and journalists turned to Facebook, Twitter, blogs, and YouTube to voice their demands, exchange news, share thoughts and opinions, send updates and news about the uprising, and document incidents as they occurred (Faris 2008, Radsch 2016).

The January 25, 2011, events that escalated into revolution started when a few people created a Facebook page called "We are all Khaled Said" in response to the case of Khaled Said, who had been tortured to death by police officers several months earlier in Alexandria. The page became the spark of the revolution when its members called for a peaceful demonstration that was attended by thousands (Radsch 2016).

As the events progressed, Internet users, especially network journalists and activists, employed Facebook, Twitter, and other applications to disseminate information about the meeting places and the way the protestors were to reach Tahrir Square, where the ministries

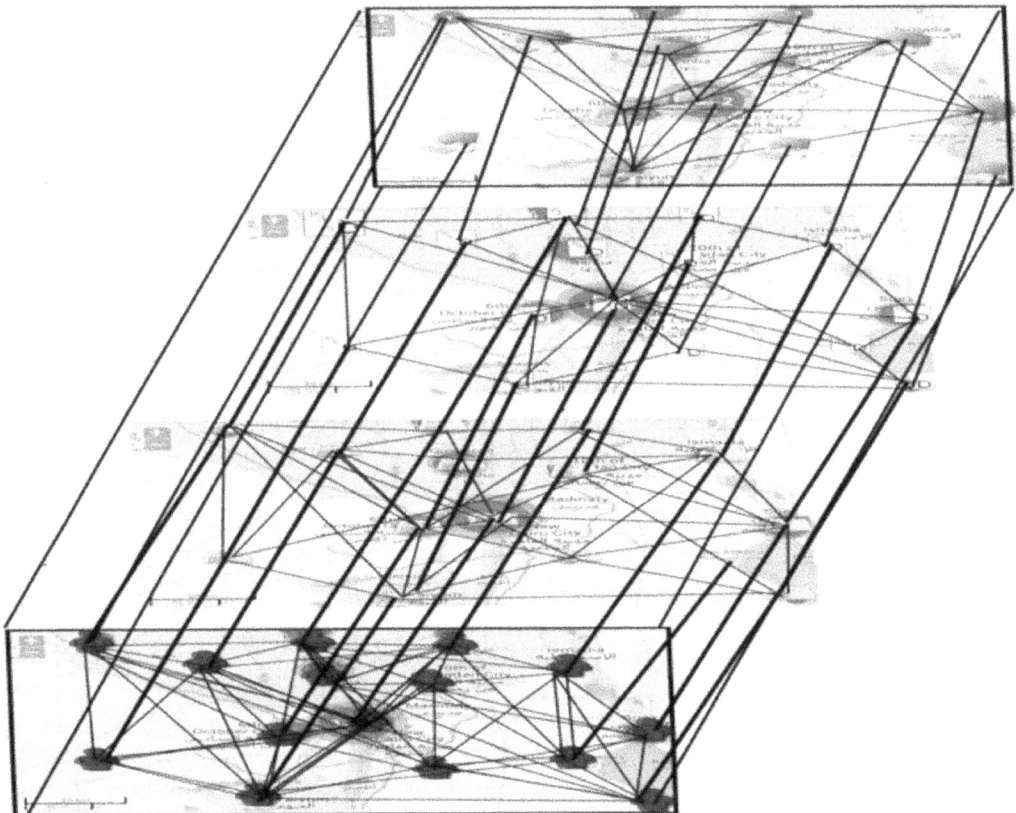

Figure 15.2.   Convergence of real and virtual communication during 2011 revolution.

and parliament are located. Status updates and tweets played a very important role in providing information to the protestors about the police formations and plans. Users provided information on how to protect oneself from the bombs that the police used. In an effort to suppress the uprising, the regime blocked more than 3,500 Border Gateway Protocol routes (Internet connections) operated by Egyptian service providers and shut down approximately 88% of the country's Internet access (Ackerman 2011, Ben Moussa and Douai 2014). Skilled users accessed Facebook and Twitter from proxy sites, which allowed Internet surfing.

During Egypt's January revolution, social media became the main outlet for information about events in the streets (figure 15.2). Social media may have performed the most critical function, playing the role of mediator between the protestors and the rest of the society (El Gody 2016). The Twitter hashtags #jan25 and #Egypt attracted media attention. Social media also helped shape the international news agenda. Global media started to get information about the Egyptian revolution from online social media news accounts like RASD and Khaled Said instead of Egyptian mainstream media (Ingraham and Moynihan 2000). News media, especially opposition and independent media, started to utilize social media as an alternative source for information and a bridge between the Internet and events on the streets This convergence changed the role of journalism in Egypt, from simply reporting about the political process to being an active participant in shaping and influencing the political process (El Gody 2013).

Some researchers, however, have stated that social media alone did not facilitate the revolution, but served as a catalyst when combined with many other kinds of digital and traditional media. The success of the revolution lay in the ability of the new technologies to integrate journalism and technicians, writers and camera operators, news gatherers and news processors, and coordinate between print, radio, and television journalism and the audience (Deuze 2008). The rise of networking sites encouraged users to interact in ways that could potentially disrupt the existing social structure. The participatory culture of online media helped ordinary people to create and distribute their own content, creating a feeling of "Wow . . . I am not alone," in the words of Wael Ghoneim, moderator of the "We are all Khaled Said" page. The user-generated content encouraged political action among ordinary people, showing that the "power of the people is stronger than the people in power" (El Gody 2016).

NETWORKED JOURNALISM IN POST-REVOLUTION EGYPT

As we have seen, ICTs redefined the role of the media in democratizing societies, from simply reporting about the political process to being "an active participant in shaping, influencing upon, indeed an integral role of the political process" (Blumler and Gurevitch 1995, 141). Among the institutions that constitute the public sphere in a network society, the media perhaps perform the most critical function, playing the role of mediator in the information transactions within the networked sphere (figure 15.3). Although journalism's main role continues to be keeping citizens engaged, promoting grassroots democracy by informing, educating, and mobilizing the public, activists encourage the discussion of local issues, providing a point of view other than that of the state (Blumler and Gurevitch 1995, Radsch 2018). The media are neither neutral participants nor impassioned chroniclers. They are either legitimizers of the status quo or upsetters of the existing social equilibrium. Because of the way they facilitate the spread of information, social media have the potential to provoke and sustain political uprisings by amplifying news and information.

Figure 15.3. Audience Media/Communication Pool.

In transitional societies moving toward democracy, such as Egypt, political development is a central topic that journalists mediate with their audience. Indeed, journalists inform the audience and facilitate informed choices as "gatewatchers," not as watchdog "gatekeepers," in the power struggle between audience, media, and politics (Al-Rawi 2017). In Egypt's post-2011 era, journalism is expected to be more than a source for news (El Gody 2013). Journalists need to cut in on the mainstream government media with material from the margins. Radsch discussed the need for journalists to be agents for social change, engaging in public argument on sociopolitical concerns, as well as a body to enhance interaction among various groups and actors in order to influence public opinion and mobilize support (Fahmy 2010, Radsch 2016).

Between 2011 and 2015, several political parties and activist bodies were formed. Similarly, so were a number of media outlets. Media organizations started to expand their presence to social media so that, besides providing news content, they also provided a space for interactivity. Three main groups benefited most from the new technologies after the Egyptian revolution. The first group was political activists, especially Islamists, the military, liberals, and civil-society and human-rights groups that were historically deprived of their freedom of expression and coerced into silence for decades. The second was the social groups that challenge social norms and traditions, who used the Internet to create pressure groups to make their voices heard. Finally, the third was the religious groups, especially the Salafis and Da'wa, who found in social media a venue where they could express their ideologies and concerns to a wider audience. Social media, especially Facebook, became the new arena for political parties, activists, and groups embracing various ideologies to "online spaces of flows" to address the emerging needs of the readers. Post-revolution political actors started to create Facebook pages to attract communities and to enable these communities to interact with each other (El Gody 2016).

CONCLUSION

A surge of social media innovations is altering the Egyptian media landscape, creating parallel communication networks. On average, Egyptians have access to over 1.6 million Egyptian websites; thousands of mobile applications; hundreds of online radio, television, and video stations; and tens of thousands of blogs and other websites for activists and citizen journalism. This fusion of information networks has introduced new network spaces where Egyptians cluster, thus moving their activities online and focusing on politics, economics, human rights, and social issues that had earlier been ignored. Online activists have provided detailed descriptions of street politics by posting multimedia material, thus generating public interest and reinforcing citizen power and democracy. This wave of convergence is considered to be more truthful and reliable than the mainstream media, starkly raising the question of where the journalism industry fits within this network society.

This new type of journalism is different because it requires different listening skills, looking out for content rather than for quotes in order to build a story. It requires a conscious sense of how to reach out to citizens to listen to them, and to have them listen and talk to each other. The new role of journalism is to allow citizens to participate in identifying newsworthy events. This shift in journalistic values requires a fundamental shift in the traditional agenda-setting role of journalists. They must give up some control over who sets the agenda, what issues will be covered, and how they will be covered. This is in direct conflict with traditional news values, which place the agenda-setting responsibility squarely on the shoulders of the elite, with the public playing only a marginal role.

The success of a journalist in an active network society lies in his or her ability to be a node among different stakeholders. In Egypt, journalists are required to act as gatewatchers over the process of network communication, helping to construct meaningful messages. News organizations have come to be forums for debate in order to create a networked sphere where opinions can travel back and forth among nodes. Similarly, the success of a newsroom lies in its ability to manage a multi-skilled, multimedia work center that is capable of converging new technologies in news creation and production. During this process, newsrooms need to understand that print and online journalism have different routines, rituals, practices, and cultures. Convergence means that each sector needs to learn how the other works, and that both of them need to acquire new technological and conceptual skills in order to work in this new media environment.

REFERENCES

Abbott, L. M. 2016. "The conceptual public sphere and its problems: Habermas, political action and the Arab states." *Journal of International Political Theory* 12 (3): 365–79.

Ackerman, S. 2011. "Egypt's internet shutdown can't stop mass protests." Wired, January 28, 2011. http://www.wired.com/dangerroom/2011/01/egypts-internet-shutdown-cant-stop-mass-protests.

Allan, S., and E. Thorsen. 2014. *Citizen Journalism: Global Perspectives.* Vol. 2. New York: Lang.

Amin, H. 2010. "The Making of the Journalist and Journalism of the Next Decade." Paper presented at Operational Policies and Developing Media in Africa, Nairobi, Kenya.

Anderson, J. 2003. "New media, new publics: Reconfiguring the public sphere of Islam." *Social Research: An International Quarterly* 70 (3): 887–906.

Anderson, J., and D. Eickelman. 2008. "New Media and New Publics in the Arab World." Paper presented at Nouveaux médias dans le monde arabe: Colloque organisé par le GREMMO, University of Lyon, France.

Ardic, N. 2012. "Understanding the 'Arab Spring': Justice, dignity, religion and international politics." *Afro Eurasian Studies* 1 (1): 8–52.

Arquilla, J., and D. Ronfeldt. 2001. "Emergence and Influence of the Zapatista Social Netwar." In *Networks and Netwars: The Future of Terror, Crime, and Militancy*, edited by D. Ronfeldt and J. Arquilla, 171–99. Santa Monica, CA: RAND.

Atton, C. 2010. "Alternative Media Theory and Journalism Practice." In *Digital Media and Democracy: Tactics in Hard Times*, edited by M. Boler, 517–31. Cambridge, MA: MIT Press.

Ayish, M. 2008. *The New Arab Public Sphere*. Berlin: Frank & Timme.

———. 2018. "A youth-driven virtual civic public sphere for the Arab world." *Javnost—The Public* 25 (1-2): 66–74.

Beckett, C., and R. Mansell. 2008. "Crossing boundaries: New media and networked journalism." *Communication, Culture & Critique* 1 (1): 92–104.

Beltrame, J. 2001. "Whose news? TV guys say convergence can make the product better. Tell that to the CRTC." *Maclean's*, May 28, 2001, 34.

Ben Moussa, M., and A. Douai. 2014. "The digital transformation of Arab news: Is there a future for online news after the 'Arab Spring'?" *Applied Journalism and Media Studies* 3 (2): 133–54.

Blumler, J., and M. Gurevitch. 1995. *The Crisis of Public Communication*. London and New York: Routledge.

Bruns, A. 2005. *Gatewatching: Collaborative Online News Production*. New York: Peter Lang.

Castells, M. 2008. "The new public sphere: Global civil society, communication networks, and global governance." *Annals of the American Academy of Political and Social Science* 616 (1): 78–93.

———. 2015. *Networks of Outrage and Hope: Social Movements in the Internet Age*. Cambridge and Malden, MA: Polity.

Dahlberg, L. 2001. "The internet and democratic discourse: Exploring the prospects of online deliberative forums extending the public sphere." *Information, Communication, and Society* 4 (4): 615–33.

Dahlgren, P., and C. Sparks. 1992. *Journalism and Popular Culture*. London: Sage.

Deuze, M. 2008. "The professional identity of journalists in the context of convergence culture." *Observatorio (OBS*) Journal* 7: 103–17.

Duffy, M. 2011. "Networked journalism and Al-Jazeera English: How the Middle East network engages the audience to help produce news." *Journal of Middle East Media* 7 (1): 1–23.

Fahmy, N. 2010. "Revealing the 'Agenda-Cutting' through Egyptian Blogs: An Empirical Study." Paper presented at the Online Journalism Symposium, Austin, Texas.

Faris, D. 2008. "Revolutions without revolutionaries? Network theory, Facebook, and the Egyptian blogosphere." *Arab Media & Society*, September 29, 2008. https://www.arabmediasociety.com/revolutions-without-revolutionaries-network-theory-facebook-and-the-egyptian-blogosphere.

Fraser, N. 1990. "Rethinking the public sphere: A contribution to the critique of actually existing democracy." *Social Text* 25/26: 56–80.

Garrison, B. 2004. "Online Newspapers." In *Online News and the Public*, edited by B. Salwen, B. Garrison, and P. Driscoll, 3–46. Mahwah, NJ: LEA.

El Gody, A. 2008. "US Image in Arab Blogsphere." Paper presented at the International Communication Association (ICA) Conference, May 20–25, 2008, Chicago, Illinois.

———. 2013. *Journalism in a Network: The Role of ICTs in Egyptian Newsroom*. Sunnyvale, CA: Lambert Academic Publishing.

———. 2016. "Network Journalism and the Egyptian Revolution." In *Mediated Identities and New Journalism in the Arab World: Mapping the "Arab Spring,"* edited by M. Ben Mousa and A. Douai, 185–204. London: Palgrave Macmillan.

Habermas, J. 1997. *The Inclusion of the Other: Studies in Political Theory*. Cambridge, MA: MIT Press.

———. 2006. "Political communication in media society: Does democracy still enjoy an epistemic dimension? The impact of normative theory on empirical research." *Communication Theory* 16 (4): 411–26.

Hamdy, N. 2009. "Arab citizen journalism in action: Challenging mainstream media, authorities and media laws." *Westminster Papers in Communication and Culture* 110 (1): 6, 92–112.

Heinrich, A. 2012. "What is 'network journalism'?" *Media International Australia* 1 (144): 60–67.

Hofheinz, A. 2009. "Arab Internet: Popular Trends and Public Impact." In *Arab Media and Political Renewal: Community, Legitimacy and Public Life*, edited by N. Sakr, 1417–34. London: I. B. Tauris.

Ingraham, P., and D. Moynihan. 2000. "Evolving Dimensions of Performance from the CSRA to the Present." In *The Future of Merit: Twenty Years after the Civil Service Reform*, edited by J. Pfiffner and D. Brook, 205–21. Baltimore, MD: Johns Hopkins University Press.

Jenkins, H. 2003. "Quentin Tarantino's Star Wars? Digital Cinema, Media Convergence, and Participatory Culture." In *Rethinking Media Change: The Aesthetics of Transition*, edited by D. Thorburn and H. Jenkins, 281–314. Cambridge, MA: MIT Press.

Kolodzy, J. 2006. *Convergence Journalism: Writing and Reporting across the News Media*. Lanham, MD: Rowman & Littlefield.

Lynch, M. 2007. "Blogging the new Arab public." *Arab Media & Society*, March 12, 2007. https://www .arabmediasociety.com/blogging-the-new-arab-public.

McLuhan, M. 1994. *Understanding Media: The Extensions of Man*. Cambridge, MA: MIT Press.

Murphy, E. 2011. "The Arab state and (absent) civility in new communicative spaces." *Third World Quarterly* 32 (5): 959–80.

Pepe, T. 2011. "From the blogosphere to the bookshop: Publishing literary blogs in Egypt." *Oriente Moderno* 91 (1): 75–90.

Quandt, T., and J. Singer. 2009. "Convergence and Cross-Platform Content Production." In *The Handbook of Journalism Studies*, edited by K. Wahl-Jorgensen and T. Hanitzsch, 130–46. New York: Routledge.

Radsch, C. 2016. *Cyberactivism and Citizen Journalism in Egypt: Digital Dissidence and Political Change*. London: Palgrave Macmillan.

———. 2018. *World Trends in Freedom of Expression and Media Development: Regional Overview of the Arab Region*. Paris: UNESCO Information and Communication Section.

Al-Rawi, A. 2017. "News values on social media: News organizations' Facebook use." *Journalism* 18 (7): 871–89.

Rosen, J. 2011. "The 'Twitter can't topple dictators' article." PressThink, February 13, 2011. http:// pressthink.org/2011/02/the-twitter-cant-topple-dictators-article.

Russell, A. 2011. *Networked: A Contemporary History of News in Transition*. Cambridge and Malden, MA: Polity.

———. 2016. "Networked Journalism." In *The Sage Handbook of Digital Journalism*, edited by T. Witschge, C. Anderson, and D. Domingo, 149–63. London: Sage.

Salah-Fahmi, W. 2009. "Bloggers' street movement and the right to the city: (Re)claiming Cairo's real and virtual 'spaces of freedom.'" *Environment and Urbanization* 21 (1): 89–107.

Salvatore, A. 2013. "New media, the 'Arab Spring,' and the metamorphosis of the public sphere: Beyond Western assumptions on collective agency and democratic politics." *Constellations* 20 (2): 217–28.

Shah, D. V., J. Cho, W. P. Eveland, and N. Kwak. 2005. "Information and expression in a digital age: Modeling internet effects on civic participation." *Communication Research* 32 (5): 531–65.

Sicilia, M., S. Ruiz, and J. Munuera. 2005. "Effects of interactivity in a web site: The moderating effect of need for cognition." *Journal of Advertising* 34 (3): 31–44.

Teel, L. 2007. "Souk al-Afkar." Paper presented at the Arab-U.S. Association for Communication Educators, Amman, Jordan.

Toulouse, C., and T. Luke. 1998. *The Politics of Cyberspace*. New York: Routledge.

Van Dijk, J. 2012. *The Network Society*. London: Sage.

Volkmer, I. 2003. "The global network society and the global public sphere." *Development* 46 (1): 9–16.

Warren, M. 1995. "The Self in Discourse Democracy." In *The Cambridge Companion to Habermas*, edited by S. White, 167–200. Cambridge: Cambridge University Press.

VI

CULTURAL EVOLUTION

Media's Effects on Societal Norms and Expectations

16

The Image of Emirati Culture in the Eyes of Non-Arab Expatriates

Khaled S. Gaweesh

Due to ongoing globalization, being immersed in another culture is an experience lived by a growing number of individuals worldwide and will continue in the decades to come. When moving to the host country, expatriates are faced with the challenge of adapting to a new culture, lifestyle, and norms.

In the past few years, the United Arab Emirates (UAE) has increasingly become a home for expatriates from all around the world. In fact, the number of expatriates in the UAE is greater than the number of native citizens. According to the UAE Federal Competitiveness & Statistics Authority, the UAE population was 9,121,167 at the end of 2016. According to the *United Arab Emirates Yearbook 2013*, UAE citizens represent 11.4% of the total population. If we assume the stability of this percentage, the number of UAE citizens would reach almost 1 million. The expatriates in the UAE account for 88.6% of the population, representing more than 119 nationalities from all over the world. People from all Asian countries constitute 70.4% of the total UAE population; the Indians alone are 28.5% and Pakistanis 13%. Arab expatriates are 17.4%, while all other nationalities form less than 1% of the total population.

This diversity of nationalities and the sheer number of expatriates in the UAE make the country an interesting and unique environment for cultural studies. Despite the number of studies that have been conducted on specific nationalities, there are still some unexplored areas, especially when it comes to the image of the country.

THE IMAGE OF THE UAE AMONG NON-ARAB EXPATRIATES

Because of the diversity in the UAE and the efforts the UAE government is exerting to make the country an attractive and pleasant destination for foreigners, the image that non-Arab expatriates hold of this country is an interesting and important question. It has become even more important because the UAE is the host country for Expo 2020 (which will be held in 2021 because of COVID-19). This study excludes the Arab expatriates, as they come from cultures very similar to that of the UAE, and focuses exclusively on the non-Arab expatriates.

The main goal of the research was to explore the image of UAE culture among the non-Arab expatriates. Hofstede's cultural dimensions theory and information integration theory guided the development of the questions and the discussion of the findings. Another concern was to explore the variables that may influence the image built by non-Arab expatriates.

THEORETICAL BACKGROUND

A number of different theories in the field of cross-cultural communication can be applied in this case. I will use Hofstede's cultural dimensions theory (1980), because of its established legitimacy and its simple yet accurate definition of culture. In addition, the information integration theory developed by Norman Anderson (1981) will explain the relationships among the images the expatriates receive from different sources of information to build their overall image about the country they are living in.

Hofstede defined culture (1980) as the collective programming of the mind distinguishing the members of one group or category of people from others. He developed his original model by using factor analysis to examine the results of a worldwide survey of employee values by IBM in the 1960s and 1970s. The theory was one of the first that could be quantified and used to explain observed differences among cultures. The original theory proposed four dimensions along which cultural values could be analyzed: Power Distance Index (PDI), Individualism versus Collectivism (IDV), Masculinity versus Femininity (MAS), and Uncertainty Avoidance Index (UAI). Later research in Hong Kong led Hofstede to add a fifth dimension, Long-Term Orientation versus Short-Term Orientation (LTO), to cover aspects of values not included in the original paradigm. In 2010, Hofstede added a sixth dimension, Indulgence versus Restraint (IND). These six dimensions will be the guideline for the study questions that shaped the questionnaire.

Power Distance Index

The first dimension is the Power Distance Index (PDI). It describes how a culture deals with inequalities. Hofstede (1980/2001, 83) defines power distance as "the extent to which less powerful members of a society accept and expect that power is distributed unequally." The social hierarchy is obvious in large power distance cultures where everyone has his/her established position within this hierarchy. The more hierarchical a society, the larger the power distance. In contrast, small power distance cultures tend to emphasize equality in rights and opportunities. People in these cultures prefer democratic processes and decentralized management structure; they see superiors as being similar to them and accessible.

Individualism versus Collectivism

The second dimension is Individualism versus Collectivism (IDV). It refers to how people define themselves and their relationships with others. Hofstede (1980/2001) defines individualism as a preference for a loosely knit social structure in which individuals take care of themselves and their immediate families. In short, individualism is the societal predilection for independence.

Masculinity versus Femininity

Masculinity versus Femininity (MAS) is the third dimension. It is defined as the distribution of emotional roles between genders, and identifies the characteristics of one gender role that are favored culturally, relative to the characteristics of the other gender role. Masculine cultures' values are competitiveness, assertiveness, materialism, ambition, and power, whereas feminine cultures place more value on relationships and quality of life.

Uncertainty Avoidance Index

Uncertainty Avoidance Index (UAI), which is the fourth dimension, is defined as "society's tolerance for uncertainty and ambiguity, and the extent to which the members of a culture feel threatened by uncertain or unknown situations and try to avoid these situations" (Hofstede 1980/2001). Hofstede states that in cultures with strong uncertainty avoidance, people have a higher level of anxiety, stress, and tension. In contrast, low uncertainty avoidance cultures accept and feel comfortable in unstructured situations or changeable environments and try to have as few rules as possible.

Long-Term Orientation versus Short-Term Orientation

The fifth dimension, which was added in 1991, is Long-Term Orientation versus Short-Term Orientation (LTO), initially called "Confucian dynamism." It is defined as the extent to which a society exhibits a pragmatic future-oriented perspective rather than a conventional or short-term point of view. According to the Chinese Value Survey (Hofstede and Bond 1988), cultures with a higher score in long-term orientation tend to have more persistence, perseverance, thrift, and a strong sense of shame, as well as ordered relationships. Conversely, cultures with a lower score tend to spend more to keep up with social pressure, have less savings, and prefer quick results.

Indulgence versus Restraint

The sixth dimension, Indulgence versus Restraint (IND), is essentially a measure of happiness: whether or not simple joys are fulfilled. Indulgence is defined as "a society that allows relatively free gratification of basic and natural human desires related to enjoying life and having fun." Its counterpart is defined as "a society that controls gratification of needs and regulates it by means of strict social norms" (Hofstede 2011). Indulgent societies believe themselves to be in control of their own life and emotions; restrained societies believe other factors dictate their life and emotions.

It is very important to note that the Hofstede paradigm has been used in this study not to describe the UAE culture itself, but to guide the measurement of the perception of this culture by the non-Arab expatriates.

Information integration theory, which was developed and extensively tested in a variety of experiments by Norman Anderson, explores how attitudes are formed and changed through the integration (mixing, combining) of new information with existing cognitions or thoughts. Information integration theory considers the ideas in a persuasive message to be pieces of information, and each relevant piece of information has two qualities: value and weight. The value of a bit of information is its evaluation (favorable or unfavorable), and the weight is the information's perceived importance.

Information integration theory states that when we obtain new information (often from persuasive messages), those new pieces of information will affect our attitudes. They will not replace our existing attitudes, but when we learn new positive information, negative attitudes tend to become less negative and positive attitudes are likely to become somewhat more positive. Furthermore, the weight and value of each bit of information influence our attitudes. Therefore, new information is mixed, combined, or integrated with existing information to create a new attitude.

CULTURE AND IMAGE

The United Arab Emirates has been enriched by a pool of cultures that interact with one another. The culture is continuously changing due to openness to the world and the mix of nationalities within its borders. But what is culture, really? The word has a wide range of sometimes contradictory definitions. One definition is "the shared knowledge and schemes created by a set of people for perceiving, interpreting, expressing and responding to the social realities around them" (Lederach 1995). Another is "the set of attitudes, values, beliefs, and behaviors shared by a group of people, but different for each individual, communicated from one generation to the next" (Matsumoto 1996).

Hofstede's definition takes quite a different approach. He states that "culture is the collective programming of the mind which distinguishes the members of one category of people from another" (Hofstede 1991/1994). His cultural dimensions theory puts his definition into a structured model that can be applied to any country to define its culture compared to other cultures in the world.

The literature on culture and adaptation has mainly focused on cross-cultural differences, influenced by the work of Hofstede (1991/1994) and Schwartz (1999). Most studies focus on social behavior. For example, Fletcher and Fang (2006) suggest that in order to study culture and social behavior, two basic approaches may be used: the etic approach (culture-general) and the emic approach (culture-specific). The etic approach focuses on identifying universal dimensions that cause cultural differences; it is usually quantitative and uses large-scale surveys. The emic approach uses a series of case studies, tends to be qualitative, and finds that "attitudes and behaviors are expressed in a unique way in each culture" (Chan and Rossiter 2003).

In a country such as the UAE, where there is such a diversity of people from different ethnicities and cultures, many people acquire several identities. According to Epps and Demangeot (2013), "there is much mixed heritage, long-term western 'expats' with their own Gulf-state culture, an intermingling of cultures." Moreover, "multiculturalism in UAE is a shared, lived experience where being different is the norm, rather than a politicized ideology." In the literature, it is more common to find comparisons between countries rather than studies of ethnic diversity within the same borders. Their tendency is to focus on cultural differences, whereas they should focus more on the commonalities that could ease the communication process between cultures.

There are many theories that address the concept of building an image. Many research papers use destination images to understand how people choose their travel destination. The same may be applied when expats try to learn about the country's culture ahead of time to decide whether they will accept a job offer or not. Destination branding is defined as "selecting a consistent element mix to identify and distinguish it through positive image building" (Cai 2002). Destination image is defined as "a concept formed by the consumer's reasoned and emotional interpretation as the consequence of two closely interrelated components:

perceptive/cognitive evaluations referring to the individual's own knowledge and beliefs about the object, and the effective appraisals relating to the individual's feelings towards the object" (Beerli and Martin 2004).

The image formation is a process that is defined as a "construction of mental representation of a destination on the basis of information cues delivered by the image formation agents and selected by a person" (Tasci and Gartner 2007). According to Gartner (1993), destination image is created using three components: cognitive, affective, and conative. The literature shows that the cognitive component is an antecedent of the affective component, and discusses the evaluation responses of the consumers stemming from their knowledge of the objects (Holbrook 1978, Russel and Pratt 1980, Anand et al. 1988, Stern and Krakover 1993). But the absence of a universally accepted, valid, and reliable scale led to the proposition of incorporating all possible aspects of a destination that could be used as instruments to measure the perceived image of a place.

The UAE is a country that is rapidly advancing because of its cultural input from all over the world. One would expect this to place pressure on the local customs and traditions, yet the local people seem to be able to maintain them with no difficulty (AlMazrouei and Pech 2015). We will examine the image of UAE culture according to Hofstede's cultural dimensions and compare it with the non-Arab expatriates' image.

In terms of the Power Distance Index, the hierarchy in the UAE is high and is expressed as inherent inequalities, centralization, autocratic leadership style, and subordinates' expectation to be told what to do (Alteneiji 2015). In addition, the UAE is a collective society with strong ties. From birth, people are integrated into strong, cohesive in-groups, which protect them throughout their lifetime in exchange for unquestioning loyalty (Hofstede 2011, 92). On the other hand, the UAE is considered to be neither masculine nor feminine. This means that while the society is propelled by concerns of achievement, success, and competition, it relies equally on the kinds of values that ensure quality of life coupled with caring for other people (Aljerjawi 2016).

Emiratis have a high preference for avoiding uncertainty. They have strong traditions and rituals and tend toward formal, bureaucratic structures and rules (Alteneiji 2015). Such cultures avoid uncertainty by means of harsh behavioral codes, laws, and rules; disapproval of unusual opinions; and a belief in absolute truth (Hofstede 2011). In addition, cultures with low long-term orientation have high preferences for personal steadiness and stability, high respect for culture, and an expectation of reciprocation of favors and gifts (Alteneiji 2015). Finally, the UAE can be considered a restraint society because it suppresses or restricts the indulgence of needs and regulates it by means of social norms (Ourfali 2015).

RESEARCH QUESTIONS

The aim of this study is to answer a number of questions. First, what is the image of UAE culture among non-Arab expatriates according to Hofstede's dimensions of culture? Second, what sources of information have the non-Arab expatriates used to build their image of the UAE culture? And finally, do non-Arab expatriate opinions about the UAE culture differ across demographic variables?

A structured survey was developed to measure the variables and answer the study questions. A convenient sample of 121 non-Arab expatriates was interviewed. Eighteen Likert-scale statements were developed to measure the image of UAE culture according to Hofstede's dimensions. (The statements measure the image of the UAE among the non-Arab expatriates; they do not measure the UAE culture per se.) The statements were tested for comprehensibility and clarity; they were deleted, altered, or kept according to the pretesting results. One statement that does not belong to any of the dimensions was added to measure the ease of adapting to UAE culture from the respondents' perspective.

The respondents rated the statements on a five-point scale from "strongly agree" to "strongly disagree." Completing the survey took an average of twelve to fifteen minutes. The data were collected from the Emirates of Dubai, Sharjah, and Ajman, but the respondents who participated were working and living in Dubai, Sharjah, Ajman, Ras Al Khaima, and Umm al-Quwain; no respondents were working or living in Abu Dhabi. The sample included males and females, different age groups, all levels of education with a majority of high school and above, and people from all over the world, with a majority from Asian countries.

The statements used in the questionnaire are as follows.

A.   Power Distance Index (PDI):

- There is an unequal distribution of power in UAE society.
- There is a big difference in UAE society between people in terms of rights and opportunities, and I notice that people accept the differences.
- I think that individual freedom in UAE society is restricted.

B.   Individualism versus Collectivism (IDV):

- I find that people of the UAE have strong social and family relationships with each other.
- People of the UAE appreciate the group's rights more than the individual's rights.
- Individuals in the UAE care about themselves more than their families.

C.   Masculinity versus Femininity (MAS):

- Both men and women compete equally for leadership and power in UAE society.
- I think that UAE society is a masculine society (men are superior).
- Men and women in professions in UAE society work together equally.
- I feel that the UAE culture treats both genders equally.

D.   Uncertainty Avoidance Index (UAI):

- I believe that people of the UAE feel threatened by unknown situations that may occur in the future.
- In my opinion, UAE nationals suffer from stress and tension because of the fear of what might happen in the near future.
- UAE society is intolerant of new ideas and behavior, as they lean toward traditions.
- UAE society highly respects traditions, codes of behavior, and beliefs.

E.   Long-Term Orientation versus Short-Term Orientation (LTO):

- I believe that UAE people have good insight into the future.

F. Indulgence versus Restraint (IND):

* I find that UAE society has strict social norms that limit people from enjoying life and having fun.
* UAE society allows people to freely enjoy life and have fun.

G. Adjusting to UAE culture is easy.

THE FINDINGS

Power Distance Index (PDI)

According to the responses of the participants, the UAE culture is perceived as high in the PDI. Nearly half of the respondents (48.8%) think that there is unequal distribution of power in UAE society, versus 11.6% who disagree. Furthermore, 62.8% think that there is a big difference in UAE society between people in terms of rights and opportunities and notice that people accept these differences. These results coincide with those of Alteneiji (2015), who reported that the hierarchy in UAE culture is high and is expressed as inherent inequalities, centralization, auto-cratic leadership style, and subordinates' expectation to be told what to do.

On the other hand, the respondents split equally regarding "the restrictions on individual freedom in UAE," which may be explained through their understanding of the meaning of "individual freedom." Some may understand the freedom from a social perspective (you are free to go wherever you want, dress as you wish, etc.), while others may see it from a political perspective. In conclusion, it is quite clear that non-Arab expatriates perceive UAE culture as high in the PDI.

Individualism versus Collectivism (IDV)

It is very clear from the responses that the non-Arab expatriates strongly perceive that the UAE culture is collective. The majority of respondents believe that UAE people have strong social and family relationships with each other (100%), appreciate the group's rights more than the individual's rights (51.2%), and care about their families more than themselves (53.7%). All these behaviors—as perceived by the respondents—characterize an environment of collectivism more than individualism. This result has been supported by previous studies (Hofstede 2011, Aljerjawi 2016), which found that the UAE is a collective society with strong ties, where people are integrated from birth into strong, cohesive in-groups, which continue to protect them throughout their lifetime.

Masculinity versus Femininity (MAS)

In selecting this dimension, I was not concerned with the characteristics related to each gender, such as competitiveness, materialism, relationships, or quality of life, but wanted to understand more specifically the extent to which non-Arab expatriates tend to see UAE culture as differentiating between men and women.

The image of UAE culture among non-Arab expatriates from this perspective is interesting and perhaps confusing. In general, the expatriates tend to perceive the UAE society as a masculine society. This may be because the UAE is an Arab Muslim country and this stereotype may be in place for all such countries. On the other hand, when the respondents were asked about their opinion regarding competition between men and women for leadership and power, the majority agreed that this competition is equal (56.8% versus 11.6%). On the professional level, the vast majority think that the two genders work together equally (71.9% versus 6.6%). This is consistent with all UAE labor laws, which do not differentiate between men and women in terms of work rights and duties. On the contrary, they provide advantages for working women with regard to childbirth and breast-feeding (paid leave of absence and shorter working hours). The level of agreement is even higher on the issue of whether both genders are treated equally in UAE culture in general (87.6% versus 2.5%). These results suggest that the "masculinity" of UAE society is a stereotype more than an image among non-Arab expatriates.

Uncertainty Avoidance Index (UAI)

In general, the respondents perceive Emiratis as having a high preference for avoiding uncertainty: 44.6% disagree with the statement "UAE nationals suffer from stress and tension because of the fear of what might happen in the near future," while 22.3% agree with the statement. Furthermore, 38% of the respondents agreed that "UAE society leans toward traditions," versus 30.6% who disagreed. The vast majority of respondents (87.6%) agreed that "UAE society highly respects traditions, codes of behavior, and beliefs." According to Hofstede (2011), these are indicators of a culture with a high preference for avoiding uncertainty.

The only item that slanted in the other direction was statement no. 3, where 36.3% of the respondents agreed that "the people of the UAE feel threatened by unknown situations that may occur in the future," while 25.6% disagreed. This may be explained by the unstable political situation in the Gulf region that may affect the perception of the respondents.

Long-Term Orientation versus Short-Term Orientation (LTO)

It is very clear that the respondents believe that the UAE has a long-term orientation; 88.4% agreed with the statement. This may be interpreted by the response to plans announced to the public through different media outlets, and the new projects executed across the country.

Indulgence versus Restraint (IND)

It seems that the respondents tend to view UAE society as allowing people to freely enjoy life and have fun: 71.9% agree, versus 7.5% who disagree. Meanwhile, 48.7% (versus 34.8%) thought that UAE society has strict social norms that limit people from enjoying life and having fun. One of the possibilities of this little contradiction is that respondents have created a kind of distinction between the restrictions that UAE nationals must abide by and the freedom that expatriates enjoy because they are not bound by the restrictions that apply only to UAE nationals. Here, we should understand how the expatriates differentiate between the social norms of the UAE nationals and the fact that these norms do not affect the expatriates' freedom to enjoy life and have fun. This result reflects the multinationalism of the UAE population, and explains the apparent contradiction.

Adjusting to UAE Culture

The statement "Adjusting to UAE culture is easy" was added to the survey in order to find out how easy it is for expatriates to adapt. The results (table 16.1) show that 73.5% of the

Table 16.1.   Respondents' answers to the statements

Statements	Strongly Agree %	Agree %	Neutral %	Disagree %	Strongly Disagree %
1. I find that people of the UAE have strong social and family relationships with each other.	60.3	39.7	0.00	0.00	0.00
2. Both men and women compete equally for leadership and power in UAE society.	26.4	31.4	30.6	9.9	1.7
3. I believe that people of the UAE feel threatened by unknown situations that may occur in the future.	10.7	25.6	38.0	21.5	4.1
4. Adjusting to UAE culture is easy.	25.6	47.9	18.2	6.6	1.7
5. I find that UAE society has strict social norms that limit people from enjoying life and having fun.	19.8	28.9	16.5	26.4	8.3
6. There is an unequal distribution of power in UAE society.	9.1	39.7	39.7	9.1	2.5
7. People of the UAE appreciate the group's rights more than the individual's rights.	16.5	34.7	35.5	11.6	1.7
8. I think that UAE society is a masculine society (men are superior).	12.4	41.3	24	20.7	1.7
9. I believe that UAE people have good insight into the future.	56.2	32.2	10.7	0.8	0.00
10. In my opinion, UAE nationals suffer from stress and tension because of the fear of what might happen in the near future.	6.6	15.7	33.1	31.4	13.2
11. UAE society allows people to freely enjoy life and have fun.	24.8	47.1	20.7	5.8	1.7
12. Men and women in professions in UAE society work together equally.	27.3	44.6	21.5	6.6	0.00
13. There is a big difference in UAE society between people in terms of rights and opportunities, and I notice that people accept the differences.	13.2	49.6	27.3	9.1	0.8
14. Individuals in the UAE care about themselves more than their families.	7.4	15.7	23.1	37.2	16.5
15. UAE society is intolerant of new ideas and behavior, as they lean toward traditions.	14.9	23.1	31.4	19.0	11.6
16. UAE society highly respects traditions, codes of behavior, and beliefs.	41.3	46.3	9.9	2.5	0.00
17. I feel that the UAE culture treats both genders equally.	26.4	47.1	15.7	10.7	0.00
18. I think that individual freedom in UAE society is restricted.	14.0	23.1	25.6	23.1	14.0

respondents agreed that adjusting to UAE culture is easy, which emphasizes the fact that the UAE is a welcoming country to people with different backgrounds.

THE SOURCES OF INFORMATION USED BY NON-ARAB EXPATRIATES TO BUILD THEIR IMAGE OF UAE CULTURE

"Personal contacts with UAE nationals" is at the top of the most important sources of learning about UAE culture, indicating the importance of personal experiences. It is apparent that many of our respondents built their image on real experiences with people, not through exposure to the media. When it comes to learning about other cultures, it seems that face-to-face communication with family and friends is still an important and trusted source of information. New technologies come third (27.3% for both social media and Internet), while traditional media ranked last at 11.3%.

It is also evident that our respondents obtained their information about UAE culture from more than one source, as suggested by information integration theory. Seventy-three respondents (60%) mentioned more than one source of information. These data support the notion that people add pieces of information together, and that this combined information tends to affect their attitudes.

THE RELATIONSHIP BETWEEN THE DEMOGRAPHIC VARIABLES AND THE IMAGE NON-ARAB EXPATRIATES HAVE OF UAE CULTURE

Seven demographic categories have been tested using ANOVA (Analysis of Variance) and chi-square to determine whether there is a significant relationship between any of them and the components of the image. These demographics are gender, age, marital status, educational level, country of origin, place of residence in the UAE, and the number of working years in the UAE. Each of these variables has been tested statistically to see whether there is a significant correlation with any of the Likert statements which reflect the expatriates' image. When ANOVA produced a significant variance, it was double-checked with chi-square in order to understand the details. Any significant variance not supported by significant chi-square has been discarded. This section will present only the significant relationships that were found.

Gender

There is no significant difference between men and women in their answers on any of the statements.

Age

Age as an independent variable has a significant effect ($P \leq 0.05$) on two of the statements.

- Statement 5: "I find that UAE society has strict social norms that limit people from enjoying life and having fun." (Sixth dimension: indulgence versus restraint.)
- Statement 17: "I feel that the UAE culture treats both genders equally." (Third dimension: masculinity versus femininity.)

I found that the younger respondents (18–25 and 26–35) tend to agree that UAE society has strict social norms more than older respondents (36–45 and 46+) (chi-square = 18.203, P $\leq$ 0.05). It seems that young people are more liberal than older people, who are more conservative and do not see the UAE social norms as limiting enjoyment and fun. On the question of gender equality, older respondents (46+) tend to disagree that the UAE culture treats both genders equally, more than younger age groups (chi-square = 28.159, P $\leq$ 0.01).

Marital Status

Marital status caused no significant difference on any of the statements.

Educational Level

There are four significant correlations with respect to educational level as an independent variable.

- Statement 2: "Both men and women compete equally for leadership and power in UAE society." (Third dimension: masculinity versus femininity.)
- Statement 17: "I feel that the UAE culture treats both genders equally." (Third dimension: masculinity versus femininity.)
- Statement 5: "I find that UAE society has strict social norms that limit people from enjoying life and having fun." (Sixth dimension: indulgence versus restraint.)
- Statement 14: "Individuals in the UAE care about themselves more than their families." (Second dimension: individualism versus collectivism.)

The correlations between education and each statement show that the higher the educational level, the greater the disagreement on gender equality (chi-square = 38.757, P $\leq$ 0.05), and the lower the educational level, the greater the agreement on the existence of strict social norms that limit people from enjoying life and having fun (chi-square = 46.568, P $\leq$ 0.01). In addition, the higher the educational level, the greater the disagreement on statement 14: "Individuals in the UAE care about themselves more than their families" (chi-square = 58.237, P $\leq$ 0.01).

Country of Origin

There are three significant correlations with respect to country of origin as an independent variable.

- Statement 5: "I find that UAE society has strict social norms that limit people from enjoying life and having fun." (Sixth dimension: indulgence versus restraint.)
- Statement 14: "Individuals in the UAE care about themselves more than their families." (Second dimension: individualism versus collectivism.)
- Statement 17: "I feel that the UAE culture treats both genders equally." (Third dimension: masculinity versus femininity.)

The correlation between nationality and the answers on statement 5 is significant (chi-square = 49.412, P $\leq$ 0.01). The expatriates from Asian countries and Russia tend to agree with this statement much more than expatriates from North America, Western Europe, and Australia (the average of those who agree is 10.7%). It seems that the majority of those who are from Asian countries have less education, lower-class jobs, and less income. These factors may contribute to this attitude, since they do not receive the same treatment as Western nationals who have better education, jobs, and income. Another explanation could be the culture of those who belong to Western nationalities: they are used to enjoying their life no matter what others might think, in contrast to Asian people, who may consider how others (specifically, UAE nationals) view them, leading them to act in a way they think will conform to the UAE culture.

The expatriates from Western Europe, North America, and Australia who disagree with statement 14 are twice as numerous as the Asians (85% for Western versus 44.2% for Asians). One of the possible explanations is the frame of reference of each group; the people from Asia compare the Emirati behavior with their own in their home countries, where they may sacrifice and do more for their families. The Western nationals, coming from a more individualistic culture, may view UAE society as more strongly collectivist (chi-square = 48.685, $P \leq 0.01$).

The proportion of Asian and Russian expatriates who think there is gender equality in the UAE is higher than those from North America and Western Europe (79.2% and 62.1% respectively; chi-square = 33.888, $P \leq 0.05$). It seems that the respondents' frame of reference has an influence on their perception of gender equality.

Emirate of Residency

There are three significant correlations with respect to emirate of residency as an independent variable.

- Statement 5: "I find that UAE society has strict social norms that limit people from enjoying life and having fun." (Sixth dimension: indulgence versus restraint.) Chi-square = 28.363, $P \leq 0.05$.
- Statement 14: "Individuals in the UAE care about themselves more than their families." (Second dimension: individualism versus collectivism.) Chi-square = 32.534, $P \leq 0.01$.
- Statement 18: "I think that individual freedom in UAE society is restricted." (First dimension: power distance index.) Chi-square = 29.979, $P \leq 0.05$.

The expatriates who live in Dubai are the least likely to agree with statement 5: 30.3% (for Dubai residents) versus the average of 82.2% (in other emirates). This result reflects Dubai's cosmopolitan atmosphere and the freedom that expatriates who live there enjoy in terms of their personal behavior. For example, Dubai has many public beaches where they can wear whatever they want without any restrictions. Foreigners can eat and drink according to their cultures in restaurants, bars, and other public places, and there are many places for fun and nightlife.

Those who live in both Dubai and Sharjah disagree with statement 14 much more than those who live in Ajman (average of 60% versus 28.5%). We may conclude that there are differences between UAE nationals who belong to Dubai and Sharjah, on the one hand, and those who belong to Ajman, on the other hand.

The expatriates who live in Sharjah are the most likely of all to agree with statement 18. This makes sense, as Sharjah is well known for being the most conservative of the emirates. For example, it is the only emirate that bans shisha in cafés and other public places.

Number of Working Years in the UAE

There are four significant correlations with respect to the number of working years in the UAE as an independent variable.

- Statement 11: "UAE society allows people to freely enjoy life and have fun." (Sixth dimension: indulgence versus restraint.) Chi-square = 35.818, P ≤ 0.01.
- Statement 9: "I believe that UAE people have good insight into the future." (Fifth dimension: long-term orientation.) Chi-square = 29.027, P ≤ 0.01.
- Statement 16: "UAE society highly respects traditions, codes of behavior, and beliefs." (Fourth dimension: uncertainty avoidance.) Chi-square = 18.258, P ≤ 0.05.
- Statement 18: "I think that individual freedom in UAE society is restricted." (First dimension: power distance index.) Chi-square = 27.143, P ≤ 0.01.

The expatriates who are least likely to agree with statement 9 are those who stayed for one year or less (61.1% versus an average of 91.4%), which makes sense because they perhaps did not witness the execution of any of the plans announced by the UAE government.

The longer the respondents stayed in the UAE, the greater their agreement with statement 11 (84.9%, 72%, 64%, 44.5%, starting with those who spent more than five years and ending with less than one year). This suggests that, year after year, the expatriate becomes more familiar with the UAE culture and finds that he/she is enjoying life and having fun without restrictions.

Again, it is obvious that the short time spent in the UAE may affect the judgment of the respondents. Those who stayed for one year or less are the least likely to agree with statement 16 (77.8% versus an average of 88.3%). In addition, neutral answers were most frequent among respondents who stayed for one year or less (22.2%); perhaps they felt unable to decide.

The respondents who stayed in the UAE for one year or less are the most likely to agree that individual freedom in UAE society is restricted (72.2% versus an average of only 30% among other categories). There are three possible explanations. First, if you spend only a short time in the country, you might not see the full picture. Second, those who stay for a longer time grow accustomed to the culture of the UAE and no longer notice restrictions. Third, those who stayed for a longer time were more conservative in their answers. Generally, it is obvious that there is a significant correlation between the number of years spent in the UAE and the image built by respondents.

DISCUSSION

The goal of this chapter was to measure the image of UAE culture among its non-Arab expatriates. As previously explained, Hofstede's paradigm was not used to observe the UAE culture itself, but to guide the measurement of the perception of this culture by the respondents.

UAE culture is perceived as high in the Power Distance Index (PDI), which coincides with Alteneiji's (2015) findings.

The UAE culture was described as a collective culture by Hofstede (2011) and Aljerjawi (2016) because of the strong and continuous ties that integrate people into groups from birth to death. The results here confirm this finding: the respondents believe that UAE people have strong social and family relationships with each other, appreciate the group's rights more than the individual's rights, and care about their families more than themselves.

As a stereotype of Arab and Muslim countries, the respondents see the UAE as a masculine society, although they believe that the competition for leadership and power is equal between the two genders. They also think that both genders work together equally. Perhaps the respondents were drawing a distinction between "social status" and "women's rights and opportunities as guaranteed by law." Socially, the respondents still believe that the UAE culture tends to be masculine, although women in the UAE have equal opportunities in terms of work, leadership, power, and education. The law guarantees this equality, and there are many everyday examples of successful female leaders and professionals in the UAE.

The respondents believe that UAE society highly respects traditions, codes of behavior, and beliefs. Hofstede (2011) stated that these are indicators of a culture with a high preference for avoiding uncertainty. As a result of media coverage of new plans and projects for the country, the respondents believe that the UAE has a long-term orientation. In fact, Dubai won the bidding for hosting Expo 2020, and many new projects since then have been launched and finished.

It seems that the respondents differentiate between UAE nationals and expatriates with respect to the freedom of enjoying life and having fun. The respondents think that social norms may hamper UAE nationals in this regard, as they are expected to abide by the norms of a collective culture. However, the respondents feel that these social norms have no influence on expatriates, and that the local environment provides plenty of opportunities for enjoyment and entertainment. The respondents also view the UAE culture as an easy one to become accustomed to.

One of the advantages of the image perceived by the respondents is that it has been built mainly by two forms of interpersonal communication. The first of these is direct contact with UAE nationals, and the second is contacts with family and friends of the respondents. When an image has been built by direct communication and real-life experiences, we can assume it will be more precise and reflective of what our respondents really think; it is not a "remote" built image. It also minimizes the influence of traditional media, which came in last on the list of our respondents' sources for learning about UAE culture.

In general, we may say that age, education, nationality, emirate of residence, and number of working years in the UAE created some differences among certain groups of our respondents in all dimensions. In some cases, variances emerged even between statements within the same dimension. Other statements have no significant correlations because every dimension except the fifth has been measured by more than one statement. The sixth dimension (indulgence versus restraint) appears to be the one most susceptible to individual influence, as it has correlations with all demographics except marital status. It seems that the single most influential demographic is the number of working years in the UAE, which makes sense: the variance in living experience will obviously cause a variance in the answers of our respondents. The only demographic characteristic that did not have any correlation with any of the dimensions is the marital status. In conclusion, we confirm that there is a significant correlation between the demographic variables (except marital status) and the image that non-Arab expatriates have of UAE culture.

REFERENCES

Aljerjawi, K. 2016. "Cultural dimensions' impact on performance management in the UAE market." *Innovative Journal of Business and Management* 5 (3): 62–71.

AlMazrouei, H., and R. J. Pech. 2015. "Working in the UAE: Expatriate management experiences." *Journal of Islamic Accounting and Business Research* 6 (1): 73–93. https://doi.org/10.1108/JIABR-08-2013-0032.

Alteneiji, E. A. 2015. "Leadership Cultural Values of United Arab Emirates: Case of United Arab Emirates University." Master's thesis, University of San Diego.

Anand, P., M. B. Holbrook, and D. Stephens. 1988. "The formation of affective judgments: The cognitive–affective model versus the independence hypothesis." *Journal of Consumer Research* 15: 386–91.

Anderson, N. 1981. *Foundations of Information Integration Theory.* New York: Academic Press.

Beerli, A., and J. D. Martin. 2004. "Tourists' characteristics and the perceived image of tourist destinations: A quantitative analysis—a case study of Lanzarote, Spain." *Tourism Management* 25 (5): 623–36.

Cai, L. 2002. "Cooperative branding for rural destinations." *Annals of Tourism Research* 29 (3): 720–42.

Chan and Rossiter. 2003. "Information integration theory." Communication Institute for Online Scholarship (CIOS). Accessed May 15, 2015. http://www.cios.org/encyclopedia/persuasion/Finformation_integration_1theory.htm.

Epps, A., and C. Demangeot. 2013. "The rainbow of diversity versus the rain of fragmentation: The futures of multicultural marketing in the UAE." *Foresight* 15 (4): 307–20.

Fletcher, R., and T. Fang. 2006. "Assessing the impact of culture on relationship creation and network formation in emerging Asian markets." *European Journal of Marketing* 40 (3/4): 430–46.

Gartner, W. C. 1993. "Image formation process." *Journal of Travel and Tourism Marketing* 2 (2/3): 191–216.

Hofstede, G. 1980/2001. *Culture's Consequences.* Thousand Oaks, CA: Sage.

———. 1991/1994. *Cultures and Organizations: Software of the Mind.* New York: HarperCollins Business.

———. 2011. "Dimensionalizing cultures: The Hofstede model in context." *Online Readings in Psychology and Culture* 2 (1). https://doi.org/10.9707/2307-0919.1014.

Hofstede, G., and M. Bond. 1988. "The Confucius connection: From cultural roots to economic growth." *Organizational Dynamics* 16 (4): 5–21.

Holbrook, M. B. 1978. "Beyond attitude structure: Toward the informational determinants of attitude." *Journal of Marketing Research* 15: 545–56.

Lederach, J. P. 1995. *Preparing for Peace: Conflict Transformation across Cultures.* Syracuse, NY: Syracuse University Press.

Matsumoto, D. 1996. *Culture and Psychology.* Pacific Grove, CA: Brooks/Cole.

Ourfali, E. 2015. "Comparison between Western and Middle Eastern cultures: Research on why American expatriates struggle in the Middle East." *Otago Management Graduate Review* 13: 33–43. http://www.otago.ac.nz/management/otago632081.pdf.

Russel, J. A., and G. Pratt. 1980. "A description of affective quality attributed to environment." *Journal of Personality and Social Psychology* 38: 311–22.

Schwartz, S. H. 1999. "A theory of cultural values and some implications for work." *Applied Psychology: An International Review* 48: 23–47.

Stern, E., and S. Krakover. 1993. "The formation of a composite urban image." *Geographical Analysis* 25 (2): 130–46.

Tasci, A. D. A., and W. C. Gartner. 2007. "Destination image and its functional relationships." *Journal of Travel Research* 45 (40): 413–25.

17

Women's Self-Representation Online

A Dramaturgical Interpretation of Identity Performance through Social Networking Websites

Meriem Narimane Noumeur

Social media tools, particularly social networking sites (SNSs), have become leading tools for social interaction and interconnection. These websites generally provide several services, giving users a space for identity formation rather than merely representing the personality they might wish to be.

Facebook is the largest social media site, with more than two billion people using it every month (Statista 2019). In Algeria, there were about 19 million Facebook users as of April 2019—44.1% of its entire population. The majority of users (64%) were men. The largest usage gap between men and women occurs within the age range of 25 to 34 (Napoleoncat 2019).

Facebook has quickly become a natural part of everyday life. Its users use it for a variety of purposes, such as creating an online self-image, representing themselves, and creating specific impressions. When Mark Zuckerberg (2012) introduced the new Timeline feature at a public event in September 2011, he described it as follows: "Timeline is the story of your life. It has three pieces: all your stories, all your apps, and a new way to express who you are." He explained how Timeline lets you "tell the whole story of your life on a single page" (van Dijk 2013, 204).

Despite the constant scrutiny of women's usage of Facebook, it is generally considered a normal activity. The use of social networking websites by Arab women has been discussed in terms of the concept of virtual space. It is generally acknowledged that Arab women are affected by societal constraints and stereotypes that are difficult to eradicate, and that strongly influence how women view themselves and present themselves in different contexts.

Using Goffman's dramaturgy, this chapter discusses the way Algerian women construct their online identities on Facebook, as well as the effect of the existing social context on their identity performance, by examining a sample of Algerian women who are consistent Facebook users.

SOCIAL NETWORKING SITES AND SELF-REPRESENTATION

Social media, as a new culture, are changing the perception of social norms and traditions (Al-Sharqi et al. 2015). Boyd and Ellison (2007) define social network sites as "web-based services that allow individuals to (1) construct a public or semi-public profile within a bounded system, (2) articulate a list of other users with whom they share a connection and (3) view and traverse their list of connections and those made by others within the system."

Users of online platforms have adopted various strategies as they became savvier in deploying new "technologies of the self" (van Dijk 2013, 201). Technology accelerates change and creates a "liquefaction" process affecting identity and the self (Bauman 2004, 51).

Studies have recognized that individuals have multiple identities (e.g., James 1890, Gergen 1991, Goffman 1961), and the performance of these identities varies in relation to the kinds of people with whom we interact. One of the most important self-presentation studies was Goffman's work, which focuses on the context of human behavior based on a viewer's impression of the action or behavior. In his seminal work, *The Presentation of Self in Everyday Life*, Goffman (1959) analyzed interpersonal interaction and how individuals "perform" in order to present a desirable image, using the image of the theater to illustrate the contrast between a person's front stage and backstage behavior. In other words, he emphasized the ways in which people routinely mold and monitor the presentation of themselves—almost like actors on a stage—in social situations (Bruce and Yearley 2006).

Existing research suggests that cyberspace has extended into a virtual environment in the Goffmanian tradition of presentation of the self to others (Turkle 1995, Zhao 2003). In this new setting, the performance of identity has developed in new directions, and the fields of "backstage" and "front stage" need to be redefined in the absence of the individual's physical presence.

Eakin (2015), in his study on self and self-representation online and offline, discusses the boundaries between virtual and real identity by stating that while the Internet has brought ease and speed to the way we express ourselves, and invented new ways of constantly manipulating that expression, performing identity work online is really not radically different from doing so offline. For this reason, self-representation on the Internet cannot be properly understood in isolation from the offline world.

Agunbiade et al. (2013) point out that the construction of identity is done simultaneously in both the virtual and the physical spheres, thereby making a plural identity for the same individual possible. Baptista (2003) considers that new identities are not created online, but that division of the self "can be found in everyday face-to-face interaction" (212).

Caffrey (2017) concludes that we increasingly become more hybrid beings, informed and influenced by our social networking platforms. He argues that human beings are rapidly becoming dependent on an intricate relation with material devices and online connections, thus internalizing these devices' mechanisms and environments until they finally become extensions of the "self."

Bareket-Bojmel et al. (2016) point out that self-presentation methods used to cater to the online "individual self" are closely linked to the feedback process that is amplified within these social platforms. Charles Cooley (1902) suggests that we will "come to know ourselves through the mirror of others' reactions to us" (Belk 2016). This mirror is even more evident through social networking sites, where users project themselves and manipulate people's perception of them.

Ellison et al. (2006) find that the greater control over self-presentational behavior in computer-mediated communication (CMC) allows individuals to manage their online interactions more strategically, and in some cases, participants describe how they or others create profiles that reflect an ideal image as opposed to the actual self: "Many people describe themselves the way they want [to be] . . . their ideal selves" (426).

The majority of studies have highlighted the gender differences in practicing self-presentation online. These studies have focused on the ways men and women create their online identities and their self-performance in cyberspace. The debate within the Arab world has been specifically linked with the limits of online representations, especially for women, and has therefore raised several questions regarding the identity constructed by women on social networking websites and the ways in which they sustain it.

The construction of a virtual identity is often affected by the sociocultural context, which in the Arab case imposes a number of limits on women, leading women to move from a real to a virtual space to find a free space to articulate the self. A study published by the Center of Arab Women for Training and Research indicates that the sociocultural context (social value systems) may compel female users to hide their identity in order to enjoy a margin of freedom that enables them to carry out certain activities: expressing opinions, building virtual ties with users, and communicating with them (CAWTAR 2017, 134).

Using data collected from Algerian women about their performance of their virtual identity, the present study investigates the extent to which identities overlap (online and offline) when actors choose to perform differently in one environment (backstage and front stage), where the self-performance oscillates between the real and the virtual environment. It aims to answer the following questions:

RQ1: To what extent do Algerian women use privacy settings when they interact with different groups of people on Facebook?

RQ2: How do Algerian women represent themselves on Facebook?

RQ3: How do Algerian women perform their online identities and manage their impressions of the self?

RQ4: To what extent does the sociocultural context affect Algerian women's self-representation on Facebook?

METHODOLOGY

The study used a mixed-method approach via an "Explanatory Sequential Design," by collecting data through an online survey, then conducting an online focus group discussion to validate the results of the study and its interpretation. The study is based on the following approaches.

Quantitative Approach

An online survey was carried out to examine real and virtual identity performance among Algerian women. A total of 550 Algerian women participated in this study. The majority (53%) of the respondents' ages ranged from 18 to 26 years, and 47% were 27 or older. Among the respondents, 380 (69%) were single, 158 (29%) were married, and 11 (2%) were divorced.

Qualitative Approach

Twelve Algerian women from different Algerian cities participated in an online focus group discussion about the construction of online identities and the social constraints that inhibit self-representation as desired by the female Facebook user.

ANALYSIS

The Use of Facebook among Algerian Women

Most respondents (53%) checked their pages at least five times a day, 45.5% of them spent more than three hours a day on Facebook, 40.4% spent from one hour to three hours, and 14% spent less than one hour.

The majority of the women (71.5%) had fewer than 150 Facebook friends, 19.6% had from 150 to 300, and only 8.9% had more than 300 friends. Their network contains a range of social ties such as family members, close friends, classmates, and some virtual friends whom they have never met in the real world.

Algerian Women and Privacy Settings

Privacy settings can be used to control access to personal profiles, so that only designated users within a shared network have access to profiles. For users who do not wish to apply privacy settings, however, profiles are accessible to any Facebook member (Nosko et al. 2010, 407). To examine their concerns about their privacy settings, the Algerian women were given a list of Facebook groups and were asked to indicate the extent to which they allowed those groups to access their entire Facebook profile. The results in figure 17.1 show that the majority of the respondents only allowed a few groups to see their entire Facebook profile without any restriction: families (57.3%), close friends (71.8%), other friends (66%), and classmates (50.2%).

Some respondents limited access to their Facebook posts and information for certain groups, such as their classmates (34.5%) and teachers (34%). A majority (54.18%) did not allow strangers to view their entire Facebook profile.

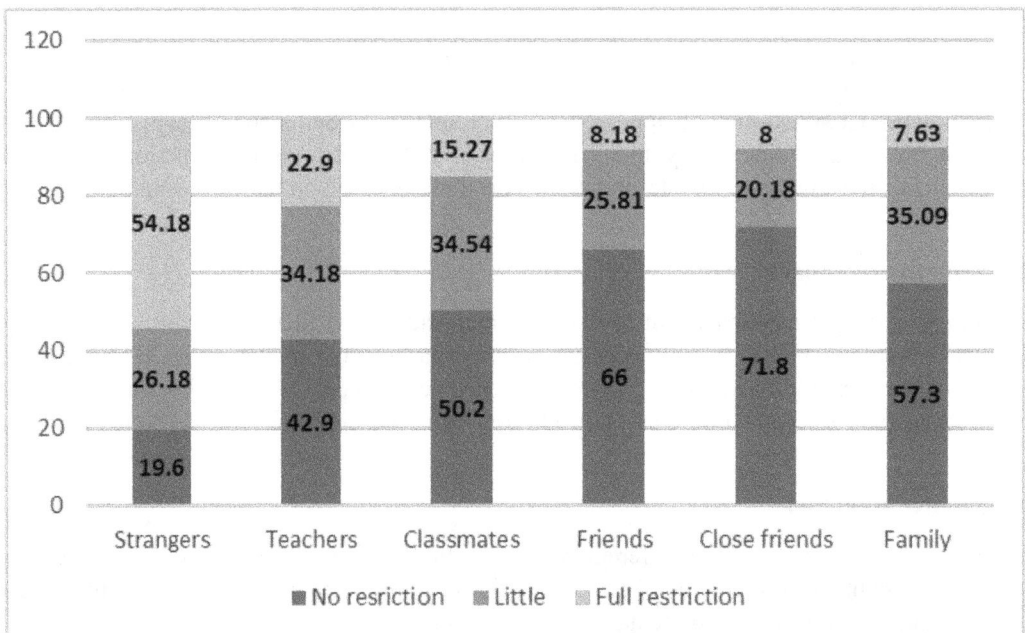

Figure 17.1.   Facebook disclosure among different groups of people.

The findings of this study showed that some respondents have only disclosed a limited amount of their Facebook information to family (35%), friends (26%), and close friends (20%), and about 8% of the women were not friends on Facebook with these groups.

By setting these restrictions, the users choose those groups of people to whom they desire to project their virtual identity. They believe that restricting family members or friends from seeing their entire Facebook profile has helped them create and enact a new, imaginative version of the self in front of the selected audience on Facebook. According to Goffman (1959), an actor on front stage is conscious of being observed by an audience, and performs to that audience by committing to certain rules and social conventions. Failing to do so means "losing face" (Goffman 1955) and failing to project the image/persona they wish to create.

Algerian Women's Performance of Online Identity

Developed by Goffman (1959), identity-as-performance is seen as a part of the flow of social interaction, where individuals construct their identity performances to fit their milieu (Pearson 2009). Online, users can claim to be whoever they would wish to be. Similar to an actor playing a role, they create their identities by selecting user names and profile pictures, and present themselves the way they want—reflecting either their own personality or the personality of the person they wish to be.

Self-Representation through User Names

About 54% of the respondents used their real names on Facebook, and 46% used nicknames. Of those who used invented names, 54% said it was for fear of harassment, 21% said it was so they could express themselves freely, and 14% were not allowed by their families to use their real identity if they wish to interact on Facebook (figure 17.2).

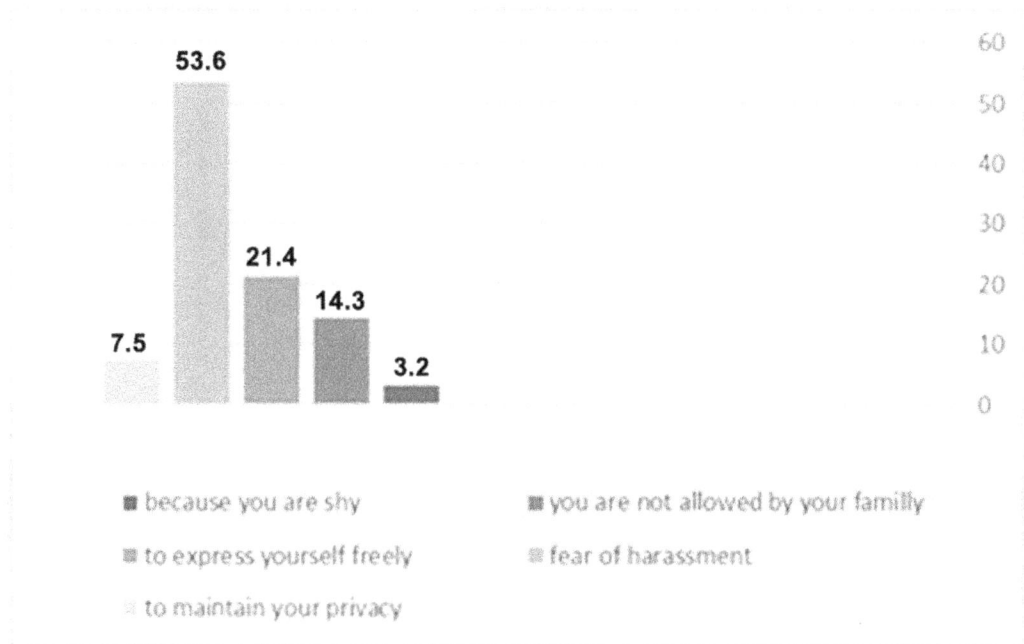

Figure 17.2. Reasons for using nicknames on Facebook.

In the focus group discussion, most of the participants reported that the majority of Algerian women use pseudonyms on Facebook because certain members of their family (such as a father or brother) do not allow them to use their real names. Others said that they adopted pseudonyms only in order to express themselves freely and to remain anonymous to some people.

Self-Representation through Profile Pictures

The profile picture is usually the first thing to be seen, and thus is arguably one of the most important features of the user's Facebook page. The profile picture offers online friends their first impression of the user's appearance and perhaps their character. The findings of this study revealed that almost all the respondents (88%) did not provide their real photos. About 32% of the 88% used meaningful images as a profile picture, 20% used flowers or other pictures of nature, 10% used images of celebrities or family members, 8% used quotes, 5% used photos of children, and 3.1% used historical characters or other kinds of pictures (figure 17.3).

Numerous reasons prevent Algerian women from providing their own pictures on Facebook. The most important are social traditions (48%), fear of harassment (25%), not being permitted by someone (9%), a personal wish not to share her picture (7%), religious reasons (6%), or simply to incarnate a new personality (3%) (figure 17.4).

One of the primary goals of social networking sites is to encourage the disclosure of personal information to others online. This personal information can include full name, address, date of birth, contact information, and photos. The results of the present study demonstrate the influence of social tradition and culture on self-presentation online. The majority of the respondents prefer to use a meaningful image, which could be an expression of their psychological state (love, sadness, anger, solitude, etc.) or to show support of a specific issue.

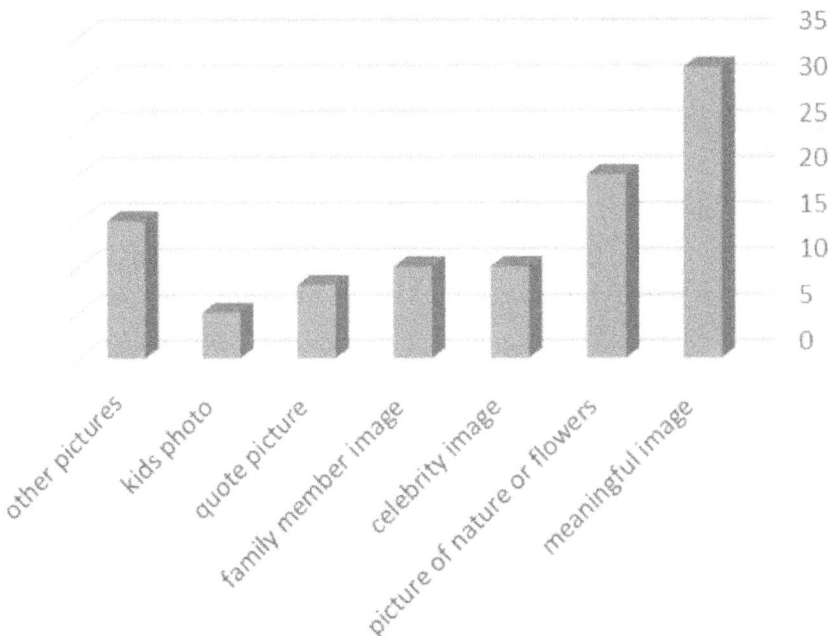

Figure 17.3. Women's identity expression via profile picture.

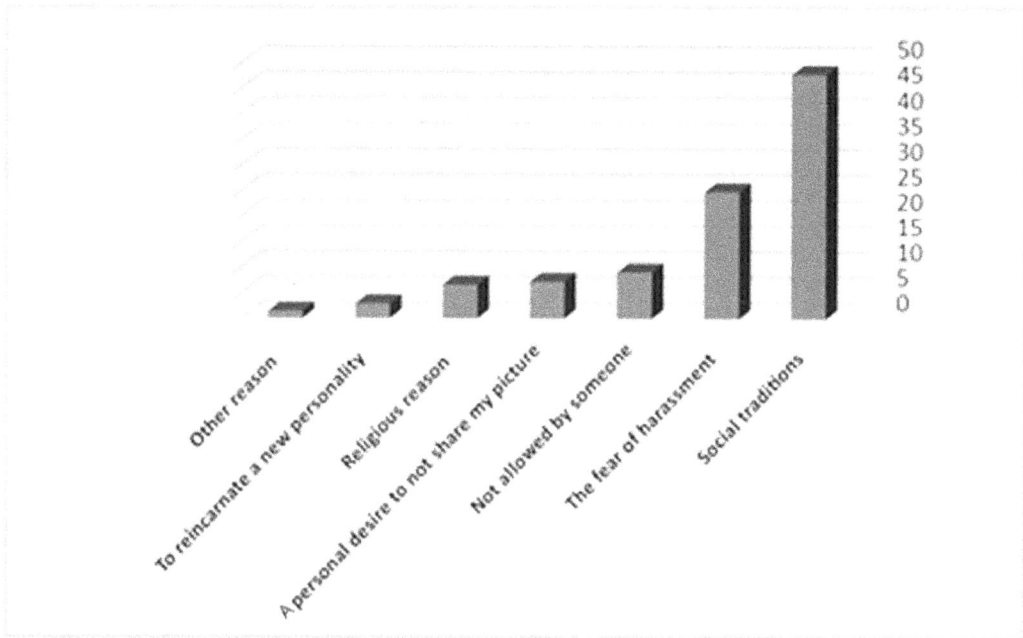

Figure 17.4. Algerian women's reasons for not sharing their real photos on Facebook.

In Algeria, as in other Arab societies, women are subject to traditional social values that make them represent modesty, and therefore using their real photos may affect their perception by others. Four participants in the focus group discussion reported that they were forbidden to use their own photos as profile pictures by their fathers or brothers, or in some cases by their husbands. However, one of the participants said: "My husband certainly gave me permission to share my photos but I personally feel this is not allowed in our society, maybe because I was not allowed to do that by my father or maybe because we are living in a patriarchal society."

The women's reasons for not sharing their photos online confirm that women's identity construction in Arab societies has been affected by the sociocultural context: the importance of cultural and religious values, the relative value of freedom, and the individual's social position.

Reinforcing the findings of the present study, the CAWTAR study states that "the study of digital identity construction in the Arab cultural context must deal with the cultural constraints that have variable effects in Arab societies and within the same society (urban vs. rural for instance), the socialization roles of educational institutions, women's sociopolitical role representations, and the social media context itself" (CAWTAR 2017, 77).

REPRESENTATION AND MISREPRESENTATION

To reveal the relationship between the Algerian women's online identities and their offline ones, they were asked to describe the extent to which their virtual identity reflects their real selves. More than half of the participants said that their Facebook identity reflects their real one only to some extent, while 32% reported that their Facebook shows their real identity, and 12% reported that it did not. Respondents who answered that their self-representation online did not match their real one gave different reasons. Fifty-seven percent reported that they could not represent themselves adequately by the use of words (written self-representation), 16% thought that their use of images is not enough to express their true selves, and 26% said that Facebook is a place for acting out multiple identities and not presenting the true one.

Almost none of the participants in this study provided actual wrong information about themselves. Of those who did (14% of the respondents), 32% said that it was because they wanted to play new roles on the virtual stage, 22% to imitate someone else, 20% to draw the attention of someone, and the rest for a number of other reasons.

Impression Management

Using a five-point Likert scale, we examined the concern about managing a positive impression online. The results (table 17.1) showed that the highest mean (3.77), with an SD of 1.15, is found in item 6 ("It is important for you to have a positive Facebook account"). This result made it clear that the women were trying to maintain a positive impression of themselves.

On the other hand, the lowest mean (1.69), with an SD of 0.85, occurred in item 2 ("You can publish wrong information about yourself if you know that no one will know the truth"). These results were supported by the participants in the focus group discussion, all of whom confirmed that it is important for them to have a positive Facebook account. One of the participants mentioned that Facebook allowed her to manage new impressions about herself: "Facebook helped me present a new aspect of my personality that I cannot reveal in my offline interactions with my family and friends, so I always try to manage new impressions about myself online which are not well known offline."

Table 17.2 shows the means and standard deviations for the effect of the social context on women's self-representation on Facebook. The highest mean (3.06), with an SD of 1.27, was found in item 5 ("You want your family to be satisfied with the image you present on Facebook"), followed by item 2 (mean 2.96, SD 1.20) ("Changes in your personal status [engaged, married, etc.] affect how you represent yourself on Facebook"). The lowest mean (2.17), with an SD of 1.12, occurred in item 4 ("A woman who publishes her real photos on Facebook presents a negative self-image"). The results of this study showed that Algerian women cannot perform their online identities in isolation from the offline one, that they are trying to manage a positive impression about themselves when they interact in cyberspace, and that their self-representations have in fact been affected by social constraints.

Moreover, all twelve of the women in the focus group discussion reported that the social context affected their self-representation online; they were not completely comfortable expressing themselves even if they used false names or graphic photos. One of the participants

Table 17.1.   The extent to which Algerian women tried to manage impressions about themselves through Facebook

Item	Mean	Standard Deviation
1. You are trying to correct a wrong impression about yourself	2.43	1.15
2. You can publish wrong information about yourself if you know that no one will know the truth	1.69	0.85
3. You can change your profile picture to draw someone's attention	2.02	1.06
4. You change or delete what you post on Facebook if you receive negative comments	2.14	1.16
5. You manage your Facebook account so you can join certain groups (intellectuals, housewives, etc.)	3.28	1.33
6. It is important for you to have a positive Facebook account	3.77	1.15

Table 17.2. The effect of social context on Algerian women's self-representation online

Item	Mean	Standard Deviation
1. The fear of your parents' reaction to your updates on Facebook affects the way you represent yourself	2.92	1.21
2. Changes in your personal status (engaged, married, etc.) affect how you represent yourself on Facebook	2.96	1.20
3. Your Facebook friends list (real or virtual) affects the way you represent yourself online	2.37	1.14
4. A woman who publishes her real photos on Facebook presents a negative self-image	2.17	1.12
5. You want your family to be satisfied with the image you present on Facebook	3.06	1.27

confirmed: "I cannot show my real self on Facebook or express myself freely, because I belong to a community with values and taboos that should not be bypassed, and since our behaviors are regulated by the norms, rules, laws, and social structures of society."

Another participant revealed: "The restrictions imposed on us by our society have led us to create different Facebook accounts, one account for real friends (family, work) and another one with a nickname and unknown identity, so that we could freely represent our real selves in cyberspace anonymously."

The study revealed that Algerian women may create multiple identities, one to perform their real identities in front of a mixed audience (real friends and virtual friends with no prior social ties) and a second to perform new identities in front of new people by creating a new version of

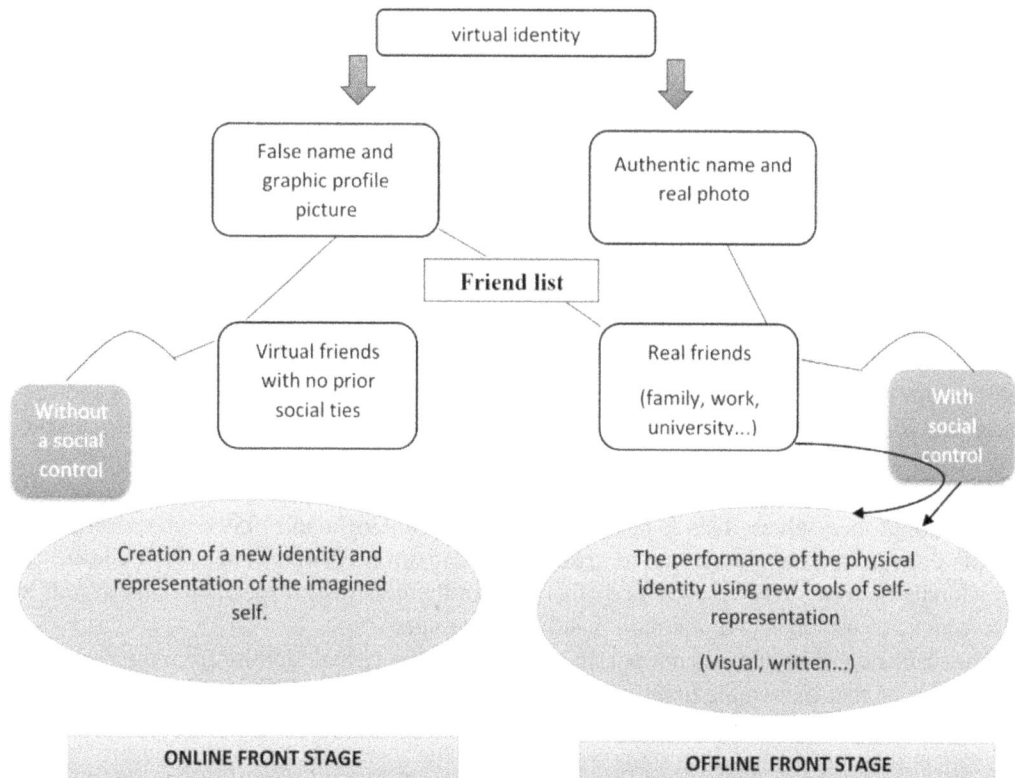

Figure 17.5. False and real identity and the effect of friend list on self-representation online.

themselves, making their physical identities unknown to others and thereby becoming anony-mous. Thus, even the creation of an account with a fake identity does not mean that women can behave freely. Their degree of freedom depends on the people with whom they wish to interact within this environment, which determines the relationship between the women's virtual and real identity performance and the overlap of the backstage and front stage between the two spaces (figure 17.5).

DISCUSSION

This study examines the way Algerian women represent themselves online through the perfor-mance of their virtual identity on Facebook. The findings show that Algerian women disclose their Facebook identities only to their families and close friends; other friends and classmates did not enjoy this privilege, and the majority of them did not disclose their Facebook identi-ties to strangers. The literature suggests that the reasons why some women restrict access to their information, while others do not, can vary. The effect of different factors, such as gender, cultural background, digital skills, and the extent of online activity, has frequently been ana-lyzed (Bellman et al. 2004, Cho 2007, Fogel and Nehmad 2009, Lewis et al. 2008, Sun and Wu 2012, Thelwall 2011, Weiqin et al. 2016, Youn and Hall 2008; all cited in Farinosi and Taipale 2018, 54).

This study reveals that although the majority of the respondents used their real names in their online identities, most of them did not use their real photos because of social constraints and the fear of harassment. These results were confirmed during the focus group: we observed that the female users were not comfortable portraying themselves on Facebook even if they used pseudonyms; they felt that they were socially controlled. Even pseudonyms do not allow the women to represent themselves freely. Furthermore, their representations could also be affected by the people (audience) they interact with, so that their identity performance online is actually affected by the audience in their friend list (both real and virtual friends).

The female users might have felt themselves performing their virtual identity as if they were performing their real one on the front stage of real life, but when they used pseudonyms and performed their identity in front of virtual friends, they expressed themselves freely with no sense of social control (figure 17.5). Goffman, in his work on dramaturgy, assumes that when humans are engaged in any interaction, they are performing for those with whom the interaction takes place (Ritzer 2007). Therefore, hiding identity helps women enjoy a measure of freedom that enables them to express opinions, build virtual ties with other users and com-municate with them, and re-create themselves and reconstruct their identity in the virtual space.

The present study thus confirms that female users do try to manage a positive impression of themselves through their Facebook profile, but without actually publishing any wrong infor-mation about themselves. This idea is also supported by Goffman (1959), who asserted that people engage in strategic actions to create and maintain a desired image. He believed that individuals not only tried to convince others to see them as just, respectable, and moral, but also wanted to establish and maintain positive impressions.

The results confirm that it is not possible to separate the virtual identity from the real one. It was observed that the female users perform their virtual identity within the real context; they could not isolate their virtual identity from the real one. Most of them answered that Facebook did reflect their real identity "to some extent."

Eakin (2015) argued that individuals construct themselves whenever they engage in self-narration online or offline. The quality of the identity and the properties of its representation are two different faces of a single phenomenon of self-experience. Similarly, Cover (2014) says, "Online social networking behavior is as performative as 'real-life' acts, and just as equally implies a stabilized inner core self behind the profile. The interplay of the two identities (virtual and real) produces a new self-image with well-known impressions about the real self and new impressions, which have been managed in the virtual space." Baker (2009) introduces an alternative perspective through the concept of "blended identity," whereby the offline self informs the creation of a new, online self which then re-informs the offline self in further interactions with people whom the individual has first met online.

The main contribution of this research, specifically, was the presentation of the Algerian women's self-representation process online and its relation with the performance of their physical identity in the social context.

Algerian women are certainly affected by the constraints of the social context. The majority of them took social tradition and values into consideration when they represented themselves online, sometimes even using fake accounts in order to express themselves freely. Research by the Center of Arab Women for Training and Research found that "the constraints of the socio-cultural context (social value systems) may compel female users to hide their identity and enjoy a margin of freedom that enables them to carry out certain activities" (CAWTAR 2017, 134). This result was also supported by the work of Goffman, who claims that "individuals are inclined to present idealized impressions to their audiences, modifying and adapting their performances to suit the understandings, expectations, and values of the society" (Goffman 1956, 10).

CONCLUSION: RELATIONSHIP BETWEEN BACKSTAGE AND FRONT STAGE IN ONLINE AND OFFLINE ENVIRONMENTS

In order to meaningfully interpret the findings of this study, we propose a relationship between the front stage and backstage in the online and offline platforms. If the front stage is the interactions that women perform on their Facebook wall or on other pages or groups using their virtual identity, the backstage is then the life behind the screen where the reality appears. But these stages may sometimes overlap. Based on Goffman's dramaturgy, we suggest the following relationships (figure 17.6).

Self-Representation on the Front-Backstage

When the self is divided between the front stage of the real world and the backstage of the virtual space, we assume that the person performs her virtual identity on Facebook while she is alone in her room behind the screen performing her real self (the backstage of life). Therefore, the real backstage meets the virtual front stage in one self-performance.

Self-Representation on the Front-Front Stage

We assume that a woman is sitting somewhere interacting with some people and performing her virtual identity through her phone. She is performing two roles at the same time, the first one using a certain appearance and accessories (according to her imagined-self requirements)

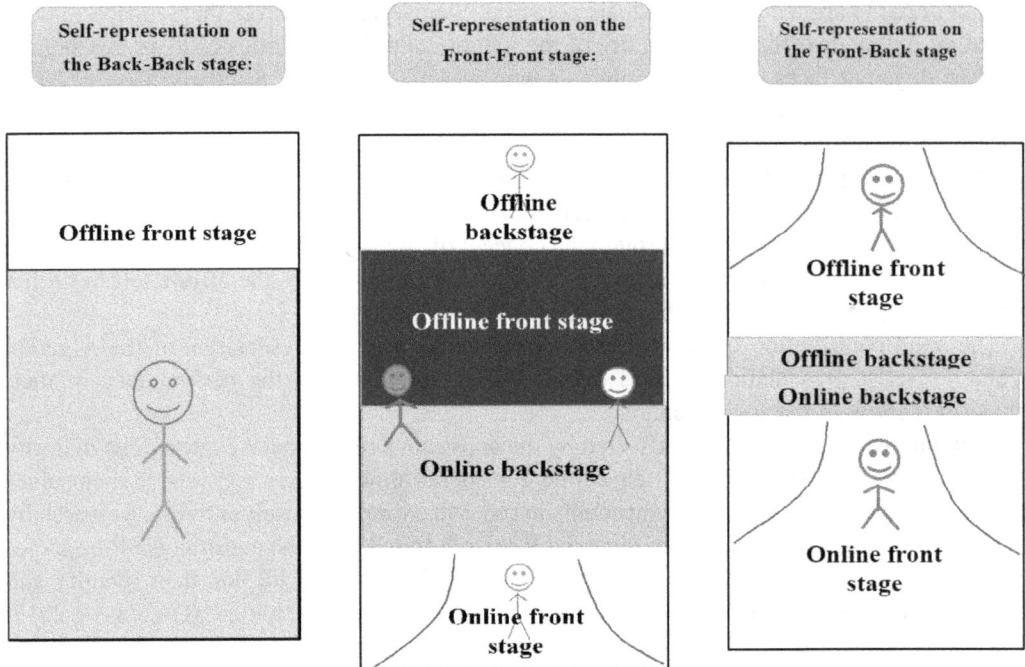

Figure 17.6. Relationship between backstage and front stage in online and offline environments.

on Facebook, and the second one in which she plays another role depending on what the audience finds attractive. This indicates that the performance of identity and self-representation may be on two different platforms at the same time, the first realistic and the second virtual; the self divides to perform two roles and act two different personalities. Here, the real backstage does not meet the virtual one, but the performance on the front stage is almost the same with the use of different tools for self-representation. This possibility applies mostly to those who use their real identities on Facebook.

Self-Representation in the Back-Backstage

We assume that a woman is sitting alone in her room performing her virtual identity, which is a fake one with strange people (no prior social ties). Therefore she acts freely, showing her real self, as if she is performing these roles on the backstage of life with an audience who does not know anything about the actor, whereas actually this role is being performed on the front stage of life as demanded by the character she is representing. Here the concept of the front stage fades because it overlaps with the concept of the backstage.

The study of self-representation through social networking sites raises many issues, especially in the context of dramaturgy and the relationship between the front stage and backstage. These questions require further in-depth studies to understand how they work in different settings.

Furthermore, recent decades have seen a dramatically accelerating pace in the development and adoption of new technologies, which have affected all areas of social, personal, and global life in an ever-changing pattern. These new technologies have imposed a new lifestyle where the elements of identity have changed. This has allowed individuals to find new ways for shaping a new identity, free from sociocultural restrictions. This is especially significant for women in the Arab countries, who are exposed to social surveillance to a great degree.

The virtual identity of Arab women in general, and Algerian women in particular, is related to the opportunities that virtual space provides them in terms of the ability to express themselves more openly and to play different roles. Studies have revealed that the impact of social and cultural restrictions persists in the virtual space; women always seek to manage their virtual identity in a way that satisfies the community first before satisfying themselves. They put considerable effort into beautifying their image in this parallel society where they live under the same social restrictions as in the real world. Therefore, the women's presence in the virtual space actually did not change much in their lives.

In some cases, Arab women consider the use of a fake identity in the virtual space as an opportunity, where they can find pleasure by forming a new identity and choosing new people to perform it in front of. It amounts to a second life away from social surveillance. Through this identity, they can express their thoughts and feelings; it gives them a chance to practice everything that is forbidden in society.

Finally, Arab women's presence in the virtual space always remains under control. Her virtual identity is considered as a mirror: for some, it reflects their real life, while for others, it is a reflection of their inner world. Women in virtual communities do just about everything they do in real life, but they leave their bodies behind. They cannot touch anybody, but a lot can happen within those boundaries.

REFERENCES

Agunbiade, O. M., M. O. Obiyan, and G. B. Sogbaike. 2013. "Identity construction and gender involvement in online social networks among undergraduates in two universities, Southwest Nigeria." *Inkanyiso: Journal of Humanities and Social Sciences* 5 (1): 41–52.

Baker, A. J. 2009. "Mick or Keith: Blended identity of online rock fans." *Identity in the Information Society* 2 (1): 7–21.

Baptista, L. 2003. "Framing and Cognition." In *Goffman's Legacy*, edited by A. Treviño, 197–215. Lanham, MD: Rowman & Littlefield.

Bareket-Bojmel, L., S. Moran, and G. Shahar. 2016. "Strategic self-presentation on Facebook: Personal motives and audience response to online behavior." *Computers in Human Behavior* 55: 788–95.

Bauman, Z. 2004. *Identity.* 2nd ed. Cambridge: Polity Press.

Belk, R. 2016. "Extended self and the digital world." *Current Opinion in Psychology* 10: 50–54.

Boyd, D., and N. Ellison. 2007. "Social network sites: Definition, history, and scholarship." *Journal of Computer-Mediated Communication* 13 (1).

Bruce, S., and S. Yearley. 2006. *The SAGE Dictionary of Sociology*. London: Sage.

Caffrey, L. (2017). "Social Media and the Construction of 'Self': How Our New Sociotechnical Environment Is Changing the Construction of Identity." Master's thesis, Dublin University.

CAWTAR (Center of Arab Women for Training and Research). 2017. *Arab Women in Virtual Debate: A Study of Women's Representations in Traditional Media Facebook Pages.* https://www.academia .edu/29077720/Arab_Women_in_Virtual_Debate_A_Study_of_Women_s_Representations_in_Tra ditional_Media_Facebook_Pages.

Cooley, C. H. 1902. "Looking-Glass Self." In *The Production of Reality: Essays and Readings on Social Interaction*, 5th ed., edited by Jodi O'Brien, 126–28. Thousand Oaks, CA: Pine Forge Press.

Cover, R. 2014. "Becoming and Belonging: Performativity, Subjectivity, and the Cultural Purposes of Social Networking." In *Identity Technologies: Constructing the Self Online*, edited by A. Poletti and J. Rak, 55–69. Madison: University of Wisconsin Press.

Eakin, P. J. 2015. "Self and self-representation online and off." *FRAME, Journal of Literary Studies* 28 (1): 11–29.

Ellison, N., R. Heino, and J. Gibbs. 2006. "Managing impressions online: Self-presentation processes in the online dating environment." *Journal of Computer-Mediated Communication* 11 (2): 415–41.

Farinosi, M., and S. Taipale. 2018. "Who can see my stuff? Online self-disclosure and gender differences on Facebook." *Observatorio (OBS*)* 12 (1): 53–71.

Gergen, K. J. 1991. *The Saturated Self: Dilemmas of Identity in Contemporary Life*. New York: Basic Books.

Goffman, E. 1955. "On face-work: An analysis of ritual elements in social interaction." *Psychiatry* 18 (3): 213–31.

———. 1956. *The Presentation of Self in Everyday Life*. Monograph no. 2. Edinburgh: University of Edinburgh Social Sciences Research Centre.

———. 1959. *The Presentation of Self in Everyday Life*. New York: Doubleday Anchor.

———. 1961. *Encounters: Two Studies in the Sociology of Interaction*. Oxford: Bobbs-Merrill.

James, W. 1890. *The Principles of Psychology.* Vol. 1. New York: Holt.

Napoleoncat. 2019. "Facebook users in Algeria." Accessed May 9, 2019. https://napoleoncat.com/stats/facebook-users-in-algeria/2019/04.

Nosko, A., E. Wood, and S. Molema. 2010. "All about me: Disclosure in online social networking profiles: The case of Facebook." *Computers in Human Behavior* 26 (3): 406–18.

Pearson, E. 2009. "All the World Wide Web's a stage: The performance of identity in online social networks." *First Monday* 14 (3). https://doi.org/10.5210/fm.v14i3.2162.

Ritzer, G. 2007. *Contemporary Sociological Theory and Its Classical Roots: The Basics*. New York: McGraw-Hill.

Al-Sharqi, L., K. Hashim, and I. Kutbi. 2015. "Perceptions of social media impact on students' social behavior: Comparison between arts and science students." *International Journal of Education and Social Science* 2 (4): 122–31.

Statista. 2019. "Most popular social networks worldwide as of April 2019, ranked by number of active users (in millions)." Accessed May 9, 2019. https://www.statista.com/statistics/272014/global-social-networks-ranked-by-number-of-users.

Turkle, S. 1995. *Life on the Screen: Identity in the Age of the Internet*. London: Weidenfeld and Nicolson.

van Dijk, J. 2013. "'You have one identity': Performing the self on Facebook and LinkedIn." *Media, Culture & Society* 35 (2): 199–215.

Zhao, S. 2003. "Toward a taxonomy of copresence." *Presence: Teleoperators & Virtual Environments* 12 (5): 445–55.

Zuckerberg, M. 2012. "Mark Zuckerberg unveils Facebook Timeline." YouTube, September 23, 2011. http://www.youtube.com/watch?v=v67PFmVvqDs.

18

An Analysis of YouTube Users' Reaction to the Tunisian President's Call for Gender Equality in Inheritance

Aliaa Dawoud

In August 2017, Tunisian president Beji Caid Essebsi called for legal changes in order to give women equal inheritance rights. Many Muslim feminists have been calling for this change for many long years, but their calls were easily dismissed; they hardly ever received much media attention and the women were usually accused of aping the West. However, a call to the same effect by an incumbent president was not something that could be as easily ignored or dismissed. Indeed, it sent shock waves through the region and several local and regional television networks devoted a lot of airtime to discuss the issue. In addition, large numbers of people—both men and women—took to social media to express their views on the matter.

This chapter will analyze a sample of a thread of comments on a YouTube video of an episode of an Egyptian talk show in which an Islamic scholar and a secular journalist discuss the proposed changes to women's inheritance. The chapter will argue that Islamic ideology—in the broader sense of the term—is dominant among most of the YouTube users who commented on the episode. That is why so many of them opposed the proposed changes to women's inheritance. It will also argue that secular users are in the minority. In addition, the chapter will show how some users' stances on the proposed changes to women's inheritance are related to various social, political, and economic factors rather than simply religious ones.

HOW EGYPTIAN FEMINISM AND NEOCOLONIALISM AFFECTED THE EGYPTIAN FAMILY STRUCTURE

In order to arrive at a comprehensive understanding of why any changes in women's rights in the private sphere are so problematic in the Middle East, it is crucial to consider how the region's postcolonial history and its neocolonial present are adversely related to women's status. The first subsection of the literature review will provide some historical background about how Egyptian feminism developed in correlation with British colonizers' views on Egyptian women's status. The same subsection will also point out how this correlation had a long-term negative impact on the way women's rights were perceived by many members of Egyptian society. The second subsection of the literature review will show how much of the region remains subject to neocolonialism today, while also explaining how this is adversely related to family structures.

Historical Factors That Fuel Resistance to Changes in Women's Status

One of the factors influencing the manner in which a particular society views feminism is its history (Badran 1995). Indeed, during the British occupation of Egypt, the colonizers proclaimed that they would liberate Egyptian women from the oppressive culture in which they lived and promoted the adoption of aspects of Western culture (Baron 2005, 218). This critically impacted the discourse used to frame women's rights at the time. This is because secular nationalists, who were mostly Western-educated members of the elite, deprecated women's status and the manner in which they were treated in Egypt, describing it as backward and oppressive (Badran 1995, Ahmed 1992). In fact, the discourse that these secular nationalists adopted to voice these criticisms and the changes they called for were largely similar to those of the colonizers.

These arguments were initially voiced by men, but soon many women's voices made similar arguments. These women were secular nationalists who grounded their feminist discourse in secular terms and often called for the adoption of European laws and ways of life. Furthermore, these female activists also cooperated with Western feminist organizations (Ahmed 1992). This attitude tainted feminism and feminists in the eyes of many natives of postcolonial countries, including Egypt.

In fact, this chapter will illustrate how some Egyptians—as well as some citizens of other Arabic-speaking Middle Eastern countries—seem to continue to have a very negative perception of secular Arabs who call for changing Muslim women's status to resemble Western women's status. It will also show how, in some cases, this negative perception is fueled by the idea that this is a form of neocolonialism.

Contemporary Factors That Fuel Resistance to Changes in Women's Status

Resistance to changes in women's status seems to be strengthened by ongoing international interference in the local affairs of many Middle Eastern countries. In fact, the economies and political systems of many countries in the region are subject to much foreign interference by powerful Western countries and international organizations, such as the World Bank and the International Monetary Fund. The economic approach promoted by this process has meant that several Middle Eastern countries are stuck in a vicious cycle of foreign debt. It has also brought about striking disparities in living standards, which have in turn fueled a lot of resentment.

In contrast to this intense interference in the political and economic systems of most countries in the region, the Personal Status Laws, or the laws governing the private sphere, including women's inheritance, are the only laws that have not been secularized and remain based on Islamic principles. Indeed, in many cases they are also the only area in which the official religious establishment still has a say. In this environment, it is therefore perhaps not surprising that this set of laws is perceived as the last bastion of cultural authenticity and that any attempt to amend them in collaboration with the West is usually ferociously attacked and opposed (Kandiyoti 1991).

Several forces make it increasingly difficult for many Arab men to continue to play the traditional role of sole provider for their families. In this part of the world, as in other traditional societies, Arab men have long been perceived as naturally superior over women and men are accustomed to assuming the role of provider for their families. However, many men are no longer able to do so, partly due to the economic difficulties described above. Other factors contributing to this phenomenon include globalization, women joining the workforce, and poverty, as well as some women's expressions of independence.

This inevitably means that power dynamics within families are changing, and that men's natural superiority and authority over women in the private sphere are under threat (Lodhia 2014, Wyrod 2008). In such a dire situation, it comes as no surprise that any suggested changes in inheritance favoring women would be met with fierce resistance, because they are bound to be perceived by many men as yet another threat to their natural superiority and authority over women in the private sphere. Indeed, this chapter will indicate that some YouTube users framed their opposition to changing the inheritance laws in social and economic terms rather than religious ones.

DEFINITION OF IDEOLOGY

An overview of the operational definition of an ideology is important because it will enable a more thorough analysis of some of the comments in the YouTube thread that will be analyzed in this chapter. An ideology has been defined as a socially shared set of ideas that constitute a belief system to a particular group of people. Ideologies are very important because they "define the social identity of a group." In other words, ideologies define, control, and organize the group's "shared beliefs about its fundamental conditions and ways of existence and reproduction," or its cultural values (Van Dijk 2006, 123). Indeed, this study shows that many YouTube users seem to believe in an Islamic ideology in the broader sense of the term, while a small number of users seem to align themselves with secular ideology.

One of the important social functions of an ideology is that it provides an "ultimate basis" for both the discourse and the social practices of its followers. Indeed, many of the comments by YouTube users were framed in either Islamic or secular discourse. Another important function of an ideology is to provide a basis for people to come together around shared goals (Van Dijk 2006, 122). As will be shown below, this particular function of an ideology is crucial to understanding why some of the YouTube users who came across as Islamist were so angered by the proposed changes to women's inheritance.

Scholars have noted how the believers in a particular ideology do not all share the same level of knowledge of it. That is why a certain subgroup of believers tends to act as teachers, experts, or leaders for the rest of the group, which can in turn allow this subgroup to dominate other members of the group, or society at large (Van Dijk 2006). Indeed, this chapter will argue that Islamic scholars in general, and al-Azhar scholars in particular, seem to clearly play this role of leaders, teachers, and experts. It will further argue that many people seem to fully accept their assumption of this role, largely because for many of these users, Islamic ideology seems to have surpassed its status as an ideology to be perceived simply as common sense, or the only way things could or should be.

When any ideology reaches this stage, scholars refer to it as "common ground" (Van Dijk 2006, 128). In this environment, an ideology that counters the dominant one may provide a basis for people to resist the dominant ideology. Indeed, this chapter will argue that secular ideology seems to enable some people in the region to resist in this way, but the matter is not that simple.

METHODOLOGY

As stated at the beginning of the chapter, several Egyptian talk shows dedicated one or more episodes to discussing the Tunisian president's call to make Muslim women equal to men in inheritance. One such case was an episode of the program *Akher al-nahar* ("At the End of the Day"), which is aired on the channel al-Nahar ("The Day"). It was uploaded on YouTube on August 22, 2017. It featured a discussion between Abdalla Roshdy, an Islamic scholar from al-Azhar, and Sherif El Shobashi, an Egyptian secular journalist. When this study was conducted, the episode had been viewed 273,266 times and had received more than 1,200 comments from people from various Arab countries, including Egypt, Tunisia, Algeria, Mauritania, and Saudi Arabia.[1] Due to time constraints, only the first 204 comments in the thread were analyzed. The unit of analysis was one comment, regardless of its length. All of the comments were translated from Arabic by the author.

Since the issue under study is a discussion about the fact that Muslim men inherit twice as much as Muslim women, critical discourse analysis (CDA) was used to analyze the YouTube thread. CDA is a qualitative research method used to analyze how discourse is used to justify, maintain, and reproduce social inequalities in general, including gender inequality. CDA rests on the notion that language is not neutral, but is always embedded in contexts and used to perform various power-related functions in society. One such function is maintaining a particular social order, such as a gender order (Mullet 2018).

A core element of CDA is that, in any society, power is hierarchically organized as well as institutionalized, so that certain power elites play specific roles in the enactment of power. One such role is dominance, which involves indirectly controlling people's ideologies. That is why CDA is helpful in analyzing how linguistic expressions of power are used to influence people's ideologies (Mullet 2018). Thus, it could be argued that Islamic religious scholars are the institutionalized power elite, who influence many Muslims' ideological stances on how inheritance should be divided. This is a particularly crucial point in this study because, as will be shown in the results section, a large number of YouTube users from various Arab countries, including both men and women, seemed to fully accept the authority of religious scholars in this area.

Furthermore, one of the tactics used to justify inequality is the portrayal of one's own group in a positive light, while simultaneously representing the other group in a negative light. This is described by CDA scholars as a "paired complementarity strategy" (Van Dijk 2006, 130). As will be shown in the results section of this chapter, this tactic was used quite often by YouTube users who supported the status quo regarding women's inheritance. However, it should be noted that it was also used by many of those who supported the changes proposed by Essebsi.

The 204 YouTube comments were initially divided into eleven different themes. After further analysis, they were then grouped under five main themes, each with a set of subthemes. At a later stage, the five main themes were further reduced to four, and the number and categorization of the subthemes were also refined.

RESULTS AND DISCUSSION

This section of the chapter is divided into four main subsections, which correspond to the four main themes identified in the YouTube comments under study.

Commending or Attacking One of the Show's Speakers

The first theme consists of comments in which the users either commended or attacked one of the two interviewees on the show. In fact, a countless number of users commended Roshdy, the Islamic scholar. Indeed, this was by far the most recurrent subtheme in the entire sample of threads under study. A large number of users attacked or even insulted El Shobashi, the secular intellectual being interviewed. Furthermore, the sample under study did not contain a single comment in which a user praised El Shobashi, nor did any of the users in the sample criticize Roshdy himself, even though many users argued against everything that he stood for. However, since this study only analyzed the first 204 comments, out of 3,200 comments made by YouTube users on the episode, the possibility that some other users may have spoken well of El Shobashi, or directly criticized Roshdy, cannot be ruled out.

Commending the Islamic Scholar Interviewed on the Show

The strikingly large number of comments that spoke very highly of Roshdy came from both male and female users. For example, one user wrote, "God bless you, Sheikh Abdallah. May God always enable you to benefit [others]" (Shams Shams). Another user wrote, "God bless Dr. Abdallah Roshdy. He is confident and swiftly provides convincing answers to any questions. If you agree with me, [press] like" (Chedia Bouchlaghem). Indeed, 436 people responded by liking the latter comment, which happened to be written by an Egyptian female user. In fact, many of the comments in this particular subtheme also received a large number of likes. For example, another comment that received 95 likes read: "Sheikh Abdallah Roshdy, may God bless you. Long live Egypt with its honorable scholars of al-Azhar" (Ahmed Gamal Eldin).

Even though most of the comments were rather brief and simply contained some form of praise for Roshdy, in some cases the users also touched upon some other thorny issues. For example, one user wrote: "Dr. Sheikh Abdallah is excellent. Greetings from Algeria. We are at a loss without al-Azhar's scholars. The *umma* [Islamic nation] needs the input of al-Azhar's scholars in all of the issues facing the *umma*. Al-Azhar should not be marginalized any more" (Sana H). The idea that al-Azhar should have a say in the affairs of other countries is something that several other users, especially Tunisian users, forcefully argued against, as will be shown in a subsequent subsection.

In any case, due to the recurrence of comments praising Roshdy, and building on Van Dijk's (2006) argument, it could be argued that Roshdy seemed to play the role of expert, teacher, or leader of Islamic ideology in general, and in the area of women's inheritance in particular. It could also be further argued that many of the YouTube users who appeared to believe in this ideology seemed also to accept not only Roshdy's assumption of that leading role in this area, but also al-Azhar's institutional assumption of such a role.

Attacking the Secular Speaker on the Show

In addition to the massive praise for Dr. Roshdy, a considerable number of users harshly criticized El Shobashi, and some even insulted him. For example, one Egyptian female user wrote: "What kind of college did Sherif graduate from? Why is he talking about religion? Does it make any sense to ask a plumber about blacksmithing or carpentry? You are really getting on our nerves; we have had enough of this" (Mariam Tamer). This particular comment received 61 likes, and it was part of a series of comments questioning why Egyptian television networks gave secular intellectuals like El Shobashi so much airtime.

Another comment, which received 157 likes, read: "Hey, Sherif, you obviously have not memorized any verses of the Quran. Shut up because you are in a very weak position" (Abeer Hijaze). Other comments, such as the following one, used even more inappropriate language:

Does this man called Sherif even know how to think? His arguments are not convincing and do not even make any sense. He can't even put a proper sentence together. All he keeps saying is that [Dr. Roshdy] will accuse me of being a nonbeliever and my status should be respected. To hell with you and your status and [to hell with] all those who uphold stupid views like yours. (Amir Oraby)

These comments seem to reinforce the argument that for many of these users only al-Azhar scholars can be regarded as acceptable leaders of the Islamic ideology. They also support the idea, as mentioned in the literature review section, that some Egyptians and Arabs continue to have an unfavorable view of secular Arabs who call for changes in women's status in their societies.

Arguments Using Secular versus Religious Discourse

The second main theme is how users framed their arguments using secular versus religious discourse. In many cases, the religious versus secular arguments were part of a long subthread in which multiple proponents of secularism and Islamism engaged in a heated back-and-forth debate. As this subsection will show, most of their comments were perfect examples of using the "paired complementarity strategy," and in many cases they also included insults and inappropriate language.

Valorizing Secularism

Many of the Tunisian users who seemed to be supportive of the changes proposed by their president tended to ground their arguments in secular discourse. Some of the comments were very brief and simply stressed that Tunisia is a secular state. For example, a female user called Lilia Telili wrote: "Tunisia is a secular state, not a religious or an Islamic state. Tunisia is a secular state. I repeat, Tunisia is a secular state." Meanwhile, another user wrote: "Hey, you Mauritanian, why don't you mind your own business? The Tunisian people follow an interpretation of the true faith [Islam] which respects women, people's rights, and their freedom" (Iness Afel).

In fact, many other Tunisian users argued that other Arabs should mind their own business, and some of them directed this argument specifically to al-Azhar. In the words of one such user, "We are doing fine on our own. We do not want al-Azhar [which resembles] ISIS [an abbreviation for the Islamic State of Iraq and Syria] to interfere in our affairs" (Kudo Shinishi). Indeed, this user was not the only one who linked al-Azhar to ISIS in some way, as other comments in this section will illustrate.

Meanwhile, other users who came across as secular wrote some lengthy comments such as the following:

Countless [televised] programs in countries like Egypt and France devoted a lot of airtime to addressing this topic. This was not the case in Tunisia. This is because the Tunisian Parliament will have the final say when it comes to this issue, so there is no need for such chatter. The Tunisian public has moved beyond such trivial issues, and it entrusts such matters to legal [and constitutional experts]. . . . We chose [our constitution]. . . .

Other Arabs do not know the Tunisian people or Tunisian women well. . . . Tunisian women were not brought up to be pampered like other Arab women. They are well educated and are fully aware of their rights and duties. They were brought up to hate Islamists and ISIS. They were taught by atheist professors. [Tunisian women] work hard and excel in their careers. Good for them. We are not like you. You have your own faith. God bless Tunisia.

[Mind your own business] and your one million prostitutes in Mohamed Ali Street and others. We have our own constitution, country and beliefs.

I may disagree with Beji [the Tunisian president] in some issues, and I may support him in others, because we are a democracy. But I will never accept any insults to my nation. (Oas Academy)

This lengthy comment received 12 likes. It is representative of the detailed comments from other Tunisian users. Almost all such comments reiterated the idea that Tunisians are different from other Arabs, better educated and with a more modern and/or enlightened understanding of Islam. Many of them also called on other Arabs to mind their own business.

This comment is a perfect example of what some CDA scholars call the "paired complementarity strategy," because the user clearly went to great lengths to portray the Tunisian people as far superior to all other Arabs. In addition, he also directly insulted Egyptians by referring to the notion of "one million prostitutes" and "Mohamed Ali Street." Some background information is necessary to explain what this user probably meant.

Mohamed Ali is a street in Cairo that used to be considered a cultural center because it was once full of restaurants featuring performance artists, poets, and belly dancers. The reference to "one million prostitutes" has to do with what has been described as "the World Cup hate match," which took place between Egypt and Algeria in 2009 (Oliver 2009). In the buildup to the match, the Egyptian media led a ferocious campaign against Algeria, and many commenters made inappropriate comments about Algeria and its people on Egyptian television. Since many Arabs refer to Algeria as "the country of one million martyrs," because of the large number of Algerians who lost their lives in the country's struggle for colonial independence from France, some Algerians started referring to Egypt as the country of "one million prostitutes," in reference to Egypt's vibrant entertainment industry, whose products are broadcast throughout the Arab world. This is largely because many of the Egyptian actresses and belly dancers who are part of this industry are perceived by both Egyptians and other Arabs as loose women. Thus, this user refers to them indirectly as prostitutes.

Using Religious Discourse to Justify the Status Quo

One user wrote in response to the last comment cited in the previous section: "Hey you, what is at stake is the *umma*'s doctrine . . . and not the doctrine of that man called . . . [Beji]. This is not about interfering in internal Tunisian affairs. Wake up and see clearly. You have crossed the red line" (Momo Khaldi). This comment received 10 likes and is a clear example of what Van Dijk (2006) calls one of the cognitive functions of ideologies. In this case, the Islamic ideology seems to have given its followers a common understanding of the interests and goals of the *umma*, or the group as a whole. Other examples to this effect will be cited in the subsection that analyzes comments relating women's inheritance to various political factors, especially neocolonialism.

Other users who grounded their arguments in religious discourse also resorted to the paired complementarity strategy to try to shame the Tunisian people. For example, one user wrote:

Shame on you, Tunisians! They are tampering with the Quran . . . and you are not trying to do anything about it. I am from Algeria and thank God we care about our faith. If they tried to implement such a disgraceful law [in our country] we would stop them. We love Islam and we will never allow anyone to tamper with it because we fear God Almighty and we do not want God to humiliate us. (Fathi Rmd)

Relating Women's Inheritance to Political Factors

Some YouTube users related women's inheritance to a number of thorny political issues. This subsection will look at three such factors.

Proposed Changes to Women's Inheritance as a Manifestation of Neocolonialism

Some users directly linked the proposed changes to women's inheritance to the West, and wrote rather negatively about secular Arabs calling for changing women's status to resemble that of Western women. One user commented:

I am Mauritanian, and I know the Tunisian people well. I attest to how pious they are. However, a small number of Tunisians who are anti-Islam and anti-Sharia have a say in the way the country is run, and their arguments are well received in the West. Thus, they impose their views on the vast majority of Muslims. I hope that things don't head in the same direction in Egypt and beyond. [I hope that] those who hate Islam don't end up having it their way. (Sidi Med)

Another user put it even more bluntly:

By the way, no one is trying to interfere in Tunisia's internal affairs. What we are truly after is defending the Islamic faith and standing up for Muslim women. The seculars want Muslim women to be just like Western women, [they want them to be] areligious and non-Islamic. They want [Muslim women] to [stop thinking and simply follow what they say.] Don't you realize that a war is being waged against Islam? Don't you understand? With all due respect for everyone. (Mohamed Talaat)

In other words, these users seemed to perceive the proposed changes to women's inheritance as a manifestation of neocolonialism. Furthermore, many other users seemed to agree with them, because one of the comments along these lines received as many as 138 likes. But it is interesting to note that hardly any Tunisians put forward arguments along these lines. This begs the question of whether some Tunisians do indeed have a different take on women's status, and Islam as a whole for that matter, as some Tunisians who have been quoted in previous subsections have indeed argued.

Islamic Scholars Ignore How Many Other Aspects of Sharia Go Unimplemented

Other users questioned why there was so much commotion about some topics relating to Muslims, but not others. One Tunisian user commented:

Why is this any of your business? The *umma* [Islamic nation] only comes together when the issue at stake is one that has to do with women. But it didn't budge when the [Egyptian] army killed [its own] people, when the Zionists kill our brothers and sisters, nor when the evil [countries] came together to impose an embargo on another Arab country. It doesn't budge when women and children suffer due to *urfi* [undocumented] marriage, when Iraqi and Syrian women are sold in ISIS [territory] nor when [former Iraqi President] Saddam [Hussein] was killed during Eid al-Adha

[Festival of the Sacrifice]. You pick and choose the aspects of religion that help you achieve your political goals, not those that are in the *umma*'s interest. (Amelya Amelya)

The user was probably referring to the ongoing trade embargo on Qatar, which started in June 2017, when he wrote "when the evil [countries] came together to impose an embargo on another Arab country." The embargo was imposed by four Arab countries, namely Saudi Arabia, the United Arab Emirates, Egypt, and Bahrain. The quartet severed all economic and diplomatic ties with Qatar on the grounds that it allegedly supports terrorism, disseminates fake news, and engages in state-sponsored hacking (Dudley 2018). This comment received 16 likes and provides another interesting example of one of the cognitive functions of an ideology, namely how it allows its followers to have a common understanding of the interests and goals of the group as a whole (Van Dijk 2006). But in this case, it was used in the opposite sense, because the user argued that the *umma* only came together on selected issues which he thought were less important.

Yet another user wrote:

Muslim rulers do not govern their countries using Sharia. The only aspect [of Sharia] that they abide by is inheritance. Why is inheritance the only area of Sharia [deemed important]? A lot of other aspects of Sharia [are important too, such as] banks giving interest, [and allowing for the existence of] prostitution, drinking and nightclubs [in majority-Muslim countries]. So, are we Islamic countries only when it comes to inheritance? . . . I wonder why they are not concerned about all of God's law. Why do we implement some of them but not others? Why don't we talk about the [other] laws that have been neglected for a hundred years? (Tourab Adam)

Clearly, these two users were looking at a much broader picture instead of simply focusing on the controversy regarding women's inheritance.

Al-Azhar Is a Co-opted Institution

Other users who similarly addressed the broader picture argued that al-Azhar is a co-opted institution. In the words of one user:

Al-Azhar is an institution which does as al-Sisi [the current Egyptian president] says. I swear that you are a bunch of idiots. Each [Arab] country has its own religious authority and its Islamic scholars. The problem is that the ruling regimes do not support them. They imprison them if they stand up for what is right. Open up your mind, brother. (Mohamed El-Mahdyi)

In response, an Egyptian user wrote:

You are absolutely right. Al-Sisi controls most of the high-ranking positions in al-Azhar and the [Egyptian] Christian [official] establishment. . . . However, al-Azhar has been around for 1100 years and it is an important religious authority. And as so many other users have said, al-Azhar is not imposing its views on you or on anybody else. It is merely clarifying the Islamic stance on the matter. Your actions are not in line with Islam. But you can do whatever you like; no one forced you to become a Muslim in the first place. (Habibi Rabhi)

Relating Women's Inheritance to Social and Economic Factors

The final theme links women's inheritance to some pressing social and economic factors.

Relating Women's Inheritance to Men's Increasing Difficulty in Playing the Role of Sole Provider

Some male users defended the status quo regarding women's inheritance based on social and economic factors rather than religious ones. For example, one user wrote:

> Malika [the female user he was responding to], let us assume that you have a son and a daughter, both of whom are married. Your daughter's husband is the one who provides for her, in compliance with [the Quranic verse] that men are the protectors and maintainers of women. So, if you pass away, [is it fair] if your daughter inherits as much as your brother, even though your daughter does not provide for her husband and children, even if she is a millionaire? You have to be more realistic and take [some] social issues into consideration. (Mohamed Amin)

This particular comment suggests that men find it increasingly difficult to play the role of sole provider for their families. It seems to be one of the factors that affects some men's perception of the debate surrounding inheritance in Islam. In fact, another user put it even more bluntly: "If a man does not fulfill his duty of providing for his family, and his wife is the one who works [outside the home] and provides for the family, then in that case [women should inherit more]" (Hassan Akamih).

Anti-Feminist Discourse

A final subtheme that also seemed inspired by the dire state of the economy in many Arab countries revolved around anti-feminist discourse. For example, one user wrote:

> I feel sorry for women, you have destroyed them. . . . They start working while they are still in elementary school, and even when they grow up, they end up working like men, inside the house and outside the house. You have burdened and overwhelmed women. They can no longer find men to protect them and provide for them. Some fathers force their daughters to work, and then when they get married, their husbands want to take their money, leading to marital problems. Men have neglected their duties toward women . . . I am talking about some men, not all of them. (Islam Rizk)

Another user took it to a new level:

> I am from Algeria. Many men have noticed how women compete with men in the job market. That is why many of them choose to marry working women. This way a man can wake up at noon, to find that lunch and coffee have been served. He won't give a damn about his exhausted wife, and probably does not even care if she sleeps with the CEO of the hospital. . . .
> I have a program which proves that men are toying with you. [It contains] crying, screaming and the like. The more you call for freedom, the less worthy you become. Go on, compete with men. This is what men want. And as soon as you have kids, you find yourself torn between working inside and outside the home, and you end up having to give your husband your salary, otherwise he will leave you. (Zaibi Labib)

These comments are indications of how feminist and women's rights discourses continue to be unacceptable to many Arab men. They also seem to paint a very rosy picture of what

Muslim-majority countries would look like if men and women abided by the traditional gendered division of labor.

CONCLUSION

This analysis of a sample from a thread of comments by YouTube users from various Middle Eastern Arabic-speaking countries indicates that Islam seems to function as an ideology that defines the social identity of many of the commentators. In fact, it serves as a common ground for some users, so that dividing inheritance according to Sharia seems to be the only way things can or should be done. Furthermore, comments such as the ones that refer to the concept of an *umma* and the ones that frame the proposed changes to women's inheritance as "a war against Islam" suggest that for some of the commentators, Islamic ideology also serves the function of uniting people around a shared goal. The most recurrent theme—praise for the Islamic scholar featured on the show—as well as comments like the one in which an Algerian user called for al-Azhar to be allowed to play a greater role in the *umma*, indicate that many users seem to be fully on board with the idea that Islamic scholars in general, and al-Azhar scholars in particular, should have the right to act as leaders of the Islamic ideology, and should therefore dominate society in this regard. It is noteworthy that all of these findings seemed to be applicable to male and female users alike.

All of these findings combined could be interpreted as an indication of the growing Islamization of the Egyptian and/or Arab populace. The fact that the study's results also indicate that proponents of secular ideology seemed to be clearly outnumbered can be taken as further evidence to support this argument. However, these results may very well be a reflection of an entirely different phenomenon. It could be that because Islamists have little, if any, access to traditional media outlets, they may be better organized and more adamant about making their voices heard on social media. Clearly more cross-sectional and comparative studies are necessary in order to determine whether or not this is indeed the case.

By focusing on the comments of YouTube users rather than the content of the video itself, which was adapted from a mainstream television station, this study sought to shed light on how social media enable virtual discussions on sensitive topics, which may not be as easily addressed offline. One cannot help but wonder how easy it would have been for the secular users to express their views in offline discussions, given how outnumbered they seemed to be. In addition, as the results of the study indicated, some of the YouTube users who delved into the political and social factors affecting the inheritance laws ended up addressing some interesting taboos. For example, some of them talked about how religious institutions in various Arab countries are loyal to the ruling regimes and simply issue religious verdicts at the whim of those regimes. It is clearly beyond the scope of this study to investigate the implications of breaking such taboos on social media. But as the recent anti–sexual harassment campaigns on social media in Egypt indicate, when some taboos are broken in the virtual world, this is sometimes a first step toward enacting change in the real world.

NOTE

1. By the time the study was submitted for publication, the episode had been viewed 1,100,562 times and had received more than 3,600 comments.

REFERENCES

Ahmed, L. 1992. *Women and Gender in Islam: Historical Roots of a Modern Debate*. New Haven, CT: Yale University Press.

Badran, M. 1995. *Feminists, Islam, and Nation: Gender and the Making of Modern Egypt*. Princeton, NJ: Princeton University Press.

Baron, B. 2005. *Egypt as a Woman: Nationalism, Gender and Politics*. Berkeley: University of California Press.

Dudley, D. 2018. "As Qatar prepares to mark a year under the Saudi embargo, it looks like the winner in the dispute." *Forbes*, May 17, 2018. https://www.forbes.com/sites/dominicdudley/2018/05/17/as-qatar-prepares-to-mark-a-year-under-the-saudi-embargo-it-looks-like-the-winner-in-the-dispute.

Kandiyoti, D. 1991. Introduction to *Women, Islam and the State*, 1–21. Edited by D. Kandiyoti. London: Palgrave Macmillan.

Lodhia, S. 2014. "'Stop importing weapons of mass destruction!' Cyberdiscourses, patriarchal anxieties, and the men's backlash movement in India." *Violence Against Women* 20 (8): 905–36.

Mullet, D. R. 2018. "A general discourse analysis framework for education research." *Journal of Advanced Academics* 29 (2): 116–42.

Oliver, B. 2009. "Twenty years on, the 'hate match' between Egypt and Algeria is on again." *The Guardian*, October 10, 2009. https://www.theguardian.com/football/blog/2009/oct/10/egypt-algeria-repeat-hate-match.

Van Dijk, T. A. 2006. "Ideology and discourse analysis." *Journal of Political Ideologies* 11 (2): 115–40.

Wyrod, R. 2008. "Between women's rights and men's authority: Masculinity and shifting discourses of gender difference in urban Uganda." *Gender & Society* 22 (6): 799–823.

YouTube. 2017. "*Akher al-nahar*: hiwar khas bad al-gadal hawl karar Tunis mosawat almara bi al-ragol fi-l-mirath" (*Akher al-nahar*: A special discussion held in light of the controversy surrounding the Tunisian decision to equate women with men in inheritance). August 22, 2017. https://www.youtube.com/watch?v=UGmxyiTr3jQ.

19

Binge-Watching and Its Implications in the Global Media Flow

Azza A. Ahmed

The ability of digitalization to allow "interoperability" between television and other technologies has gradually led to a transformation of multiple aspects of television, including its technology, distribution, economics, associated media policy, and use (Mikos 2016). The convergence between television and computers was a key outcome of interoperability (Lotz 2009). Rather than only being received using the conventional television set, television content can now be accessed from various platforms and technical devices (Mikos 2016). As viewers began to use new technologies to watch TV content in different ways, they discovered that they had access to huge amounts of new content that they had never seen before (Colin 2015). The result was a new era of TV watching behavior, binge-watching.

Binge-watching has been supported by a phenomenon known as media symbiosis, where people are using new media to watch traditional TV content more than ever before (Ahmed 2017). Further, the continuing evolutions in new technology and Internet services allow users greater control over the time and duration of their consumption of televised content. Television binge-watching has arisen as a new behavioral phenomenon (Walton-Pattison et al. 2016) and marks a new era of TV-watching behavior among youth. It is a result of dependence on new media and the widespread usage of smartphones connected to the Internet (Ahmed 2017).

Considering the extent and impact of this change, it is important to review the literature and theoretical frameworks that have been used to study this phenomenon in various countries over the globe. This chapter presents a review of the literature on this crucial topic. It also sheds light on the results of three recent studies on marathon TV-watching—that is, binge-watching—in the United Arab Emirates. In these three studies (Ahmed 2017, 2019, 2021) investigating binge-watching in the Emirates, there is an indication of an increasing number of people in the UAE watching serialized TV fiction in a compressed timeframe through applications, platforms, and websites.

The first study (Ahmed 2017) marks the earliest research on binge-watching in the Arab world. It investigated binge-watching among a sample of Arab residents in the UAE, focusing on how it might correlate to depression and loneliness. The data were collected from a sample of 260 Arab residents living in Abu Dhabi, the UAE capital, from different age groups.

The second study (Ahmed 2019) used quantitative and qualitative techniques to examine the expected outcomes for binge-watching and the possibilities of anticipating regret after such activity, among a sample of 229 Emiratis. In-depth interviews were conducted with twenty of the respondents to further understand this recently developed behavior.

The results of the 2017 and 2019 studies showed that foreign (non-Arab) TV content, especially U.S. drama, was the favorite and most frequent type of TV content that the Emiratis and UAE Arab expats binge-watch. These findings led to the third study (Ahmed 2021), which investigated perceptions of the possible negative effects of U.S. drama binge-watching on the respondents' own cultural values as compared with its perceived effects on the cultural values of others. The study helped in understanding the extent to which Arab residents in the UAE perceive media imperialist influence upon themselves and others. It examined the perceptual and behavioral components of the third-person effect in relation to TV binge-watching. Cultural background traits (individualism and collectivism) were studied as an intervening variable.

FROM TRADITIONAL TO ONLINE TV CONTENT VIEWING

It is becoming apparent that traditional television viewing is declining while other technologies that provide access to televised content keep growing. Studies have shown that online video-watching among young adults is skyrocketing (Ahmed 2017).

Bury and Li (2015) discussed three modes of TV-watching that the world has witnessed over the past decade. They provided an overview of these three modes connected to specific stages of digital convergence. The first mode is digitally time-shifted viewing, which recorded television programming using devices such as the DVR, PVR, and VCR, from the 1970s until the 1990s. The second mode is online viewing associated with computer technologies; however, this mode blurs the boundary between television and new media. This mode developed from the mid-1990s until the early 2000s. The third and most recent mode to emerge as a result of digital convergence is mobile viewing. It is enabled by streaming and downloading technologies but involves a device such as a smartphone, iPod Touch, or tablet. Such devices permit viewing for a longer time than via the traditional TV screen.

Since 2010, online streaming services and similar viewing platforms have become portals for viewers to immerse themselves in hours of endless content. Binge-watching is transforming the way people view television, and it might change the economics of the industry (Moore 2015). Binge-watching is now the most popular TV-viewing habit among people of many ages and nationalities.

DEVELOPMENT OF TV BINGE-WATCHING HABIT

Binge-watching is a very different experience from consuming regular TV shows. It originated in the 1980s when some TV stations in the United States started featuring reruns of episodes of certain series in marathon sessions. When DVDs become available for home viewing, their high storage capacity allowed viewers to watch entire seasons, making it easy to say to oneself "just one more" (Statista 2016). Bury and Li (2015) concluded that while the majority of viewing still takes place in front of a television screen, the computer has achieved secondary screen status among North Americans and equal status among younger viewers and Europeans. Therefore, media-bingeing is quickly becoming the viewing habit of choice for many television fans, thanks to the intensive usage of the Internet among teenagers (Devasagayam 2014).

In 2012, Patricia Phalen and Richard Ducey introduced a new concept, "multi-screen environment," in which an individual can watch any TV content once s/he is connected to the Internet using mobile devices, computer screens, tablets, or iPads. As technology advanced, more people began using DVRs and the Internet to watch television on their own schedule without commercial interruptions. Recently, "companies such as Netflix and Hulu have made fortunes on giving U.S. people and others all over the world the ability to watch almost any show at the touch of a button" (Devasagayam 2014).

The Netflix platform has been the preferred content delivery network among binge-watchers in the United States (Dickinson 2014). Jenner (2014) stated that Netflix not only offers a large online library of film and TV in the United States and most European countries, but also offers original content in the form of serialized drama and comedy. Netflix has moved into territory that sets it apart from the familiar structures of production, broadcasting, or branding of television (Jenner 2014).

Devasagayam (2014) explained that the word "bingeing" was originally related to food and obesity, defined as "a rapid consumption of a large amount of substance in a short period." Applying the same notion to TV, "binge-watching" is the experience of watching multiple episodes of a program in a single sitting. Because of advances in technology and the relatively low cost of unlimited bandwidth, more people are binge-watching their favorite television shows and movies than ever before (Pittman and Sheehan 2015).

Media-bingeing is quickly becoming the viewing habit of choice for many television fans in the United States. In the United Kingdom, Stamatakis et al. (2009) found that over one-third of adults spend at least four hours a day watching television. In a survey conducted by Walton-Pattison et al. (2016), participants reported binge-watching a mean of 1.42 days/week. On the other hand, Netflix stated in June 2016 that instead of one episode per week, Netflix members choose to binge-watch their way through a series—that is, finishing an entire season in one week. It seems that the same is true among teenagers and youth in the Middle East. In the United Arab Emirates, approximately 50% of viewers spend between one and three hours per day watching TV. Emirati nationals watch the greatest amount of television, with 53% watching between three and six hours per day (Arab Media Outlook Annual Report 2015). With the recent emergence of online streaming television services in the UAE, watching television has never been this easy.

There are signs that binge-watching has become a daily habit for most teenagers. Petersen (2016) found that the schedule of the participants in his qualitative research is determined to a large extent by their binge-watching habit. In the Emirates, Ahmed (2017) found that 82.3% of the UAE residents who were surveyed binge-watch for five hours or more a day. Ahmed (2019) also found that 84% of 229 Emiratis binge-watch a TV program for four hours per session a day; clearly, this habit has become widespread among Emiratis.

The binge-watching experience can be described as involving continuous cueing of subsequent episodes and a built-in contingent reward mechanism, without the need for conscious decision making, thus leading to more automaticity-driven behavior (Walton-Pattison et al. 2016).

Memmott (2013) cites Pamela Rutledge, head of the Media Psychology Research Center in Boston, who says, "We associate the word 'binge' with being out of control." She explains instead that it allows viewers to watch TV the same way they might read a book. "Whenever a choice is in the hands of the consumer, it's a good thing."

Binge-watching suggests an entirely different media experience from what "traditional" scheduled television can offer. Control over scheduling, previously in the hands of the broadcaster, is turned over to the viewer (Jenner 2015). Binge-watching is a different viewing experience from traditional TV viewing in that the ability to watch whenever, wherever, whatever, and however one wishes has become a preferred form of consumption for both content consumers and creators (Warren 2016).

Several technical definitions of binge-watching have been proposed. Walton-Pattison et al. (2016) defined it as "viewing multiple episodes of the same television show in the same sitting." Dickinson (2014) defined it as watching two to six episodes of the same show in one sitting or within twenty-four hours. Warren (2016) suggested that five episodes are a better cutoff point for examining how binge-watching affects viewers. Castro et al. (2021) defined binge-watching as consumption of at least two complete episodes of the same serialized TV fiction. The binge-watching behavior includes selecting a show, the viewing time, and the number of episodes to watch (Hallinan and Striphas 2014).

BINGE-WATCHING HABITS

Ahmed (2019) has shown that the Internet is the most common method for binge-watching, used by 55% of Emirati respondents. The favored TV programs are foreign drama (watched by 38% of the respondents), dubbed Turkish drama (28.4%), documentaries (24%), comedy programs and Khaleej drama (20% each), sports (20%), Japanese anime (16.2%), and then adventure programs, Egyptian drama, talk shows, reality TV shows, cooking, and scientific programs (each with 10% or less).

In the U.S. context, Dickinson (2014) found that drama is the preferred TV genre for millennials to binge on (63%). The second most favored was comedy (25%). Other categories included reality (2.2%), animation (1.6%), documentary (2.7%), and "other" (5%). Moore (2015) found that the most favorite shows for U.S. university students to binge-watch were fantasy (*Game of Thrones*), drama (*The Walking Dead*), crime (*Sons of Anarchy*), comedy (*Big Bang Theory*), and action (*Arrow*).

In 2017, Ahmed reported that Turkish drama had the highest percentage for UAE binge-watchers (68.5%), followed by Western drama (31.2%), comedy programs (26.1%), Khaleej drama (21.9%), documentaries (16.5%), and Egyptian drama (14.6%), with some scattered low percentages for Japanese anime, cooking programs, talk shows, puzzles, reality shows, and scientific programs.

Ahmed's research (2017, 2019) also revealed that respondents use multiple media to binge-watch. YouTube was identified as the most frequent, followed by TV channel websites, OSN-TV, Torrent downloads, Shahid.net, and Internet streaming services. The fewest number of respondents mentioned Netflix and DVDs. These results are similar to what was reported by Sung et al. (2015), who found that most of their respondents use Internet streaming for binge-watching, then the program's website, then download services.

Ahmed (2019) found that respondents tend to binge-watch during weekends (68.1%), watching up to four episodes and sometimes more per session (72%), mostly at home (77.7%). Binge sessions lasted just over two hours on average, and participants watched more than they had originally intended in nearly half of the sessions. By contrast, Castro et al. (2021) found that participants most often binge-watched on weekday evenings and nights, mostly in the living room and bedroom. Ahmed (2017) confirmed that home is the most popular place for binge-watching, which probably explains the fact that 66.5% of respondents binge-watch alone and 21.9% with family members. People also binge-watch on airplanes, to kill time during the long journey. Unexpectedly, 31.1% of respondents mentioned "university" as the place to binge-watch.

The in-depth interviews conducted by Ahmed (2019) reported that most Emiratis started binge-watching more than ten years ago. They began by using Internet websites to watch five to ten episodes from a TV series in one session. Each episode might last up to two hours, as with Turkish soap opera. The duration of binge-watching ranged from six to fourteen hours a day, from three episodes in a row to a whole season (about twenty-four episodes). Most of the Emiratis interviewed said that they prefer free websites such as Shahid.net, YouTube, or Kisat Esh'q, among others. They also use mobile applications, such as the Turkish soap opera app.

Some examples of foreign TV content binge-watched by Emiratis, as reported by Ahmed (2019), were *How to Get Away with Murder*, *The Tonight Show Starring Jimmy Fallon*, *The Tomorrow People*, *The Ellen DeGeneres Show*, *Baby Daddy*, *Young and Hungry*, *The Walking Dead*, *Supernatural*, *Friends*, and *Full House*. For Arabic content, the interviewees mentioned the Turkish dramas *al-Azhar al-hazena* ("Sad Flowers"), *Hoab a'ma* ("Blind Love"), and *Motazwgat ghadebat* ("Angry Wives"), among others.

As for the devices used for binge-watching, Ahmed (2017, 2019) found that the laptop is the most popular, followed by mobile smartphones, Internet TV, iPads, and finally desktop personal computers. These results are similar to those reported by Dickinson (2014), who found that TVs and laptops were the most preferred devices for binge-watching. Warren (2016) reported that, on average, respondents who watched primarily on tablets tended to watch more episodes in subsequent weeks than those who watched primarily on a computer.

BINGE-WATCHING ALONE OR WITH COMPANY

Ahmed's results (2017, 2019) showed that most respondents prefer to binge-watch alone rather than with friends and family members. Dickinson (2014) and Castro et al. (2021) found the same. A MarketCast study (PRWeb 2013) revealed that 98% of 1,022 American TV viewers ages 13–49 binge-watch at home and 56% say they only binge-watch by themselves.

Ahmed (2019) found an increase in the mean score of the number of hours spent on binge-watching for those who watch alone, 7.95, compared to the mean score of those who watch with others, 7.0. Warren (2016) found a statistically significant positive relationship between the number of episodes watched with others and hours per viewing session. He also found that respondents who viewed all of their binge-watched episodes with others had levels of mental rumination higher than those who watched by themselves. This suggests that binge-watching with others might make the experience even more enjoyable.

The results of in-depth interviews by Ahmed (2019) indicated that respondents have a number of reasons for preferring to binge-watch alone. Some of these are: to concentrate on the dramatic events and scenes unfolding without interruption, to feel more involved, to avoid interruption from someone asking questions or commenting while watching, to be able to freely stop any scene and re-watch it, and to feel as if one is watching in a movie theater. Several of the females interviewed in this study reported a new behavior of online binge-watching: a group of women would agree to watch certain episodes at the same time, but each one alone on her own device. While watching, they would discuss the content via WhatsApp. This is an indication of how dramatically the current technology has affected TV-watching behavior.

This tendency to watch alone is a new form of TV-watching behavior. Especially in the Arab world, it used to be that the whole family would watch TV dramas and newscasts together, exchanging comments and sharing interpretations of what they were watching. This no longer seems to be the case.

OUTCOME EXPECTATIONS FROM BINGE-WATCHING

Outcome expectations are defined as the satisfaction the respondents might presume to gain from binge-watching (Ahmed 2019). The "uses and gratifications" approach is valuable in gaining understanding of a new media environment (Rubin 2009). Uses and gratifications literature strongly suggests that "escape from reality" is one of the major motivations for intensive TV-watching. Viewers watch more TV to forget temporarily about everyday life stress caused by work, school, or social life in general.

Uses and gratifications is the most helpful model to understand the expected outcomes for binge-watchers. Katz et al. (1974) explained the difference between the gratification sought and the gratification obtained. The first is the expectation about content formed in advance of the exposure, and the second is the satisfaction subsequently secured from consumption of it. Studying the satisfaction of television viewers with an episode-by-episode examination, Dennis and Gray (2013) found that program performance was the most significant predictor of audience satisfaction. Expectation was the second-strongest predictor, and connectedness was a more limited predictor.

People gave different reasons for binge-watching. Dickinson (2014) reported that 50% of his sample binge-viewed TV shows "for fun." The second-most-common reasons were "to escape" and "to pass time"; others included "shows are addicting," "to relax," and to "wind down" at the end of the day. Peña (2015) found that a primary gratification of binge-watching is escapism. In fact, binge-watching is a particularly effective form of escape, because the prolonged periods of time in front of the screen allow the viewer to become completely immersed in the show.

Avoidance of advertisements was given as a reason by 60% of the respondents in a Marketing Charts survey (2014). Kubey and Csikszentmihalyi (2002) reported that the sense of relaxation ends when the TV set is turned off, but feelings of passivity and lowered alertness continue. Castro et al. (2021) found that participants binge-watch to relax, relieve boredom, and escape. Devasagayam (2014) found that the formation of one-sided, unconscious bonds between viewers and characters is one of the major motives for binge-watching.

Tsay-Vogel (2016) introduced the concept of "togetherness" as an important element in teens' motivations for binge-watching. He explained that by using online platforms, audiences achieved a sense of togetherness in two ways: by connecting to others with the same interests in foreign programs and by re-associating with their home when they are abroad by consuming domestic programs. Kolotkin et al. (1987) concluded that people try to re-create feelings of happiness when bingeing on media. People may find themselves thinking obsessively about a show's events during the day.

Many participants in Petersen's (2016) research reported specific positive outcomes of their binge-watching: it is a reward for hard work; it is a powerful way to experience a story; it allows stressed-out students to relax. Another positive aspect is the apparent lack of physical side effects on the viewer (Devasagayam 2014). Ahmed (2019) found a positive significant correlation between binge-watching and outcome expectations. Devasagayam (2014) pointed out that the availability of shows without commercials makes it enjoyable to view long strings of episodes, and is one of the motives for binge-watching. All of this research suggests that binge-watching increases when the outcome expectations are higher.

On the other hand, Petersen (2016) pointed out that university students recognized the benefits of binge-watching but failed to recognize the dangers of this new TV-watching habit. Walton-Pattison et al. (2016) indicated that binge-watching may itself have either a conflicting or a facilitating effect on the pursuit of other personal goals (e.g., facilitating socializing or preventing the completion of other work).

Ahmed's in-depth interviews (2019) showed that the enthusiasm and suspense in TV shows and drama were the most frequent reason for binge-watching. The other reasons mentioned were to enjoy watching beautiful vistas from different countries; to learn quickly how the series ends before others can tell you; to strengthen English-language skills by watching foreign shows; to satisfy curiosity about the next steps of the drama; to escape from the pressures of study; to enjoy the real-life stories of certain series; to be entertained; to pass time; and to gain knowledge from watching historical TV series and documentary programs.

In Wagner's (2016) study, participants mentioned a number of other binge-watching motivations, such as background noise for multitasking, avoiding spoilers, maximizing social currency, and escapism. Pittman and Sheehan (2015) concluded that the salient factors for regular bingers are relaxation, engagement, and hedonism. They added that those who binge on an entire series in one or two days particularly value engagement, relaxation, hedonism, and aesthetics.

PSYCHOLOGICAL EFFECTS OF BINGE-WATCHING

Sung et al. (2015) point out that binge behaviors are thought to be closely related to negative feelings. Finn (1992) identified intensive television-viewing as a form of addiction; however, Devasagayam (2014) found that binge TV-watchers do not consider themselves TV addicts due to the lack of visible side effects that other forms of bingeing produce. However, LaRose et al. (2003) stated that addicted media consumers feel compelled to consume media despite potentially negative consequences that make continued use appear irrational or out of control, even in their own eyes. Kubey and Csikszentmihalyi (2002) specified some addiction-related criteria that might apply to heavy TV-watching: "using it more often than one intends; thinking about reducing use or making repeated unsuccessful efforts to reduce use; giving up important social, family, or occupational activities to use it; and reporting withdrawal symptoms when one stops using it."

On the other hand, Kubey and Csikszentmihalyi (2002) claim that watching television, per se, is not problematic. The transition to problematic usage can begin if the behavior acts as an important or exclusive mechanism to relieve stress, loneliness, depression, or anxiety. When this problematic media use becomes excessive, it, in turn, can cause problems, confrontations with significant others, and an inability to stop media consumption once started (LaRose et al. 2003).

In a focus group study conducted by Devasagayam (2014), one individual admitted that he had watched full seasons in a single day "several" times. The focus group members shared that the free time they had over the summer forced them to watch out of sheer boredom. Binge-viewers may fail to control their time spent watching, although they can make a negative judgment on the binge behavior. They find themselves clicking the "next" button for one episode after another, even though they realize that there are things to do the next day or they need to sleep (Sung et al. 2015). As mentioned earlier, Kubey and Csikszentmihalyi (2002) reported that the sense of relaxation ends when the TV set is turned off, but the feelings of passivity and lowered alertness continue.

Petersen (2016) examined how binge-watching affects the social and academic lives of college students.

> For many participants, the rhythm of their day was built around binge-watching. They scheduled a time to binge-watch and rewarded themselves after accomplishments. While the participants downplayed or were unaware of the effects of this new watching experience, their grades suffered, their social lives are ignored, and the schedule is determined to an extent by their binge-watching habit. (86)

LaRose et al. (2003) demonstrated that media habits formed to alleviate depressed moods undermined self-regulation and led to increased Internet usage in a sample of 465 college students. Consistent with this, Kim et al. (2005) found that the levels of depression and suicide ideation were highest in the Internet-addicted group in a sample of 1,573 Korean high school students. Ha et al. (2007) reported that Internet addiction was significantly associated with depressive symptoms and obsessive-compulsive symptoms among a Korean sample. However, Shaw and Gant (2004) concluded that Internet use was found to decrease loneliness and depression significantly, while perceived social support and self-esteem increased significantly.

Many recent studies have proved that there is a relationship between the amount of time spent watching television and the likelihood of eventually being diagnosed with depression. This means that if TV-viewing habits are excessive, a person is putting him/herself at greater risk of suffering from this debilitating and life-altering condition. Wheeler (2015) found that the higher participants scored in depression and loneliness, the more they reported watching television for both ritualistic and instrumental purposes, and the more they reported watching back-to-back episodes of television programs. Sung et al. (2015) also found that depression and loneliness were related to binge TV-watching among 316 respondents between 18 and 20 years old. The more an individual was lonely and depressed, the more episodes the individual watched.

Derrick et al. (2009) found that watching favorite television programs buffered against feelings of loneliness more than other activities, including eating, surfing the web, listening to music, and watching regular programming on television. Ahmed's results (2017) revealed that more than half of binge-watchers (61.5%) scored higher on the loneliness scale than non-binge-watchers, especially among females and among the "30 years and above" age group.

Kubey and Csikszentmihalyi (2002) found that survey participants commonly report that television has somehow absorbed or sucked out their energy, leaving them depleted. They have more difficulty concentrating after viewing than before. In contrast, they rarely indicate such difficulty after reading. After playing sports or engaging in hobbies, people report improvements in mood, but after watching regularly scheduled TV, people's moods are about the same or worse than before.

Among Emiratis, Ahmed (2017) found a significant difference between high and low binge-watchers in their level of depression. The respective mean values suggested that high binge-watchers tend to be more depressed than low binge-watchers. This result supports the research of Wheeler (2015), who found that the higher the study subjects scored in depression, the more they reported watching back-to-back episodes of television programs.

However, the cause and effect between binge TV watching and negative psychological effects cannot be claimed; it is unknown whether depressed people tend to binge-watch more for the reasons mentioned, or the binge-watching leads to depression as viewers might regret spending many hours in one session watching a whole season of a TV program. (Ahmed 2017, 204)

ANTICIPATED REGRET AND FEELING GUILTY

One major unexpected outcome from binge-watching that is frequently cited in U.S. press articles is guilt (Wagner 2016). Anticipated regret can be defined as the feeling of guilt and regret of doing something upon finding out that it was not the right practice at a specific time (Ahmed 2019). The unplanned shift from casual watching to bingeing has some unintended consequences for bingers that may reinforce the choice to watch by themselves (PRWeb 2013). Walton-Pattison et al. (2016) proposed that anticipated regret is one of the factors that might represent potentially useful constructs to help understand binge-watching. Peña (2015) reported that many viewers who binge-watch see it as the new normal with no guilty feelings. Walton-Pattison et al. (2016) stated that binge-watching may generate feelings of regret, such as when this activity extends into the early hours of the morning, affecting sleep and the day ahead. They explained that since prolonged binge-watching may lead to regret, the anticipation of this emotion before binge-watching might help to explain anticipated regret.

Panek (2014) studied the association between self-control and feeling guilty after watching TV. He explained that students with lower self-control spent more time watching leisure media such as television than doing their schoolwork. They then felt guilty for that decision after they experienced the consequences of choosing media over the long-term benefits of studying. Similarly, Reinecke et al. (2014) found that people suffering from stressful workdays who used media as a stress reducer tended to feel guilty for doing so. They stated that those who used television as a stress reducer for their overworked lives paradoxically experienced guilt more frequently, as media usage felt like a form of procrastination rather than attempted relaxation. In this case, busy work schedules caused media relaxation to backfire and guilt to grow. On the contrary, Castro et al. (2021) found that increasing hours of binge-watching did not increase feelings of guilt.

Ahmed (2019) stated that most participants in her in-depth interviews said that they never feel regret after they binge-watch. She explained that the interviewees seemed to exaggerate their ability to prioritize, while some of them gave some justification for not feeling regret. Those who admitted feeling regret said that it was often apparent in the morning, when they suffered from a severe headache or had not done their assignments.

SELF-REGULATION DEFICIENCY AND BINGE-WATCHING

Self-regulation deficiency is defined as the inability to direct one's TV binge-watching behavior (Ahmed 2019).

PRWeb (2013) pointed out that 71% of bingers admit that their binge sessions are mostly unplanned. They start out intending only to watch one or two episodes but then get "sucked in" to a much longer viewing session. Bandura (1991) pointed out that self-regulation—the ability to direct one's own behavior instead of being passively affected by external influences—plays a critical role in influencing human behaviors. Three interactive stages are usually involved in the self-regulatory process:

- Self-monitoring: People pay attention to or observe their performances as well as the various effects caused by their conduct.
- Self-judgment: People evaluate a given performance, either using personal standards or comparing it with the performance of others.
- Self-reaction: Based on the outcome of self-judgment, people either reinforce the behavior that is positively evaluated or abstain from pursuing an action that results in negative self-judgment. It directly affects a person's behavior change.

Liu and Peng (2009) investigated self-regulation in the context of massively multiplayer online games (MMOGs). They found that deficient self-regulation results in the negative consequences associated with MMOG playing. LaRose et al. (2003) argued that the essential problem of Internet dependency is a deficiency in self-regulation. Dickinson (2014) found that binge-viewing results in bargaining, aggression, lethargy, neglect, sleeplessness, and isolation. He added that millennials' sense of control through the use of technology makes excessive TV viewing, renamed "binge-viewing," an accepted ritual.

People might want control over their media consumption, but for some, binge-viewing signals a loss of control (PRWeb 2013). In the Emirates, Ahmed (2019) reported a positive significant correlation between binge-watching and self-regulation deficiency—that is, the more the respondents practice binge-watching, the more deficient they are in their self-regulation.

Most of the participants in Ahmed's in-depth interviews (2019) confirmed that it is difficult to quit binge-watching unless there is something necessary or urgent to do. When asked about their opinions of people who postpone work till they finish watching consecutive episodes of the same program, the interviewees, who were binge-watchers themselves, described such behavior as "not good" and said it should be stopped immediately.

This finding led to Ahmed's third research project (2021), which studied marathon TV-watching of U.S. drama in the context of Philip Davison's third-person effect (TPE) theory (1983). TPE hypothesizes that an individual underestimates the likelihood of harmful and socially undesirable effects of media content on himself and those close to him while overestimating the likelihood that the same content will negatively affect others.

TPE, BINGE-WATCHING OF U.S. DRAMA, AND CULTURAL BACKGROUND

Most media content, including TV dramas, flows mainly from the Global North and West to the East. Foreign soap operas were among the most preferred types of televised content binge-watched online among Emiratis and UAE residents (Ahmed 2017, 2019). U.S. drama was marked as a top favorite among various age groups in the Arab world. This is a sign of the emergence of new technologies that make U.S. media products available to audiences all over the world 24/7 through Internet live-streaming and platforms like Netflix.

Investigating beliefs about positive and negative media influences, Lee (1998) found that few people in Hong Kong believed that foreign programs had negative effects on their values, behaviors, or way of living. Instead, many of the respondents thought that foreign programs could increase their knowledge of foreign cultures and enrich their own culture. Attitudes about positive or negative influences also differ cross-culturally based on how strongly such influence was experienced within the local culture or society. For example, Willnat et al. (2002) found that European respondents tended to believe that U.S. media negatively affected the cultural values of others more than their own, while this was not the case with Asian respondents.

Davison's (1983) perceptual hypothesis states that people tend to believe they are less influenced than others by content perceived as negative and deleterious to one's cultural values. TPE theory has been applied to a wide range of media content, such as pornography (Lo and Wei 2002), music clips (Ahmed 2004), advertisements (Henriksen and Flora 1999), political advertising (Cohen and Davis 1991), defamation (Cohen et al. 1988), and violence (Hoffner et al. 2001). Asian and European students who were exposed to U.S. traditional media (newspapers, magazines, or TV) were more likely to believe that violent U.S. media content affected others more than themselves (Willnat et al. 2002).

The cognitive processes underlying TPE have generally been related to how and why social comparisons and contrasts are made (Tsay-Vogel 2016). U.S. drama, particularly examples that include violence, has been perceived as TV content that might affect its Arab audiences negatively. This subject has attracted the attention of some scholars who studied this phenomenon in Europe and Asia, including Hong Kong, Malaysia, and Singapore, among other places (Lee 1998, Hoffner et al. 2001, Willnat et al. 2002, Willnat et al. 2007). However, this subject and related issues have been investigated primarily for traditional series or spontaneous TV watching, and not for binge-watching, nor for viewers from the UAE and elsewhere in the Middle East.

Hoffner et al. (2001) examined the third-person effect in perceptions of the influence of television violence and found that the more people liked violent television, the less effect they saw on themselves relative to others on average around the world. Willnat et al. (2002, 188) concluded that respondents in eight Asian and European countries likewise perceived the effects of U.S. violence in the media to be stronger on others than on themselves. Ahmed (2021) found that U.S. drama binge-watchers tend to perceive the negative effect of U.S. drama as higher on others (63%) compared to themselves (12.8%), while they perceive the positive impact as higher on themselves (55.6%) compared to others (21.8%). For violent U.S. drama, Ahmed (2021) found that binge-watchers tend to perceive the negative effect as higher on others (79.4%) compared to themselves (42.4%), while they perceive the positive impact as higher on themselves (53.3%) compared to others (17.5%).

Davison (1983) discussed the relationship between third-person perception and censorship attitudes. He emphasized that those who strongly supported censorship believed that the general public is adversely influenced by media messages, but did not admit to being affected themselves. The third-person effect's behavioral hypothesis predicts that people who are more likely to exhibit third-person perception are also more likely to support restrictions on media messages (Lee and Yang 1996). The relationship between TPE and censorship support has been examined and confirmed by many researchers (Chia et al. 2004, Hoffner et al. 1999, Salwen and Dupagne 1999, Ahmed 2004, McLeod et al. 1997). Willnat et al. (2007) found that Malaysian respondents were more likely to support censorship of U.S. TV drama content because of its negative effect on Malaysian society.

Taking for granted a direct correspondence between the presumed exposure of others to a media message and its impact on them, individuals are more likely to participate in actions aimed at regulating the distribution and/or production of supposedly harmful media messages (Sun et al. 2008). Willnat et al. (2002) stated that European policy makers have tried to restrict the amount of U.S. television programming shown in Europe through the 1989 Television

Without Frontiers directive, as per the Commission of the European Communities 1989. While the quota limiting U.S. programming to 50% of European broadcasting was ignored by many E.U. members, countries such as France and Great Britain strongly supported limits on U.S. media imports. Ahmed (2021) found that binge-watchers of U.S. drama in Arab countries overall tend to agree on imposing censorship on U.S. drama (51%), compared to 40.9% in the UAE, while 33.9% of respondents in the UAE disagree that these shows should be censored, compared to 20% in other Arab countries.

Culture affects the way its members view themselves, their social environment, and their relationships with others (Markus and Kitayama 1991). Cultural imperialism theory suggests that media from one country will invade and colonize another, and the culture of the invading nation will seep into the receiving/victim nation as a result. The victim nation is imagined to be culturally autonomous before the invasion, then under siege and culturally disenfranchised (Gray 2014). Unlike the colonial enterprise, which was imposed in many instances by force of arms, cultural imperialism acts subtly until it gets to the critical stage of addiction (Akpabio and Mustapha-Lambe 2008).

Communication imperialism, as a form of cultural imperialism, suggests that Global North political and economic powers not only control the political and economic management of the world, but also have worldwide control over means of communication, and thus rule over communication flow (Sabir 2013). Consequently, communication imperialism reduces cultural interaction to a one-sided process, instead of a two-party exchange of culture and values.

The closely related term "media imperialism" also implies a situation whereby the media system of one geographical area is subjected to the dictates of the media system of another area. The pertinent issue here is the effect of media imperialism on culture (Omoera and Ibagere 2010). Media imperialism emerged from the West, and it created an entirely new phenomenon—a degree of media dominance that has controlled, managed, and changed the culture of developing countries around the world (Sabir 2013).

Boyd-Barrett (1977) described several features of media imperialism: the shaping of the communication vehicle (communication technology), a set of individual arrangements for the continuation of media production, the body of values about ideal practice, and special media content. Omoera and Ibagere (2010) have argued that in many countries compelled to view the world through the prism of Western values, ideas, and civilization, the influence of American media content only intensifies consumption values rather than production values. Consequently, the developing world has been relegated to the status of mere consumers of American media content.

The negative impact of U.S. media on local cultures has been studied in various environments, such as in Nigeria (Omoera and Ibagere 2010), Malaysia (Willnat et al. 2007), and among Asian and European students (Willnat et al. 2002). The authors of these studies have discussed a number of reasons for the invasion of U.S. media production in developing countries, along with ways to reduce negative impacts on local culture and traditions.

Willnat et al. (2007) proposed that culturally bound conceptualizations of self and others are likely to be good predictors of people's perceptions of how self and others are influenced by specific media content. Mikos (2016) considered binge-watching television series as a cultural practice that viewers integrate into their everyday lives and adapt to their circumstances. The social conditions of their lives, such as work, partners, and children, demand a share of their time and thus limit their television consumption.

Kim (1995) describes how individuals with independent cultural self-construal tend to see themselves as unique and value the ability to express themselves and act independently. On the other hand, individuals with an interdependent self-construal have the desire to be part of a social group and are less likely to behave in a way that disrupts the social order (Triandis 1989). Gudykunst et al. (1996) point out that, while one culture can vary internally in terms of individualist or collectivist self-construal orientations, people in the United States are more likely to perceive themselves as individualists, while Middle Eastern people are more likely to perceive themselves as collectivist.

Willnat et al. (2007) concluded that the perceptions of U.S. TV drama in Europe and Asia are influenced by respondents' cultural values and, to a somewhat smaller degree, their exposure to U.S. media. Lee and Tamborini (2005) found that students who perceived themselves as more collectivist (or interdependent) exhibited smaller third-person effects and were less likely to support Internet pornography censorship.

In the UAE, Ahmed (2021) concluded that the perception of the negative effect of U.S. drama and its violent content is not affected by the individual's perception of cultural self-construal, whether individualist or collectivist. Similarly, Willnat et al. (2007) found that the differences in perception between the two groups (individualist and collectivist) were not significant. However, Malaysian respondents who exhibited an interdependent self-construal were less likely to exhibit TPE and more likely to support censorship of U.S. drama, unlike Ahmed's study (2021), where no difference was found between the two groups' support of censorship. While age and gender do not have a significant effect on binge-watching of U.S. drama and the third-person effect, English fluency and number of visits to the United States had a significant effect. The results revealed that the more often the respondents had visited the United States, the less likely they were to perceive a harmful effect of U.S. drama and its violent content on themselves and others.

THE GLOBAL MEDIA FLOW IN THE TWENTY-FIRST CENTURY AND BINGE-WATCHING OF TV

Communication has changed drastically in the twenty-first century, especially in Arab countries. It has shifted from traditional media to new media not only in methods of producing media content, but also in its consumption. The consequences of this shift affect media production, its distribution, Arab preferences in the language of the media content, and the audience's psychology.

Global media flow has emerged with a unique shape because of advanced technologies. As shown in the TV binge-watching research in the Arab world, audiences tend to use laptops, smartphones, iPads, and other modern devices to binge-watch their preferred TV content via the Internet at their convenience. New types of Internet platforms facilitate global media flow to the Arab region. In particular, Netflix is among the most preferred platforms that the Arab audience uses to reach the global TV content, mostly U.S. production, which is believed to affect their values and identity.

Today, the Arab audience's ability to limit both the time spent binge-watching online videos and the type of content they choose is decreasing. The strong tendency to binge-watch non-Arab more than Arab drama suggests that the Arab audience is becoming increasingly vulnerable to the global flow of communication.

In 2018, Netflix started broadcasting existing series in Arabic and producing original Arabic series of its own. The first of these was *Jinn*. The first Egyptian one was *Ma wara'a al-tabya'a* ("Paranormal"), which first aired in 2020. Simultaneously, Arab online streaming platforms have been emerging, including WATCH iT! and Shahid VIP. This might be a step toward creating a balance in the global media flow in the coming years.

Examining TV binge-watching with the third-person effect approach provides significant insights into the perception of the effects of binge-watching U.S. drama. If a person perceives that the negative effects of U.S. drama are higher on others than on him/herself, he or she will resume binge-watching while denying its effects on his or her cultural identity. This suggests that the tendency of Arab youth to consume U.S. televised media production will continue to grow.

There is an undeniable impact of foreign media content flow on the Arab countries that results from intensive TV binge-watching. The positive impacts include improving English fluency and enriching the audience's cultural background. However, some serious negative impacts are also foreseen. Examples include disrupting the Arab identity and adopting new behavior that might contradict the traditional lifestyle, beliefs, and values.

Recent research in the Arab region indicates that the more Arabs binge-watch foreign TV dramas, (1) the less they regret spending many hours watching back-to-back episodes, (2) the more they lack self-regulation, and (3) the more they suffer from loneliness and depression. There are also indications that the cultural structure and identity of Arab youth are affected by the intensive watching of U.S. drama. The Arab audience is starting to foster individualism, which has traditionally been more associated with U.S. identity, and straying away from their collectivism. This is an initial indication that binge-watching U.S. drama affects the cultural structure and identity of Arab youth, which used to be more interdependent than independent.

Binge-watching TV is still a rich and evolving interdisciplinary research area for media and psychology scholars to study its possible effects on individuals and communities. Future research should investigate the impact of foreign media content flow to the Middle East. In particular, the influence of U.S. and European media content on cultural identity should be studied. Media imperialism should also continue to be investigated in the light of the novel forms that have been made possible by modern technologies and content availability.

REFERENCES

Ahmed, A. 2004. "UAEU students' perception of the effects of music clip satellite channels on Arab societies: A study on third-person effect." *Egyptian Journal for Public Opinion Research* 2 (5): 79–134 (in Arabic).

———. 2017. "New era of TV watching behavior: Binge watching and its psychological effects." *Media Watch* 8 (2): 197–207. https://mediawatchjournal.in/mwj/may17-5.pdf.

———. 2019. "Marathon TV watching among Emiratis in the interactive media environment." *Arab Media & Society* May 15, 2019. https://www.arabmediasociety.com/marathon-tv-watching-among -emiratis-in-the-interactive-media-environment.

———. 2021. "Impact of US drama binge-watching in the Emirates: Third-person effect and cultural self-conceptual." *Arab Media & Society*, March 22, 2021. https://www.arabmediasociety.com/impact -of-us-drama-binge-watching-in-the-emirates-third-person-effect-and-cultural-self-conceptual.

Akpabio, E., and K. Mustapha-Lambe. 2008. "Nollywood films and the cultural imperialism hypothesis." *Perspectives on Global Development and Technology* (*PGDT*) 7 (3-4): 259–70.

Arab Media Outlook Annual Report. 2011–15. *Arab Media: Exposure and Transition*. Dubai Press Club. Accessed October 23, 2016. https://fdocuments.in/document/arab-media-outlook-2011-2015.html.

Bandura, A. 1991. "Social cognitive theory of self-regulation." *Organizational Behavior and Human Decision Processes* 50: 248–87.

Boyd-Barrett, O. 1977. "Media Imperialism: Towards an International Framework for the Analysis of Media Systems." In *Mass Communication and Society*, edited by J. Curran, M. Gurevitch, and J. Woolacott, 116–35. London: Edward Arnold.

Bury, R., and J. Li. 2015. "Is it live or is it time shifted, streamed, or downloaded? Watching television in the era of multiple screens." *New Media & Society* 17 (4): 592–610.

Castro, D., J. M. Rigby, D. Cabral, and V. Nisi. 2021. "The binge-watcher's journey: Investigating motivations, contexts, and affective states surrounding Netflix viewing." *Convergence* 27 (1): 3–20. https://doi.org/10.1177/1354856519890856.

Chia, S. C., L. Lu, and D. M. McLeod. 2004. "Sex, lies, and video compact disc: A case study on third-person perception and motivations for media censorship." *Communication Research* 3 (1): 109–30.

Cohen, J., and R. G. Davis. 1991. "Third-person effects and the differential impact in negative political advertising." *Journalism Quarterly* 68 (4): 680–88.

Cohen, J., D. Mutz, V. Price, and A. Gunther. 1988. "Perceived impact of defamation: An experiment on third-person effects." *Public Opinion Quarterly* 52 (2): 161–73.

Colin, L. T. 2015. "There Goes the Weekend: Understanding Television Binge-Watching." Doctoral dissertation, University of Alabama.

Davison, W. P. 1983. "Third-person effect in communication." *Public Opinion Quarterly* 47 (1): 1–15.

Dennis, D., and D. Gray. 2013. "An episode by episode examination: What drives television viewer behavior? Digging down into audience satisfaction with television dramas." *Journal of Advertising Research* 53 (2): 166–74.

Derrick, J. L., S. Gabriel, and K. Hugenberg. 2009. "Social surrogacy: How favored television programs provide the experience of belonging." *Journal of Experimental Social Psychology* 45: 352–62.

Devasagayam, R. 2014. "Media Bingeing: A Qualitative Study of Psychological Influences." Paper presented at the Marketing Management Association, Chicago.

Dickinson, K. 2014. "Confessions of the Millennial Binge-Viewer: An Examination of the TV Show Binge-Viewing Phenomenon." Master's thesis, California State University, Fullerton. https://www.proquest.com/openview/eacdb52658c544f6c3582bddfca19cdc/1?pq-origsite=gscholar&cbl=18750&diss=y.

Finn, S. 1992. "Television 'addiction'? An evaluation of four competing media-use models." *Journalism Quarterly* 69 (2): 422–35.

Gray, J. 2014. "Scales of cultural influence: Malawian consumption of foreign media." *Media, Culture and Society* 36 (7): 982–97.

Gudykunst, W. B., Y. Matsumoto, S. Ting-Toomey, K. Nishida, K. Kim, and S. Heyman. 1996. "The influence of cultural individualism-collectivism, self-construal, and individual values on communication styles across cultures." *Human Communication Research* 22 (4): 510–43.

Ha, J. H., S. Y. Kim, S. C. Bae, et al. 2007. "Depression and Internet addiction in adolescents." *Psychopathology* 40 (6): 424–30.

Hallinan, B., and T. Striphas. 2014. "Recommended for you: The Netflix Prize and the production of algorithmic culture." *New Media & Society* 18 (1): 117–37.

Henriksen, L., and J. A. Flora. 1999. "Third-person perception and children: Perceived impact of pro- and anti-smoking ads." *Communication Research* 26 (6): 643–65.

Hoffner, C., M. Buchanan, J. D. Anderson, et al. 1999. "Support for censorship of television violence: The role of third-person effect and news exposure." *Communication Research* 26: 726–42.

Hoffner, C., R. S. Plotkin, M. Buchanan, et al. 2001. "The third-person effect in perceptions of the influence of television violence." *Journal of Communication* 51 (2): 283–99.

Jenner, M. 2014 . "Is this TVIV? On Netflix, TVIII, and binge-watching." *New Media & Society* 18 (2): 257–73.

———. 2015. "Binge-watching: Video-on-demand, quality TV, and mainstreaming fandom." *International Journal of Cultural Studies* 20 (3): 1–17.

Katz, E., J. G. Blumler, and M. Gurevitch. 1974. "Utilization of Mass Communication by the Individual." In *The Uses of Mass Communications: Current Perspectives on Gratifications Research*, edited by J. G. Blumler and E. Katz, 19–31. Beverly Hills, CA: Sage.

Kim, K., E. Ryu, M. Chon, et al. 2005. "Internet addiction in Korean adolescents and its relation to depression and suicidal ideation: A questionnaire survey." *International Journal of Nursing Studies* 43 (2): 185–92.

Kim, M. S. 1995. "Towards a Theory of Conversational Constraint: Focusing on Individual Level Dimension of Culture." In *Intercultural Communication Theory*, edited by R. L. Wiseman, 148–69. Thousand Oaks, CA: Sage.

Kolotkin, R. L., E. S. Revis, B. G. Kirkley, and L. Janick. 1987. "Binge eating in obesity: Associated MMPI characteristics." *Journal of Consulting and Clinical Psychology* 55 (6): 872–76.

Kubey, R., and M. Csikszentmihalyi. 2002. "Television addiction is no mere metaphor." *Scientific American*, February 2002, 75–80. http://sites.oxy.edu/clint/physio/article/televisionaddiction.pdf.

LaRose, R., C. A. Lin, and M. S. Eastin. 2003. "Unregulated Internet usage: Addiction, habit, or deficient self-regulation?" *Media Psychology* 5: 225–53.

Lee, B., and R. Tamborini. 2005. "Third-person effect and Internet pornography: The influence of collectivism and Internet self-efficacy." *Journal of Communication* 55 (2): 292–310.

Lee, C., and S. Yang. 1996. "Third-person perception and support for censorship of sexually explicit visual content: A Korean case." *Bangkok Journalism Review* 7: 21–39.

Lee, P. S. N. 1998. "Foreign Television in Hong Kong: Little Watched but Favorably Received." In *Television without Borders: Asian Audiences Speak Out*, edited by A. Goonasekera and P. Lee, 141–70. Singapore: AMIC.

Liu, M., and W. Peng. 2009. "Cognitive and psychological predictors of the negative outcomes associated with playing MMOGs (massively multiplayer online games)." *Computers in Human Behavior* 25: 1306–11.

Lo, V. H., and R. Wei. 2002. "Third-person effect, gender, and pornography on the Internet." *Journal of Broadcasting & Electronic Media* 46 (1): 13–33.

Lotz, A. D. 2009. "What is U.S. television now?" *ANNALS of the American Academy of Political and Social Science* 625: 49–59.

Marketing Charts. 2014. "TV binge-viewers hold mixed attitudes to advertising." July 16, 2014. http://www.marketingcharts.com/television/tv-binge-viewers-hold-mixedattitudes-to-advertising-44113.

Markus, H. R., and S. Kitayama. 1991. "Culture and self-implications for cognition, emotion, and motivation." *Psychological Review* 98: 224–53.

McLeod, D. M., W. P. Eveland Jr., and A. I. Nathanson. 1997. "Support for censorship of violent and misogynic rap lyrics: An analysis of the third-person effect." *Communication Research* 24: 153–74.

Memmott, C. 2013. "10 great TV series to binge-watch." AARP, October 8, 2013. http://www.aarp.org/entertainment/television/info-10-2013/10-great-tv-series-tobinge-watch.html.

Mikos, L. 2016. "Digital media platforms and the use of TV content: Binge-watching and video-on-demand in Germany." *Media and Communication* 4 (3): 154–61.

Moore, A. E. 2015. "Binge Watching: Exploring the Relationship of Binge-Watched Television Genres and Colleges at Clemson University." Graduate Research and Discovery Symposium (GRADS), Paper 138. http://tigerprints.clemson.edu/grads_symposium/138.

Omoera, O. S., and E. Ibagere. (2010). "Revisiting media imperialism: A review of the Nigerian television experience." *International Journal of Research and Review* 5: 1–18.

Panek, E. 2014. "Left to their own devices: College students' 'guilty pleasure' media use and time management." *Communication Research* 41 (4): 561–77.

Peña, L. L. 2015. "Breaking Binge: Exploring the Effects of Binge-Watching on Television Viewer Reception." Master's thesis, Syracuse University.

Petersen, G. T. 2016. "To binge or not to binge: A qualitative analysis of college students' binge-watching habits." *Florida Communication Journal* 44 (1): 77–87.

Pittman, M., and K. Sheehan. 2015. "Sprinting a media marathon: Uses and gratifications of binge-watching television through Netflix." *First Monday* 20 (10). http://firstmonday.org/ojs/index.php/fm/article/view/6138/4999.

PRWeb. 2013. "MarketCast study finds TV 'binge-viewing' creates a more engaged viewer for future seasons and not a bingeing habit." March 8, 2013. http://www.prweb.com/releases/2013/3/prweb10513066.htm.

Reinecke, L., T. Hartmann, and A. Eden. 2014. "The guilty couch potato: The role of ego depletion in reducing recovery through media use." *Journal of Communication* 64 (4): 569–89.

Rubin, A. 2009. "Uses and Gratifications: Perspective on Media Effects." In *Media Effects: Advances in Theory and Research*, edited by J. Bryant and M. B. Oliver, 525–48. 3rd ed. New York: Routledge.

Sabir, M. 2013. "Imperialism of media and developing countries." *South Asian Studies* 28 (2): 283–94.

Salwen, M. B., and M. Dupagne. 1999. "Effects of US television on foreign audiences: A meta-analysis." *Journalism Quarterly* 71: 947–59.

Shaw, L. H., and L. M. Gant. 2004. "In defense of the Internet: The relationship between Internet communication and depression, loneliness, self-esteem, and perceived social support." *CyberPsychology & Behavior* 5 (2): 157–71.

Stamatakis, E., M. Hillsdon, G. Mishra, et al. 2009. "Television viewing and other screen-based entertainment in relation to multiple socioeconomic status indicators and area deprivation: The Scottish Health Survey 2003." *Journal of Epidemiology & Community Health* 63: 734–40.

Statista. 2016. "The statistics portal." http://www.statista.com/topics/2508/binge-watching-in-the-us.

Sun, Y., L. Shen, and Z. Pan. 2008. "On the behavioral component of the third-person effect." *Communication Research* 35 (2): 257–78.

Sung, Y. H., E. Y. Kamg, and W. N. Lee. 2015. "A Bad Habit for Your Health? An Exploration of Psychological Factors for Binge-Watching Behavior." Conference proceedings, the 65th Annual Conference of the International Communication Association, San Juan, Puerto Rico, May 21–25, 2015.

Triandis, H. C. 1989. "The self and social behavior in differing cultural contexts." *Psychological Review* 96: 506–20.

Tsay-Vogel, M. 2016. "Me versus them: Third-person effects among Facebook users." *New Media & Society* 18 (9): 1956–72.

Wagner, C. N. 2016. "'Glued to the sofa': Exploring guilt and television binge-watching behaviors." Communication honors thesis, Trinity University. https://digitalcommons.trinity.edu/comm_honors/11.

Walton-Pattison, E., S. U. Dombrowski, and J. Presseau. 2016. "'Just one more episode': Frequency and theoretical correlates of television binge watching." *Journal of Health Psychology* 23 (1): 17–24.

Warren, S. M. 2016. "Binge-Watching Rate as a Predictor of Viewer Transportation Mechanisms." Master's thesis, Syracuse University. https://core.ac.uk/download/pdf/215708917.pdf.

Wheeler, K. S. 2015. "The Relationships between Television Viewing Behaviors, Attachment, Loneliness, Depression, and Psychological Well-Being." Georgia Southern University Honors Program Theses. Paper 98. https://digitalcommons.georgiasouthern.edu/honors-theses/98.

Willnat, L., Z. He, T. Takeshita, and E. López-Escobar. 2002. "Perceptions of foreign media influence in Asia and Europe: The third-person effect and media imperialism." *International Journal for Public Relations* 14: 175–92.

Willnat, L., E. Tamam, and A. Aw. 2007. "Perceptions of Foreign Media Influence in Asia: Cultural Self-Construal and the Third-Person Effect." Paper prepared for presentation at the Annual Meeting of the International Communication Association, San Francisco, May 2007.

Index

Abdelhamid, Bassam, 144
Abdelwahab, Meddeb, 152
Abdullah (king), 55
Abidi, Hasni, 163
Abu Dhabi Media, 179
Abu Dhabi Vision 2030, 134
Abu Hizam, 145
Abu Sbaih, Ibrahim, 6
accountability, transparency and, 128–30, 134
ADG. *See* Arab digital generation
advertising, 68, 172, 177–78, 182, 201
Afkar Media, 194
Agence France Presse, 22
Agency for Global Media, U.S., 101
Agha, S., 101–2
Agunbiade, O. M., 248
al-Ahdath al-Maghribia, 27
Ahmed, Azza, xx, 275–85
Al Ahram Regional Press Institute, 4, 9–11
Al-Ahrar, 4
Akher al-nahar, 264
Alam, Magdi, 10
Alam al-Masrin (Egyptian Media Group), 69–70
Alexandria, Egypt, 3–4
Alexandria Cotton Exporters, 86
Algeria, xiii; Arab Spring and, 43–44, 162;
    ARPT, 153–55, 158–59; colonial radio in,
    35–36; cybercrime in, 159–60, 162; DTT in,
    40–41; Egypt and, 267; Facebook in, 156–58,
    160–64, 247; French colonial occupation, xvi,
    20–21, 35–36, 41, 163; French colonization
    of, 35, 37–38, 41, 45; ICT in, 153, 157–58;
    independence, 35–37, 42, 44–45; Internet

in, 152–59, 161–64; journalists, national
press and, 42–43; liberalization of, 37,
43; Morocco and, radio broadcasts, 36;
MPTIC, 153; National Coordination for
Change and Democracy, 160; network
extension, administrative restructuring
and, 39–40; newspapers in, nationalization
of, 42; Organic Law of 2012, 43–44;
political instrumentalization of radio and
TV, 41–43, 45; popular revolts in, 151–52;
private channels, in audiovisual landscape
of, 43–45; radio in, 35–39, 41–43, 45–46;
RCSTI/CERIST, 153; RTA in, 37, 39–40,
43; RTF in, 38–39; social media in, xviii,
154, 156, 160–65; state-controlled media,
44; telecommunications sector in, 152–55,
158–59; television in, 35, 38–46; women,
on Facebook, 247, 249–57, *250*, *251*, *254*,
255, 259
Algerian Academic and Research Network
    (ARN), 153
Algerian Radio, 36–37
Algerian Radio-Diffusion and Television (RTA)
    Company, 37, 39–40, 43
Algérie Télécom (AT), 153, 158
Algiers Radio Club, 35
Al Hadith, xiv
Al Hurrah Television, 97, 100–101, 103
Al-Ittihad Al-Ichtiraki, 5–6
Al Jazeera, xi–xiii, 57, 102–3, 139
Al Jazeera Arabic, 54
Al-Jenaibi, B., 133–34
Aljerjawi, K., 243

About the Contributors

Inas Abou Youssef, PhD, is professor of journalism and dean of the Mass Communication Faculty at Ahram Canadian University, and editor in chief of the *Arab Journal of Media & Communication Research*. Her main interests are international communication and media & gender. She was a board member of the Egyptian National Council of Women (2006–2009) and the technical consultant for Media Women Watch, National Council of Women and UNICEF (2004–2011). Professor Abou Youssef is also one of the founders of AREACORE. She is currently running a student exchange program with the Free University in Berlin.

Azza A. Ahmed, PhD, is professor of communication at Zayed University in the United Arab Emirates and the Faculty of Mass Communication at Cairo University in Egypt. Her research interests include media effects, television studies, media credibility, binge-watching, and new media usages and impacts. She was the Arabic editor of the *Journal of Middle East Media* 2005–2016 and a board member of the Arab-U.S. Association for Communication Educators (AUSACE).

Philip Auter, PhD, is the Hubert Bourgeois Endowed Professor of Communication and graduate coordinator for the Department of Communication at the University of Louisiana at Lafayette. He offers both traditional and distance learning communication courses—some of which have been partnered with international universities via the Internet. Dr. Auter has authored more than forty journal articles, book chapters, and other contributions—many on the Middle East and North Africa region. He has presented at regional, national, and international communication conferences and was the lead author of a USAID Middle East Partnership Initiative grant. Auter is a member of the board of the Arab-U.S. Association for Communication Educators (AUSACE).

Mohammad Ayish, PhD, holds a doctoral degree in mass communication from the University of Minnesota, Twin Cities (1986). He is professor and head of the Department of Mass Communication at the American University of Sharjah (AUS), United Arab Emirates. Before joining AUS in fall 2012, he had served as dean of the College of Communication at the University of Sharjah and had worked as an advisor for the UAE National Media Council. His research interests include satellite broadcasting, digital communications, social media, media ethics, mobile journalism, and digital diplomacy. Ayish writes frequently on Arab media and has been widely published as a scholar in the field.

Tayeb Boutbouqalt, PhD, is Professor of Contemporary History and Communication Studies and head of the French Department at the King Fahd Advanced School of Translation in Tangier, Morocco. He is the CEO of the International Center for Translation and Intercultural Communication, and a founding member of the Arab-U.S. Association of Communication Educators (AUSACE). He is the author of over 120 articles related to intercultural communication and contemporary Moroccan history and communication, most of which appeared as opinion columns in the daily Moroccan newspaper of *Al Ittihad Al Ichtiraki*, and has published four books on this topic.

Aliaa Dawoud, PhD, is assistant professor of mass communication. She received her doctorate in philosophy from the School of Media, Arts & Design at the University of Westminster in 2010. She is currently pursuing a second MA degree in Middle East studies at City University of New York. Dr. Dawoud has taught in several universities, including the University of Westminster in London and the American University in Cairo.

Khaled S. Gaweesh, PhD, has been associate professor of mass communication at Abu Dhabi Campus of Zayed University since August 2020, and associate professor in the Faculty of Mass Communication at Cairo University in Egypt. He has participated in a number of institutional accreditation processes, presented at conferences, served as a peer reviewer for many journals, and published in the areas of advertising, image, corporate reputation, and communication technologies. He holds a PhD from Cairo University and has spent two years at the University of South Carolina as visiting scholar.

Ahmed El Gody, PhD, is assistant professor of media and communication studies at Örebro University, Sweden. El Gody has authored two books, *African Media and ICT4D* (2003, coauthor) and *Journalism in a Network* (2012), and several academic articles and refereed chapters in the areas of newsroom operation, media liberation and the democratization process in the Middle East, social media, the Arab Spring, and migration and integration policies in the E.U.

Naila Nabil Hamdy, PhD, is associate dean for the School of Global Affairs and Public Policy at the American University in Cairo. She has authored numerous articles in international journals covering the fields of journalism, global communication, and political engagement. A media commentator, public speaker, and guest lecturer, she has also frequently been invited to lecture at several universities worldwide including the Arhus School of Journalism in Denmark, the University of Louisiana at Lafayette, Thomas Moore University in Belgium, the Free University of Berlin, the University of Qatar, and the American University of the Emirates, among others. She is a member of the board, and a former president, of the Arab-U.S. Association for Communication Educators (AUSACE).

Kamal Hamidou, PhD, is associate professor in mass communication and head of the mass communication department at Qatar University. He has taught at several other universities including Metz University, France, and the UAE University. He is widely published in peer-reviewed journals in several languages. His major research interests are inter-corporate communication, the sociology and usages of legacy media and new media, and the influence of communication contents, process, and systems on social change, perception, and cognition processes.

Fran Hassencahl (PhD, Case Western Reserve University) is associate professor of communication at Old Dominion University in Norfolk, Virginia. She directs the minor in Middle Eastern studies and teaches communication and culture in the Middle East, contemporary Turkish politics, and intercultural communication. Her research interest is in the area of framing through political cartoons, press stories, and debate and the construction of identity in novels. She has served as visiting faculty at the University of Aleppo and Al Akhawayn University, Morocco.

Tara Al-Kadi, PhD, earned her degree from Roehampton University in London in 2017. Her published research examines the Egyptian broadcasting landscape in relation to prominent media theories and international broadcast models. Dr. Al-Kadi has been teaching mass communication at the American University in Cairo (AUC) and the October University of Modern Sciences and Arts (MSA) since 2010. She is particularly passionate about the subject of Egyptian media ethics and conducts media training for government and private media Arab professionals.

Kyung Sun Lee received her PhD in media studies from the University of Texas at Austin. She is assistant professor in the College of Communication and Media Sciences at Zayed University in Dubai. Her research explores the areas of global communication, social change, and critical political economy. Lee's work has appeared in major journals in the field and in edited collections including the *International Journal of Communication* and *Computers in Human Behavior*.

Deanna Loew is an award-winning publicist and marketing expert. She has worked on many successful media campaigns for a variety of international clients. She has a special interest in social media, crisis mitigation, and search-engine optimization and has been awarded the Gold Medal at the Florida Public Relations Association's Global Image Awards for her professional work in the field.

Noha Mellor holds a PhD from Copenhagen University, Denmark. She is professor of media at the University of Bedfordshire, U.K., and adjunct professor of Middle Eastern studies at Stockholm University, Sweden. She is the author of several books about Arab media and journalism including *The Making of Arab News* (2005), *Modern Arab Journalism* (2007), *Arab Media* (2011), and *Voice of the Muslim Brotherhood* (2017).

Hesham Mesbah, PhD, is associate professor and chair of the Department of Communication at Rollins College in Winter Park, Florida. He received his doctoral degree in mass communication from Cairo University in 1996. His research agenda includes comparative cognitive effects of news media, new media, and the impact of media use on social capital, public opinion, and social openness. He had been actively engaged in training journalists and providing research and public relations consultations in Egypt and Kuwait. Currently, he is senior editor of the *Journal of Middle East Media* (*JMEM*) and past president of the Arab-U.S. Association for Communication Educators (AUSACE).

Meriem Narimane Noumeur received her PhD in formation and new technologies of information and communication from Batna 1 University in Algeria. She is a lecturer in the Department of Sciences of Information and Communication at the same university. Dr. Noumeur has published and presented papers in the fields of virtual citizenship, virtual identity, digital violence, digital religiosity, and online self-representation. Meriem is also a novelist.

Saddek Rabah, PhD, is professor of communication and media studies at Qatar University. He holds a PhD in media studies from the Panthéon-Assas University Paris II, France. His main research areas include social media studies, Internet studies, media convergence, media and social change, and media discourse. He has published and translated several books and book chapters on these subjects, as well as more than thirty articles in Arabic, French, and English. He is a member of the board of the Arab-U.S. Association for Communication Educators (AUSACE).

Abeer Salem is the Egypt Country Director of the International Higher Education Teaching and Learning Association (HETL) and is a member of the advisory board of the *Journal of Applied Research in Higher Education*. She teaches development communication and international communication at October University for Modern Sciences and Arts (MSA) in Egypt. Her recent publications address sustainability issues in relevance to leadership, communication, indigenous learning, indigenous entrepreneurship, and higher education. She holds a PhD in sustainability education from Prescott College for the Liberal Arts and the Environment in Arizona.

Hend El-Taher holds a BA and MA in journalism and mass communication from the American University in Cairo with minor specialization in Islamic studies. She also received a diploma in Islamic Shari'a from the Higher Institute for Islamic Studies. She currently teaches at the Arab Academy for Science, Technology & Maritime Transport in Aswan and previously taught at the British University in Egypt. Her research interests are in media, religion, and development.

Leonard Ray Teel, PhD, is professor emeritus of communication at Georgia State University. He is the founding director of the GSU Center for International Media Education and a founding member and first president of the Arab-U.S. Association for Communication Educators (AUSACE). He is also the founding editor of the *Journal of Middle Eastern Media*. Teel previously worked as an award-winning journalist and has also received the Journalism Historians Association's Excellence in Research Award on four occasions. Teel's research interests include U.S. and international media history and international/global communication. He is the recipient of more than $1 million in funding to lead journalism training and faculty exchanges with the Middle East and other regions.

Oshane Thorpe holds a PhD from the Institute of Communication Studies at the Communication University of China with a specialization in communication (2017). He has authored numerous peer-reviewed articles in journals such as *Sustainability, Data*, and the *Journal of Educational Social Research*. His current research focuses on the usage of social media apps in mediatizing traditional beliefs, as well as social media and privacy. Prior to joining the University of Wollongong in Dubai, he worked at the American University in the Emirates in Dubai, as well as having taught at the Beijing University of Technology and at the Tianjin Foreign Studies University, China.

Karin Wilkins (PhD, University of Pennsylvania) is dean of the School of Communication at the University of Miami. Previously, she was associate dean for Faculty Advancement and Strategic Initiatives with the Moody College of Communication at the University of Texas at Austin. She was awarded the Cale McDowell Award for Innovation in Undergraduate Studies for creating degrees in global studies, Middle East studies, and communication and leadership. She previously served as editor in chief of *Communication Theory*. Her work addresses scholarship in the fields of development communication, gender, and global communication. Wilkins is a member of the board of the Arab-U.S. Association for Communication Educators (AUSACE).